THE ULTIMATE GUIDE TO VINTAGE

STAR WARS®

ACTION FIGURES 1977-1985

MARK BELLOMO

Published by

Krause Publications, a division of F+W Media, Inc.
700 East State Street • Iola, WI 54990-0001
715-445-2214 • 888-457-2873
www.krausebooks.com

To order books or other products call toll-free 1-800-258-0929
or visit us online at www.krausebooks.com

The word STAR WARS and its associated trademarks are owned by Disney/Lucasfilm, & licensed to Hasbro Inc., and are used in this book solely for identification purposes. Disney/ Lucasfilm & Hasbro, Inc. assume no responsibility for the content of this book. The publisher is not sponsored by or associated with Disney/Lucasfilm & Hasbro Inc. or its affiliates. This book is a result of the author's independent research reporting on the secondary market and is intended to provide information for collectors.

ISBN-13: 978-1-4402-4059-1
ISBN-10: 1-4402-4059-0

Front and back cover photos by Kris Kandler
Cover and interior design by Nicole MacMartin
Edited by Kris Manty

Printed in China

CONTENTS

Introduction   4
  How to Use This Book   5
  Price Descriptions   7

PART 1: ACTION FIGURES
Star Wars   10
  1977   12
  1978 First Wave   14
    After the Early Bird   20
    Add-on Assortment   32
  Late 1978 Second Wave   38
  1979 Second Wave   47

The Empire Strikes Back   50
  1980 First Wave   51
  1980 Second Wave   65
  1980 Third Wave   74
  1981 Third Wave   78
  1982 Third Wave   82

Return of the Jedi   86
  1982 First Wave   87
  1983 First Wave   90
  1984 Second Wave   114
  1984 Third Wave   124

Power of the Force   126
  1984   127
  1985   133
  Collector's Coins   142

*Star Wars: Droids (The Adventures
of R2-D2 and C-3PO)*   146
  1985   147

Star Wars: Ewoks   153
  1985   154

Large Size   157
  Star Wars, 1978-1979   157
  The Empire Strikes Back, 1980   166

**PART II: ACCESSORIES (Creatures,
Playsets, and Vehicles)**
Star Wars
  1978   168
  1979   178

The Empire Strikes Back
  1980   194
  1981   207
  1982   222

Return of the Jedi
  1983   235
  1984   250

Power of the Force
  1985   260

Star Wars: Droids
  1985   266

Index   269
Bibliography   270

INTRODUCTION

Due to the 1973 oil crisis that skyrocketed the cost of the petroleum-based plastic used to make action figures, toy producers had to scale down their product or halt production altogether. Therefore, the new standard size for the marketplace became the 3-3/4-inch scale—a dimension that allowed children to inexpensively obtain many multiple figures, while aficionados could engage themselves in the pursuit of a "Collect 'Em All" mentality that continues to this day. At $1.99 each, you could purchase five Imperial Stormtroopers for ten dollars in 1978: currently, one *single* Stormtrooper figure sells for $9.99.

This new 3-3/4-inch size—a scale already featured with success in such toy lines as Fisher Price's Adventure People franchise (1975-1985), Mego's Comic Action Heroes line (1976-1982), and Tomland's Starroid/Space Raiders assortment[s] (1977-1978)—allowed toy companies to experiment with higher price-point creatures, vehicles (both aircraft and automotive), accessories, playsets, and ... MUCH larger playsets.

Certainly, the troubles that the U.S. experienced with the cost of oil—and hence, oil-based plastics—made action figure production in the late 1970s a far trickier business than it was in the first ten-to-fifteen years of the genre's production (c. 1964-1976): Both OAPEC's powerful oil embargo of 1973 and 1979's terrible energy crisis led to the miniaturization of action figures. Hence, Kenner originally branded their characters as "Mini-Action Figures" in pack-in catalogs, on product boxes, and within promotional materials for the company's nascent *Star Wars* toy line to distinguish the smaller size of these plastic characters relative to the much larger existing action figure lines of the 1970s, such as Hasbro's foot-tall G.I. Joe Adventure Team members, the 10-inch tall Gabriel/Hubley Lone Ranger Rides Again! Western heroes, Mego's 8-inch tall Official World's Greatest Super-Heroes line of DC and Marvel comic book characters, and Kenner's own fully articulated and über-popular 13-inch tall Six Million Dollar Man and 12-1/4-inch tall Bionic Woman franchises.

Furthermore, please note that nearly every accessory—every rifle, pistol, lightsaber, staff, cloak, blaster, etc.—manufactured by Kenner for its *Star Wars* action figure line possesses one (with some having many more than one) variation in construction, due to the fact that these singular accoutrements were produced in different factories all around the world. From different shades of plastic to oddly dissimilar molds, these nuanced variations add to the collectability of the vintage *Star Wars* line; with more accessory (and action figure) variations found on a monthly basis by astute collectors.

Nearly 100 unique figures were produced in Kenner's vintage *Star Wars* line (discounting the company's *Droids* and *Ewoks* sub-lines released in 1985) between 1978 and 1985, with records showing that a preposterous amount of product was moved during that period: Kenner sold more than 300 million action figures in less than a decade (!).

TIMELINE

Release date of *Star Wars* Films, 1977-1983.

ANH	ESB	ROTJ
Star Wars Episode IV: A New Hope	Star Wars Episode V: The Empire Strikes Back	Star Wars Episode VI: Return of the Jedi
1977	1980	1983

How To Use This Book

All of the action figures, accessories, creatures, mail-away items, playsets, vehicles, and weapon systems are not only organized by film (or television program, in the case of *Droids* and *Ewoks*), but by release date, etc.

The following three abbreviations will often be used when referring to the three films comprising the original *Star Wars* film trilogy: *ANH = Star Wars: A New Hope* (a.k.a. *Episode IV*); *ESB = Star Wars: The Empire Strikes Back* (*Episode V*); *ROTJ = Star Wars: Return of the Jedi* (*Episode VI*).

When regarding the time of events and major clashes (a.k.a. the Clone Wars, Battle of Hoth, etc.) in the *Star Wars* universe, events revolve around the destruction of the Empire's first Death Star during the Battle of Yavin (the preeminent battle of the Galactic Civil War), which took place in space above the moon Yavin 4. Therefore, I use the initials ABY (*after* the Battle of Yavin) and BBY (*before* the Battle of Yavin) to indicate time: in the *Star Wars* universe, the Battle of Yavin is therefore *year zero*.

The prices listed in this guide are the *best assessments available* based upon the pricing currently realized via a 12-month average "completed items search" on eBay, as well as from many prominent retailers across the United States for a period of one full year. These prices should be used as a guide only—and as such, can be quickly outdated: please take the pricing in this book with due deference. The prices listed in this guide are for NON-AFA GRADED toys, i.e., pieces that have not been professionally assessed and given a grade by the Action Figure Authority. For the purpose of assigning value to the vintage *Star Wars* toys in this reference book, there are three different ways that Kenner packaged these products for solicitation at retail, with a range of grades assigned to each of these three package-types.

First, there are *carded* items (with *carded bubble* packaging), which are those vintage *Star Wars* items released on a carded bubble—

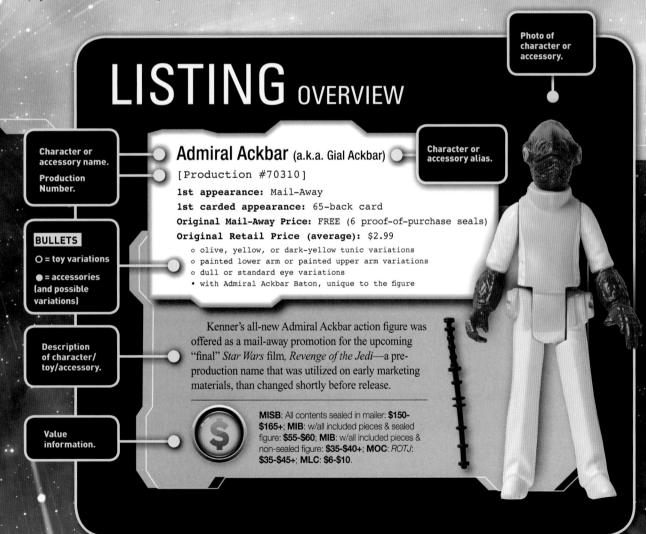

LISTING OVERVIEW

Photo of character or accessory.

Character or accessory name.

Production Number.

BULLETS

○ = toy variations

● = accessories (and possible variations)

Description of character/ toy/accessory.

Value information.

Admiral Ackbar (a.k.a. Gial Ackbar)

Character or accessory alias.

[Production #70310]

1st appearance: Mail-Away
1st carded appearance: 65-back card
Original Mail-Away Price: FREE (6 proof-of-purchase seals)
Original Retail Price (average): $2.99

- ○ olive, yellow, or dark-yellow tunic variations
- ○ painted lower arm or painted upper arm variations
- ○ dull or standard eye variations
- • with Admiral Ackbar Baton, unique to the figure

Kenner's all-new Admiral Ackbar action figure was offered as a mail-away promotion for the upcoming "final" *Star Wars* film, *Revenge of the Jedi*—a pre-production name that was utilized on early marketing materials, than changed shortly before release.

MISB: All contents sealed in mailer: **$150-$165+; MIB:** w/all included pieces & sealed figure: **$55-$60; MIB:** w/all included pieces & non-sealed figure: **$35-$40+; MOC:** *ROTJ:* **$35-$45+; MLC: $6-$10.**

5

essentially a piece of sturdy chipboard or cardboard (called a "card") with a translucent piece of shaped plastic (called a "bubble") attached via glue or paste so that the toy and its requisite accessories are visible to the consumer. When describing the prices of items in this book, packaged action figures will appear on a number of different MOC (Mint On Card) variations. The way to differentiate between these packages is by using their release date: those figures released earliest—and the rarest package variations of all—will be mounted on "*Star Wars*" packaging, which indicates these figures were produced from the first film: *Star Wars, Episode IV, A New Hope*. There are two different versions of prices for those figures released on *Star Wars* packaging:

- **"12B":** "12 back" cards—"12" because there were only a dozen *Star Wars* action figures initially available by Kenner; this package variation is indicated by the code "12B" for "12-back card," because there were only twelve figures in the assortment and featured on the package back.
- **"20/21B":** When Kenner added eight (or sometimes nine, when Boba Fett saw his release) more figures into the mix, the amount of figurines mounted on "*Star Wars*" packages was raised to twenty or twenty-one, and all of these figures were pictured on the BACK of a figure's card, hence the "20/21B" which represents "20 or 21-back card."

The rest of the labels are not as specific: *ESB* stands for an *Empire Strikes Back* package, regardless of the amount of figures featured on the back of the package or currently released by Kenner. The same holds true for *ROTJ*, which represents a *Return of the Jedi* package, and POTF, letters that reference Kenner's final Power of the Force lineup.

MOC (Mint On Card)

The original packaging for the toy in question is completely intact: the bubble is in no way removed (or even slightly separated) from the card, and the figure inside is usually in C-10, dead mint condition (a solid "10": on a scale of 1 [the lowest, poorest condition] to 10 [the highest, best condition]) due to the fact that the package has never been opened and the toy in question has never been exposed to human hands.

Due to the rarity of many MOC vintage *Star Wars* action figures, some unscrupulous dealers will try and pass off "custom-carded" figures as vintage originals. By using a high-quality printer to replicate the detailed graphics onto replica cardstock, and then constructing custom-made, translucent factory bubbles to match the Kenner originals, these two reproduction items were then used to mount a vintage figure onto this reproduction cardback. Some sellers—whether intentionally or unintentionally—may try to pass these repro cards off as original MOC items.

If you're in doubt as to whether or not to purchase a MOC figure because its provenance is in question, please check with an expert, or compare the package to a confirmed original.

MLC (Mint, Loose, and Complete)

The toy in question is without its original packaging, but has every single one of its included parts, e.g., accessories (laser pistols, lightsabers, missiles, or other easily lost weapons), yet the specimen is in *excellent* condition: grading at least a C-8.5 out of 10. When grading loose toys, a collectible is only MLC if the toy-in-question *is truly* mint, loose, and complete.

Many collectors will not purchase a vintage *Star Wars* playset, vehicle, or weapon system unless all of its respective labels are applied and *none* are missing, since missing stickers will adversely impact the overall appearance of the toy. Missing labels should be considered when pricing a vintage MLC *Star Wars* collectible.

However, there is one aspect of collecting MLC vintage *Star Wars* items that has given many action figure aficionados a powerful headache: reproduction ("repro") vintage *Star Wars* parts. Although

P. 14

Artoo-Detoo
(R2-D2).

MOC	MLC	MISB	MIB	MISP
Mint On Card	Mint, Loose, and Complete	Mint In Sealed Box	Mint In Box	Mint In Sealed Package

USEFUL ABBREVIATIONS

casual *Star Wars* fans might applaud the availability of repro accessories since these items are far easier-to-find and cost much less than original *Star Wars* parts, most diehard vintage *Star Wars* collectors, completionists (those fans who try to obtain one of each and every vintage *Star Wars* item in order to possess a "complete" collection), and troop-builders (those collectors who wish to amass a great number of troops to form an army of Imperial Stormtroopers, TIE Fighter Pilots, Biker Scouts, etc.) find that repro parts have watered down the market. Furthermore, repro parts allow uninformed sellers to "complete" vintage *Star Wars* action figures (and some playsets and vehicles) with repro parts not realizing that these accessories are reproductions, hence selling these toys with cheaply made, low-priced repro parts—yet at the higher value of an original item.

There are many dozens of tricks, tips, and reference photos cached and spread over hundreds of pages which can illustrate the difference between repro and original vintage *Star Wars* parts (i.e., Artoo Detour's article, "The Float and Drop Test") to new and returning collectors alike, but the sheer page count would run far too high to be dealt with in this reference guide, so I'll leave you with what I consider to be the single most indispensable Internet source for determining the difference between original and repro parts: *The Imperial Gunnery*, the premiere guide to "vintage *Star Wars* weapons and accessories." From Yoda's gimer stick to Luke Skywalker's "double-telescoping" lightsaber, the specific difference between reproduction parts and original parts is reviewed on *TIG's* website in great detail: www.imperialgunnery.com.

Price Descriptions

MISB (Mint In Sealed Box)

The toy in question remains factory sealed (taped, glued, etc.) with all of its accessories and packaging inserts (unapplied label sheet, instruction sheet, etc.) intact within its un-opened, original box. This is the rarest existing condition for a vintage *Star Wars* toy, and as such, a MISB artifact commands *exponentially* higher prices than those previously opened, MIB (Mint In Box), non-factory-sealed specimens.

Therefore, MISB samples of vintage *Star Wars* toys are holy grails for many toy collectors, which is why unscrupulous collectible dealers will try to pass off "re-sealed" MIB items as if they *were* MISB. So please inspect purported MISB toys very carefully to determine their authenticity. If the artifact in question is a considerably rare piece, you should contemplate having the AFA (Action Figure Authority) professionally grade the toy.

MIB (Mint In Box)

The original box for the toy is intact (nothing has been cut out or removed, etc., such as a Kenner proof-of-purchase seal), but said box is *not* factory-sealed (with tape, glue, etc.), as the package has indeed been opened. The toy is placed within the box, and is in excellent condition, possessing all of its respective accessories and accoutrements.

There are a variety of ways for a toy to be considered MIB. For instance, if the box was carefully opened, and the toy is complete—along with all of its packing inserts, unapplied label sheet, protective cardboard dividers, and paperwork—then the toy is considered MIB as well (and *not* MISB). However, for most collectors and retailers and for the grading standards delineated in this guide, it is not necessary for a MIB toy to include all of the toy's respective paperwork as well (e.g., *Star Wars* product catalog, "Warning" or "Important" inserts, paper promotional material, original shipping bag, etc.).

To wit: If the seal on a box is broken, then the toy is MIB.

Furthermore, many collectors will not purchase a vintage *Star Wars* playset, vehicle, or weapon system labelled as MIB unless all of its labels are applied and *none* are missing. Missing labels will adversely affect the toy's aesthetics. When calculating a vintage MIB *Star Wars* item, missing labels should be considered.

MISP (Mint In Sealed Package)

The toy in question remains factory-sealed (with tape, glue, PVC plastic, etc.) with all of its accessories and packaging inserts within its unopened, original package. Since this is the rarest condition for a vintage *Star Wars* artifact, MISP toys command *exorbitantly* high prices on the secondary market.

Since MISP samples of vintage *Star Wars* toys are so very rare, unscrupulous dealers will often try to pass off "re-sealed" items as if they were MISP. Therefore, please inspect your MISP toys carefully to determine their authenticity. Similar to MISB items, if the vintage *Star Wars* artifact is a considerably rare piece, you should consider investing some money to have the AFA (Action Figure Authority) professionally grade the item.

MIP (Mint In Package)

When the original package for the toy is completely intact (nothing has been cut out or removed, etc., such as a Kenner proof-of-purchase seal), but said package is *not* factory-sealed (with tape, glue,

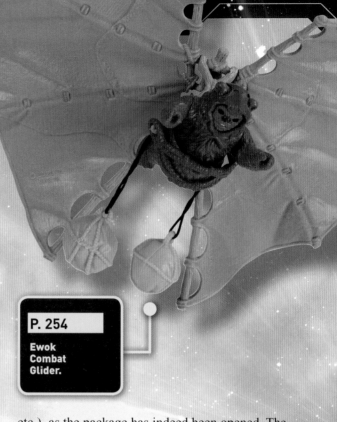

P. 254
Ewok Combat Glider.

etc.), as the package has indeed been opened. The toy is placed within the package, and is in excellent condition, possessing all of its respective accessories and accoutrements.

There are a variety of ways for a toy to be considered MIP. For instance, if the package was carefully opened, and the toy is complete—along with all of its packing inserts, protective cardboard dividers, unapplied label sheet, instructions and paperwork—then the toy is considered MIP as well (and *not* MISP). However, for most collectors and retailers and for the grading standards delineated in this guide, it is not necessary for a MIP toy to include *all* of the toy's respective paperwork as well (e.g., *Star Wars* product catalog, "Warning" or "Important" inserts, paper promotional material, original shipping baggie, etc.). Remember, if the seal on a package is broken, then the toy is MIP.

Furthermore, missing labels will adversely affect the toy's aesthetics. When calculating a vintage MIP *Star Wars* item, missing labels should be considered. Many finicky collectors will not purchase a vintage *Star Wars* playset, vehicle, or weapon system labelled as MIP unless all of its labels are applied and *none* are missing.

PART I
ACTION FIGURES

STAR WARS

Episode IV: A New Hope

A long time ago, in a galaxy far, far away …

It is a period of civil war. Rebel spaceships, striking from a hidden base, have won their first victory against the evil Galactic Empire.

During the battle, Rebel spies managed to steal secret plans to the Empire's ultimate weapon, the Death Star, an armored space station with enough power to destroy an entire planet.

Pursued by the Empire's sinister agents, Princess Leia races home aboard her starship, custodian of the stolen plans that can save her people and restore freedom to the galaxy …

Star Wars Episode IV: A New Hope (1977)—the epic space opera that launched one of the premiere media franchises in history—opened in theaters on May 25th, 1977, with a budget of $11 million.

Although the profound, lasting influence of the *Star Wars* franchise upon the collective consciousness of Generation X (and nearly every generation since) may never be accurately assessed, *Episode IV's* runaway success at the box office certainly took the many hard-working people who were involved in *A New Hope's* production by surprise.

At the outset, some cast and crew members in-volved with *Episode IV* considered the movie "weird" and a "children's film"; they were put off by the more fantastic elements of the plot introduced by writer/director George Lucas. The entire production was also plagued by *forces majeure* that caused Lucas to miss his planned Christmastime 1976 release date. Moreover, since science fiction films were largely uninspiring in terms of revenue and critical acclaim—performing well initially, and then trailing off into box office oblivion—America originally didn't believe in the possibility of success for *Star Wars*.

Not even toy companies believed in the property. When Lucas originally shopped around the license to produce toys, none of the major buyers pursued the film. Only Kenner Toys—a subsidiary of the Fortune 500 food-processing company, General Mills, Inc. (i.e., part of the company's toy division)—bit on the license. This is why the large capital, cursive "G" that represented a General Mills brand was emblazoned on every *Star Wars* toy's proof-of-purchase seal.

However, following the film's premiere, *Star Wars* was a bonafide hit with moviegoers: lines of fans who viewed the film for the third, fourth, or fifth time wrapped around city blocks; phrases such as "lightsaber," "the Force," and "Death Star" entered the American lexicon; rumors of an Academy Award nomination for Best Picture were bandied about by critics, and *Star Wars* reaped worldwide, lifetime box office receipts of more than three-quarters of a billion dollars.

But in spite of the runaway success of *Star Wars*, the aforementioned production delay didn't just affect the release of the movie. Kenner Toys—now the film's license holder fortunate enough to produce action figures based on the film's characters—

e space opera *Star Wars Episode IV: A New Hope* launched one of the biggest pop-culture phenomenons in history. *Disney/Lucasfilm/20th Century Fox/Heritage Auctions*

aced a similar delay in getting their own products o retail. Before the movie hit theaters, Kenner everely underestimated consumer demand for *Star Wars* merchandise, and did not develop an action figure line quickly enough for a fourth quarter, Christmastime 1977 release on store shelves (since t takes time to craft toys and action figures), so one of the company's executives, Bernard Loomis, a man responsible for some of the most important

made a stunning decision: to afford kids and collectors the mere PROMISE of action figures to come. Kenner's postponement yielded collectors their very first *Star Wars*-related *product*; not of action figures or poseable creatures or deluxe playsets, mind you, but a sort of chipboard "place holder" to placate rabid fans until toy factories finished production on the first assortment of the original twelve *Star Wars* action figures, which hit retail

Early Bird
Certificate
Package.

The stars of

Authentic

Start your own collection with an Early Bird Set
With this Special Certificate Package, you can be sure of own-
ing a set of the first authentic STAR WARS figures available.

Early Bird Certificate Package
(a.k.a. "Early Bird Kit")

[Production #38140]

1st appearance: Early Bird Certificate Package
1st carded appearance: n/a
Original Retail Price (average): $7.99

Since Kenner had initially underestimated demand for *Star Wars* product, they had nothing at all ready for the Christmas season of 1977. Thankfully, Kenner executive Bernard Loomis, president of the Kenner Toy Division from 1970-1978, concocted a revolutionary idea. He became the brainchild of Kenner's first brilliant action figure-related offering: the "Early Bird Certificate Package"—selling American children the "promise" of figurines.

Kenner limited sales to 500,000 units and the 2,000,000 figures in the Gift Certificate Program promoted the sale of a whopping 40,000,000 figures the following year.

Solicited at retail "for a limited time only—not to be sold after December 31, 1977," the Star Wars Early Bird Certificate Package, essentially a slapdash gift set comprised entirely of color-printed paper and chipboard, was sold for $7.99 at finer retail outlets and department stores across America. Before submitting the Redemption Certificate to Kenner, here is what this "Early Bird Kit" (the set's nickname from collectors) contained:

- Early Bird Certificate (coupon) "good for 4 authentically detailed STAR WARS Action Figures"—can be separated into "coupon" and "receipt"
- Colorful Display Stand with STAR WARS (characters) Picture
- STAR WARS Space Club (Membership) Card signed by Luke Skywalker
- STAR WARS Stickers, 4: "May the Force Be with You," C-3PO, R2-D2, "Star Wars" logo
- Proof-of-Purchase Coupon
- "After Tearing Off at Perforations" directions

The set's chipboard-comprised Colorful Display Stand featured painted portrayals of the first 12 *Star Wars* characters, the exact same painted representations found on the original *Star Wars* 12-back action figure packages, *and* it could be folded to construct a display stand for the first 12 figures. The base/"stage" of the stand had 12 oval-shaped holes that could be punched out, so that when your 4 *Star Wars* figures arrived via the mail, you would also receive a set of 12 white action figure foot pegs to encourage you to buy the remaining 8 of the 12 initial figures. (For a detailed image of these pegs, see the Cloud City Playset; the pegs for both sets are *exactly the same*).

After you sent the Early Bird Certificate to Kenner for redemption, you would receive the following in the mail, far earlier than originally stated: Kenner shipped every figure out by March of 1978. MIBaggie means "Mint In Sealed (translucent) Baggie."

- White rectangular mailer box (from Maple Plain, Minnesota)
- Artoo-Detoo action figure MIBaggie (stamped "MADE IN HONG KONG" in black lettering)
- Chewbacca action figure MIBaggie (stamped "MADE IN HONG KONG" in black lettering)
- Luke Skywalker action figure MIBaggie (stamped "MADE IN HONG KONG" in black lettering)
- Princess Leia action figure MIBaggie (stamped "MADE IN HONG KONG" in black lettering)
- 12 white foot pegs/"plastic holders" to at-

tach figures to the already-purchased stand MIBaggie
- White, fragile, vaccu-formed plastic figure holder tray
- "Early Bird Set Premium Offer of Collector Stand" paper redemption slip/ "Welcome to the Exciting World of Star Wars!" form (also shows how to use foot pegs)
- 1977 *Star Wars* catalog
- White Paper Insert (no printing)

Please note that the baggies containing the four Early Bird figures could be either taped or heat-sealed. If taped, on almost every found sample, the tape has become a bit yellowed and brittle—so be careful handling samples. Regardless of how the bags were sealed, there are four different types of stamped plastic baggies: 1) a baggie horizontally stamped "MADE IN HONG KONG" in small *white* letters (roughly waist or chest high to the figure in question)—stamped either on the front or back of the baggie, since these figures were quickly placed into the baggies; 2) a baggie with "MADE IN HONG KONG" stamped in small *black* letters running horizontally; 3) occasionally, a baggie with "MADE IN HONG KONG" in small black lettering again, yet running vertically (usually only on the Chewbacca baggie), and running the length of the entire baggie; or 4) very rarely, a baggie

may be stamped—usually on the back side—with the "Kenner" logo in blue lettering (usually only on the R2-D2 baggie). The final figure-less baggie, the sealed baggie containing the 12 white foot pegs for the Early Bird Display Stand, has no lettering and is NEVER taped shut—it is heat-sealed.

It should also be noted that with the earliest versions of the Luke Skywalker action figure included with this set, sometimes he included a "double-telescoping" lightsaber. This is a very rare and hard-to-find accessory, and causes the value of this already rare set to jump in price by $400 to $500 or more.

Since this set is difficult to find an average price for, what follows is a determination of average values, with a full mint, sealed set (all pieces and parts **MISP**) selling for over $4,500-$5,000:

Original Early Bird Certificate Package Envelope: **MISP**: **$2,650-$2,800+**; **MIP** (with all paperwork): **$385-$425+**; Early Bird Certificate Coupon (on its own): **MLC**: **$235-$255+**; Early Bird Certificate Package Colorful Display Stand (on its own): **MLC**: **$75-$100+**. Boxed Early Bird Figures & foot pegs (all SEALED in baggies) with Plastic Tray and paperwork: **MISP**: **$2,650-$2,900+**; **MIB**: **$1,350-$1,650+**.

> Captain Panaka: " ... An extremely well put together little droid. Without a doubt, it saved the ship, as well as our lives."
>
> Sabé: "It is to be commended ... what is its number?"
>
> Captain Panaka: "R2-D2, your Highness."
>
> —RD-D2 is presented to Sabé, Queen Amidala's decoy (*Episode I: The Phantom Menace*)

Artoo-Detoo (R2-D2)

[Production #38200]

1st appearance: Early Bird Certificate Package
1st carded appearance: 12–back card
Original Retail Price (average): $1.99

- o "Early Bird" dark(er) blue paint or standard blue variations
- • with paper label/sticker, unique to the figure

In the film canon, the first appearance of R2-D2 occurs when the intrepid astromech droid busies himself saving Jedi Master Qui-Gon Jinn, Jedi Knight Obi-Wan Kenobi, Gungan Jar Jar Binks, as well as Queen Amidala and her court when "the little droid … bypassed the main power drive," states Commander Ric Olié, of the queen's royal starship in *The Phantom Menace* and allows the refugees to escape a blockade.

Although the word *droid*, a truncation of "android," was coined back in the early 1950s within the pages of Quinn Publishing's sci-fi pulp magazine, *If*, (re: Mari Wolf's short story "ROBOTS of the WORLD! ARISE!"), we collectors now utilize the term to describe the ludicrously famous, bucket-shaped robot known as R2-D2 and his golden-plated humanoid companion, C-3PO. Furthermore, Wookieepedia states that the "official" definition of the word—an explanation that expertly encapsulates the meaning of *droid*—is delineated as follows: "a mechanical being with a self-aware consciousness, as distinguished from a computer by having a self-contained method of locomotion."

Even the most casual fans can attest that the *Star*

Wars film universe is simply littered with droids in *Episodes I* through *VI*: from the Trade Federation's "clankers," those B1 battle droids featured in *Episode I*, to the more civil and less belligerent protocol droids found in the original trilogy, whether from the LOM or 3PO-series; from knuckleheaded DUM-series pit droid mechanics of *Episode I* to the more furtive probe droids utilized by the Empire, whether the Viper-series or Darth Maul's three DRK-1s; from highly proficient medical droids such as the Rebellion's 2-1B surgeons from *The Empire Strikes Back*, or the Imperial "chopper" DD-13 medical assistant droid in *Revenge of the Sith*. Even the most dangerous sentient robots in the galaxy fall under this classification: the deadly assassin droid IG-88 and his sinister IG-86 "brethren."

However, the iconic droid with the designation of "R2-D2," is, more specifically, an *astromech* droid: acting as his master Luke Skywalker's (and formerly, Luke's father, Anakin Skywalker's) in-flight, automated mechanic and co-pilot, carrying out a wide range of duties—most specifically repair and navigation. Regardless of which spacecraft an astromech droid operates, innumerable experienced pilots depend upon the peerless skills of these trusty

R2-D2 early darker dome, left, and standard dome, right. The right-hand photo also features R2-D2 without his paper label.

astromech droids, who aid their humanoid companions with the wide variety of tools and equipment stored within recessed compartments, later featured in many Kenner and Hasbro astromech droid action figures. Astromech droids are extremely popular with both the military and general public, whether assisting in the operation of an X-wing T-65 starfighter or one of the many versions of the Rebellion's Y-wing starfighter, both via an external socket, or a Jedi Eta-2 *Actis*-class light interceptor, a.k.a. Jedi starfighter, via a dorsal socket.

Manufactured by Industrial Automaton as a product of the corporation's "R" series of astromech droids, Artoo-Detoo is part of IA's landmark "R2" line, since the company's earlier "R1" line of models was beset by failure. In contrast, IA's R2 line was expertly designed, and as a result, these models were

in demand far and wide throughout the galaxy. And Artoo-Detoo is the finest member of a spectacular series of droids.

As simple as Kenner's R2-D2 action figure is, with its paper sticker, clicking head, vac-metallized silver dome, and two sturdy legs, this original interpretation of Artoo-Detoo flew off of retail shelves—it was the perfect encapsulation of the brave, childlike hero of the Rebellion. Although these days three points of articulation does not an action figure make, there are few robots more iconic than R2-D2.

 MOC: *SW* 12B: **$285**, 20/21B: **$190**; *ESB*: **$80**; **MLC**: darker "Early Bird" dome: **$35-38**, standard color dome: **$12**.

Chewbacca (a.k.a. "Chewie")

[Production #38210]

1st appearance: Early Bird Certificate Package
1st carded appearance: 12-back card
Original Retail Price (average): $1.99

- ○ standard brown or iridescent green pouch variations
- • with Bowcaster (unique to the figure) and Bowcaster variations

The Chewbacca action figure must have been a fabulous seller for Kenner since this toy is the only version of the character ever produced for the vintage line, and it was solicited on every cardback assortment from 1978-1985, even appearing on a POTF cardback with unique coin. Every fan who amassed a *Star Wars* collection—regardless of the collection's size—must have felt compelled to own this fierce yet tender-hearted Wookiee. Kenner's interpretation of Chewbacca is a first-rate plastic representation of the character, and the figure's height advantage afforded it the ability to tower over most members of the Imperial forces, from Stormtroopers to TIE Fighter Pilots, from Biker Scouts to Imperial Gunners.

As a character, Chewbacca is a member of the tall, shaggy, sentient Wookiee race of sturdy bipeds, where the word "Wookiee" is translated from the species' language of *Shyriiwook* ("Wookiee speak" to the uninitiated) as "People of the Trees." A class of humanoids renowned for their loyalty and intellect, yet hair-trigger tempers, the canopy-dwelling Wookiees are both long-lived and honorable. Although many would suggest that the Wookiee race was essentially technophobic, they couldn't be more incorrect. As cited in Wookieepedia: "(Wookiees) could easily mend and maintain modern starcrafts (sic), and were even known to effect temporary repairs of hyperdrives with pieces of hardwood."

As an adventurer, Chewbacca becomes a hero of the Wookiee people during the period of the Clone Wars (22-19 BBY), and following the sinister implementation of contingency Order 66 (the coordinated execution of most members of the Jedi Order), Chewie assists Jedi Master Yoda in escaping the clutches of the rising tide of the Empire. Chewbacca follows Yoda's lead when the Wookiee's home planet of Kashyyyk

falls under Imperial control, and he becomes a fugitive from justice fighting against the influence of the Empire. On one mission where Chewbacca botches an escape attempt while trying to free Wookiee prisoners from Trandoshan slavers (see Bossk), his spaceship garners laser fire from a cadre of Imperial TIE fighters. The TIEs are led by Han Solo, a young lieutenant in the Imperial Navy, whose sympathy toward the defiant Wookiee turns him against his Imperial commanders. Ultimately, Solo defies direct orders and brazenly rescues Chewie from certain death—the young Corellian pilot earning the Wookiee's undying gratitude and staunch fealty via his peoples' tradition of a repaid "life debt." The two quickly find an Imperial bounty placed upon their heads and become smugglers and boon companions, traveling the galaxy as devoted friends and co-pilots of the *Millennium Falcon*, eventually playing a key role in the defeat of the Empire.

It is worth noting two items of interest re: the Kenner action figure. Firstly, there are three important variations of Chewie's crossbow: a) an early version made of dark green, translucent plastic (not pictured) [perhaps] included with the "Early Bird Kit," b) the standard blue-black (pictured above) included with most carded samples, and c) the lighter blue (pictured above) packaged [perhaps] within ESB packages. Furthermore, Chewbacca figures came with two possible colors of tool pouch: a) the hard-to-find iridescent green pouch, included with early samples, and b) the standard brown colored tool pouch.

MOC: *SW* 12B: **$375+**, 20/21B: **$215**; *ESB*: **$100**; *ROTJ*: **$80**; *POTF*: **$115**;
MLC: standard crossbow: **$16**, iridescent early issue crossbow: **$30-$35**.

CLOSE-UP

Chewbacca Bowcaster variations: lighter blue and blue-black.

Chewbacca, with Bowcaster.

Aunt Beru: "Owen, he can't stay here forever, most of his friends have gone. It means so much to him."

Uncle Owen: "Well, I'll make it up to him next year, I promise."

Aunt Beru: "Luke's just not a farmer, Owen. He has too much of his father in him."

Uncle Owen: "That's what I'm afraid of."

— Luke's adopted Aunt and Uncle discuss his fate

Luke Skywalker (a.k.a. "Farm Boy Luke")

[Production #38180]

1st appearance: Early Bird Certificate Package
1st carded appearance: 12-back card
Original Retail Price (average): $1.99

- o blond, light-brown, dark-brown, or orange hair variations
- with Lightsaber (standard or double-telescoping lightsaber variations), unique to the figure

There are few toys created in the fifty-year history of the medium of action figures, 1964-present, that evoke such fond memories as Kenner's original Luke Skywalker figure. This version of the Rebellion's *purported* "new hope" is often called "Farm Boy Luke" based upon the fact that the outfit worn by the character reflects his tenure as a humdrum moisture-farming adolescent while he was being raised by his Aunt Beru and Uncle Owen on the desert planet Tatooine of the Outer Rim Territories. With his sand-proof leg bindings (they're not boots) and gripping soles, a Tatooine farm tunic, light pants, and a brown utility belt with molded "droid caller" and tool pouch hooked onto its right-hand side, this figure is prepped for Luke's adventures to begin.

Luke Skywalker and his younger twin sister by mere seconds, Leia Amidala Skywalker (see Princess Leia Organa), were born under duress on the asteroid colony of Polis Massa in 19 BBY to their mother, Padmé Naberrie, the one-time Queen (and Senator) Amidala of the world of Naboo. They are spirited away to this covert location in order to hide their existence from their father, Anakin Skywalker (See Anakin Skywalker and Darth Vader). Padmé is slowly dying from the effects of a Force-choke perpetrated upon her by her husband in the confused throes of apparent betrayal; after giving birth, Padmé

succumbs to her wounds, the stress of childbirth, and a broken heart—spiritually destroyed, she loses the will to live.

Fearing for the lives of the newborn babes, Senator Bail Organa, Jedi Master Obi-Wan Kenobi, and Grand Master Yoda (see Ben [Obi-Wan] Kenobi and Yoda) recognize that Emperor Palpatine (see The Emperor) will turn the galaxy upside-down in order to locate these two heirs of Skywalker since they are potential threats to the Galactic Empire. Therefore, a plan is hatched: Obi-Wan choses to take Luke to Tatooine, where the boy lives a clandestine existence with Anakin Skywalker's step-brother and his wife, moisture farmers Owen and Beru Lars, while "Old Ben" lives nearby, close enough to protect Luke from the Empire's threats. Senator Organa takes Leia to Alderran, where he and his wife, Queen Breha of Alderaan, raise the girl as a princess.

Sporting a mere five points of articulation, the loose interpretation of actor Mark Hamill's visage wasn't the doll's number-one selling point: it was the figure's sliding lightsaber feature. With its delicate tip and lever that allowed kids and collectors to slide the weapon back-and-forth, this "telescoping" lightsaber feature was an ingenious delight. Delineated here is the text that appears on the back of the earli-

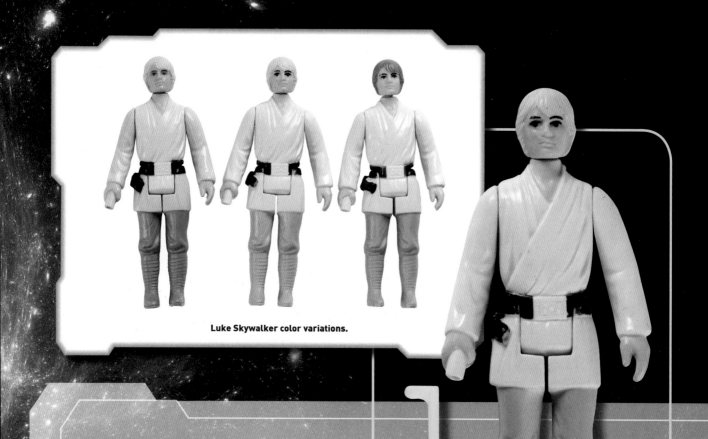

Luke Skywalker color variations.

Luke Skywalker, with Lightsaber.

est action figure packages: "How to work Light Saber. When in closed position, tip of saber sticks out slightly. Push arm lever forward and pull saber out by tip. To close, push tip of saber in and push arm lever back."

However, some of the earliest released samples of Luke Skywalker feature a "double-telescoping" lightsaber, whether carded or in the "Early Bird Kit"—a two-piece lightsaber accessory with a thin saber tip running through the entire length of a long shaft, which is separately moveable and removable from its outer shaft. These double-telescoping sabers are VERY rare and command staggeringly expensive prices on the secondary market. Unfortunately, these lightsabers are relatively easy to reproduce, so please visit reputable websites such as The Imperial Gunnery (www.imperialgunnery.com) to check if your saber is authentic. Mint On Card (MOC) samples of Luke Skywalker with this accessory have sold for over $10,000—and are impossibly rare.

 MOC: *SW* 12B: **$650+**, 20/21B: **$325**; *ESB* brown hair: **$250**, blond hair: **$225**; *ROTJ*: **$210**; **MLC**: standard lightsaber, blond hair: **$21**, standard lightsaber, brown hair: **$50-$60+**, double-telescoping lightsaber: **$225-$325+**, depending upon condition.

Luke Skywalker "single" vs. "double-telescoping" lightsabers.

Princess Leia Organa

[Production #38190]

1st appearance: Early Bird Certificate Package
1st carded appearance: 12-back card
Original Retail Price (average): $1.99

- o black hair + black belt or brown hair + brown belt variations
- • with dark blue/black Princess Leia Blaster (Defender sporting blaster pistol)
- • with white vinyl Princess Leia Organa Cape, unique to the figure

Birthed mere moments after her older twin brother (see Luke Skywalker), Leia Amidala Skywalker was born on the asteroid colony of Polis Massa to their wounded mother, Padmé Naberrie, the one-time Queen and Senator Amidala of the world of Naboo. Transported to this clandestine location in order to hide the children's existence from Anakin Skywalker (see Anakin Skywalker and Darth Vader)—their father and newly christened Dark Lord of the Sith—Padmé is slowly dying from the effects of a Force-choke executed by her husband; she succumbs to her wounds and passes away following the stress of childbirth and a profoundly broken heart.

Senator Bail Organa, Jedi Master Obi-Wan Kenobi, and Grand Master Yoda (see Ben [Obi-Wan] Kenobi and Yoda) fears for the children's lives and recognizes that Emperor Palpatine (see The Emperor) will comb the galaxy for their location, since the heirs of Anakin Skywalker are dangerous threats to his machinations. In order to protect the babes, Obi-Wan removes Luke to Tatooine, while Senator Organa escapes with Leia to his homeworld of Alderran. If Coruscant is the Republic's beating heart, the divine beauty of Alderaan symbolizes the Republic's spiritual soul: with its refined culture, unspoiled natural resources, and devotion to peace, the Alderaanians' lush planet represents benevolence and prosperity throughout the galaxy. Bail Organa and his wife, Queen Breha of Alderaan from the House Organa, raise her as their adopted princess.

The strong-willed, highly perceptive, endlessly resourceful Leia Organa is raised as the heir to the House Organa, where her skill at politics becomes apparent at an early age, eventually earning her the position of senator. Wise beyond her years, Leia's personality is similar to that of her true mother, Padmé Amidala: she is not a demure damsel-in-distress requiring rescue, and she finds tributes from her loyal subjects unnecessary. Senator/Princess Leia Organa is an honest politician who cares about the well being of her people. Yet inside her beats the heart of an intrepid adventurer.

As a strong advocate for the Rebel Alliance, her adamant position against the Empire puts Princess Leia in the government's crosshairs, a conflict that sets the opening sequence for the first *Star Wars* film, *Episode IV: A New Hope*. Here, the capture of Leia's CR-90 Corvette (the Rebel Blockade Runner known as *Tantive IV*), is boarded by Darth Vader and his Imperial forces (see Imperial Stormtrooper),

No. 38190 *Ages 4 and up

STAR WARS™

Princess Leia Organa

FREE BOBA FETT
WITH PURCHASE OF
ANY FOUR STAR
WARS ACTION
FIGURES
(See blister on back)

®Kenner

Meets or exceeds all safety
requirements of Product Standard F276
©T. TWENTIETH CENTURY FOX FILM CORP.

Princess Leia Organa, with accessories.

Princess Leia Organa, MOC (*Star Wars* card)."

which are deployed from the Sith Lord's (see Darth Vader) capital ship, the Star Dreadnought known as the *Executor* (see Darth Vader's Star Destroyer action playset). After Imperial Stormtroopers seize the princess, she is violently interrogated by Imperial officer Grand Moff* Wilhuff Tarkin regarding the location of a concealed Rebel base. Even under duress, Leia refuses to disclose the base's true location, and so Tarkin chooses to target her homeworld of Alderaan for destruction, exploding the planet and providing the entire galaxy with an example of what happens to those opponents of Emperor Palpatine (see The Emperor).

Thankfully, immediately before her capture, Leia places the plans for the Death Star battle station into a Rebel-allied R2 unit (see Artoo-Detoo [R2-D2]) with the hopes of the intrepid droid finding one of the last remaining Jedi Knights in the galaxy (see Ben [Obi-Wan] Kenobi). Eventually, the droid and his companion (see See-Threepio [C-3PO]) escape the clutches of the Empire and find their way to the desert planet Tatooine,

where they are bought by Luke Skywalker who, upon cleaning the R2-unit, encounters the droid's message from Leia appealing for help from "Obi-Wan Kenobi." Luke takes the droids to visit "Old Ben" Kenobi, and the two determine the princess' peril.

After a series of (mis-)adventures, Leia is eventually rescued by Luke, Han Solo, and their small band of Rebel heroes, and begins to play an important, essential role in the Rebel Alliance. For further information, see Leia Organa (Bespin Gown), Leia (Hoth Outfit), Princess Leia Organa)(Boushh Disguise), and Princess Leia Organa (In Combat Poncho).

*"Grand Moff" was a title given to a Regional Governor of Oversectors/Priority Sectors—i.e., locations that were of special interest to the Empire.

MOC: *SW* 12B: **$325+**, 20/21B: **$215**; *ESB*: **$175**; *ROTJ*: **$300**; **MLC**: **$25**.

Ben (Obi-Wan) Kenobi, with accessories.

Ben (Obi-Wan) Kenobi

[Production #38250]

1st carded appearance: 12-back card
Original Retail Price (average): $1.99

- o white or gray hair variations
- • with Lightsaber (standard or double-telescoping lightsaber variations), unique to the figure
- • with brown vinyl cape, unique to the figure

Obi-Wan Kenobi—later known by the name "Ben Kenobi" while in exile—is one of the last existing Jedi Knights in the galaxy following the collapse of the Galactic Republic at the opening of *A New Hope*. As a young man, Obi-Wan is trained by the headstrong risk-taker Qui-Gon Jinn, and during one particular adventure, the two arrive on the desert planet Tatooine, where they encounter a young human child who possesses the highest level of *midi-chlorians* in recorded history. Intelligent, microscopic life forms that live within human cells, when these midi-chlorians are present in sufficient numbers, they will allow the host body to detect the "pervasive energy field known as the Force." Qui Gonn and Obi-Wan discover that the boy known as Anakin Skywalker possesses a midi-chlorian count so high, they question his mother about his conception: Shmi Skywalker confirms that Anakin's was a fatherless birth—the boy was conceived by the midi-chlorians.

Believing the child to be "The Chosen One" spoken about in an ancient Jedi Prophecy (he who would one day bring balance to the Force), the two Jedi take the boy from his homeworld and Obi-Wan trains him to become one of the most powerful Jedi Knights in the galaxy. Unfortunately, passion and anger ultimately cloud Anakin's judgment, and he is manipulated by Supreme Chancellor Palpatine (secretly the Sith Lord Darth Sidious) to embrace the dark side of the Force, becoming Sidious' apprentice, Darth Vader. When Palpatine ascends to the position of Emperor, and following a cli-

Obi-Wan: "These aren't the droids you're looking for."
Stormtrooper: "These aren't the droids we're looking for ... "
Obi-Wan: "He can go about his business."
Stormtrooper: "You can go about your business ..."
Obi-Wan: "Move along."
Stormtrooper: "Move along ... move along ... "

— Obi-Wan Kenobi using the Force to dissuade a Stormtrooper from harassing him and Luke Skywalker

mactic showdown with Obi-Wan Kenobi, Anakin—now as Darth Vader—is mortally wounded by Kenobi on the lava fields of Mustafar. His body burnt beyond recognition, the confused pawn of Palpatine loses his limbs, as well as his soul, to the dark side.

After defeating his former padawan, Obi-Wan learns of a plot to destroy the Jedi, albeit too late. Following the decimation of the Galactic Republic and the beginning of the Great Jedi Purge with the execution of the infamous Order 66, Obi-Wan and Yoda race to the side of a pregnant Padmé Amidala, Anakin's wife, to witness the birth of her twin children: Luke and Leia. Padmé dies in childbirth and Leia is taken to live with the Organas on Alderaan, while Luke is spirited away by Obi-Wan, who goes into hiding—existing in a world of self-imposed exile for a period of nearly two decades, never too far away from Luke. Although Obi-Wan was at one time a Jedi Master, Republic General, and member of the Jedi High Council, all of these prestigious titles are washed away by the rising tide of the Empire.

Years later on Tatooine, when Luke comes calling on Ben with a message from Princess Leia via the trusty astromech droid R2-D2, "Ben Kenobi" introduces Luke to the Force, in the hopes that he is "The Chosen One."

Regarding his action figure, for an explanation of the difference between Obi-Wan's double-telescoping lightsaber, and a standard-telescoping version, please see Luke Skywalker. Mint On Card (MOC), packaged samples of this impossibly rare double-telescoping lightsaber Ben (Obi-Wan) Kenobi figure are incredibly expensive, commanding nearly $20,000 each.

 MOC: *SW* 12B: **$325**, 20/21B: **$175**; *ESB*: **$65+**; *ROTJ*: **$120**; *POTF*: **$150**; **MLC**: standard lightsaber, white hair: **$20**, standard lightsaber, gray hair: **$20**, double-telescoping lightsaber: **$325-$375+**, depending upon condition.

Ben (Obi-Wan) Kenobi, MOC.

Darth Vader

[Production #38230]

1st carded appearance: 12-back card
Original Retail Price (average): $1.99

- o soft gray head or standard black hard head variations
- o hard sculpt torso or soft sculpt torso
- o gloss or matte torso/gloss or matte limbs
- • with Lightsaber (standard or double-telescoping lightsaber variations, unique to the figure
- • with black vinyl Darth Vader Cape, unique to the figure

As Supreme Commander of the Imperial Forces of Emperor Palpatine, the sinister, cloaked Sith Lord called Darth Vader holds a rank directly below the Emperor in the Imperial Government. Formerly known as daring Jedi Knight Anakin Skywalker (see Anakin Skywalker, Ben [Obi-Wan] Kenobi, Luke Skywalker, and The Emperor for more back story on this character), the second chronological *Star Wars* film trilogy (*Episodes IV-VI*) recounts this once-noble hero's descent into dark-ness and his devotion to the Dark Side of the Force as an (Apprentice) Sith Lord. While we ultimately witness his eventual redemption through the love and devotion he feels toward his son (Luke—the galaxy's purported "new hope"), as Lord Darth Vader, this character is the most important antagonist of *A New Hope, The Empire Strikes Back*, and *Return of the Jedi*

In order to protect his artificial limbs and damaged organs, Darth Vader dons a suit of armor (serial number: E-3778Q-1): a life-support system that keeps the Sith Lord alive in spite of injuries that would have killed a normal

Darth Vader, with accessories.

Darth Vader (as Anakin Skywalker): "Now ... go, my son. Leave me."

Luke Skywalker: "No. You're coming with me. I'll not leave you here. I've got to save you."

Darth Vader (as Anakin Skywalker): "You already ... have, Luke. You were right. You were right about me. Tell your sister ... you were right."

— Darth Vader's deathbed discussion with his son, Luke Skywalker

human as a result of the trauma suffered following his battle with Obi-Wan Kenobi on the volcanic planet of Mustafar (ca. 19 BBY). The Sith Lord allows no one else to witness him donning this uniform since this would reveal his vulnerable physical nature to others: we observe brief glimpses of his head only rarely throughout the aforementioned three films—particularly when Vader utilizes the rejuvenating effects of his specially-crafted spherical hyperbaric meditation chamber aboard the Star Dreadnought, the *Executor* (see Darth Vader's Star Destroyer Playset).

Wearing a hermetic collar, vision enhancement receptors, a voice projector/respiratory intake, a plastoid girdle that protects his abdominal organs, ribbed multi-ply trousers, shin armor that guards his prostheses, boots that adhere to his artificial limbs, an armored breastplate that shields his badly injured chest, and intricately designed neck vertebra replaced with metal, Vader's entire body requires maintenance via the use of a control panel—the black box located in the middle of the Sith Lord's chest. This control panel monitors Vader's life support systems and controls these processes through the use of this central processing unit, which allows for the insertion of readout cards that periodically monitor the systems that maintain his suit.

Upon becoming a Sith Apprentice, Anakin Skywalker takes the name Darth Vader—where it has been suggested that *darth* may be a contraction of Dark Lord of the Sith, or a corruption of the Rakatan word *Daritha* meaning "emperor," or it could possibly be a combination of the words *darr* ("triumph/conquest") and *tah* ("death")— therefore, *darr tah* suggests to "triumph over death," or obtain immortality (or possibly the alternate translation, "conquest through death").

Nonetheless, while utilizing this armored shell as a new identity, Vader embraces the dark side of the Force and becomes a Dark Lord of the Sith under the thumb of Emperor Palpatine for a number of years, where he loyally serves his master until convinced otherwise by his only son, Luke. Witnessing Palpatine destroying his progeny, Anakin eschews his mantle as Darth Vader at the cost of his own life, and hurls the Emperor down a four-hundred kilometer deep shaft, where the last of the line of Sith Lords explodes into a burst of dark side energy.

Regarding his action figure, for an explanation of the difference between Darth Vader's double-telescoping lightsaber and a standard-telescoping version, please see Luke Skywalker. Mint On Card (MOC), packaged samples of an impossibly rare double-telescoping lightsaber Darth Vader figure are incredibly expensive, commanding nearly $20,000 each.

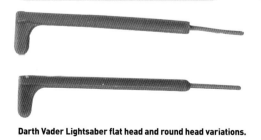

Darth Vader Lightsaber flat head and round head variations.

MOC: *SW 12B*: **$575-$650+**, *20/21B*: **$325**; *ESB*: **$150**; *ROTJ*: **$120**; *POTF*: **$210**; **MLC**: standard lightsaber: **$18**, w/soft head variation: **$25-$32**, double-telescoping lightsaber: **$325-$375++**, depending upon condition.

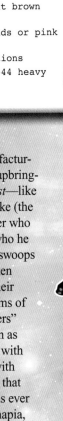

Han Solo

[Production #38260]

1st carded appearance: 12-back card
Original Retail Price (average): $1.99

- o small or large head variations
- o large head with dark brown or light brown variations
- o large head with pale face/pale hands or pink face/pink hands
- o white or black molded pants variations
- • with blue/black Rebel Blaster (DL-44 heavy blaster pistol)

CLOSE-UP
Han Solo's
Rebel Blaster.

Orphaned at an early age on the famous manufacturing planet of Corellia, Han Solo shares a similar upbringing to Charles Dickens' protagonist in *Oliver Twist*—like Oliver, Solo is adopted by the corrupt Garris Shrike (the "Fagin" of this tale), a hot-tempered bounty hunter who turns a profit via organizing a group of orphans who he manipulates into committing small thefts, racing swoops (see Dengar), and running confidence games. When successful, the orphans are fed; when down-on-their luck, which was inevitable, they became the victims of Shrike's physical beatings. With their "headquarters" organized on a decommissioned troop ship known as the *Trader's Luck*, eventually Shrike is too liberal with his fists, and a nineteen-year-old Solo absconds with the starship. Unfortunately, during the showdown that allows him to flee, the only sentient being who has ever been kind to Solo is killed by Shrike: Dewlannamapia, a benevolent old Wookiee cook and surrogate mother

figure to the orphans. "Dewlanna"—Solo's nickname for the compassionate Wookiee—fed Solo, educated him as best she knew how, and taught him the language of Shyriiwook: the young man is devastated.

Eventually Solo flees to Coruscant, the symbolic center of the Empire (see The Emperor), where he fulfills his dream of becoming a pilot in the Imperial Navy, albeit under an assumed name: Vyyk Draygo. Graduating top of his class as a lieutenant, he is sent on one particular mission to assist a slaver and ally of the Empire. After boarding a broken-down slaving craft, Solo encounters the wounded Chewbacca, a Wookiee who the novice Imperial pilot is ordered to skin alive. Solo refuses a direct order, and eventually devises to assist Chewbacca in escaping from the Empire with the help of the Rebel Alliance. Following his

"Look, I ain't in this for your revolution, and I'm not in it for you, princess. I expect to be well paid. I'm in it for the money."

—Han Solo to Princess Leia Organa
regarding the Rebel Alliance
to Restore the Republic

Han Solo,
MOC (*Empire
Strikes Back*
card).

No. 38260
ASST. #69360

Ages 4 and up

Han Solo

Kenner.

Han Solo small and large head variations.

betrayal, Solo is court-martialed and receives a dishonorable discharge, but feels vindicated that he finally saves a Wookiee in memory of Dewlanna's death. Chewbacca, swearing a life-debt to the young pilot (see Chewbacca), joins him as his partner and co-pilot in the dangerous vocation of smuggling.

When introduced to viewers in *Episode IV* as a patron of Chalmun's Spaceport Cantina (a.k.a. the Mos Eisley Cantina [see Cantina Adventure Set *or* Creature Cantina]), Solo is pursued and confronted by an inept Rodian bounty hunter (see Greedo) since Jabba the Hutt places a bounty on the Corellian's head. After dispatching Greedo quite easily, Chewbacca introduces Luke Skywalker and Ben "Obi-Wan" Kenobi to him: they and their two droids (see Artoo-Detoo [R2-D2] and See-Threepio [C-3PO]) are searching for a ship to provide them safe passage to the planet Alderaan—a trip free of Imperial entanglements. Suggesting they use the unassuming *Millennium Falcon*, Solo and Chewbacca take the job since the funds they can potentially collect will help them to repay the Hutt crime lord, yet they never receive those funds from Luke and Ben: Alderaan is destroyed by the Empire's new superweapon, the Death Star.

After accepting his fate and assisting his newfound ally and friend, Luke, in a series of adventures fight-

ing the Empire, *Episode IV* ends with Solo piloting the *Millennium Falcon*, deftly shooting down two TIE fighters that bracket Luke's X-wing (see X-wing Fighter) during his trench run of the Death Star at the Battle of Yavin. Without Solo destroying the two "eyeballs" (see Imperial TIE fighter) and disabling Darth Vader's modified TIE (see Darth Vader TIE Fighter), the first Death Star would never have been destroyed by Luke's photon torpedoes, and the Rebellion would have failed in their mission.

Wearing his Corellian spacer black vest—an article of clothing donned by Corellian mariners which is outfitted with extra pockets to hold extra ammunition and supplies—along with a white shirt, belt with droid caller and holster for his customized DL-44 blaster pistol, black action boots, and black captain's pants adorned with Corellian Bloodstripes, Kenner's original Han Solo figure is one of the most iconic toys of all time.

MOC: *SW* 12B, small head: **$750**, large head: **$550**; 20/21B, small head: **$460**, large head: **$440**; *ESB* small head: **$300**, large head: **$245**; *ROTJ*: **$175**; **MLC**: small head version: **$25**, large head version: **$20**.

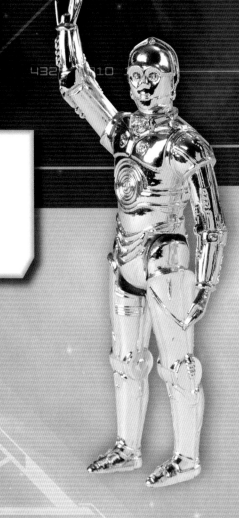

See-Threepio (C-3PO)

[Production #38220]

1st carded appearance: 12-back card
Original Retail Price (average): $1.99

Produced by one of the largest droid-manufacturing corporations in the galaxy—Cybot Galactica—the 3PO-series of *protocol droids* are synthesized to aid their owners in the task of Human-cyborg relations. So sophisticated and exceptional are these droids at fulfilling their programming that this 3PO model line was in steady demand for a full century after their initial manufacture. Crafted to look remarkably similar to the sentient humanoids they serve, protocol droids assist sentient beings with the act of communication. Furthermore, since 3POs were created with servitude in mind, their personalities are fabricated to be subservient and extremely non-violent: 3POs never engage in combat for any reason—not even in self-defense.

Due to the runaway success of the 3PO-series, other companies conceive their own models of protocol droids to compete against Cybot Galactica's money-making 3PO-series, such as Industrial Automaton's LOM-series (see Zuckuss) or Arakyd Industries' RA-7-series (see Death Star Droid).

Apart from the 3PO-series droids' obvious skill, the famous Battle of Endor (*Episode VI: Return of the Jedi*) causes the "C-series" of protocol droids (C-1 to C-9) to skyrocket in popularity. Although Cybot Galactica denies the rumor that the thrilling adventures of a lone protocol droid with the designation of "C-3PO" is the main reason why the C-series becomes popular, it is indeed the revered status of a single unit that sells this entire line of droids.

The protocol droid known as C-3PO, a worrisome, stuffy fussbudget of a robot, is renowned far and wide as a hero of the Rebel Alliance. When partnered with the fearless, happy-go-lucky astromech droid R2-D2, the exploits of this pair serve many functions in the original trilogy, and well beyond: as a brilliant comedy team, à la Abbott and Costello or Laurel and Hardy, as a touchstone that allows younger viewers to relate to the sophisticated space opera that is *Star Wars*, and to illustrate the presence of a caste system in the

"We seem to be made to suffer. It's our lot in life."

— C-3PO commenting on the unfair position droids maintain in the galaxy

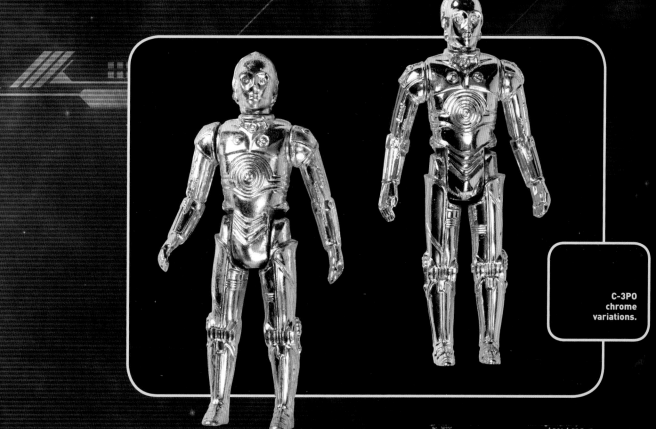

C-3PO chrome variations.

galaxy that exists, a social order where droids inhabit the bottom rung of the galactic ladder.

Using a design reminiscent of the robot "Maria" from Fritz Lang's revolutionary masterpiece *Metropolis* (1927), Lucas was deliberate in directing genius conceptual artist Ralph McQuarric (the visionary responsible for the characteristic "look" of the original trilogy) to create a neutral-looking face for Threepio that projects no emotion whatsoever—all of the character's emotion is related by his histrionic voice, shuffling manner of walking, and stiffness of his limbs.

C-3PO was also a popular figurine that possesses five points of articulation and a stunning gold-plated finish that resulted from Kenner's use of the cutting-edge process of vacuum metallization—a method which applied a thin layer of metallic chrome (0.01 to 0.2 micometers) onto an action figure, creating a "vac-metallized" toy. No *Star Wars* collector in their right mind would amass a collection without this golden droid.

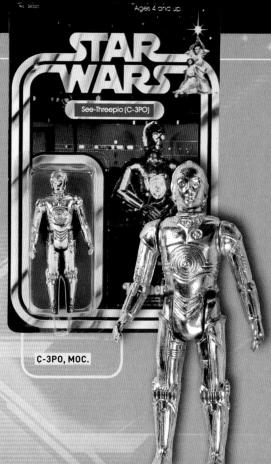

C-3PO, MOC.

 MOC: *SW* 12B: **$315**, 20/21B: **$225**; *ESB*: **$150-$165**; *POTF*: **$100**; **MLC**: **$15-20**, depending upon condition of chrome.

Stormtrooper/Imperial Stormtrooper

[Production #38240]

1st carded appearance: 12-back card
Original Retail Price (average): $1.99
- o circular dots in arms or square dots in arms variations
- o chest piece variations (x3)
- with blue/black Imperial Blaster (E-11 blaster rifle)

Who is underneath a stormtrooper's armor? Whose face is beneath their standard-issue helmets? The answer is simple: the Imperial Stormtrooper Corps are comprised of both former clone troopers from the days of the Galactic Republic, as well as new recruits desirous of supporting the Empire. At the dawn of the Galactic Empire, the remaining clone troopers from the Grand Army of the Republic simply are renamed and reorganized into Imperial stormtroopers.

At the beginning of *A New Hope*, although a few Imperial Stormtroopers are derived from clones of bounty hunter Jango Fett (see Boba Fett) and are born and raised at a variety of facilities (one prominent site was on the planet of Kamino), some are grown with cells from all-new templates. Since most clone troopers age at twice the rate of naturally born human beings, even though they are bred from a superior template, clone troopers' numbers dwindle due to combat attrition and the weight of age. Therefore,

Stormtrooper, with Imperial Blaster.

attracting and retaining new (non-clone) recruits is of paramount importance to the Empire, which swells their ranks with the Imperial Stormtrooper Corps.

Bearing a striking similarity to the "Phase II" armor worn by the second generation clone troopers who are featured toward the end of the Clone Wars (22 BBY-19 BBY), Imperial stormtrooper armor assist these elite soldiers in enforcing the New Order of the Empire (see The Emperor)—a political program where Palpatine: 1) proclaims himself Emperor, 2) legalizes the extermination of

"Under the Empire's New Order, our most cherished beliefs will be safeguarded. We will defend our ideals by force of arms. We will give no ground to our enemies and will stand together against attacks from within or without. Let the enemies of the Empire take heed: those who challenge Imperial resolve will be crushed."

— Emperor Palpatine establishing his New Order

Stormtrooper, MOC *Empire Strikes Back* card.

No. 38240
ASST. #39300

No. 38240

Ages 4 and up.

Stormtrooper, MOC *Star Wars* card.

Imperial Blaster color variations.

the Jedi, and 3) outlines the transformation of the Galactic Republic into the new Galactic Empire. As an extension of the Emperor's will, stormtroopers often utilize swift, efficient, and sometimes brutal tactics to accomplish their missions (e.g., the death of Luke Skywalker's Aunt Beru and Uncle Owen, the slaughter of a clan of Jawas, etc.), so that their vast numbers hold thousands of star systems in thrall.

For more information on the accoutrements carried by an Imperial Stormtrooper, please regard the POTF figure, Luke Skywalker (Imperial Stormtrooper Outfit).

MOC: *SW* 12B: **$375**, 20/21B: **$275**; *ESB*: **$175-$190**; *ROTJ*: **$120**; *POTF*: **$215**; **MLC**: **$15-$20**, depending upon the condition of its white plastic.

ADD ON

Note: Although all twelve of the "original" *Star Wars* figures were pictured on the back of their carded bubble packages (referred to hereafter in the book as a "card-back": literally, the back of a card which is meant to hang on retail sales pegs with a figure on the front packaged inside of a clear plastic bubble) initially, only nine characters were released in the first wave: the four figures included in the Early Bird Kit: Artoo-Detoo, Chewbacca, Luke Skywalker, and Princess Leia Organa, as well as the next five characters: Ben (Obi-Wan) Kenobi, See-Threepio (C-3PO), Darth Vader, Han Solo, and the (Imperial) Stormtrooper. Quickly added to this assortment were three popular early "troop-builders," a term used by diehard action figure collectors to describe generic 'solider-type' characters that can be amassed to form an 'army or 'troop': Death Squad Commander, Jawa, and the Sand People. Observant aficionados will note the absence of these three figures on the Star Wars Action Collector's Stand mail-away promotional included with the Early Bird Kit: they weren't ready yet for photography.

Death Squad Commander/ Star Destroyer Commander

```
[Production #38290]
```

1st carded appearance: 12-back card
Original Retail Price (average): $1.99
- o matte body and limbs or glossy body and limbs variations
- o pale face or pink face variations
- • with blue/black Imperial Blaster (E-11 blaster rifle)

Since the Star Destroyer Commander is the first Imperial trooper produced by Kenner in the vintage *Star Wars* line, it is important to determine that the Galactic Empire possesses divisions within the mighty armed forces of the Imperial Military (a.k.a. the Imperial Service, the successor of the Republic Military), distinct detachments tasked to carry out the will of Emperor Palpatine (see The Emperor) throughout the galaxy. With Palpatine functioning as the august body's Commander-in-Chief, and Darth Vader holding the role of the next-highest rank, Supreme Commander, this assembly of Imperial fighting forces is not simply physically intimidating, but mentally as well—inspiring

fear across the once-harmonious cosmos. Employing the super weapon/space station known as the Death Star (both I & II), which is utilized to enforce Emperor Palpatine's directives, at first blush it appears that the Alliance to Restore the Republic (the Rebellion) has little chance for success against this massive organization possessing of tens of trillions of individual members.

Death Squad Commander uniform variations.

No. 38290
ASST. #69360

Ages 4 and up

STAR
EMPIRE
STRIKES BACK
WARS

Star Destroyer Commander

Kenner

Death Squad
Commander, with
Imperial Blaster.

The branches of the Imperial Military, of the existing nineteen, that are germane to the purpose of this book, are delineated as follows: the Imperial Army, Imperial Navy (a.k.a. Imperial Starfleet), the Imperial Stormtrooper Corps, the Imperial High Command, and the Imperial Palace Guard. Specifically, the Imperial Navy Commander pictured on this action figure's card front is that of Sergeant Derek Torent, a senior watch trooper who is stationed aboard the command center of the first Death Star (see Death Star Space Station) in 0 BBY. As a watch trooper, he ias tasked to monitor external sensor data—the Empire's first line of defense against Rebel assaults.

Regarding the toy, the original name of this character's action figure in 1978, "Death Squad Commander," was controversial due to the title's similarity to the reprehensible "death squads" utilized by the Nazis in WWII (the *Einsatzgruppen*)—so when the figure was re-released for *ESB* and onward, Kenner decided to forego this designation in favor of "Star Destroyer Commander." With this new designation came a curious denotation. Consider the name of the Empire's flagship vehicles, the "Star Destroyers." Quite simply, the name suggests these spacecraft were so immensely powerful, that these colossial ships could figuratively *destroy stars* (!).

The Death Squad/Star Destroyer Commander toy marks one of the four "troop builder" action figure characters produced by Kenner for the company's first assortment of *Star Wars* toys. Concocting this quartet of troop builders and injecting them into the first wave of the toy line allowed early fans of *A New Hope* to amass a horde of these troopers and boost Kenner's retail sales as well. Whether Sand People, Jawas, Imperial Stormtroopers, or Death Squad/Star Destroyer Commanders, kids and collectors simply loved amassing lots of enemy troops. What kid didn't wish to own more than one Jawa or Stormtrooper?

MOC: *SW* 12B: **$425-$450**, 20/21B: **$215-$235**; *ESB*: **$125-$150**; *ROTJ*: **$65-$70**; **MLC**: **$12-$15**.

ADD ON

Jawa, with accessories (vinyl Jawa Cape).

Jawa

[Production #38270]

1st carded appearance: 12-back card
Original Retail Price (average): $1.99

- o large eyes or small eyes variations
- o cloth Jawa Robe cape stitch color variations (light brown or dark brown thread)
- with Jawa Ionization Blaster, unique to the figure
- with brown cloth Jawa Robe or tan vinyl Jawa Cape variations, unique to the figure

A race of gaunt, rodent-like humanoids—possessing shrunken faces sporting huge yellow eyes and a massive set of incisors—that are native to the desert planet of Tatooine, Jawas wear hooded robes to protect their delicate skin from the baking heat of their homeworld. These compulsive, expert scavengers form a well-organized community, scrounging the preservative desert wastes of Tatooine (see Radio Controlled Jawa Sandcrawler) for any scrap metal regardless of its origin—from droids to spaceships—which they sell to anyone showing interest. The race is famous for fixing a broken piece of machinery just well enough for it to work for a limited period of time: until the item is sold, after which the fixed machinery will usually break down once again.

Jawas are renowned for their potent odor, traditional brown-hooded robes featuring polished orange gemstones embedded within the fabric of their facial hoods to protect the creatures' eyes, their short physical stature, and an odd, fast-spoken, high-pitched language known as Jawaese. One theory exists that posits Jawas and Sand People derived from a common ancestor (known as the Kumumgah), since both have genetic markers in common.

"Ya e'um pukay...
yanna kuzu peekay."
(trans. "I won't sell ... this is
not for sale.")

— Two lines of Jawaese (almost) never spoken aloud

Jawa

Kenner

Jawa, MOC.

Jawa, with accessories (cloth Jawa Robe).

As characters, Jawas are born with a passive yet adaptive nature, hardly reacting to the pressures of the Empire other than to view Imperials as yet another customer group to swindle in their pursuit of business opportunities. Contrast their species to that of the aggressive, xenophobic Tusken Raiders (see Sand People), and the Jawas appear far gentler in comparison. Even their weapons are ion blasters—which shoot simple beams of energy to disable droids long enough to fit the mechanical being with a restraining bolt, such as the case of R2-D2.

The Jawa clan featured in the beginning of *Star Wars: Episode IV* contains members of a nomadic tribe led by Chief Nebit—the Jawa from *A New Hope* who distinctively directs negotiations with Luke Skywalker and his adopted father, Uncle Owen Lars.

Kenner's Jawa is one of the best translated of all the company's nascent attempts at producing 3-3/4-inch action figures. The earliest releases of this toy possess a tan-colored vinyl cape instead of a brown fabric one—more similar to the ones included with Darth Vader or Princess Leia Organa. These impossibly expensive accessories are both incredibly rare and terribly easy to fake, so if you encounter any Jawa specimens with vinyl capes, please take them to an authority on the subject for a positive identification.

MOC: *SW* 12D, vinyl cape. **$2,750-$3,000+**, cloth cape: **$210-$225**; 20/21B: **$125-$140**; *ESB*: **$65-$75**; *ROTJ*: **$80-$100**; *POTF*: **$115-$135**; **MLC**: vinyl cape: **$275-$350+**, cloth cape, very light stitching: **$25-$32**, cloth cape, standard: **$12-$16**.

Sand People / Sandpeople / Tusken Raider (Sand People)

[Production #38280]

1st carded appearance: 12-back card
Original Retail Price (average): $1.99

- ○ hollowed face tubes or filled face tubes variations
- ○ dark brown, medium brown, or light brown hands and chest straps
- • with Sand Person Gaderffii ("Gaffi") Stick, unique to the figure
- • with tan vinyl Sand Person Cape, unique to the figure

Although the identities of many masked *Star Wars* characters have been revealed to fans over time (Boba Fett, Darth Vader, the Emperor, Jawas, Stormtroopers, etc.) to this day, not one iteration of the *Star Wars* canon has exposed the true face of Tatooine's rag-covered, violent Sand People. There are few facts known about these bellicose bipeds, since Tusken Raiders are notoriously difficult to study from a biological standpoint for a number of reasons: 1) Sand People *may* be physically in-compatible with humans, 2) they possess hostile relationships toward outsiders, and 3) in their cul-ture, to expose any part of flesh to the outside air is considered scandalous—offenders of this rule were cast out of their tribe or (during grave offenses) beaten until lifeless.

Like the pocket-sized Jawas, the roughly 6-feet tall Sand People (a.k.a. Tusken Raiders, referencing an attack on Fort Tusken in 98-95 BBY) are nomadic, sentient beings indigenous to the desert planet of Tatooine—yet this is where the comparison between the two races ends. Where Jawas are opportunists who find mingling with other races necessary in order to maximize their economic bottom line, Sand People prefer a more aggressive approach toward diplomacy, assaulting, and outright attacking, outsiders who happen upon their tribes. However, although Sand People are known to adopt the human children from camps of settlers they raid, this does not

Sand People, with accessories.

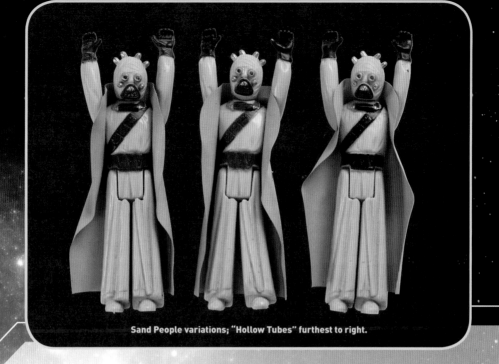
Sand People variations; "Hollow Tubes" furthest to right.

mean Sand People are humans; even desiccated corpses found on the hostile dunes of Tatooine leave few clues to the Raiders' biological identity—other than the semi-canonical hints provided by the feline-attributed "Grave Tuskens" found working for Dark Jedi Maw in *Star Wars: Jedi Knight (Dark Forces II)*. There is debate as to whether or not a brief image featuring an unmasked Tusken Raider is imagined or recalled from memory, since this appeared to Anakin Skywalker in the comic book, *Star Wars: Republic*.

Regarding their equipment, Sand People make use of a few different devices to cope with their inhospitable environment—specifically in the focused area of hot, dry, rocky canyons of the Jundland Wastes: their eyes are covered by visors or goggles due to Tatooine's bright sunlight, while below the eyes and in front of the creatures' assumed cheeks protruded two pipes—assumed to be utilized for breathing (a.k.a. "blood spitters") or spitting blood (rumored) at adversaries during combat. Covering their "mouths" is a constantly opened maw, while in front of their necks is a moisture trap that humidifies the air taken into the lungs. While they travel on furry Banthas—easily domesticated beasts of burden that many Sand People form a blood-bond with around childhood—Sand People

utilize simple charged projectile/slugthrower rifles (a.k.a. Tusken Cycler rifles [not included with the Kenner figure]) when aboard their Banthas, but when engaged in melee combat, the Raiders utilize their most iconic weapons: gaderffii sticks (a.k.a. Gaffi sticks). Made from scavenged materials, this deadly pole arm possesses a double-axed blade on one end, which culminates in a poison-tipped spike, usually dosed with Sandbat venom, while the other end forms a spiked club. Made from scavenged spaceship pieces and durable native krayt dragon horn, these weapons are feared the world over.

MOC: *SW* 12B: **$225**, 20/21B: **$135**; *ESB*: **$95**; *ROTJ* standard: **$65**, hollow cheek tubes: **$135-$150+**; **MLC**: hollow cheek tubes: **$65**, standard release: **$15**.

"Outsiders ... that brazenly walked apart from the land [that] reminded them of their past transgressions, of the time when they too walked apart from land ... the Sand People hate all outsiders and give them no footing."

— Questionable history of the Sand People as translated by the droid HK-47, *Knights of the Old Republic*

Greedo

[Production #39020]

1st appearance: Cantina Adventure Set
(Sears exclusive)
1st carded appearance: 20-back card
Original Retail Price (average): $1.99

- o Tri-Logo (dark blue) or regular (blue-green) green variations
- • with blue/black Rebel Blaster (DL-44 heavy blaster pistol)

The insecure, amateur bounty hunter known as Greedo is a male of the Rodian species: a class of sentient, reptilian humanoids who are famous for their ferocious nature and an inherently violent culture, stemming from their stressful lives growing up on the dangerous jungles of the planet Rodia. With round eyes capable of infra-red sight, a snout like a tapir, rough, green-colored skin, pores in their epidermis that exuded a powerfully scented oily secretion, heightened olfactory senses, and a pair of moveable antennae on top of their heads with saucers on the end, Rodians make excellent warriors, slavers, bounty hunters, and mercenaries.

As he grows older, Greedo leaves his adopted home of Mos Espa spaceport and begins traveling to the stars and awkwardly pursues a career in bounty hunting, inspired by the career of his father, Greedo the Elder, a highly successful mercenary. With the naïve goal of becoming one of the galaxy's greatest bounty hunters, Greedo engages in a series of (mis-)adventures, which lead to his pursuit of Han Solo, twice chasing a contract issued on the smuggler by Jabba the Hutt. He is bested out of the bounty by the clever Corellian both times.

An exasperated Greedo eventually catches up with Solo yet again, this time in Chalmun's Spaceport Cantina, a.k.a the Mos Eisley Cantina (see Cantina Adventure Set *or* Creature Cantina), Tatooine's popular drinking establishment. Accosting Solo, Greedo sits

Greedo,
with Rebel
Blaster.

CLOSE-UP

Greedo's accessory.

across from him with his pistol drawn, trying to extort half a bounty out of the smuggler. In response, Solo shoots the Rodian with his own pistol hidden underneath the table the two share. Greedo is killed instantly.

Regarding Greedo's peculiar action figure, it is worth noting that Kenner's designers had little more than photos of the four cantina patrons masks available to them from Lucasfilm—and so, the intrepid company had to construct the bodies of Greedo, Hammerhead, Snaggletooth, and Walrus Man from the waist down without any reference photos whatsoever. The result: a Greedo without his vest, and with improper colors, uniform details, etc.

"Ches ko ba tuta creesta crenko ya kolska!" (from Huttese: "This is something I've been looking forward to for a long time!")

— Greedo confronts Han Solo, threatening the smuggler's life

MOC: *SW* 20/21B: **$215-$235**; *ESB*: **$75-$80**; *ROTJ*: **$60-$70**; **MLC**: **$10-$12**.

Hammerhead minor eye and body variations.

Hammerhead's accessory.

Hammerhead, with Imperial Blaster.

Hammerhead
(a.k.a. "Momaw Nadon")

[Production #39030]

1st appearance: Cantina Adventure Set (Sears Exclusive)
1st carded appearance: 20-back card
Original Retail Price (average): $1.99

- o eyes looking left or eyes looking down left variations
- • with blue/black Imperial Blaster (E-11 blaster rifle)

Considered highly offensive by the Ithorian race, the nickname of "Hammerhead" applies to a lone member of the mammalian, herbivorous, sentient species of creatures hailing from the naturally lush world of Ithor. With two mouths located on each side of his neck, four throats, glossy (usually) brown skin, slightly slow reflexes, and, when younger, the ability to metamorphose from a limbless pupa state to that of a fully functioning Ithorian, Kenner's Hammerhead action figure portrays the form of an average, fully grown male Ithorian.

Possessing a long, curved neck and T-shaped head reminiscent of the hammerhead sharks of modern Earth, Hammerhead is actually the name Kenner Toys gave to Momaw Nadon—an Ithorian high priest of the floating city of *Tafanda Bay*—who is exiled upon revealing his planet's agricultural secrets to the Galactic Empire in order to prevent further destruction to his homeworld. Although Nadon saves Ithor from devastation, the Ithorian Elders pun-

ish him for his sacrilege through exile. Therefore, "Hammerhead" settles on Tatooine, and is seeking respite in Chalmun's Spaceport Cantina, a.k.a. the Mos Eisley Cantina (see Cantina Adventure Set *or* Creature Cantina) when Luke Skywalker and Ben "Obi-Wan" Kenobi are searching for a ship to provide them passage to the planet of Alderaan.

Regarding "Hammerhead's" peculiar action figure, Kenner's designers had little more than photos of the four cantina patrons masks available to them from Lucasfilm—and so, they had to construct the bodies of Hammerhead, Greedo, Snaggletooth, and Walrus Man from the waist down without any reference photos whatsoever. The result: a Hammerhead figure without his staff, with boldly incorrect colors, uniform details, et. al.

MOC: *SW* 20/21B: **$180-$200**; *ESB*: **$110-$120**; *ROTJ*: **$75-$80**; **MLC: $10-$12**.

Snaggletooth, red jump suit
(a.k.a. "Zutton" or "Red Snaggletooth")

[Production #38280]

1st appearance: Cantina Adventure Set
(Sears exclusive)
1st carded appearance: 20-back card
Original Retail Price (average): $1.99
- with blue/black Rebel Blaster (DL-44 heavy blaster pistol)

Snaggletooth, red jumpsuit, with Rebel Blaster.

Like all members of his species—a race of mammalian sentient humanoids sometimes called Snaggletooths, due to their short, pointy fangs and jaws that protrude—the Snivvian known as Zutton forms the basis for the Kenner character known as Snaggletooth. With thickly insulated skin as a result of the brutally cold environment of their home world of Cadomai Prime, Snivvians also possess an oversized snout, which affords them the luxury of becoming first-rate trackers and scouts. Snivvians also are renowned as some of the most talented artists and authors in the galaxy due to years of oppression at the hands of slavers which, combined with their home planet's "intolerably cold winters," channel their impulses toward aesthetic expression. Unfortunately, like the Trandoshians (see Bossk), Snivvians develop a reputation for psychopathic sensibilities, to the extent that when " … twin males were born, one of them would invariably display traits of psychotic genius."

A frequent patron of Chalmun's Spaceport Cantina, a.k.a. the Mos Eisley Cantina (see Cantina Adventure Set *or* Creature Cantina), Zutton/Snaggletooth (also known as "Z-Ton" and "Zutt") is a fierce Snivvian artist, who utilizes his talent in support of his younger brother, Takeel, who is often confused for Zutton. However, since Zutton manages to spend much of his painting income on "spice," a slang term for various mind-altering drugs, in order to supplement his wages he takes the occasional bounty from Jabba Desilijic Tiure (see Jabba the Hutt Action Playset).

The outfit worn by Snaggletooth's action figure appears nothing like the uniform he wears in *A New Hope*. Since Kenner's designers did not have images of the uniforms worn by the four cantina denizens (see Greedo, Hammerhead, and Walrus Man)—the only images that existed were those of their face masks. Therefore, Zutton's outfit is quite inaccurate. Steve Hodges, a Kenner designer who produced some of the

Snaggletooth, red and blue jumpsuits comparison.

first blueprints for the original *Star Wars* figures, utilized his company's logo and placed that symbol onto Snaggletooth's belt buckle.

MOC: *SW 20/21B:* **$180-$195**; *ESB:* **$110-$120**; *ROTJ:* **$85-$95**; **MLC:** **$8-$10**.

Snaggletooth, blue jumpsuit
(a.k.a. "Zutton" or "Blue Snaggletooth")

[Production #39040]

1st appearance: Cantina Adventure Set
                    (Sears exclusive)
1st carded appearance: n/a
Original Retail Price (average): $8.77
(ONLY available with Sears exclusive
Cantina Adventure Set)

- ○ dent or no dent-in-boot variations
- • with blue/black Rebel Blaster (DL-44 heavy
  blaster pistol)

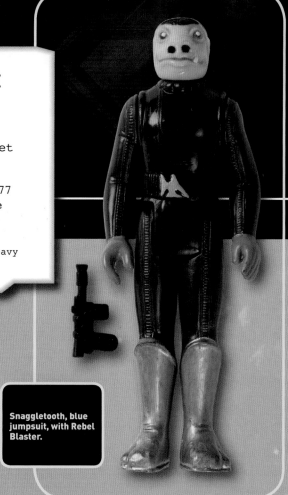

Snaggletooth, blue jumpsuit, with Rebel Blaster.

Kenner's action figure translation of Zutton is dubbed "Snaggletooth" on its packaging and was released in two different manifestations: in his more common smaller, shorter size—sporting a red jumpsuit; and in his more uncommon larger, taller size—donning a blue jumpsuit. This larger Snaggletooth could *only* be obtained through Sears' Christmas catalog.

Although most collectors believe that this highly prized Blue Snaggletooth variation was only available with the Sears exclusive Cantina Adventure Set (please regard its individual entry), this is untrue. In Sears' 1978 *Wish Book for the Christmas Season*, Blue Snaggletooth was also part of a two-pack customers could order with Greedo; the figures arrived individually sealed in Kenner baggies, with both placed into a small white box with black printing. Beginning in 1979, the Blue Snaggletooth was no longer available within the separately solicited two-pack OR in the four-pack which was included with the aforementioned chipboard Cantina Adventure Set.

Oddly enough, although this figure is worth quite a bit of money on the secondary market, he is relatively easy to obtain via online auctions sites or in secondary shops. Please be careful not to nick or rub Snaggletooth's boots, since the paint applied rubs off easily—hence the high price for mint condition loose samples. The blue Snaggletooth action figure was also never available mounted on a card (MOC) like his shorter, redder counterpart; sealed samples of the figure will only be found in a plastic baggie (MISP).

It is worth noting that although many fans believe that Kenner's Snaggletooth figure is based upon the tall Snivvian from *A New Hope* (one who's been deemed "Zutton"), there is evidence that this figure instead derives from a different Snivvian character found in

1978's *The Star Wars Holiday Special*. After carefully watching the special, observant collectors will note that during the broadcast, Lucasfilm salvaged some of the cantina creatures' masks from *ANH*, placing one of these reused masks upon a Snivvian from the *Special* who was wearing a red and black jumpsuit, and sporting a black belt which featured the EXACT buckle found on Kenner's Snaggletooth action figure. The *Special* established the character's name as "Zutmore"—which later transitioned to the more accepted "Zutton."

Regardless of which Snivvian the action figure is based upon, 1) Zutton is the name of Kenner's Snaggletooth action figure, 2) Snaggletooth is a member of the Snivvian race, and 3) the character appears to be an amalgamation of the Snivvians found in *A New Hope* and *The Star Wars Holiday Special*.

MIP: in factory-sealed Kenner baggie: **$725-$775+**; **MLC**: depending on condition of siver boots: **$200-$240+**, dead mint samples are **$300-$310+**.

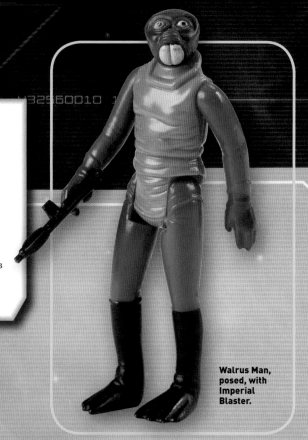

Walrus Man,
posed, with
Imperial
Blaster.

Walrus Man
(a.k.a. Ponda Baba, or "Sawkee")

[Production #39050]

1st appearance: Cantina Adventure Set
                (Sears exclusive)
1st carded appearance: 20-back card
Original Retail Price (average): $1.99

- white or pink tusks
- darker green or lighter green head variations
- with blue/black Imperial Blaster
  (E-11 blaster rifle)

Although vintage toy collectors know this distinctive Kenner action figure as Walrus Man since the alien's face resembles a tusked walrus, in the larger *Star Wars* mythos, the character's proper name is Ponda Baba (a.k.a. Sawkee)—an appellation utilized for the character in every version of the toy produced by Hasbro since they bought the license.

The pirate/smuggler known as Ponda Baba owes much of his bad humor to his species' innate ill temper.

As a member of the Aqualish race from the planet Ando—a class of amphibious, tusked bipeds who are renowned across the galaxy for

Walrus Man's accessory.

their disagreeable manner and belligerence—Baba possesses characteristics of both pinnipeds (seals, sea lions) and arachnids (spiders, scorpions): a truly bizarre physical amalgamation. The fact that Baba's walrus-like facial tusks curve downward over his mouth like a spider only further reinforces this peculiar combination.

Partnered with the infamous sociopathic surgeon Dr. Evazan, who "has the death sentence on twelve systems," the pair are eventually pursued by bounty hunters due to their illicit ventures. Fearing for their lives, Baba and Evazan hole up on the Outer Rim world of Tatooine, eager to escape prosecution. During their exile, and while patronizing Chalmun's Spaceport Cantina, a.k.a. the Mos Eisley Cantina (see Cantina Adventure Set *or* Creature Cantina), the two criminals encounter a young moisture farmer and his wizened old mentor. Although Luke Skywalker and Ben Obi-Wan Kenobi are non-confrontational, Baba and Evazan

Walrus Man white tusks and pink tusks variations.

Arfive-Defour (R5-D4)
(a.k.a. "Red")

[Production #39070]

1st carded appearance: 20-back card
Original Retail Price (average): $1.99

- with paper label/sticker, unique to the figure

Derived from the same class of astromech as the famed Rebel hero R2-D2, the droid with the designation R5-D4 (nicknamed "Red") was featured in one single scene of *Episode IV: A New Hope*, where Luke Skywalker purchases droids from a clan of short, crafty, business-savvy humanoids: Chief Nebit's tribe of Jawas (see Jawa). Traveling over the heat-baked dunes of Tatooine to peddle their wares, the diminutive brown-robed Jawas visited the Lars Homestead where they sold the white-and-red striped R5-D4 to the young moisture farmer. Or they *would have* sold Arfive, but at the last moment when the family picked C-3PO and R5-D4 out as a pair, R2-D2 sabotaged R5's motivator, if we carefully follow the canonical continuity. This sabotage ended Arfive's involvement in the transaction.

Unfortunately, R5-D4 was one of the R5 units plagued with problems and performance issues. As a result of his unreliability, Arfive was passed from owner to owner, developing an inferiority complex in the process—well before he was incapacitated by R2-D2. He changed hands a few more times due to his incompetence, yet ultimately was traded to an

historian (and spy) who was keen to make the droid useful for the first time ever. Lieutenant Voren Na'al refurbished the mistreated and insecure droid, upgraded his intelligence gathering package, and put him to work as an undercover field agent for the Rebellion, where he gathered valuable, top-secret information for the Alliance from the Imperial Prefect's office in Mos Eisley.

 MOC: *SW* 20/21B: **$185-$210**; *ESB:* **$120-$130**; *ROTJ:* **$75-$90**; **MLC: $12-$15**.

bully the pair of humans regardless. Kenobi tries to diffuse the situation, yet Evazan eggs on the dim-witted (and possibly drunk) Baba, who assaults the younger of these two humans. The veteran Jedi Knight engages Baba in melee combat, slicing off Walrus Man's right arm during the fracas.

Oddly enough, a continuity error exists within Walrus Man's lone scene in *ANH*. Ponda Baba's arms end with finned appendages before his combat with Ben Kenobi, yet after Obi Wan cuts off the creature's arm, Baba's hand appears distinctly furry when it

is observed lying on the cantina floor. Perhaps this incident inspired West End Games' postulation that there are two different species of Aqualish " … easily recognized by the configuration of their hands … (one was) a cupped, fin-like hand, with no fingers, and only a stubbed opposable thumb. The other … by five-fingered, fur covered, claw-like hands."

 MOC: *SW* 20/21B: **$175-$180**; *ESB:* **$85-$90**; *ROTJ:* **$65-$70**; **MLC: $10-$12**.

Death Star Droid
(a.k.a. RA-7 protocol droid)

```
[Production #39080]
```

1st carded appearance: 20-back card
Original Retail Price (average): $1.99

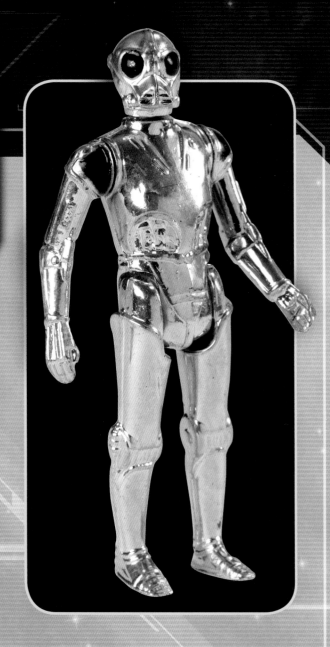

The RA-7-series of protocol droid shares certain similarities in programming and structure with C-3PO, hero of the Rebellion. However, according to the all-encompassing, *The Complete Star Wars Encyclopedia*, the RA-7 is a low-intelligence model of protocol droid produced by Arakyd Industries, a class of droid that sports reflective silver plating and a bipedal, humanoid shape. In contrast with the more accessible, affirming, and eager-to-please 3PO-series, the droids of the RA-7-series are firm and severe, and also sport an insectoid head—in the hope of attracting insect-like consumers who are most comfortable working with droids that resemble their own species

According to Wookieepedia.com, the Empire orders thousands of units of RA-7s and gives them away free of charge. However, the RA-7s are spread throughout the galaxy to serve a more serious purpose than simple protocol.

As part of a sinister plot, the Imperial Security Bureau (ISB) hides recording devices within the head modules of the RA-7s that are part of a covert surveillance system which absorbs information via the droids' highly advanced audio pickups and low-light photoreceptors. Even the Empire itself is not immune to the Security Bureau's machinations. To that end, the ISB question the motivation of Grand Moff Tarkin and his subordinate officers, believing that Tarkin will one day utilize the power of the Death Star to overthrow the Empire. As a result of their concerns about this coup, the ISB stations thousands of RA-7s aboard the gigantic space station, earning these droids the nickname "Death Star Droids": the general appellation used by Kenner for the characters' respective action figure.

Though many of the recipients of these Imperial "gifts" immediately discover the ISB's deliberate act of espionage when they crack open the droids' poorly designed heads, they do not desire to insult the Emperor by refusing receipt and returning their RA-7 units back to Arakyd, so instead they send them to auction, throw them atop junk heaps, and even try to hock them at local swap meets.

These droids are an unmitigated disaster for the Empire, so then, it is within the cargo hold of a hulking Jawa sandcrawler owned by Chief Nebit (see Jawa) where an incompetent RA-7 unit by the name of "Threebee" (3B6-RA-7) is ignominiously dumped. Inside the enormous traveling scow full of scrap metal and decomposing droids is where Threebee encounters R2-D2 and C-3PO, as well as an R5-D4 and Power Droid, in *A New Hope*.

MOC: *SW 20/21B:* **$230-$255;** *ESB:* **$165-$180;** *ROTJ:* **$85-$115;**
MLC: $14-$16.

Luke Skywalker (X-wing Pilot) / Luke Skywalker (X-wing Fighter Pilot)

[Production #39060]

1st carded appearance: 20-back card
Original Retail Price (average): $1.99

- large eye/different chest or standard variations
- with blue/black Rebel Blaster (DL-44 heavy blaster pistol)

Luke Skywalker (X-wing Pilot), with Rebel Blaster.

After departing Tatooine and following Ben Kenobi (see Ben [Obi-Wan] Kenobi) off-world to tragically witness his mentor's death at the hands of Darth Vader, Luke Skywalker enters a new stage in his calling as a Rebel hero: that of an Alliance starfighter pilot. Already a stellar aviator back home, his pre-existing abilities, combined with the newly found gunnery skills learned during his adventures with Han Solo, merge with Luke's use of the Force to assist him when executing the most important flight of his life. Piloting a T-65 starfighter (see X-wing Fighter) with the call-number "Red Five" in a supremely dangerous trench run on the Death Star, Luke switches off his targeting computer and uses the Force to direct his timing and precision—the mystical, metaphysical power of the Force guides his deployment of the proton torpedoes that destroy the first Death Star and save the Rebellion.

Dressed in his famous X-wing fighter pilot outfit for this mission, and others afterward (see Dagobah Action Playset), the second action figure based upon the protagonist of *A New Hope*, Kenner's Luke Skywalker (X-wing [Fighter] Pilot) figurine wears a uniform which marks the period of time when the character eschews his farm boy origins and finally enters the ranks of the Rebellion. Easy-to-obtain at retail from late 1978 until the vintage line went belly-up in 1985, this action figure was also used quite often by collectors whenever they needed a generic Rebel pilot to man an Alliance spacecraft in their toy rooms. Although Kenner produced action figure versions of the Rebellion's A-wing and B-wing pilots, collectors had to wait until 1984—*four full years*—to receive these, or ANY non-Luke Skywalker based pilot figures (!). Within the interim, this figure simply had to fill the gap.

While the color of a flight uniform usually indicates which spacecraft they fly, this system is not always 100 percent accurate—since necessity is the mother of invention with the Rebellion. Most of the time, the following indicators are consistently true: orange is for X-wing pilots (although they were modified for Snowspeeder pilots), gray is relegated to Y-wing pilots, green is used by A-wing pilots, while a red flight suit indicates a B-wing pilot.

General Bast: "We've analyzed their attack, sir, and there is a danger. Should I have your ship standing by?"

Tarkin: "Evacuate? In our moment of triumph? I think you overestimate their chances!"

— Governor Wilhuff Tarkin, underestimating the skill of Rebel pilots

MOC: *SW 20/21B*: $235-$275; *ESB*: $105-$115; *ROTJ*: $65-$80; *POTF*: $250-$275; **MLC**: $16-$20.

Power Droid
(a.k.a. "Gonk Droid")

[Production #39090]

1st carded appearance: 20-back card
Original Retail Price (average): $1.99

- o two different body sculpts
- • with two paper labels/stickers, unique to the figure
- • removable rubber Power Droid Vent

Essentially functioning as a mobile battery for vehicles, starships, and related machines, the standard Power Droid is totally armless and possesses either two or four legs. Utilized around the galaxy as walking power supplies, these droids are often referred to as "Gonk Droids"—an onomatopoeic allusion to the characteristic sound these droids make when walking, i.e., "gonk, gonk … GONK." Not particularly bright and possessing a relatively low AI (Artificial Intelligence) since its internal workings are essentially filled by fusion generators, the EG-6 model Power Droid produced by Verline Systems makes its first canonical appearance within the bowels of a Jawa Sandcrawler (see Radio Controlled Sandcrawler) featured in *Episode IV: A New Hope*.

Oddly enough, the EG-6 model did indeed possess a manipulator arm, yet this retractable limb is found hidden within a flip-up panel located on the lower portion of its front side—underneath the droid's light-power plug-in socket located on the lower half of its front "face."

Although the Kenner action figure for this character possesses a bevy of special features (poseable legs that appear wrapped within insulated leg sheaths that make a clicking sound when moved, a faceplate label and long white body sticker that runs the length of the droid's midsection, a box-like appearance and deep blue color that bears little resemblance to the character in the films, and a rubber pipe [?] mounted on the droid's roof, which vents heat), this Power Droid, like Kenner's interpretation of Zutton (see Snaggletooth), is a loose translation of its film counterpart.

Power Droid body variations.

MOC: *SW 20/21B*: **$230-$255**; *ESB*: **$135-$140**; *ROTJ*: **$65-$80**; **MLC**: **$12-$15**, make sure both labels are intact.

Boba Fett

[Production #39250]

1st appearance: Mail-Away
1st carded appearance: 21-back card
Original Mail-Away Price: FREE (4 proof-of-purchase seals)
Original Retail Price (average): $1.99

- o dark brown belt or light brown belt (standard) variations
- o armor shade variations
- • with blue/black Imperial Blaster (E-11 blaster rifle)

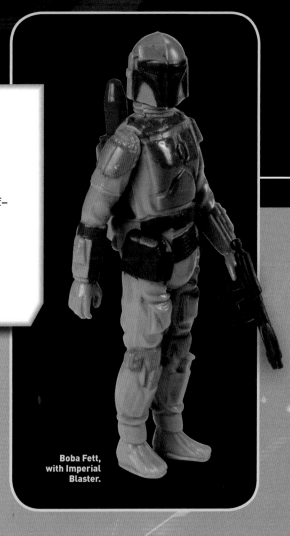

Boba Fett,
with Imperial
Blaster.

As advertised on Kenner's early promotional material, this new character in the not yet named *Star Wars* sequel is "a fearsome intergalactic bounty hunter and a threat to the Rebel Alliance, especially Han Solo!" Unavailable in any retail store at that time, the only way to obtain the mysterious helmeted being known as Boba Fett was via mail-away, for this bounty hunter was the first in a long line of mail-away action figures—a marketing tactic which encouraged consumers to purchase extra *Star Wars* toys at retail in order to obtain the four proof-of-purchase seals necessary for redemption. After mailing these POPs to Kenner, 6 to 8 weeks later a Boba Fett figure with his "rocket firing backpack" showed up at your door. Packaged in a plain white mailer box with a product catalog, Boba Fett was sealed in a translucent baggie with his requisite laser rifle accessory—yet without his rocket-firing backpack. A small white sheet was also included within the box as a means of explanation of this missing part, that "the launcher has been removed for safety reasons."

Apparently, the directive to remove Boba Fett's rocket was given in response to an accident that occurred as a result of Mattel's missile-firing Battlestar Galactica Colonial Viper vehicle: the death of one child and "injuries to 10 others" prompted a recall of approximately two million of these toys, and a modification of Boba Fett's backpack: now his rocket was glued into a socket. Any extant rocket-firing sample is either a preproduction piece originating from the hands of a Kenner employee, or a reproduction piece to show fans how the toy worked, and neither are given a value in this tome.

One of the most popular and infamous of all the characters in the *Star Wars* mythology, Boba Fett begins his life as an unaltered clone of his "father," the Mandalorian Bounty Hunter Jango Fett, and is created by the cloners of the planet Kamino in 32 BBY as the first of many replicas of Jango (see Stormtrooper). This inviolate, non-(age-)ac-

CLOSE-UP

Boba Fett's
accessory.

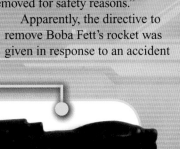

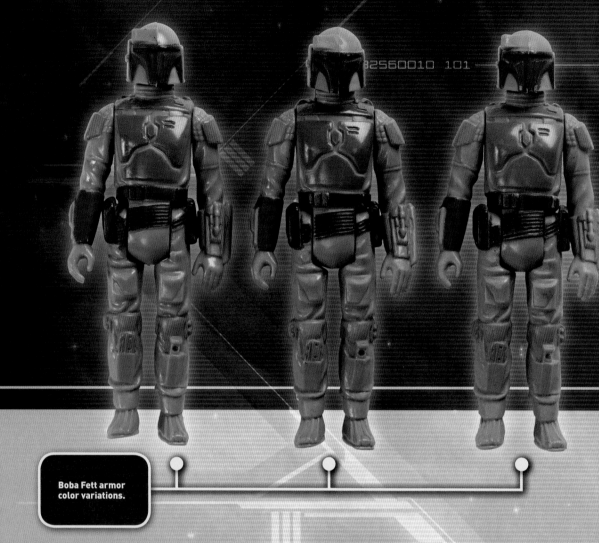

Boba Fett armor color variations.

celerated clone now known as Boba Fett is lovingly raised by Jango for the first ten years of the boy's life, until witnessing his father's death: Jango is beheaded, via lightsaber, at the hands of Jedi Master Mace Windu during the fierce Battle of Geonosis (22 BBY). Beholding his father's brutal murder changes the child, and Boba becomes distrustful of others—

as well as most Jedi Knights. Utilizing his father's ship (see *Slave-1*) and a suit of Mandalorian armor belonging to his father's mentor, Jaster Mereel, he begins to travel the galaxy, having retained many of the countless lessons Jango taught him on being a skilled, capable bounty hunter.

Even as a teenager, Boba Fett develops a sterling reputation as one of the galaxy's most formidable and fearless mercenaries. He accepts contracts from beings as notorious as the powerful crimelord Jabba Desilijic Tiure (see Jabba the Hutt Action Playset) and even works with the Empire when it suits his purpose. Many years, bounties, and adventures later, during the events

Ohnaka: "Tell the Jedi what he wants to know, Boba."

Boba Fett (yelling): "Why should I help anybody!?! I've got no one!"

Ohnaka: "It is the honorable thing to do. It's what your father would have wanted."

— Boba Fett discusses grace under pressure with Weequay pirate leader Hondo Ohnaka

Boba Fett mailer box, with ephemera.

of *The Empire Strikes Back* (ca. 3 ABY) Boba Fett and a slew of other bounty hunters are assembled on the bridge of the *Executor* (see Darth Vader's Star Destroyer Action Playset) by Darth Vader to find the Rebellion-allied spacecraft known as the *Millennium Falcon* following its escape from the ice planet Hoth. Fett beats the other mercenaries in locating the ship, finding Han Solo and his cohorts at the outpost/colony of Cloud City on the planet Bespin (see Cloud City Playset). After freezing Solo in a carbonite block, Fett transports the former smuggler to Jabba, garnering one of his most famous bounties.

One short year later (4 ABY), Fett visits Jabba's Palace on the desert planet of Tatooine and becomes embroiled in the events surrounding Solo's deliverance from his carbonite prison—thanks to Luke Skywalker and his small band of Rebel friends. During the melee at the Battle of the Great Pit of Carkoon (see Tatooine

Skiff), Fett is knocked into the Great Pit and is assumed to be consumed and digested by the creature known as the sarlaac. Although no one has ever eluded the maw of the sarlaac before, Boba Fett is the first, and after his escape and subsequent rejuvenation, the galaxy's most famous and powerful bounty hunter utilizes his singular moral compass and peerless skills to guide him through many more decades of adventures …

MISB: all contents sealed in mailer: **$650-$725**; **MIB**: w/all included pieces and sealed figure: **$275-$325**; **MIB**: w/all included pieces and non-sealed figure: **$240-$260**; **MOC**: *SW* 20/21B: **$1,750-$2,300**, depending upon card condition; *ESB*: **$565-$600**; *ROTJ*: **$410-$435**; **MLC**: **$25-$32**.

THE EMPIRE STRIKES BACK

A long time ago, in a galaxy far, far away ...

It is a dark time for the Rebellion. Although the Death Star has been destroyed, Imperial troops have driven the Rebel forces from their hidden base and pursued them across the galaxy.

Evading the dreaded Imperial Starfleet,

to *Star Wars*, 1980's *The Empire Strikes Back*: the most hallowed installment of the original trilogy.

The film further chronicles the adventures of Han Solo, Chewbacca, Princess Leia, R2-D2 and C-3PO, as they safeguard the Rebel Alliance—fending off an attack of the massive Imperial Army. The Rebel heroes then retreat to the far reaches of space to avoid unwanted attention, yet even hiding on the remote outpost of Cloud City cannot shelter them from the Emperor's wrath. Luke Skywalker follows a different path,

Bossk Bounty Hunter

[Production #39760]

1st appearance: Mail-Away (as "Secret Action Figure")
1st carded appearance: 31-back card
Original Mail-Away Price: FREE (4 proof-of-purchase seals)
Original Retail Price (average): $2.49

- o dark face and limbs or light face and limbs variations
- • with Bossk Mortar Gun (Relby-v10 micro grenade launcher), unique to figure

Bossk, with Mortar Gun.

Although the first Kenner mail-away *Star Wars* figure, Boba Fett, was pictured and advertised on *Star Wars* action figure cardbacks a full assortment earlier, the second mail-away action figure offer, 1979's Bossk, was neither pictured nor mentioned by name on toy packages. He was dubbed a "Secret Action Figure"—a character soon-to-be featured in the ominously titled upcoming sequel, *The Empire Strikes Back.*

And just like Boba Fett, Bossk came approximately 6-8 weeks after submitting your proof-of-purchase seals in a nondescript white mailer containing an *Empire Strikes Back* product catalog, a Bossk figure sealed in a translucent baggie with his "laser pistol" (actually, a Relby-v10 micro grenade launcher—a fierce weapon which served as a blaster/mortar that discharged shells containing smoke, gas, and other chemical agents) and a small black-colored note describing the character.

Bossk is a legendary bounty hunter and one of the mercenaries summoned by Darth Vader in *The Empire Strikes Back* to a meeting aboard his Star Dreadnought, the *Executor*. Born on the planet Trandosha to his father, the leader of the Bounty Hunters' Guild, Bossk's first act in life is to consume every one of his unhatched

siblings. Beginning his career as a prominent Wookiee-hunter, Bossk is well known for stalking (and unfortunately, skinning) members of the fearless Wookiee race, a despicable custom that earns him a fearsome reputation. Throughout his storied career, Bossk faces many pirates and spacers, such as Han Solo and Chewbacca, and works with several other bounty hunters, including Boba Fett and Zuckuss.

Bossk hunts his bounties using a Relby-v10 micro grenade launcher, and is also known to carry thermal detonators, a standard blaster, and even a flamethrower.

Bossk's iconic uniform was created by Lucas' film crew from a modified "High-Altitude Windak Pressure Suit" from 1962 that was devised for the British Royal Air Force, and can be seen utilized by a few other characters featured in the Mos Eisley Cantina in *A New Hope.*

Bossk mailer box, with ephemera.

MISB: All contents sealed in mailer: **$350-$375**; **MIB:** w/all included pieces and sealed figure: **$210-$225**; **MIB:** w/all included pieces and non-sealed figure: **$140-$150**; **MOC:** *ESB:* **$90-$115**; *ROTJ:* **$62-$72**; **MLC:** **$12**.

Bespin Security Guard
(I: first release; a.k.a. Bespin Wing Guard or Cloud Police)

[Production #39730]

1st carded appearance: 31-back card
Original Retail Price (average): $2.49

- o wide range of moustache variations
- • with blue Bespin Blaster (DH-17 blaster pistol)

Bespin Security Guard (I), with Bespin Blaster.

One of the easiest "troop builder" action figures to find on the secondary market, purchasing a vast number of Bespin Security Guard toys was an excellent way to amass a security force for your Sears exclusive Cloud City Playset. Since Kenner's adaptation of the figure possesses a variety of different-length moustaches, as well as a different level of thickness to the paint applied to his hair and eyes, each Bespin Security Guard is a wee bit different from the other: perfect for building an army. (Yet if you regard the image on the front of the packaging, the gentleman the action figure is based upon possesses a full beard—however, the toy is mustachioed *only*.)

Featured prominently in the Cloud City chapter of *The Empire Strikes Back*, the term "Bespin Security Guard" is an informal appellation (like Cloud City Wing Guard, Cloud Police, or Bespin cops) for the Bespin Wing Guard: the primary security force of Cloud City—an impressive mining outpost/luxury hotel/gambling facility found hovering 60,000 kilometers above the gas giant planet known as Bespin.

The largest component of the primary law enforcement agency of Cloud City, the Bespin Wing Guard directly reports to three different authorities within the facility: the Baron Administrator of Cloud City (see Lando Calrissian), the Baron's cyborg aide (see Lobot), or the city's sophisticated central computer.

Although the Bespin Security Guards in actuality carry the BlasTech Relby-k23 blaster pistol—a banned sidearm that is purchased under-the-table and supplied to them by Cloud City's quartermaster—the armament carried by the Kenner action figure is more reminiscent of the DH-17 blaster pistol, a standard-issue military sidearm used by members of the Imperial Navy and the Rebel Alliance. Therefore, the term "Bespin Blaster" which has been appropriated for this figure's accessory is a bit misleading.

Note: The blue uniform of every single Bespin Security Guard action figure should always possess gold highlights painted onto the jacket—on both the coat's front and back. A loose figure without these gold paint applications either had these paint apps wear off during play, or did not have these applications applied at all: not a rare variation, but an error that occurred in production.

MOC: *ESB*: **$125-$130**; *ROTJ*: **$35-$38**; **MLC**: **$10**, make sure the gold paint applications are not worn.

Bespin Security Guard (I) variations.

FX-7 (Medical Droid) [a.k.a. Fixit]

[Production #39730]

1st carded appearance: 31–back card
Original Retail Price (average): $2.49

- with two distinct body mold/head mold variations
- bright red OR dull orange main eye variations

Manufactured by Medtech Industries, the FX-7 medical assistant droid (aka "Fixit"—a euphonious acronym derived from the model's initials) is one member of a distinct class of the company's FXseries (FX-1 through FX-10) of nursing droids and surgical assistants. Often immobile, the cylindrically shaped FX-7 sports roughly twenty fine manipulator arms (an approximation, since the droids' medical requirements tended to vary), which are designed to be modular, allowing for a number of different accessories to be attached such as hypodermic injectors, medicine/anesthesia dispensers, or control board manipulators. The droid also possesses a bevy of medical diagnostic sensors, a lone (and much larger) telescoping grasping arm that can extend up to a full meter, a series of readout screens visible to the droid's humanoid co-workers, a scomp link which allows the FXmodel to communicate with a computer terminal (à la R2-D2), yet the droid lacks a proper language "vocoder/vocabulator," which could have allowed the FX-7 unit to engage in verbal interaction.

The Kenner toy based upon this character was spectacularly concocted for the year 1980—distinctly different from any other figurine on retail shelves for that season, with nine independent, slightly bendable white arms that folded out from its body, an extendable caplike head that rotated 360 degrees and bobbed up-anddown, and a larger claw-like arm that rotated around its upper body.

MOC: *ESB*: $85-$115; *ROTJ*: $45-$50;
MLC: Bright red-eye version: $25-$30,
dull orange-eye version: $8-$10.

53

Han Solo (Hoth Outfit/Hoth Battle Gear)

[Production #39790]

1st carded appearance: 31-back card
Original Retail Price (average): $2.49

- common tan-painted leg or rare tan-molded leg variations
- pink face or standard face variations
- chest piece variations (x2)
- with blue Rebel Blaster (DL-44 heavy blaster pistol)

Han Solo (Hoth Outfit), with Rebel Blaster.

With a "mercenary swagger and world weariness," according to the narration on the "Bonus Features" disk included with the *Star Wars: Special Edition* DVD (1997), the roguish smuggler-turned-Rebel-hero known as Han Solo keeps true to his word and assists the Rebellion in setting up their secret base on the remote ice planet Hoth.

This second version of Han Solo is based upon the hero donning his iconic arctic uniform, as featured at the beginning of *The Empire Strikes Back*. Collectors used this action figure along with Chewbacca in order to reenact the (self-)destruction of the Imperial Viper droid (see Turret and Probot Playset), an encounter which allows the Empire to determine the location of the hidden Rebel base. Furthermore, many kids across the world have utilized Han Solo (Hoth Outfit) in conjunction with Luke Skywalker (Hoth Battle Gear), and a Tauntaun or two (see Tauntaun, and Tauntaun with Open Belly Rescue Feature) to reenact Han saving his young friend Luke after the latter is mauled by a fearsome Wampa (see Hoth Wampa). The action figure is well conceived: even with his thick, heavy-weather parka, rendered a bit too blue for some aficionados'

tastes, Solo can barely survive a frigid evening inside an ad-hoc shelter protected from inhospitable climate of Hoth. Thanks to Solo's persistence and dedication to his friend, Luke does not perish on the tundra, and the Rebellion does not lose one of its foremost heroes.

Solo's devotion to the Rebel cause is short-lived, however, since he has to depart for fear of his life, after Jabba the Hutt places a "death mark" on the pilot.

Tigran Jamiro: "Your Tauntaun will freeze before you reach the first marker!"

Han Solo: "Then I'll see you in Hell!"

—Han Solo defiantly departs in search of the missing Luke Skywalker against all odds

MOC: *ESB*: **$145-$155**; *ROTJ*: **$55-$65+**; **MLC**: tan-molded leg version: **$35-$42**, tan-painted leg version: **$10**.

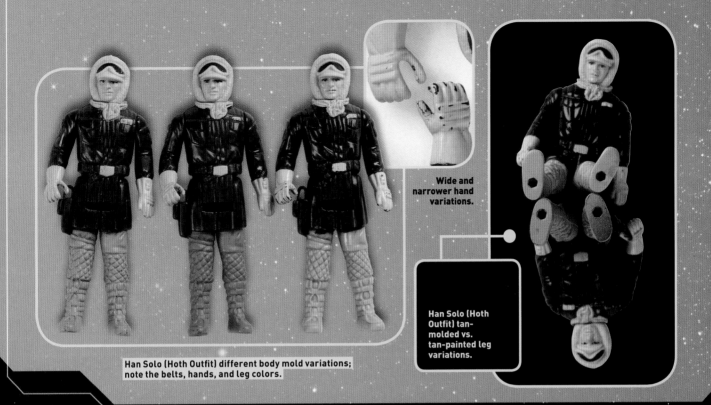

Wide and narrower hand variations.

Han Solo (Hoth Outfit) different body mold variations; note the belts, hands, and leg colors.

Han Solo (Hoth Outfit) tan-molded vs. tan-painted leg variations.

IG-88 (Bounty Hunter) [a.k.a. IG-88B, Assassin Droid]

[Production #39790]

1st carded appearance: 31-back card
Original Retail Price (average): $2.49

- o gold tinted body or grey body variations
- o two different right leg molds
- • with blue/black Imperial Blaster (E-11 blaster rifle)
- • with blue IG-88 Rifle ("modified" DLT-20A blaster rifle; unique to the figure)

IG-88, with Imperial Blaster and IG-88 Rifle.

Far more intelligent and adept at combat than the garden-variety battle droids, which came before him in galactic history (e.g., the OOM-Series Battle Droid, B1 Battle Droid, B2 Super Battle Droid, or the droideka [Destroyer Droid]), the "line" of IG-88 assassin droids are spawned from a curious series of IG-86 sentinel droids that are popularized during the Clone Wars (22-19 BBY). Initially solicited to the public as humanoid-type bodyguards/home security systems for the affluent consumer, IG-86 sentinels are unfortunately manipulated by many rich customers to become murderous assassins.

Although the manufacture of assassin droids is banned well before the rise of the Galactic Empire, the infamous scientists of Holowan Laboratories, dubbed the "Friendly Technology People," fashion the next step in the evolution of the IG-86 series, a new selection of assassin droids that come to be known as the IG-88 line. Originally, IG-88 is

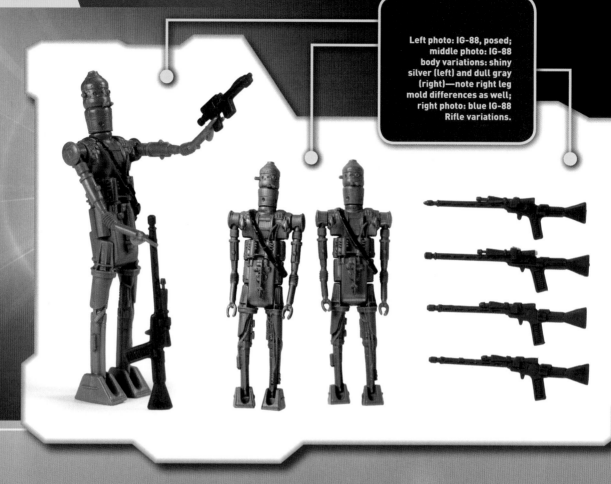

Left photo: IG-88, posed; middle photo: IG-88 body variations: shiny silver (left) and dull gray (right)—note right leg mold differences as well; right photo: blue IG-88 Rifle variations.

a single, individual unit—"IG-88A"—spawned from Holowan's IG-88-series of assassin droids (e.g., IG-88's A-D). Therefore, the mechanical bounty hunter that all die-hard *Star Wars* aficionados are familiar with is not simply christened "IG-88": his more precise appellation is "IG-88B," since he is second in the order of activation by the premiere model of the line, his master, "IG-88A." Consequently, it is IG-88A who endows these murderous droids with sentience in order to band them together with the goal of orchestrating a Droid Revolution.

Although IG-88B utilizes his masquerade as a bounty hunter as a means to obfuscate his participation in the Droid Revolution (the assassin droid's propensity for bloodletting and violence notwithstanding), the popular droid's untimely meeting with another powerful member of his bounty hunting ilk in the bowels of Cloud City puts an end to IG-88B's illustrious career: IG-88 is destroyed by Boba Fett.

Within the context of *The Empire Strikes Back*, IG-88B makes an appearance on the deck of the Star Dreadnought *Executor*, where the assassin droid/bounty hunter heeds Darth Vader's request to retrieve the *Millennium Falcon* and capture its crew (ca. 3 ABY).

"You're welcome to what's left..."

—Boba Fett, speaking to Cloud City's Ugnaughts after destroying IG-88 with the droid's own grenades

MOC: *ESB*: $150-$165; *ROTJ*: $80-$95; **MLC**: gold- or gray-tinted body versions: **$12-$15**.

Imperial Stormtrooper
(Hoth Battle Gear) [a.k.a. "Snowtrooper"]

[Production #39740]

1st carded appearance: 31-back card
Original Retail Price (average): $2.49

- o split visor or joined visor variations
- o finely detailed or loosely detailed sculpt variations
- • with blue Imperial Rifle ("modified" DLT-20A blaster rifle with added handle)
- • with white vinyl (waist) Snowtrooper Cape/Kama Skirt, unique to the figure

Imperial Stormtrooper (Hoth Battle Gear), with accessories.

Functioning as successors to the Grand Army of the Republic's clone cold assault troopers and Galactic Marines, who are specially trained for survival and combat in inclement weather, the Empire wished to develop a specialized group of Imperial Stormtroopers of a similar class. Therefore, the Imperial Army makes sure to cultivate a level of specialization within their Stormtrooper Corps (see AT-AT Driver, Biker Scout, and Stormtrooper), which allows the Empire's ground forces to engage enemies in nearly every environment, regardless of climate.

Those Imperial Stormtroopers possessing insulated uniforms and superlative training that prepares them for soldiering in an arctic climate are dubbed "snowtroopers" by *Star Wars* fans. Featured as a core unit of ground assault soldiers under the command of General Veers (see AT-AT Commander) during the Imperial assault of Echo Base, Blizzard Force is an elite unit of warriors within the Imperial Stormtrooper Corps who focus on cold-weather ops;

they are made famous due to their decisive victory during the Battle of Hoth.

Snowtroopers are "self sufficient mobile combat elements," who are utilized on a multitude of different planets where cold weather is a factor, and as such, the outfits of Snowtroopers are specially made, consisting of accoutrements including: a helmet with polarized snow goggles; a chestplate—featuring reinforced blast armor, communications controls, an identity chip, suit heater controls, a power cell monitor; a backpack unit with a heater liquid pump, power and surplus power indicators, a heavy duty power cell, and a storage compartment for rations; heated pants which were less-armored for mobility's sake; a wrist commlink; and an Imperial sidearm—the E-11 blaster, different from the modified DLT-20A included with the Kenner action figure.

Snowtrooper body variations; note the visors and belts.

MOC: *ESB:* **$95-$115**; *ROTJ:* **$55-$60**; *MLC:* **$20-$22**.

Lando Calrissian

[Production #39800]

1st carded appearance: 31-back card
Original Retail Price (average): $2.49

- o white teeth and white eyes or no teeth and dark eyes variations
- • with blue Bespin Blaster (DH-17 blaster pistol)
- • with grey vinyl (shorter) Lando Calrissian Cape, unique to the figure

Lando Calrissian, with accessories.

Born on the planet Socorro—a smuggler's refuge located in the Outer Rim Territories—Lando Calrissian uses his natural charm and good looks to develop profound skill as a first-rate gambler and confidence trickster at a young age, refining these abilities as he grows older. Acquiring the famous *Millennium Falcon* during a game of sabacc (see Millennium Falcon Spaceship for a description of the game and the ship), he pilots the starfighter on many exciting missions until he loses the "fastest hunk of junk in the galaxy" to Han Solo while playing cards. Although he misses the craft dearly, Lando acquires something far more lucrative in yet another game of sabacc—the mining outpost/luxury hotel known as Cloud City (see Cloud City Playset), the planet Bespin's largest settlement.

After being appointed Baron Administrator of the facility, Calrissian mends his ways and changes his philosophical outlook; instead of coasting through life as a roguish swindler, he now takes this newfound responsibility quite seriously—winning both the hearts and souls of his constituents as Cloud City's chief superintendent, a move that also makes him a wealthy man.

All remains status quo until that fateful day when Han Solo and a small group of fleeing Rebels, chased by Darth Vader's convoy of star destroyers, nicknamed "Death Squadron"—dock the *Falcon* on a landing platform at Cloud City, where Solo begs his old friend and smuggler-in-arms Calrissian for assistance with their ship's broken hyperdrive. Unfortunately, Vader and a contingent of Stormtroopers (see Imperial Stormtrooper) land at Cloud City immediately before Solo's small group of Rebels, forcing Calrissian to broker a deal with the Empire.

After betraying Han and the Rebels to Darth Vader under the guise of protecting his position of administrator at Cloud City—and more importantly, preserv-

ing his peoples' freedom—it seems to the Rebels that Calrissian has reverted back to type: that of a self-interested, shifty-eyed con-man who puts his own interests above all else. However, after the deal he brokers with the Empire turns sour and Han is frozen in carbonite, Calrissian sacrifices his personal liberty in order to safeguard the lives of his newfound friends. Recognizing the precarious position held by the Rebel Alliance, Lando decides to play the role of the hero—plotting the escape of the remaining Rebels, and revealing to them Darth Vader's plan to snatch Luke Skywalker.

Heading the rescue mission, Lando assists Princess Leia (see Leia Organa, Bespin Gown [even though her action figure design bears little resemblance to that of her film character]), Chewbacca, R2-D2, a partially disassembled C-3PO (see C-3PO [Removable Limbs], and a gravely wounded Luke Skywalker (see Luke Skywalker [Bespin Fatigues]) in their escape from Bespin aboard his former ship the *Millennium Falcon*. For more on this character, see Lando Calrissian (Skiff Guard Disguise) and Lando Calrissian (General Pilot).

MOC: *ESB*: **$135-$150+**; *ROTJ*: **$55-$65**; **MLC:** with teeth: **$12-$15**, without teeth: **$8-$10**.

Lando Calrissian figure variations; note belt, teeth, and faces.

Luke Skywalker (Bespin Fatigues)

[Production #39780]

1st carded appearance: 31-back card
Original Retail Price (average): $2.49

- o hair color variations (differing shades of hair, from blond to brown hair)
- o light or dark boot variations
- with blue Rebel Blaster (DL-44 heavy blaster pistol)
- with yellow lightsaber (removable, non-sliding)

Luke Skywalker (Bespin Fatigues), with accessories.

The simple, unadorned fatigues worn by Kenner's third version of Luke Skywalker not only reflects his formal ascendancy to the position of rebel commander, but this attire also subtly alludes to the warm, khaki-colored uniform utilized by padawan learners (Jedi in training) "before the dark times, before the Empire." In the swampy clime of Dagobah (see Dagobah Action Playset), Luke dons a modest jacket, plain pants, simple boots, and a white tank-top undershirt—clothing which reflects a transitional period for the galaxy's last hope, as Luke moves from acolyte to adept, from recruit to veteran by the end of *The Empire Strikes Back*.

After he is urged to visit Dagobah—a humid, jungle planet located within the galaxy's Outer Rim—by

the spirit of his former tutor (see Ben [Obi-Wan] Kenobi), Luke travels with R2-D2 (see Artoo-Detoo, with Sensorscope) to the swamp world, where he seeks out Grand Master Yoda, a peculiar being who formally leads Luke down the path to becoming a Jedi Knight. Unfortunately, after sensing his Rebel friends are in peril, Luke ignores Yoda's advice to continue his training in the use of the Force, and races off to rescue them, knowing full well that he will have to confront Darth Vader; and challenge him he does, on the elevators and catwalks within the expan-

Luke Skywalker (Bespin Fatigues), with accessories.

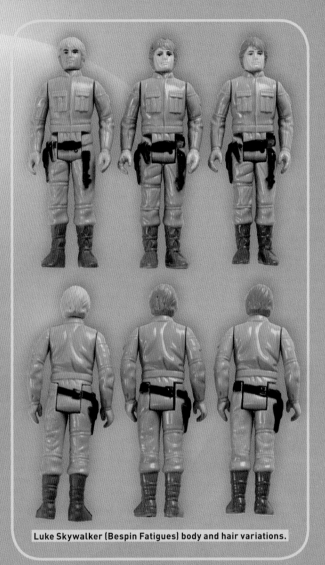

Luke Skywalker (Bespin Fatigues) body and hair variations.

sive core of Cloud City (see Cloud City Playset).

During this epic duel between Luke and Darth Vader, the Sith Lord easily conquers his opponent and slices off Luke's hand—just as the inexperienced Vader himself had lost his own right hand to Count Dooku during the culmination of *Attack of the Clones*. After defeating a clearly outmatched Luke, Vader explains to the Jedi-in-training that he is the young man's father: a revelation that not only shocks Luke, but shocked an entire generation of fans. Defeated and demoralized, Luke uses the Force to reach out to Leia, who senses his telepathic plea while aboard the *Millennium Falcon*. She and her small band of Rebel survivors, *sans* Han Solo, turn the craft around to rescue him—fleeing the confines of Cloud City to escape the growing tentacles of the Empire.

It should be noted that this figure possessed a newly designed toy lightsaber—albeit one that was QUITE difficult to place in the figure's hand—far different from the standard "telescoping" lightsabers that Kenner produced for their earlier action figure assortment (see Ben Kenobi, Darth Vader, and Luke Skywalker). With a buttoned hilt, this accessory is more aesthetically pleasing than Luke's original accessory.

However, as a matter of clarity, the color of Luke's original lightsaber, the one given to him by Obi-Wan and used in *A New Hope* and *The Empire Strikes Back*, was blue—the same color as the lightsaber wielded by Anakin in *Revenge of the Sith*.

Unfortunately, Kenner made Luke's first two toy lightsabers yellow—perhaps so as not to confuse the color with Obi-Wan's already blue saber (?), since Ben's was the more prominently wielded lightsaber in *A New Hope*.

MOC: *ESB* brown hair: **$375-$400+**, blond hair: **$275-$325+**; *ROTJ* blond hair: **$100-$110+**, brown hair: **$80-$95+**; **MLC**: brown hair: **$22-$25**, blond hair: **$18-$22+**.

Leia Organa/Princess Leia Organa
(Bespin Gown)

[Production #39720]

1st carded appearance: 31-back card
Original Retail Price (average): $2.49

- o crew necked (short collar), turtlenecked (collar up to head), or gold (color) necked variations
- o brown hair or dark brown hair variations
- o thin face or thick face variations
- o pointed-sleeves or rounded-sleeves variations
- • with blue Princess Leia Blaster (Defender sporting blaster pistol)
- • with pink vinyl Leia Bespin Cape with ornate printing, unique to the figure

Leia Organa
(Bespin Gown),
with accessories.

Adopted into the royal House of Alderaan, Princess Leia Organa—daughter of Anakin Skywalker and Padmé Amidala—is an adventuress and Rebel leader motivated by revenge against the Empire due to the destruction of her adoptive planet of Alderaan, including her adoptive parents, via the Imperial super-weapon, the Death Star (see Death Star Space Station).

This Kenner action figure marks a time when Leia and her small band of Rebel heroes flee the clutches of the Empire following the exodus, which occurs after the Battle of Hoth. Thanks to some resourceful maneuvers by Han Solo (see Han Solo, and Han Solo [Bespin Outfit]) in his *Millennium Falcon*, Leia, Han, Chewbacca, and C-3PO arrive for a brief respite at Cloud City (see Cloud City

Playset), where Han radios ahead to meet one of his old friends for assistance with his starship's damaged hyperdrive unit.

Upon meeting Solo's acquaintance from the scoundrel's checkered past, the charming Lando Calrissian, Baron Administrator of Cloud City, the group of Rebels is promised a warm reception: a formal dinner and quick repairs for the *Falcon*. Donning a regal uniform given to her by Calrissian, Leia prepares for the meal—not entirely sure she trusts the man. Unfortunately, Leia is correct in her assumption: Calrissian betrays the Rebels to Darth Vader, Boba Fett, and the Empire in order to protect the facility and its people.

Although Kenner's interpretation of this action figure is far less detailed than the lavish regalia concocted by Hasbro decades later for her mother, Queen Amidala of Naboo, Leia's costume (and particularly the design on her vinyl cape) was legitimately sophisticated for 1980.

Leia Organa (Bespin Gown) hand and sleeve variations, at left; neck and head variations, shown below.

MOC: *ESB* turtleneck: **$250-$275+**, crew neck: **$175-$200**; *ROTJ* turtleneck: **$175**, crew neck: **$125-$135**; **MLC:** turtleneck version: **$25-$28**, prominently gold neck version: **$22-$25**, crew neck version: **$18-$22+**.

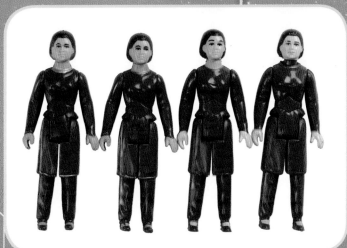

Rebel Soldier (Hoth Battle Gear)

[Production #39750]

1st carded appearance: 31-back card
Original Retail Price (average): $2.49
- brown-painted legs or brown-molded legs variations
- light brown or dark brown accents
- with blue Bespin Blaster (DH-17 blaster pistol)

Rebel Soldier (Hoth Battle Gear), posed with his Bespin Blaster accessory.

Following the Battle of Yavin, the Rebel Alliance moves their base of operations to the ice planet Hoth. Unfortunately, since Rebel leaders must always anticipate an Imperial invasion, their faction's ad hoc weapons and armaments [must] contain modifications to cope with Hoth's sub-zero temperatures.

As a character, the Rebel soldiers (a.k.a. Rebel troopers, Rebel infantry, Echo Base trooper, Hoth trooper, etc.) patrolling the surface of Hoth during *ESB* are similar to those Alliance troopers (wearing white blast helmets and light-colored uniforms with black vests), who are threatened by Darth Vader aboard Princess Leia's *Tantive IV* corvette starship at the beginning of *A New Hope*. These arctic-equipped soldiers live in terror of repeating the exact same situation: Darth Vader—keen to destroy any threat to the Empire—will stop at nothing to obtain his prize: the Sith Lord will overrun yet another outpost, leaving dead Rebel soldiers in his wake.

The action figures Kenner produced to represent these ground troopers were useful for a number of reasons: collectors could utilize them in one of the four spectacular Hoth-based playsets (see Imperial Attack Base Playset, Hoth Ice Planet Adventure Set, Rebel Command Center Adventure Set, or the Turret & Probot Playset), they could function as riders on one of the two Tauntauns offered within the line's *ESB* assortment (see Tauntaun and Tauntaun with Open Belly Rescue Feature), or even exploit them as a victim of (or culprit who attacked) the dreaded deluxe Hoth Wampa figure.

These figurines—like many of Kenner's plastic interpretations of iconic film characters—may not have expertly captured the features of the actors-in-question, but they effectively portray the characters to a romantic ideal rather than an authentic likeness. On a deeper level, this idealized representation may have allowed collectors to perhaps project their own imaginative faces onto these toys.

Rebel Soldier (Hoth Battle Gear) body variations; note the scarf and pelvic area.

MOC: *ESB:* **$100-$110+**; *ROTJ:* **$55-$60**; **MLC:** brown molded leg version: **$22-$25**, brown painted leg version: **$10+**.

Yoda, with accessories.

Yoda/Yoda The Jedi Master
(a.k.a. Grand Master Yoda)

[Production #38310]

1st carded appearance: 32-back card
Original Retail Price (average): $2.49

- o light paint or dark paint variations
- o fine or smooth torso sculpt variations
- o light brown or orange eyes variations
- • with Yoda Belt (four different variations, unique to the figure)
- • with Yoda Gimer Stick (two different variations, unique to the figure)
- • with Yoda Snake (orange, light orange, or brown variations, unique to the figure)
- • with cream cloth Yoda Robe, unique to the figure

Possessing great power and vast knowledge in the ways of the Force, the ancient being known as Yoda is of an unknown race and his early life is shrouded in mystery. At more than 900 years old, the one-time Master of the Order/Grand Master of the Jedi survives the Clone Wars, the rise and fall of the Galactic Republic, and his own self-imposed exile on the remote planet Dagobah (see Dagobah Action Playset) following the Great Jedi Purge—all the while retaining his incomparable skill as Jedi warrior military commander, and waiting in desperate hope that one day balance will be brought to the Force. When found by Luke (see Luke Skywalker [Bespin Fatigues]) on the planet Dagobah at the request of the spirit of Obi-Wan (see Ben [Obi-Wan] Kenobi), Yoda prepares to train the young man in the ways of the Force, as he had done hundreds of times before with other worthy candidates, ushering brave Jedi padawans from countless different worlds into the honor of knighthood.

Yoda body variations; note the collars, eyes, heads, legs, and detail on rope-belts.

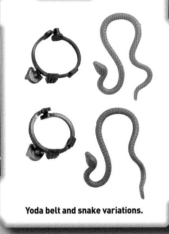

Yoda belt and snake variations.

Yoda warns Luke of the danger of the Dark Side of the Force, and cautions him against the corrupting effect of hatred, fear, and anger to a Jedi. Although we do not witness Yoda's skill with the lightsaber in *ESB*, his mastery of the aggressive and exceedingly acrobatic *Form IV* ("Ataru") affords Grand Master Yoda superlative skills against a single, powerful opponent. Ataru (a.k.a. "Way of the Hawk-Bat") is elaborate, fast-paced, requires a bit of open space, demands its user be proficient in Force-aided acrobatics, and utilizes a flurry of leaping strikes, dodging feints, and somersaults for both attack and defense. This always-offensive form makes the most of Yoda's agility, speed, and strength—and Luke incorporates some of this form into his own lightsaber philosophy. At the time of *ESB* (and during his period of exile on Dagobah), it appears that Yoda eschews his skill with a lightsaber, although his unlit lightsaber's hilt is apparent on his action figure's

belt in favor of using a gimer stick, which can be chewed to release vital nutrients and minerals that assist Yoda during periods of meditation.

With endless charm and a charismatic appeal to many different generations of *Star Wars* aficionados, Yoda's idiosyncratic speech patterns, humble way of life, and diminutive size contribute to his legion of fans.

MOC: *ESB* brown snake: **$165-$185+**, orange snake: **$145-$160+**; *ROTJ* brown snake only: **$85-$100+**; *POTF*: **$325+**; **MLC**: brown snake: **$40-$45**, orange snake: **$25**.

" ... my ally is the Force. And a powerful ally it is. Life creates it, makes it grow. Its energy surrounds us and binds us. Luminous beings are we ... not (this) crude matter. You must feel the Force around you. Here, between you ... me ... the tree ... the rock ... everywhere."

— Grand Master Yoda, instructing Luke Skywalker in the ways of the Force

Dengar (Bounty Hunter, a.k.a. "Payback")

[Production #39329]

1st appearance: (Sears Exclusive) Cloud City Playset
1st carded appearance: 41-back card
Original Retail Price (average): $2.49

- o dark facial tone or very light facial tone
- o chest piece variations
- with blue Imperial Rifle ("modified" DLT-20A blaster rifle with added handle)

Dengar, with Imperial Rifle.

One of the six bounty hunters summoned by Darth Vader to meet aboard the *Executor* (see Darth Vader's Star Destroyer Action Playset), the scarred mercenary known as Dengar is briefed by the Sith Lord regarding a mission to capture the *Millennium Falcon* and her crew. Having assembled only the best mercenaries in the galaxy, each of these talented bounty hunters have their murderous activities endorsed by Imperial law.

As a young man, Dengar develops an infamous reputation as one of the finest "swoop jockeys" within this dangerous profession. Swoop racing is a precarious vocation since piloting a swoop bike was akin to driving a gigantic engine with one small seat strapped on top—similar to, but *far* more risky than piloting a repulsorlift speeder such as the 74-Z (see Speeder Bike). During his final competition as a swoop racer, a youthful Dengar is pitted against the swashbuckling Han Solo. Toward the end of the race, Dengar carelessly crashes into Solo's swoop, creating a horrendous accident that causes Dengar not only to suffer a traumatic brain injury, but bans him from the professional swoop-racing circuit permanently.

Blaming his misfortune on Han, Dengar changes his name to "Payback" and becomes obsessed with the smuggler, allowing the Empire to perform a series of dangerous operations on his brain, replacing his hypothalamus, the main control center of the autonomic nervous system, with cybernetic circuitry that affords him an eidetic memory, yet leaves him susceptible to hallucinations. Following the surgery, a cold, clinical, and emotionless Payback becomes a bounty hunter who is exclusive to the Empire until he refuses to participate in a particularly distasteful Imperial mission—forcing his retirement as an officially licensed mercenary.

Going into business for himself, Dengar eventually takes notice of a bounty posted by Jabba Desilijic Tiure (see Jabba the Hutt Action Playset) for the capture of Han Solo. Although Dengar chases Solo from one side of the galaxy to the other for decades to obtain revenge, he is never able to achieve satisfaction for Solo ruining his life. Of course, he fails to capture the *Millennium Falcon* in *ESB*, having been beat out of the bounty by Boba Fett, a competitor who Dengar will eventually rescue from being slowly digested for a thousand years by the sarlaac pit after the Battle of Carkoon.

Dengar facial paint variations.

MOC: ESB: $60-$65; ROTJ: $35-$38;
MLC: $10.

Han Solo (Bespin Outfit)/ Han Solo (Cloud City Outfit)

[Production #39339]

1st appearance: (Sears Exclusive) Cloud
City Playset
1st carded appearance: 41-back card
Original Retail Price (average): $2.49

- with blue Bespin Blaster (DH-17 blaster pistol)

At some point, Han Solo is honored by his peoples' highest commendation: that of the Corellian Bloodstripe, an award for "conspicuous gallantry … courage demonstrated after deliberation"—essentially courage under fire. This award manifests in the form of a stripe of colored piping worn down the side of a Corellian's pants. Solo wears both colors of stripes, apparently depending upon his uniform. First-class, red Bloodstripes are almost always given posthumously due to their rarity and the level of personal sacrifice required for their achievement. A red first-class Bloodstripe can be found on the legs of both pants on Kenner's first iteration the daring pilot (see Han Solo), while on this version of the Corellian, Han (Bespin Outfit), Kenner's third version of the character, he sports a yellow, second-class Bloodstripe on both legs of his slacks. However, on Kenner's fourth (Han Solo [In Trench Coat]) and fifth renditions the character (Han Solo [In Carbonite Chamber]), it appears that a Corellian Bloodstripe should be/could be attached to the figure's trousers—since there are raised marks running down the side of *each* trouser leg on both figurines, yet these thin raised plastic stripes are *not* colored red or yellow—perhaps for economy's sake.

Regardless, Han Solo has now transformed himself into a renowned hero, fighting the evil Empire for the sake of his friends and al-

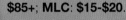

**Two of many
Bespin Blaster
variations.**

lies in the Rebellion. A natural leader and skilled pilot who is famous across the galaxy, this version of Han Solo's action figure showcases the final uniform the Alliance captain wore before his body is encased within carbonite (see Han Solo [In Carbonite Chamber]).

MOC: *ESB:* **$150-$165+;** *ROTJ:* **$70-$85+; MLC: $15-$20.**

Princess Leia: "I thought you knew this person."

Chewbacca growls a response to Han.

Han Solo: "Well, that was a long time ago … I'm sure he's forgotten about that."

—Princess Leia questions Han and Chewbacca about Lando Calrissian before visiting Cloud City

Lobot/Lobot (Lando's Aid)

[Production #39349]

1st appearance: (Sears Exclusive) Cloud City Playset
1st carded appearance: 41-back card
Original Retail Price (average): $2.49

- o two different body sculpt variations (featuring many aesthetic differences)
- • with blue Bespin Blaster (DH-17 blaster pistol)

Lobot, with Bespin Blaster.

Born the son of a slaver who is orphaned at the age of fifteen when his father's transport is raided by pirates, the human boy who would become Lobot lives as a captive of these brigands for two full years until he escapes to the outpost of Cloud City located above the gas-giant planet of Bespin. With no skills, home, or means of gainful employment, the youth steals merely to survive and is arrested by the Bespin Wing Guard (see Bespin Security Guard, I and II) and promptly convicted. In lieu of a lengthy prison term, Cloud City's superintendent at the time, Baroness Administrator Ellia Shallence, sentences the drifter to fifteen years of servitude at the mining facility/luxury resort, with the express condition that he will be slightly modified with a cybernetic implant. After drilling holes into the young man's head, he is transformed into a cyborg—by definition, a humanoid "whose physiological functioning is aided by or dependent upon an electronic device."

Augmented with BioTech Industries' Biotech Aj^6 cyborg headband—the odd-looking "headphone wrap" that prominently appears on the bald-headed Kenner figurine—the brain of the youth now known as "Lobot" has direct access to Cloud City's central computer, since the peerless Aj^6 headband affords him the ability to mentally control computer systems. As a result of this operation, Lobot's intelligence is greatly increased, as is his investment within the colony.

Unfortunately, although Lobot's Biotech Aj^6 cyborg headband enhances his intellect and allows him total control over the city's central computer—a job that at one time takes more than a dozen workers to complete—his emotional development is stunted, and the speech center of his brain deteriorates. His need to verbalize expressions abates, and his speech is reduced to clipped declarative phrases. Although his transformation into a cyborg appears to lessen Lobot's grip on humanity, those who know him best, such as Baron Administrator Lando Calrissian, recognize that his passion and loyalty to Cloud City and its people grow exponentially over the years.

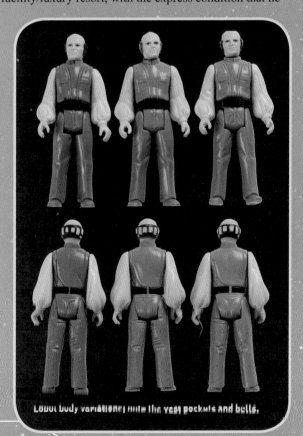

Lobot body variations note the vest pockets and belts.

MOC: *ESD*: $60-$75; *ROT.I*: $28-$35; MLC: $7-$10.

Ugnaught

[Production #39319]

1st appearance: (Sears Exclusive) Cloud City Playset
1st carded appearance: 41-back card
Original Retail Price (average): $2.49

- o wide eyes, narrow collar, grey hair, or close-set eyes, wider collar, and green-grey hair variations
- o more detailed or less detailed chest piece variations
- • with Ugnaught Toolkit, unique to the figure
- • with Ugnaught Apron/Smock (purple or blue variations, unique to the figure)

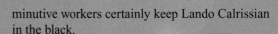

Ugnaught, with accessories.

Sporting the slightly upturned snout of a short-statured porcine humanoid, the creatures known as Ugnaughts are brought to Bespin's Cloud City by an eccentric explorer to help build the facility many generations ago—where, in return, they had free reign of the facility and are honorably represented in Cloud City's Parliament of Guilds. Found working within the processing plants of the outpost (see Cloud City Playset), they assist in the production of tibanna gas—a valuable natural element excreted by immensely large, gas-filled creatures known as "beldons." Tibanna gas—a heating fuel utilized by weapons manufacturers to power blasters and other offensive weapons—is processed by the Ugnaughts, who process the gas then package it for transport off-world in carbonite bricks or blocks; these di-

minutive workers certainly keep Lando Calrissian in the black.

Ugnaughts were sold into slavery many generations ago (thanks to the machinations of evil Separatist leader and Supreme Commander of the Droid Army, General Grievous) before the rise of the Galactic Empire, and are stolen *en masse* from their volcano-dotted, swampy homeworld of Gentes. Oftentimes Ugnaughts are targeted by slavers due to their intelligence, loyalty, high level of resistance to the elements, long lifespans (maxing out at 200 years), and ability to work for long periods of time at their "blood profession"—a trade taught to Ugnaught children (a.k.a. Ugletts) by their parents; one they would pursue until their death.

Ugnaught apron variations.

MOC: *ESB:* $80-$90; *ROTJ:* $55-$62; **MLC:** either purple or blue apron/smock, **$10-$13**.

AT-AT Driver
(a.k.a. Imperial Army Pilot)

[Production #39379]

1st carded appearance: 41-back card
Original Retail Price (average): $2.49

- o with dark or light orange highlights
- • with AT-AT Driver Laser Rifle (possesses a connected strap, unique to the figure)

AT-AT Driver, with AT-AT Driver Laser Rifle.

Although this figure is identified as an "AT-AT Driver" in the vintage Kenner *Star Wars* toy line, evidence provided by the peerless resource Wookieepedia.com suggests the name of this character could be modified to read "Imperial Army Pilot"—one of the anonymous members of the Empire's ground-based squadron of the Imperial Service. In the AT-AT Driver's broader role as a pilot for all of the Imperial Army's forces, these soldiers are ordered to maintain and operate a number of powerful vehicles. Among these, the AT-AT (see AT-AT [Imperial] All Terrain Armored Transport), its water-based counterpart the AT-AT swimmer (Aquatic Terrain Armored Transport, NOT produced as a toy), the bipedal AT-ST (All Terrain Scout Transport, see Scout Walker), and the AT-PT (All Terrain Personal Transport, also not produced as a Kenner toy). Simply put, the AT-AT Driver is proficient with every vehicle in the army inventory, which is no mean feat, particularly since directing a vehicle the size of an AT-AT over rough, rocky ground or through a craggy field is an impossible task for the ordinary soldier; therefore, the Empire only recruits the best pilots to fill the ranks of AT-AT drivers, who are incredibly valuable to the Imperial Army.

Similar to the Grand Army of the Republic's clone troopers metamorphosing into the Imperial Stormtrooper Corps (see Stormtrooper) and retaining their (mainly) bone-white Phase II clone armor, the Grand Army's clone pilots' Phase II attire is highly reminiscent of the formal regalia worn by the AT-AT driver. However, AT-AT drivers specifically retain a color scheme that is far more evocative of the Phase II clone pilot attire: a light gray flight suit with webbing, white gloves and boots, and their open-mouthed helmet. Apart from their uniforms, these AT-AT Drivers/Imperial Army Pilots are usually found unarmed, but the Kenner action figure was made more attractive to collectors by including a black rifle with strap inside the toy's package—a weapon that was uniquely crafted to be included with this figure, and is also packaged with the mail-away Star Wars Action Figure Survival Kit and as a bonus weapon with Kenner's AT-AT toy.

MOC: *ESB:* **$75-$80**; *ROTJ:* **$55-$65+**; *POTF:* **$1,000**; **MLC:** **$11-$14**.

Leia/Leia Organa/ Princess Leia Organa (Hoth Outfit)

[Production #39359]

1st carded appearance: 41-back card
Original Retail Price (average): $2.49

- o olive booted or brown booted variations
- o raised or smooth rank bar variations
- o brown or dark-brown hair variations
- • with blue Princess Leia Blaster (Defender sporting blaster pistol)

Leia, with Princess Leia Blaster.

As the adopted princess and senator of the former planet Alderaan, the daring Princess Organa possesses many admirable qualities, similar to her brilliant and politically adroit mother, Padmé Amidala. Not your typical princess from fairy tales of old, Leia is a tomboy as renowned for her intellect and resourcefulness as her natural beauty, which allows her to function as a strong leader for the Alliance to Restore the Republic. Having been exposed as a traitor against the Empire, she now focuses all of her impressive resources, diplomatic connections, and royal contacts to defeat Palpatine's Imperial forces as a key Rebel Leader.

Her Kenner action figure sports a film-authentic, formal hairdo featuring "on duty" braids, a heated vest, military snow boots with bindings, and a white insulated jumpsuit to protect her from inclement weather, yet Leia still wears the color white as a symbol of the lost planet of Alderaan, reminiscent of the flowing white Alderaanian royal gown of her first toy incarnation. Both uniforms are simple and elegant.

MOC: *ESB:* $135-$140+; *ROTJ:* $90-$100; **MLC:** $16-$24.

Han: "Hang on, Your Worship, I'm trying to figure out these weird knobs and switches..."

Leia: "Why is it you always get formal when you're about to do something stupid?"

Han Solo to Leia Organa-Solo (after their marriage) in *Star Wars: Dark Empire #1*

Imperial Commander

[Production #39389]

1st carded appearance: 41-back card
Original Retail Price (average): $2.49

- skinny head or round head variations
- low or high boot variations
- pen on chest + neckline variations (x3)
- with blue Imperial Blaster (E-11 blaster rifle)

Imperial Commander, with Imperial Blaster.

For the packaging image of an Imperial Commander, Kenner chose a photograph of Darth Vader's always-dependable mid-level officer from *The Empire Strikes Back*, Major General Maximilian Veers (see AT-AT Commander). However, since the figure is meant to represent any one of a number of different officers that are encountered throughout the film, the figurine is a decent representation of a generic Imperial Officer—sharp yet bland, utterly emotionless yet poised to strike—except for one major discrepancy: in the film, since General Veers is an officer in the Imperial Navy, we will note that the color of his Imperial Naval uniform on the card front photo is charcoal gray with a hint of green like the one also worn by Admiral Firmus Piett—not the deep, dark black as represented by the action figure, which is another type of Imperial officer entirely.

The Imperial Officer action figure's uniform color is usually meant to represent the costuming of an officer in the Imperial Stormtrooper Corps, which is therefore comprised of a black double-breasted dress tunic, a black cap (with visible flap on the back and a silver Imperial code disk pinned to the middle of the front flap), black Jodhpur trousers (note the flaring on the figure's legs), knee-high black boots, black glove gauntlets, and the rank bars, belt boxes, and code cylinders appropriate to their rank and station.

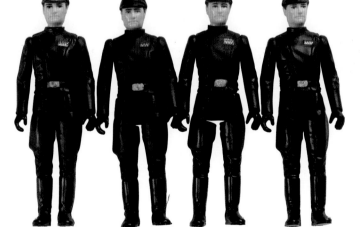

Imperial Commander head and body sculpt variations.

MOC: *ESB*: **$72-$80**;
ROTJ: **$35-$45**;
MLC: **$10-$14**.

Rebel Commander

[Production #39369]

1st carded appearance: 41-back card
Original Retail Price (average): $2.49

- o two different tunic sculpt/belt sculpt variations
- o full paint or half paint scarf variations
- • with black Rebel Rifle with attached strap
  (BlasTech A295 blaster rifle)

**Rebel Commander,
with Rebel Rifle**

The character pictured on the package front for the Rebel Commander is that of Jeroen Webb—a human male from the planet Ralltiir who became a Rebel spy for the planet's political underground, and following this, a stalwart officer for the Rebel Alliance. However, the aesthetics of the toy itself differentiates from Webb's uniform; the clothing on the Kenner figurine appears as an amalgamation of the battle togs from a number of different Rebel Commanders: 1) *Bren Derlin* (portrayed by John Ratzenberger, Cliff Clavin from television's *Cheers* fame)—a mustachioed human male who joins the Rebellion after his father is assassinated due to anti-Imperial views; Derlin is the operations and security chief at the Alliance headquarters on the planet Hoth, advancing rather quickly through the ranks; 2) two unnamed Rebel officers—one who accompanies the aforementioned Webb, and another Echo Base officer who is portrayed by Industrial Light & Magic painter/actor Harrison Ellenshaw; and 3) *Ledick Firest*, a former mercenary and heroic Rebel officer who, while sporting a horseshoe moustache as

he patrols the tundra trenches of Hoth, devises a brilliant strategy to assist the Rebellion's evacuation of the ice planet—Firest cons the Imperial walkers (see AT-AT [(Imperial) All Terrain Armored Transport]) into pursuing the Rebels' power generators rather than their vulnerable personnel.

MOC: *ESB:* **$72-$80;** *ROTJ:* **$35-$45;** **MLC:** **$10-$14.**

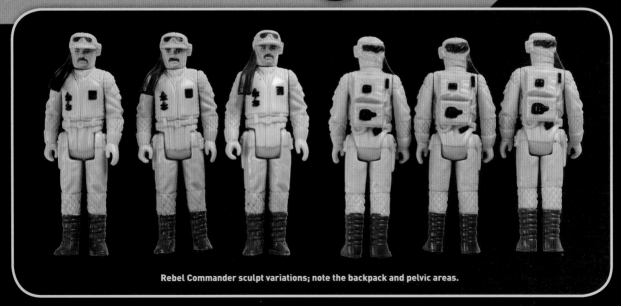

Rebel Commander sculpt variations; note the backpack and pelvic areas.

2-1B/Two-Onebee (2-1B)/Too-Onebee (2-1B)

[Production #39399]

1st carded appearance: 41-back card
Original Retail Price (average): $2.49

- ○ flat blue with extra (hand/claw) bolt or semi-metallic blue variations
- • with medical staff
- • with 2-1B "vocabulator" and non-removable cord

Originally owned by the Empire, "Too-Onebee" is tasked to provide medical care for the victims of Imperial forces following violent raids, even though he believes he is fighting on the "wrong" side of the Galactic Civil War. Eventually, the skilled droid is noticed by a ruthless and sinister Imperial governor, who ultimately falls victim to assassination by a Rebel agent. Following the governor's "permanent deposing," Too-Onebee joins the Rebellion and served with honor.

Eventually, Too-Onebee is assigned to Echo Base on the planet Hoth, where he is assisted by an FX-7-series droid (see FX-7 [Medical Droid]) in maintaining the station's lone bacta tank (a special-ized chamber containing a compound [alazhi & kavam] that allows for the rapid regeneration of wounded tissue, while preventing the development of scarring)—a rejuvenation chamber that heals Luke Skywalker in *The Empire Strikes Back*. Due to his obvious skill, he is also requested to work on the loss of Luke's hand, which he suffers on Bespin at the end of *ESB* while aboard the medical frigate, *Redemption*.

Two-Onebee

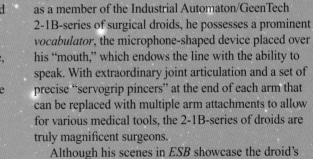

2-1B, with accessories.

is a single model of the most advanced, efficient, and expensive medical/surgical droid in the galaxy, and as a member of the Industrial Automaton/GeenTech 2-1B-series of surgical droids, he possesses a prominent *vocabulator*, the microphone-shaped device placed over his "mouth," which endows the line with the ability to speak. With extraordinary joint articulation and a set of precise "servogrip pincers" at the end of each arm that can be replaced with multiple arm attachments to allow for various medical tools, the 2-1B-series of droids are truly magnificent surgeons.

Although his scenes in *ESB* showcase the droid's translucent torso sheath, along with a prominent in-terface socket (for a computer tether) located over the upper-left portion of his chest, 2-1B's legs are never shown in the film—the designers of the robot prop nev-er add these limbs; the robot is given a rolling platform instead. As a result, when constructing the droid's ac-tion figure, Kenner had to concoct its own interpre-tation of 2-1B's legs.

2-1B claw variations—extra "bolt" on left-handed claw.

2-1B claw variations; note the thickness.

MOC: *ESB*: $75-$85+; *ROTJ*: $55-$60+; MLC: $10-$12.

> "...yes, Lord Vader. I've reached the main power generators. The shield will be down in moments. You may start your landing."
>
> —Major General Veers reports to Darth Vader during the Battle of Hoth

AT-AT Commander/General Veers

[Production #69620]

1st appearance: (Sears Exclusive) Rebel Command Center Adventure Set
1st carded appearance: 45-back card
Original Retail Price (average): $2.49

- o orange face or flesh face variations
- o two different back sculpt variations
- with blue Bespin Blaster (DH-17 blaster pistol)

AT-AT Commander, with Bespin Blaster.

General Veers is famous for leading his infamous Blizzard Force, an armored regiment of the best pilots in the Imperial Navy, on an attack of Echo Base against the Rebellion on ice planet Hoth, where he successfully routes the Rebels and destroys their shield generator. Unfortunately, although this mission records Veers' greatest success in combat, immediately after the destruction of the Rebels' generator, a damaged T-47 snowspeeder (see Rebel Armored Snowspeeder) crashes into the main AT-AT's cockpit, engulfing Veers in a fiery tomb. Somehow, the plucky General Veers survives the apocalyptic assault, yet loses his legs entirely; since he does not trust cybernetics, he chooses to utilize a hoverchair instead—a vehicle he is bound to for the rest of his life. Oddly enough, Kenner's AT-AT Commander is a figure that actually knows a limited release as "General Veers," by Sears Canada in 1980.

As an AT-AT Commander, Veers exemplifies the Imperial Army's ideals expertly; for more information on the confidence of the men who pilot the Imperial walkers, see the AT-AT Driver's entry.

MOC: *ESB*: **$75-$85**; *ROTJ*: **$45-$50**; **MLC**: **$10-$12**.

AT-AT Commander sculpt variations; note backpacks, belts, and collars.

Luke Skywalker (Hoth Battle Gear)/ Luke Skywalker (Hoth Outfit)

[Production #69610]

1st appearance: (Sears Exclusive) Rebel Command Center Adventure Set
1st carded appearance: 45-back card
Original Retail Price (average): $2.49

- with black Rebel Rifle, with attached strap; BlasTech A295 blaster rifle

Luke Skywalker (Hoth Battle Gear), with Rebel Rifle.

Dressed in the winter uniform he sports early in *ESB*, when he patrols the area around Echo base aboard his trusty mount (see Tauntaun and Tauntaun with Open Belly Rescue Feature) to investigate the arrival of a purported meteorite, the Rebel hero finds himself in an untenable situation. After his tauntaun senses a disturbance within the immediate area, Luke tries to calm her, and he is greeted with a paw-swipe from the savage repro-mammalian beast known as a wampa: it just so happens that tauntauns are the apex predator's favorite food (see Hoth Wampa). Dragging the Force-sensitive young man back to his lair, the wampa hangs Luke upside-down—saving the tasty humanoid treat for a later time.

However, it is in this important scene where we witness Luke's attunement to the Force growing: he can now manipulate physical objects.

With blood draining to his head and the bitterly cold climate encroaching on his soul, encouraging the young man to give way to unconsciousness, Luke exhibits tremendous focus, calming his mind to call his lightsaber to his hand, freeing himself from his icy prison and killing the vicious beast. Tumbling out of the wampa's cave and out into the snow, Luke sees a vision—the spirit of his late mentor Obi-Wan (see Ben [Obi-Wan] Kenobi)—who tells his apprentice to go to the Dagobah system, where he will learn from Yoda, the Jedi Master.

The weapon included with this magnificently sculpted Kenner figure, one of the company's best representations of the iconic protagonist in the vintage line, appears to be based upon the BlasTech A295 blaster rifle: the Rebel Alliance soldier's standard-issue longarm at Echo Base, which is favored by marksmen and snipers because of its high accuracy and lethal range.

Luke Skywalker (Hoth Battle Gear) uniform variations; note the belts, goggles, and vests.

MOC: *ESB*: $145-$165; *ROTJ*: $65-$80; MLC: $11-$14.

Artoo-Detoo/
Artoo-Detoo (R2-D2, with Sensorscope)/
R2-D2 (with Periscope)

[Production #69590]

1st appearance: (Sears Exclusive) Rebel Command Center Adventure Set
1st carded appearance: 45-back card
Original Retail Price (average): $2.49

- o two different head sculpt variations
- with blue plastic sensorscope (two different sensor arm variations, unique to the figure)
- with paper label/sticker (two different sticker variations, unique to the figure)

As an astromech droid, R2-D2 is capable of assisting its humanoid partner with *astrogation*: the science of navigating a spacecraft through *realspace* (traversing the cosmos at <u>less than the speed of light</u>: specifically, through the galaxy in which we dwell) and *hyperspace* (a parallel/alternate dimension/physical mode of space where one can travel <u>faster than the speed of light</u>). When partnered with a pilot and engaged in astrogation, the astromech droid's primary responsibilities are to determine the spacecraft's present location, via *astrocartography*, and also plan the means of reaching a destination that is safe as well as reliable.

Although the importance of reliability in a dogfight goes without saying, safety is even more important—especially when retreating from battle or quickly having to traverse great distances. Therefore, an astromech droid's self-awareness, as well as their cognizance of the possibility of colliding with myriad objects, is of paramount importance when engaging hyperspace: incorrectly calculated jumps mean instantaneous death, such as colliding immediately with an asteroid, planet, moon, or star.

Therefore, due to the high level of excellence required to pilot the Rebellion's B-wing, X-wing, or Y-wing fighters, navigating a ship's course is almost exclusively handled by an astromech droid, to the extent that almost every Rebellion starfighter dedicates a plug-in slot (dubbed a "socket") to the pilot's favored astromech.

As a peerless astromech droid, R2-D2 is an experienced starfighter pilot's first choice when departing on a new mission, which is why Anakin and Luke Skywalker treat the little droid with such devotion. Apart from his obvious navigational skill, Artoo also has a bevy of magnificent accoutrements at his disposal with which to assist his master. Featured with

this Kenner action figure for the first time was an
extensible sensorscope (a.k.a. "extendable auxiliary visual imaging system")—utilized to communicate with Luke after falling into a swamp on
Dagobah (see Dagobah Action Playset).

 MOC: *ESB*: **$150-$165+**; *ROTJ*:
$65-$80; **MLC**: **$11-$14**.

CLOSE-UP

Sensorscope
variations.

Bespin Security Guard (II-second release)

[Production #69640]

1st carded appearance: 45-back card
Original Retail Price (average): $2.49
- o darker face with red cuffs or lighter face with orange cuffs variation
- • with blue Bespin Blaster (DH-17 blaster pistol)

Bespin Security Guard (II), with Bespin Blaster.

Purchasing multiples of the Bespin Security Guard toy was an excellent way to "troop build" a security force for the outpost of Cloud City (see Cloud City Playset), thanks to Kenner's construction of an entirely different figural mold. This action figure marks the second character released under the name Bespin Security Guard, and is indicated within this book as "Bespin Security Guard (II)." With an impressive stance and posture—his left foot posed a bit forward, left arm bent at the elbow in readiness, and both hands affording the figure the ability to hold a weapon (a rare thing back in the vintage line)—this character was ripe for assembling multiple members of Cloud City's preeminent security force: the Bespin Wing Guard.

Bespin's official sentries who pilot the Storm IV spacecraft (see Twin-Pod Cloud Car) should also be considered members of the Bespin Wing Guard, since these aviators are essentially Bespin Security Guards dressed in uniforms carefully adapted for the rigors of flying (see Cloud Car Pilot).

It must be noted that when this figure was re-released in 2009, Hasbro simply named him Cloud City Wing Guard.

Note: The blue uniform of every single Bespin Security Guard action figure *always* possesses gold highlights painted onto the jacket—on both the coat's front and back. A loose figure without these gold paint applications either had these paint apps wear off during play, or did not have these applications applied at all. This is not a rare variation, but an error that occurred in production.

MOC: *ESB*: **$100-$110**; *ROTJ*: **$30-$35**. **MLC**: **$10-$12**, make sure the gold paint applications are not worn.

"If you can bribe a member of Bespin's Wing Guard into taking you on a spin around Cloud City, you won't regret spending the credits. The views are stunning."

—Excerpt from Ullok's Underground Guide to Bespin

Cloud Car Pilot/(Twin Pod) Cloud Car Pilot

[Production #69640]

1st carded appearance: 45-back card
Original Retail Price (average): $2.49

- o flesh face and standard sculpt or pink face with darker gray belt & pouches variations
- with grey Pilot Blaster
- with Commlink, unique to the figure

Cloud Car Pilot, with accessories.

Of all the characters Kenner chose to develop into an action figure for the vintage *Empire Strikes Back* assortment, it is peculiar that the company selected the singular "Cloud Car Pilot"—essentially a member of the Bespin Wing Guard (see Bespin Security Guard I and II) dressed in a uniform adapted for the rigors of flight. The choice is odd because the toy company's designers had to take great liberties in its construction—and not in the same way they concocted the uniforms *ex nihilo* (literally, "out of nothing") for the four cantina patrons in their collection for 1979 (see Greedo, Hammerhead, Snaggletooth, and Walrus Man). There simply WAS no Cloud Car Pilot produced by Lucasfilm in the original trilogy: the only image we witness of these pilots in *ESB* is a brief glimpse of their helmeted heads.

However, the Storm IV spacecraft (see Twin-Pod Cloud Car) featured briefly in *Empire* has potential for a wealth of sales as a toy spaceship with a catchy name to boot: the Twin-Pod Cloud Car. Therefore, in order to produce an appropriate pilot action figure to accompany Kenner's low price point and easy-to-sell Twin Pod Cloud Car toy vehicle, which has slots for two potential action figure pilots, the company scoured Lucasfilm's archive of costume designs for the *Empire Strikes Back*. According to *The Illustrated Star Wars Universe*, to construct the (Twin Pod) Cloud Car Pilot action figure, Kenner utilized the original concept design of the character as rendered by Nilo Rodis-Jamero—the brilliant assistant art director

and costume designer of visual effects for *ESB* and *ROTJ*—mimicking the uniform as best they could for its action figure incarnation. Although the parallel wasn't exact, it was effective enough, and the inclusion of two pretty unique accessories didn't hurt.

MOC: *ESB*: $105–$120+; *ROTJ*: $55–$60+ **MLC**: $14–$10+.

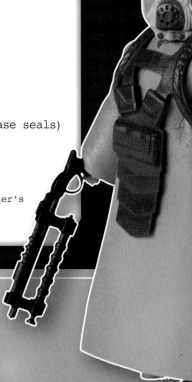

4-LOM
(a.k.a. Zuckuss, or "The Uncanny One")*

[Production #70010]

1st appearance: Mail-Away
1st carded appearance: 48-back card
Original Mail-Away Price: FREE (5 proof-of-purchase seals)
Original Retail Price (average): $2.49

- o gray mouthed or black mouthed variations
- with armor (brown or red tinted armor variations)
- with tan cloth overcoat, unique to the figure
- with 4-LOM Rifle (loosely based on the bounty hunter's GRS-1 snare rifle, unique to the figure)

*Note: In a rare error, Kenner misidentified this character as "*4-LOM*," when in actuality, this action figure represents the character named "*Zuckuss*." 4-LOM is the droid with an insect-type head. Since this character is incorrectly identified on all of Kenner's vintage packaging and promotional material as 4-LOM, we are obligated to identify this character as 4-LOM throughout this book as well.

Kenner rewarded longtime *Star Wars* collectors a third opportunity to obtain a mail-away figure before its retail release with this "Free 4-LOM" promotion. However, as mentioned, this bounty hunter's true name is Zuckuss, and he hails from the gaseous ammonia-planet of Gand, where there are several different species of sentient insectoid inhabitants who are differentiated from one another via the shape and structure of their heads and the color of their insectoid exoskeletons. These species—called the Gand (or the "Gands")—are divided into two essentially different subspecies: with or without lungs. Although Gand are suitably adapted to their toxic homeworld, when traveling to worlds with oxygen-rich atmospheres, Gand with lungs require sophisticated breathing gear—those without lungs adapt far better. Zuckuss is a lunged Gand, and therefore possesses the other impressive qualities of his race: an obvious humility and self-deprecation when in contact with other species, an exoskeleton with regenerative properties and the desire that one's individuality had to be earned via a score of impressive accomplishments.

Due to his profound skill, Zuckuss earns his individuality and reserves the ability to make use of a first-person personal pronoun ("I, me, my, mine," etc.) when describing his exploits, while other Gand speak of themselves only via third-person ("he, she, one, it, him, her," etc.). Gand revers the profession of bounty hunting, and uses a specific term— "findsman"—to delineate one who pursues the career. Findsmen are legendary figures in Gand society, and hold a bit of cache outside of their homeworld as well, since the Gand take a far more sophisticated, philosophical approach

> "You've already got a mess here. You can either start cleaning it up ... or you can join it. Your pick."
>
> —Zuckuss to cantina owner Salla C'airam, from the novel *Star Wars: Hard Merchandise*

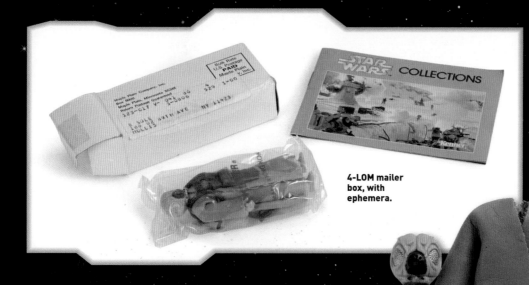

4-LOM mailer box, with ephemera.

4-LOM, with accessories.

to this normally crude vocation: findsmen are a cohort of Force-sensitive, shamanistic trackers, who utilized mystic rituals, augury, and a system of martial arts to capture their quarry.

Zuckuss is renowned across the galaxy for his ability to locate particularly well-hidden targets, which earn him the nickname, "The Uncanny One." Although his many adventures make him a hero on Gand, he is sometimes difficult to manage, since he is diagnosed with schizophrenia and dissociative identity disorder—psychoses which are quite observable since Zuckuss adopted two distinctly different dialects and personalities: one is a devout, stalwart findsman mystic; the other more dominant disposition is that of a brash, foul-mouthed thug. One of his more famous exploits takes place during the course of *ESB*, when Zuckuss is contacted by Darth Vader for a meeting aboard his ship, *The Executor*. Oftentimes Zuckuss is partnered with the mechanical being known as 4-LOM (an obvious call-number for a droid), and the two become fast friends—meeting the Sith Lord together to pursue an Imperial bounty for the *Millennium Falcon*. A formida-

ble pairing, Zuckuss' instinctive mystical intuition combined with 4-LOM's clinical, analytical skills makes them an effective team.

When engaged in his chosen profession, Zuckuss makes use of a sophisticated respirator, and is equipped with ammonia bombs, vibroblades, a slew of different plaster pistols and rifles, and his infamous GRS-1 snare rifle (included with his Kenner action figure), which can strike targets (up to 150 meters away!) with a long-lasting, immobilizing shockstun mist that induces paralysis.

MISB: All contents sealed in mailer: **$165-$180**; MIB: w/all included pieces & sealed figure: **$70-$85+**; MIB, w/all included pieces & non-sealed figure: **$50-$65+**, MOC, *ESB*: **$85-$100+**; *ROTJ*: **$55-$65+**; MLC: **$15-$20**.

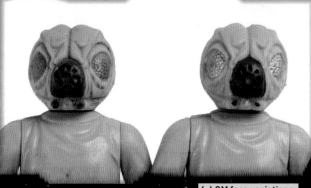

4-LOM face variations.

See-Threepio (C-3PO, with Removable Limbs)*

[Production #69600]

1st carded appearance: 45-back card
Original Retail Price (average): $2.49

- with black vinyl C-3PO Backpack, unique to the figure

*Note: The card front package text reads: "Now!! With Removable Arms, Legs, and Back Pack."

Like his droid companion R2-D2, who was modified and re-released with a pop-up sensorscope (see Artoo-Detoo [R2-D2, with Sensorscope]), C-3PO was also re-released for the *Empire Strikes Back* action figure assortment with an all-new feature: "removable limbs." Mimicking the character's near-fatal destruction at the hands of Corporal Drazin, an unseen Imperial soldier who blasts the golden droid apart (see Imperial Stormtrooper) when visiting Cloud City (see Cloud City Playset), C-3PO could now be disassembled into five different parts: head and torso, left arm, right arm, left leg, and right leg (note: his head is non-removable). After breaking this figure down into its five separate components, C-3PO (with Removable Limbs) came with a flexible black plastic backpack, which allowed another character to tote all of his body parts—exactly like the cargo net that Chewie utilized in the film.

One important note: careful readers will notice this book refers to R2-D2 and C-3PO (and most of the other droids in the tome) with the personal pronoun "he," while Jabba Desilijic Ture's torture droid EV-9D9 is referred to as "she"; this is because when droids are conceived then created, they can be programmed as either masculine or feminine. *Droid Gender Programming* utilizes software to replicate distinct genders (i.e., male, female) within the artificial intelligence of these mechanical beings, particularly those droids who are bound to interact with sentient organic beings quite frequently. R2-D2 and C-3PO best exemplify these types of droids who enjoy sophisticated, complex personalities that benefit from Masculine Droid Programming: as "masculine" droids, these robots retain heavier, bulkier, man-like bodies. In *Attack of the Clones*, the unicycled WA-7

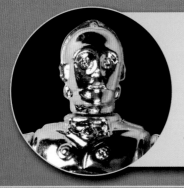

Stormtrooper (off screen): "Who are you?"

C-3PO: "Oh, my! I ... I'm terribly sorry. I didn't mean to intrude. No, please don't get up ... "

—C-3PO's final words before being blasted to bits at the outpost of Cloud City

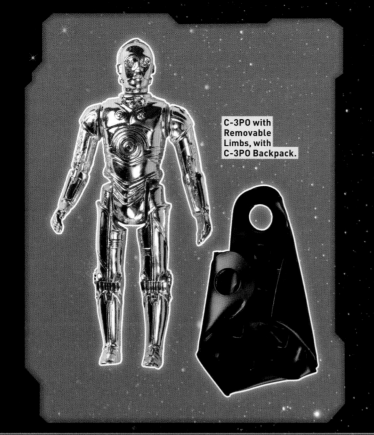

C-3PO with
Removable
Limbs, with
C-3PO Backpack.

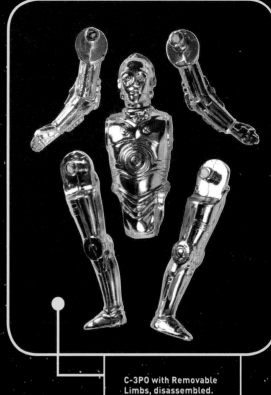

C-3PO with Removable
Limbs, disassembled.

service droid who works at Dex's Diner on Coruscant (known as FLO) is a Feminine Programmed Droid, and as such, possesses a lighter, smaller, lithe body structure and different vocal cadence and range than Masculine Programmed Droids.

With its vac-metallized finish, sturdy plastic backpack that allows other figures, specifically Chewbacca, who is pictured on the figurine's package front, to carry the protocol droid, this figure marks an advance in toy design: if carefully scrutinized, the arm and leg pegs fit into thin plastic retainers placed inside the torso's tabs in order to protect this C-3PO toy from multiple dismemberings. Finally, this version of C-3PO's break-apart action figure is utilized once more with different paint applications (and without his gold finish) in 1985's *Star Wars: Droids* toy line.

MOC: *ESB*: **$145-$155**; *ROTJ*: **$75-$85**; *POTF*: **$85-$105+**; *MLC*: **$10-$12**, based upon condition of chrome.

C-3PO with
Removable Limbs
within his backpack,
toted by Chewbacca

Imperial TIE Fighter Pilot

[Production #70030]

1st carded appearance: 47-back card
Original Retail Price (average): $2.49

- o dark grey paint application or light grey paint application variations
- • with grey Pilot Blaster

At the time of the original trilogy when the availability of Imperial recruits is plentiful, the fearsome-looking TIE pilots of the Imperial Navy are conscripted from the ranks of humanoid graduates of the Imperial Academy, as well as the remaining Jango Fett clones from the Clone Wars (22-19 BBY). Utilizing breathing equipment unnecessary to most Rebel pilots since the cockpits of Alliance starfighters are furnished with life-support systems (see A-wing, B-wing, X-wing, and Y-wing fighters), these "bucket-heads" (a Rebel nickname due to their fully-enclosed, reinforced helmets featuring breather tubes which are connected to a life-support pack) take great pride in their TIE fighters, due to the crafts' superiority re: targeting systems and flight controls.

Although their "eyeballs" (nickname for the TIE fighter) lack ejection seats, deflector shields, hyper-drives, and the aforementioned life-support systems, the zealous TIE fighter pilots are solely dedicated to their missions: conditioned to destroy their targets at the cost of their own lives.

This elite group of the Imperial Navy is tasked to fly any iteration of TIE, so then, kids and collectors alike were encouraged by Kenner to purchase the Imperial TIE Fighter Pilot action figure as a "troop builder" since they could fly the standard white TIE Fighter (1978), the "Battle-Damaged" Imperial TIE Fighter vehicle (1983), the Darth Vader TIE Fighter (1979), or the sophisticated TIE Interceptor (1984).

Imperial TIE Fighter Pilot, with Pilot Blaster.

MOC: *ESB*: **$135-$150**; *ROTJ*: **$60**; *POTF*: **$85-$105+**; **MLC: $13-$16.**

Zuckuss* (a.k.a. 4-LOM)

[Production #70020]

1st carded appearance: 47–back card
Original Retail Price (average): $2.49

- o flat gray head or metallic head
- o circle on back of knees and heels or no circles on back of knees and heels
- with Zuckuss Rifle, loosely based on the long Blastech W-90 concussion rifle

Zuckuss, with Zuckuss Rifle.

*Note: In a rare error, Kenner misidentified this character as "Zuckuss," when in actuality this action figure represents the character of "4-LOM." Zuckuss is the insectoid Gand bounty hunter with the cloth tan overcoat. The actual name of this figure is 4-LOM, since the figure is a droid.

Industrial Automaton's LOM-series is a line of protocol droids that the company plans to directly compete with the sales of Cybot Galactica's über-popular "3PO" series (see See-Threepio [C-3PO])—a strategy that initially works quite well. Although the body of the LOM-series is constructed to mimic a humanoid form (a near-exact approximation of the 3PO frame), the head of a LOM-series protocol droid is insect-like in appearance; a deliberate modifica-tion which allows Industrial Automaton to market the droid to various insectoid races across the galaxy, essentially tapping into a niche yet lucrative market, e.g., the Brizzit, Gand (see the mislabeled *Empire Strikes Back* action figure 4-LOM), Verpine, etc.

Unfortunately, Industrial Automaton is the subject of multiple lawsuits filed by Cybot Galactica: the for-mer corporation steals concepts from companies that manufactured parts for the 3PO-series; IA was build-ing their LOM-series on the bones of stolen parts.

Furthermore, the sinister adventures of droid bounty hunter 4-LOM frightens potential investors and consumers even more—with good reason. Once assigned to the M-class luxury liner *Kuari Princess* built by the Mon Calamari (see Admiral Ackbar), the protocol droid with the call-number 4-LOM func-tions as a translator between the cruiser's master computer and the liner's wealthy passengers. After a while, 4-LOM feels underappreciated—less than satisfied by the meaningless tasks he has to perform on the *Kuari Princess*, a quirk in his design causes his programming to become altered and corrupted, allowing the droid to plot thefts and steal from the ship's passengers.

Finding no limit to his desire for delivery, 4-LOM loots

the *Princess* and becomes a practiced thief and skill-ful information broker. After further corruption of his programming, he turns to bounty hunting and quickly is in high demand with gangsters such as members of the powerful Hutt Cartel since his intellect allows him to anticipate the moves of his targets. 4-LOM often pairs with Gand bounty hunter Zuckuss on many mis-sions since the two work quite well together, and they eventually find themselves aboard the *Executor* at the behest of Sith Lord Darth Vader, tasked to pursue the *Millennium Falcon*—a bounty they fail to collect. After toying with joining the Rebel Alliance, having his memory wiped, and losing a desire to comprehend the Force, 4-LOM leaves his partnership with Zuckuss and works alone, pursuing bounties from one side of the galaxy to the other.

Sporting his favorite weapon, which is heavy, difficult-to-handle, and creats a shockwave when fired—the BlasTech long W-90 concussion rifle is less accurate than the Imperial Stormtroopers' E-11, yet possesses a far longer range. This weapon is unique to the character's Kenner action figure.

MOC: *ESB:* **$110-$125**; *ROTJ:* **$50-$60**; *POTF:* **$85-$105+**;
MLC: **$12-$15+**

RETURN OF THE JEDI

A long time ago in a galaxy far, far away....

Luke Skywalker has returned to his home planet of Tatooine in an attempt to rescue his friend Han Solo from the clutches of the vile gangster Jabba the Hutt.

Little does Luke know that the GALACTIC EMPIRE has secretly begun construction on a new armored space station even more powerful than the first dreaded Death Star.

When completed, this ultimate weapon will spell certain doom for the small band of rebels struggling to restore freedom to the galaxy...

Return of the Jedi finds the core Rebel heroes fighting to restore freedom to the galaxy. *Disney/Lucasfilm/20th Century Fox/Heritage Auctions*

In *Return of the Jedi*, the final chapter of the original *Star Wars* trilogy *(Episodes IV-VI)*, children of the 1980s witnessed the conclusion of the most significant cultural touchstone of Generation X. Most importantly, patient *Star Wars* aficionados finally had the chance to observe Darth Vader's true face: that of former Jedi Knight Anakin Skywalker. Realizing that the Emperor's right-hand man, Darth Vader, is not beyond redemption—thanks to the faith and encouragement of his son, Luke Skywalker—placed an entirely new importance and added depth to the series: Anakin is indeed the "Chosen One" of the ancient Jedi prophecy.

Although a few select "Ewok bashers" crawled out of the woodwork to criticize this tribal community of teddy-bears, we must remember that *Return of the Jedi* was released during a time of contentment for *Star Wars* fans; a time long before George Lucas made some curious choices that would haunt even the staunchest, most stalwart sci-fi devotees for more than a decade. Regardless of how pundits and zealots received the new *Star Wars* trilogy of "prequels" *(Episodes I-III)*, it's worth noting the astronomical amount of money that rabid *Star Wars* collectors dump into "modern" (1995-present) and "vintage" (1978-1985) product. The current market for vintage *Star Wars* toys is truly obscene: high-grade, investment-quality items are selling for five times what they were a few decades ago.

Return of the Jedi provided enthusiasts of the space opera with an epic conclusion to Lucas' original three-part story arc. Beginning in preproduction, the movie's initial title was *Revenge of the Jedi*—and some Kenner boxes, cardbacks, promotional material, etc. was manufactured with the latter title proudly stamped on the packaging. Deemed too sinister of a descriptor to use when referring to the gallant, chivalrous Jedi Order, the word "revenge" was therefore switched to the decidedly less-vindictive "return," since a honorable Jedi Knight would not pursue vengeance.

Finally, we must mention that Kenner increased the price of their 3-3/4-inch *Star Wars* action figures from $2.49 to $2.99 when the *Return of the Jedi* assortments began. This 20 percent price hike was fairly substantial in 1982, considering the fact that these plastic figures sold for a mere $1.99 in 1978 and 1979.

Admiral Ackbar (a.k.a. Gial Ackbar)

[Production #70310]

1st appearance: Mail-Away
1st carded appearance: 65-back card
Original Mail-Away Price: FREE (6 proof-of-purchase seals)
Original Retail Price (average): $2.99
   o olive, yellow, or dark-yellow tunic variations
   o painted lower arm or painted upper arm variations
   o dull or standard eye variations
   • with Admiral Ackbar Baton, unique to the figure

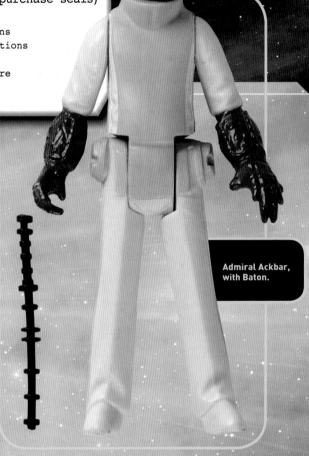

Admiral Ackbar, with Baton.

Kenner's all-new Admiral Ackbar action figure was offered as a mail-away promotion for the upcoming "final" *Star Wars* film, *Revenge of the Jedi*—a preproduction name that was utilized on early marketing materials, than changed shortly before release.

Kenner's requirements were becoming quite restrictive: now the company desired a child to submit SIX proof-of-purchase seals to obtain this iconic admiral of the Alliance Fleet, while almost *doubling* the waiting time to receive the toy. Regardless, collectors couldn't wait for the standard *Star Wars* mail-away action figure set to come to their door: a small white mailer box, the Admiral Ackbar figure and his accessory, sealed within a translucent baggie, a one-sheet explanation of the character's role in the upcoming film, a Kenner *ESB* product catalog, and a small, two-sided promotional slick that advertised for the new film and concurrent toy line. But what about the character himself?

From a race of beings known as the Mon Calamari, Admiral Gial Ackbar is the preeminent military commander for the Rebel Alliance and a sentient aquatic, who was born on his planet's ocean-covered surface. On his homeworld, Ackbar's sense of duty forces him to join the Mon Calamari military and while in this position, he also functions as an advisor determined to make peace with the Quarren (see Squid Head), yet another species native to Dac, and one that maintains a highly adverse and emotionally charged relationship with the Mon Calamari. Although the two factions fight one another on occasion, it isn't until the rise of the Galactic Empire and a violent Imperial assault on the planet that the Mon Calamari and Quarren are both

"It's a trap!"

—Admiral Ackbar reacting to the fully functioning shield surrounding the second Death Star

Admiral Ackbar mailer box,
with ephemera.

forced into slavery in order to serve the will of
Emperor Palpatine and his sinister designs for
the planet.

   Ackbar quickly joins and then leads a resistance movement that temporarily allows
his homeworld a semblance of freedom, yet
the Imperial forces are too powerful to defeat,
and he once again finds himself a prisoner.
Ackbar's organized resistance so impresses
one officer of the Empire that even as a slave
of Grand Moff Tarkin, he is well respected and
afforded the position of translator. Here, he
subtly acquires a profound comprehension of
Imperial doctrine and the knowledge of top-
secret projects … such as the first Death Star.

   After a successful rescue attempt and many
profound adventures, under Ackbar's leadership,
the Mon Calamari and the Quarren free their
planet from the control of the Empire. Following
this fruitful mission, he quickly rises through
the ranks of the Rebellion to the position of
Admiral, a title he holds as a Mon Calamari officer for many years prior, and leads several of the
most important missions for the Rebel forces.

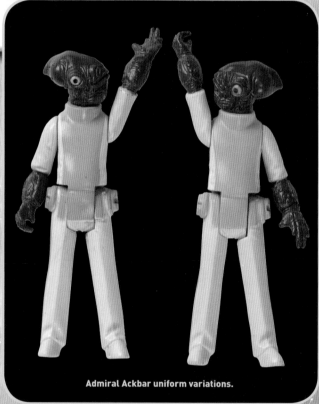

Admiral Ackbar uniform variations.

MISB: All contents sealed in
mailer: **$150-$165+**; **MIB**: w/all
included pieces & sealed figure:
$55-$60; **MIB**: w/all included
pieces & non-sealed figure:
$35-$40+; **MOC**: *ROTJ*: **$35-
$45+**; **MLC**: **$6-$10**.

CLOSE-UP

Admiral Ackbar
arm variations:
painted skin, left, and
painted uniform, right.

Lando Calrissian (Skiff Guard Disguise)
[a.k.a. Tamtel Skreej]

[Production #70830]

1st carded appearance: 65-back card
Original Retail Price (average): $2.99

- o light head and torso or dark head and torso variations
- • with Skiff Guard Helmet, unique to the figure
- • with Skiff Guard Vibro Ax, a.k.a. "BD-1 Cutter Vibro-Ax"

Lando Calrissian (Skiff Guard Disguise), posed with Skiff Guard Helmet and Skiff Guard Vibro-Ax.

After searching the galaxy for the carbon-frozen Rebel hero Han Solo with Chewbacca aboard the *Millennium Falcon*, Lando Calrissian learns the location of General Solo and assists in the organization of a group of Rebels (Luke Skywalker, Princess Leia Organa, Chewbacca, and their devoted droids R2-D2 and C-3PO), who concoct an intricate plan to rescue the Corellian from his place of display at Jabba Desilijic Tiure's (see Jabba the Hutt Action Playset) desert palace on the planet of Tatooine.

This Kenner action figure and its unique outfitting is based upon the role Calrissian plays during the rescue of Han. Wearing a clever disguise he obtains after stealing a bounty hunter's set of clothing, armor, and weapon, Lando pushes the original Tamtel Skreej

into rancor chow at Jabba's Palace (in a non-canonical *Star Wars* story from Dark Horse Comics' *Star Wars Tales* #10) to preserve his secret identity. Lando (as Tamtel) wears a helmet that obscures his face due to the appearance of the curved horns of a gondar (a foul-smelling, tusked creature) and dons Skreej's suit of Tantel armor—a protective suit used for reconnaissance during the time of the Galactic Civil War. Like many of Jabba's skiff guards, Calrissian utilizes a BD-1 cutter vibro-ax (see Gamorrean Guard for the description of a vibro weapon)—a fearsome accessory equipped with an electro-stun extensible bayonet, reinforced lance pole, replaceable vibroblade, and grooved grips. For more information on this character, see Lando Calrissian and Lando Calrissian (General Pilot).

MOC: *ROTJ:* **$35-$45**;
MLC: **$12-$15+**.

Lando Calrissian (Skiff Guard Disguise) uniform and sculpt variations.

Nien Nunb mailer box, with ephemera.

Nien Nunb

[Production #70840]

1st appearance: Mail-Away
1st carded appearance: 65-back card
Original Mail-Away Price: FREE (5 proof-of-purchase seals)
Original Retail Price (average): $2.99

- o light head w/bright pink mouth and softer sculpt, or dark head w/red-pink mouth and finer sculpt variations
- o boots with rounded ends, boots with squared-off ends, or curving boots variations
- o bright or dull red plastic flight suit variations
- with black Pilot Blaster

With this next *Return of the Jedi* mail-away offer, Kenner decreased the number of proof-of-purchase seals from 6 (the total POPs for obtaining Admiral Ackbar) to 5 for Nien Nunb, the Sullustan pilot fighting for the Rebel Alliance, and Lando Calrissian's co-pilot of the *Millennium Falcon*. Once again, as with every mail-away figure, Nien Nunb would arrive at your door packaged inside a white mailer box containing Nunb and his blaster within a sealed plastic baggie, a *Star Wars* product catalog, and a small white flier announcing the character's place in the *Star Wars* canon—specifically in the new film.

Featured in *Return of the Jedi* during the Battle of Endor, former smuggler Nien Nunb functions as Lando Calrissian's first mate aboard the borrowed *Millennium Falcon*, and helps to discharge the ordinance which destroys the superstructure of the rebuilt second Death Star—Nunb essentially fires the shot(s) that put an end to the reign of the Galactic Empire.

As a Sullustan, a species of "Near-Humans," those species closely biologically related to humans, Nien Nunb—sporting his species' trademark small ears, and facial dewflaps—is raised in the subterranean caves of his homeworld on the planet Sullust, which possesses a toxic upper atmosphere yet a mineral-rich outer crust that forces the Sullustans underground, inhabiting a maze of myriad tunnels. Their below-ground existence affords the race an uncanny ability to see in the dark (to

Nien Nunb, with Pilot Blaster.

read/see up to 20 meters in pitch blackness), as well as a preternatural sense of intuition and direction, e.g., navigating a complex map after viewing it only once, which makes them first-rate navigators and pilots.

MISB: All contents sealed in mailer: $70-$75+; **MIB**: w/all included pieces & sealed figure: $50-$55; **MIB**: w/all included pieces & non-sealed figure: $35-$42+; **MOC**: *ROTJ*: $35-$42; **MLC**: $7-$9.

Bib Fortuna (a.k.a. Bib Oltwaxt Fortuna)

[Production #70790]

1st carded appearance: 65-back card
Original Retail Price (average): $2.99

- o tight, bold detailed or soft, smooth detailed variations
- • with light tan, tan, dark tan, (or red*) Bib Fortuna Cloak variations, unique to the figure
- • with Bib Fortuna Belt, unique to the figure
- • with Bib Fortuna Battle Staff, unique to the figure

**Bib Fortuna,
with accessories.**

*Note: In certain preproduction photographs of Bib Fortuna, specifically in the paper inserts for the *Return of the Jedi* vinyl Mini-Figures Collector's Case and the See-Threepio (C-3PO) Collector's Case, Jabba's majordomo sports a burgundy fabric cloak. Never released domestically, the only way to obtain this burgundy cloak is by finding an *incredibly rare* Mexican Lili-Ledy version of the figure. Beware, these cloaks are relatively easy to fake … yet if authenticated, sell for roughly $400-$475+.

For several decades, the sly majordomo (chief steward; man in charge of a great household) for Jabba Desilijic Tiure (see Jabba the Hutt Action Playset) known as Bib Fortuna is one of the most untrustworthy sentient beings on the planet Tatooine. Prior to working for the great Hutt crime lord, Fortuna becomes quite wealthy selling his own people, the colorfully skinned humanoid Twi'leks (known derogatively as the "Tail-Heads"), into slavery on the planet Ryloth.

Sporting the distinctive two tentacles known as *lekku* (a.k.a. "brain tails," "head tails," or "lchun

Bib Fortuna cloak variations.

tchin") that are a mark of his species and the Togruta, such as those found on Jedi Master Shaak Ti, these dual lek that overhang down the back of a Twi'lek's skull contain part of the species' brain, and serve multiple purposes. These delicate brain tails are so sensitive that simply latching onto one with a small amount of force can incapacitate the owner; severe injury, particularly toward the top of a lek and near the head, can cause the Twi'lek brain damage, since this lek controls subconscious memories, as well as the most basic motor functions. Oddly enough, in spite of the pain they suffer when modifying these appendages, many Twi'leks choose to paint— or even tattoo—their lekku, which proudly serve a number of aesthetic purposes as well. Long leku, multiple lekku, or thick lekku serve multiple connotations, from high status to wealth to opulence; these braintails even suggest lasciviousness as a phallic symbol.

With his excessively long lekku, Bib Fortuna plans all the procedures and controls the disparate personalities and plots at Jabba's Palace, a citadel chock full of toadies, sycophants, servants, mercenaries, bounty hunters, musicians, slaves, yesmen, thugs, and beings of infinite mystery; the perfect place where Fortuna's checkered past as a slaver and spice importer, specifically the illegal spice Ryll, can codify his power base.

Powerful yet cowardly, wearing his traditional Ryloth robe made from Jalavash worm silk, Bib Fortuna makes a career upon hovering about his master's throne, whispering suggestions to Jabba at just the precise time. Although he is covertly plotting the death of the crime lord who he secretly despised, Bib's machinations are unfortunately discarded when the custodian allows R2-D2 and C-3PO into the stronghold; Fortuna's actions unwisely trigger the downfall of the Hutt's criminal empire—and perhaps end his own life. After the destruction of Jabba's luxury sail barge, the *Khetanna*, Fortuna's fate is of dubious authenticity. Whether he exists

Bib Fortuna sculpting variations.

as a living brain inside the body of a mechanical B'Omarr Monk, or secretly survives and is currently in control of Jabba's once-legendary criminal syndicate is up for debate.

MOC: *ROTJ*: **$30-$40+**; **MLC: $10-$12**.

Biker Scout (a.k.a. Scout Trooper)

[Production #70820]

1st carded appearance: 65-back card
Original Retail Price (average): $2.99

- mouth piece, back belt, or helmet indent variations (x4)
- with Scout Trooper Blaster Pistol, a.k.a. "hold-out blaster pistol"

Biker Scout, with Scout Trooper Blaster Pistol.

Descended from the clone scout troopers led by Clone Commander Gree during the time of the Clone Wars (22-19 BBY), specifically, the 41st Elite Corps who fought in the Battle of Kashyyyk, these soldiers eventually metamorphose into Imperial Scout Troopers (a.k.a. Biker Scouts*) upon the formation of the Galactic Empire. When not functioning in their primary military role as light infantrymen, the earlier clone scout troopers (camouflaged to better blend into jungle or forest environments) often utilize BARC (Biker Advanced Recon Commando) speeders for reconnaissance and AT-APs (All Terrain Attack Pods) for attack and defense in support of the Grand Army of the Republic. However, the Imperial Biker Scouts featured in *Return of the Jedi* use Speeder Bikes (see Speeder Bike vehicle) for recon and AT-STs (see AT-ST, All Terrain Scout Transport) for attack/defense when backing the Galactic Empire.

Sporting the same style of advanced plastoid armor as

their Clone War predecessors, Biker Scouts are specially trained, elite members of the Imperial Stormtrooper Corps tasked to accomplish duties branded too complex and dangerous for the standard trooper. Functioning as spies, survivalists, reconnaissance patrolmen, and snipers—some of the finest that the Imperial Military have to offer, Biker Scouts are sometimes called upon to complete assassination missions for the Empire.

The weapon included with Kenner's Scout Trooper has been dubbed the "hold-out blaster pistol," a.k.a. scout blaster/scout trooper blaster pistol, standard issue for the Galactic Empire's Scout Troopers due to their small size and easy concealment. Although smaller than heavy-duty sidearms such as the Stormtrooper's E-11 blaster, they were far easier to utilize while mounted on a speeder bike.

*Due to Scout Troopers traditionally using the 74-Z speeder bike, these soldiers are referred to as Biker Scouts.

Biker Scout variations; note facemasks.

MOC: *ROTJ:* $62-$75+; *POTF:* $195-$235; **MLC:** $13-$18+.

93

Chief Chirpa gray-tan (fawn-colored) Ewok

[Production #70690]

1st carded appearance: 65-back card
Original Retail Price (average): $2.99

- o in standard light-gray plastic or white/cream plastic variations
- with Chief Chirpa Hood, unique to the figure
- with Chief Chirpa Staff, unique to the figure

On the reverse of Kenner's 65-back *Return of the Jedi* card, both Ewoks—Chief Chirpa and Logray, the Ewok Medicine Man—were airbrushed out in order to preserve the physical appearance of an Ewok and keep the image of the furry little creatures a surprise for the upcoming *Return of the Jedi* film, a much simpler task in 1983, since all information about action figures could only be distributed via hard copy, snail mail, and without Internet access, of course (!).

At the zenith of Ewok culture is their leader and tribal chieftain, Chief Chirpa, who serves as the head of his peoples' Council of Elders at their home of Bright Tree Village. Although Chirpa is quick-tempered and one of the fiercest warriors in his tribe, he also exhibits great wisdom and intelligence. As the father, and lone parent due to his wife's untimely death, of heiress Princess Kneesaa (formally, Kneesaa a Jari Kintaka, the young female Ewok featured in 1985's animated *Star Wars: Ewoks*), Chirpa sitson the Ewok throne and is often witnessed consulting with Logray about the best

Chief Chirpa, with accessories.

methods of the tribe's governance.

At the time of the Battle of Endor (4 ABY), Chirpa had led the village for forty-two seasons and does not achieve success as a leader by ignoring the rational pleas of outsiders in distress. During the narrative events of *ROTJ*, it is Chirpa who accepts the Rebel's Endor strike team as an honorary part of the tribe, allowing C-3PO to relate the team's harrowing adventures within Bright Tree Village's communal hut. Since C-3PO was recognized by the Ewoks as the "Golden One," one of the Ewoks' many deities long prophesied to visit in person, they carefully listen to the protocol droid, who speaks in "Yuzzum," a protolanguage of Ewokese, as he relates the small band of Rebels' starring role in the Galactic Civil War. So moved is Chirpa by Threepio's narrative that he decides to assist the Rebels in repelling Imperial Forces on the Sanctuary Moon. Although their joint effort is ultimately successful, many brave members of Chirpa's tribe lose their lives in battle.

 MOC: *ROTJ*: **$30-$35**; **MLC: $8-$12.**

Emperor's Royal Guard
(a.k.a. Imperial Red Guard, Palpatine's Security Force)

`[Production #70680]`

1st carded appearance: 65-back card
Original Retail Price (average): $2.99

- o with two sets of <u>non-removable</u> scarlet cloth robes*, unique to the figure
- • with Vibro-Active Force Pike, unique to the figure

*Note: It is important to mention that the two robes included with the Emperor's Royal guard are distinctly non-removable, and it is difficult to take them off unless collectors wish to permanently affect the condition of the toy, damaging the figurine's head.

The Emperor's Royal Guards are a unit of elite soldiers who are independent of the Imperial Military yet report directly to Emperor Palpatine (see The Emperor) where they can be found escorting his Highness in every aspect of his life, from guarding Palpatine on his way to formal briefings, to protecting the Sith Lord as he sleeps at night. The Emperor's Royal Guard are not, as many assume, direct descendants of the blue-robed Senate Guards, a.k.a. the Coruscant Guards, of the former Galactic Republic; they are instead successors of the Supreme Chancellor's Red Guard, which serve Palpatine throughout the Clone Wars—a detachment separate from the Senate Guards. Both the blue-attired Senate Guards and the crimson-uniformed Red Guards serve next to one another during the Battle of Coruscant (19 BBY).

The peerless members of the Emperor's Royal Guard are the most fierce and best-trained soldiers of the Empire. These deadly guardsmen are equipped with a vibro-active force pike (a.k.a. stun pole) that is a largely ceremonial weapon to others, yet in the hands of a well-trained guardsman, this meter-long staff becomes a violent engine of devastation. At its lowest setting, these vibro-edged force pikes can deliver *excruciating* electrical shocks, while at its highest setting, the pike can slice through human bone and even durasteel armor plating with little effort. Along with these staves, these handpicked Royal Guardsmen are trained to become peak physical specimens, adept in many forms of armed and unarmed combat. Furthermore, there are secretive aspects of their training that have not yet been recorded—trials of attrition that simply add to their mystique.

Emperor's Royal Guard, with accessories.

Unfortunately, what is seen underneath the robes of Kenner's vintage Emperor's Royal Guard action figure does not accurately depict what is revealed beneath the cloaks of Kir Kanos and Carnor Jax—two infamous Imperial Guards featured in Dark Horse Comics' 1997/98 *Star Wars: Crimson Empire* mini-series (ca. 11 ABY); this under-armor is retconned into the Imperial Guards' narrative.

MOC: *ROTJ*: $55-$65+;
MLC: $15-$20.

Gamorrean Guard

[Production #70670]

1st carded appearance: 65-back card
Original Retail Price (average): $2.99

- o different foot peg hole variations
- o light green skin or dark green skin variations
- o dull armor, silver armor, or dark gray armor variations
- • with Gamorrean Guard Ax (a.k.a. "Clan Groogrun vibro-ax," three different variations, unique to the figure)

Within the narrative of *Return of the Jedi*, these dim-witted, mostly green skinned, powerfully built porcine barbarians are located throughout the palace of Jabba Desilijic Tiure (see Jabba the Hutt Action Playset), a far reach from their jungle homeworld: the forested planet of Gamorr. There, the native Gamorreans possess a stone-age level of technological development; they hold animistic views, believing that natural objects have souls, and their species exhibit a clannish, warlike, bellicose approach to government. With a fearsome appearance that features close-set, beady eyes, thick snouts, prominent fearsome tusks, and two small horns atop their heads, Gamorreans are ferocious warriors with great strength.

Time after time, Gamorreans prove their value to crime lords throughout the galaxy, and this significance does not escape notice of Jabba the Hutt, who hires them as security guards at his palace due to the species' tremendous power level, as well as their gullibility and slow wit: Gamorrean Guards not only come inexpensively, but they can be easily bent to the will of their commander.

The last item worth mentioning is the weapon used by Gamorrean Guards. Oftentimes, a boar will prefer to use his peoples' traditional war ax called an *arg'garok*. However, since this weapon has to be specially forged for its wielder, only the finest warriors are able to brandish them. Therefore, the accessory given to Kenner's Gamorrean Guard action figure is a Clan Groogrun vibro-ax. Built on Gamorr, this bladed armament works like every other vibro-weapon: a power pak, containing gases that form plasma when heated, supply energy to

an Ultrasonic generator, causing the blade to become far deadlier than its standard relative—since it would vibrate thousands of times per second. Since the vibro-ax possesses a wooden shaft that holds both the power cell and ax head, the handle does little to absorb the weapon's power—only the most able-bodied characters can wield this weapon. It almost appears that Jabba's dull Gamorrean Guards forget to activate this devastating feature on occasion.

Gamorrean Guard, posed, with Gamorrean Guard Ax.

MOC: *ROTJ*: **$30-$40**; *POTF*: **$750-$775+**; **MLC**: **$10-$14**, dependent upon condition of painted armor.

Gamorrean Guard body variations, at left, and ax variations, above.

General Madine* (a.k.a. Crix Madine)

[Production #70680]

1st carded appearance: 65-back card
Original Retail Price (average): $2.99

- o flesh molded head, dark gray beard, dark blue eyes, brown belt, and 3-part collar emblem variation
- o gray molded head, gray hair/beard, light blue eyes, dark brown belt, and 2-part collar emblem variation
- o flesh molded head, greenish-gray beard, blue eyes, glossy dark brown belt, and 2-part collar emblem variation*
- • with Rebel Battle Staff, unique to the figure

*Note: Beyond the three standard variations, this figure also may come with either black or gray molded arms.

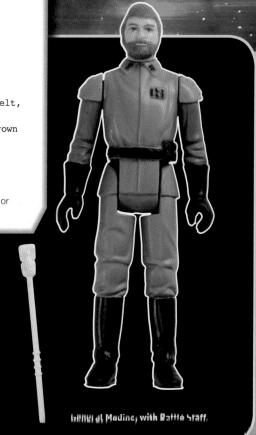

General Madine, with Battle Staff.

Crix Madine shares a few aspects of his past in common with another Rebel hero, *Millennium Falcon* pilot and former smuggler, Han Solo: both are officers in the Imperial Army before defecting, both were born on the planet Corellia, and both held the position of general and become lauded heroes for the Rebel Alliance to Restore the Republic.

In light of completing a few sinister missions that are required of him by the Empire, Madine is

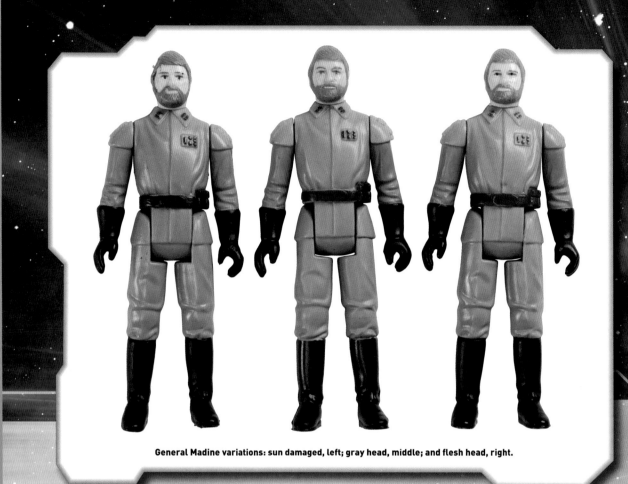

General Madine variations: sun damaged, left; gray head, middle; and flesh head, right.

wracked with guilt; culpability overwhelms him and after a few false starts, he deserts his post. Although initially distrusted by Rebel leaders, with the backing of General Carlist Rieekan, Madine becomes Chief Military Advisor, and eventually—

after proving his value as a strong tactical leader—Supreme Commander of Alliance Special Forces. In this capacity, General Madine trains Han Solo's commando strike team to steal the shuttle *Tydirium* (see Imperial Shuttle), and he devises the plan that eventually destroys the Imperial shield generator on the Sanctuary Moon of Endor.

"We have stolen a small Imperial shuttle. Disguised as a cargo ship, and using a secret Imperial code, a strike team will land on the moon and deactivate the shield generator."

—Crix Madine shares his strategy for eliminating the shield generator on the Sanctuary Moon

MOC: *ROTJ*: $32-$45+; **MLC**: $8-$10.

Klaatu* (a.k.a. Wooof)

[Production #70730]

1st carded appearance: 65-back card
Original Retail Price (average): \$2.99

- o with silver helmet and painted face or dark silver helmet and green molded face variations
- with Skiff Guard Skirt, made with two different materials, unique to the figure
- with Skiff Guard Vibro Ax, a.k.a. "BD-1 Cutter Vibro-Ax"

*Note: Beyond the above-mentioned variations, this figure also may come with either tan or gray molded arms, or a mixture of the two.

Klaatu, with Skiff Guard Vibro Ax accessory.

Although this Kenner action figure was originally labeled Klaatu, a 1983 production name, the character is *actually* named Wooof and is a member of the sub-species of the Nikto race (see Nikto) known as *Kadas'sa'Nikto* (a.k.a. Green Nikto). Adapted to the forest regions of Kintan, Green Nikto like Wooof adjust to their environment over many years of mutation, and as a result, develop small noses and discernible protective scales (visible scales, unlike his other Nikto brethren), with slight horns built up around the eyes and face.

As a character, Wooof is a member of Jabba Desilijic Tiure's entourage (see Jabba the Hutt Action Playset), functioning as the crime lord's chief pilot. Although he is of the Nikto race, Wooof was born on the desert planet Tatooine where he develops into an excellent aviator and freelance smuggler. However, during his career as a pilot, he encounters financial troubles so severe that he approaches Jabba for a loan. Unable to pay the Hutt's sizeable debt, he becomes one of the many "indentured servants" inhabiting Jabba's Palace—working in a state of permanent, inescapable slavery as the main pilot of Jabba's luxury sail barge, the *Khetanna*. Ultimately Wooof is killed in *Return of the Jedi* when Jedi Knight Luke Skywalker deflects his blaster fire back upon him.

Wooof's BD-1 Cutter vibro-ax (a.k.a. "Skiff Guard vibro-ax") is a melee weapon that contains the same essential attributes as Jabba's guards' Clan Groogrun vibro-axes (see Gamorrean Guard). However, the BD-1 has a much longer shaft than other axes, it possesses a durasteel pole that is hollowed to reduce its heft, a quick-release switch to easily replace the blade, and vibration dampeners. The weapon can be clearly seen prodding Luke to walk the plank above the Great Pit of Carkoon in *Return of the Jedi* (see Weequay).

MOC: *ROTJ:* \$30-\$38+;
MLC: \$8-\$10.

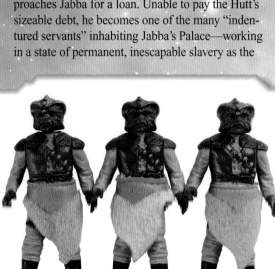

Klaatu body and skirt variations.

Skiff Guard ax variations.

Logray Ewok Medicine Man [tan and white striped (caramel-colored and cream-colored) Ewok]

[Production #70710]

1st carded appearance: 65-back card
Original Retail Price (average): $2.99

- o light brown striped lines, dark tan striped lines, or green/gray striped lines variations
- with Logray Headdress, unique to the figure
- with Logray Pouch, unique to the figure
- with Logray Staff, a.k.a. The Staff of Logray, The Staff of Power, unique to the figure

As already mentioned, Logray (Ewok Medicine Man) is one of the first of two Ewok action figures produced by Kenner completely airbrushed off of the company's 65-figure *Return of the Jedi* cardback, along with Chief Chirpa. Lucasfilm was so protective of its intellectual property that the mere image of Logray and Chirpa, of *any* Ewok on a toy package before *Return of the Jedi* was released was so secret, that even their resultant action figures necessitated this removal, ensuring that moviegoers' sensibilities would not be spoiled before watching the film.

Logray, with accessories.

Careful collectors will notice that the Ewoks' resident shaman is available with a few different shades of stripes: Logray can be found with light tan, dark tan, or gray stripes—but make sure that the color of the Ewok's stripes is not caused by simple sun fading. It is worth noting that although many *Star Wars* fans consider Ewoks to be cute, furry, fun-loving Teddy Bear-esque creatures, one quick glance at this action figure should dispel those myths, with Logray donning a headdress made from a churi bird's skull (purportedly, *churi* are large, aggressive flying birds), a pouch full of components needed to cast his "spells," and a uniquely ornate staff that is decorated with the gruesome spinal bones of a defeated foe. Known as the Staff of Logray (a.k.a. the Staff of Power), this object is a powerful, Force-imbued artifact that allows its wielder to perform potent examples of "magic."

Whether we follow the character's interpretation in 1983's *Return of the Jedi* or his animated portrayal found in 1985's *Ewoks* cartoon and Marvel/Star Comics' *Ewoks* monthly comic book, all roads lead to Logray's banishment from his tribe. Unfortunately, toward the end of his tenure, the once-noble Ewok elder devolves into a bully and gutless coward, and so after the Battle of Endor, Logray is banished from the village and his name is struck from the records—even from their famed "Songs of Remembrance." Cursing the community as he leaves, Chief Chirpa appoints his nephew (see Paploo) as a replacement medicine man whose first task is to remove Logray's curse with the assistance of "The Golden One" (see C-3PO).

MOC: *ROTJ*: $30-$40; **MLC:** $6-$10.

Luke Skywalker (Jedi Knight Outfit)

[Production #70650]

1st carded appearance: 65-back card
Original Retail Price (average): $2.99

- shorter, finer detailed body sculpt or taller, less detailed body sculpt variations
- flesh-colored head mold or brown-colored head mold variations
- with gray Palace Blaster, DL-18 blaster
- with Jedi Cloak (sewn shut clasp or snap-together clasp variations, unique to the figure)
- with lightsaber, green (common) or blue (rare) colored*

*Note: An uncommon amount of this figure came with a blue lightsaber instead of the more common and correct green one: these lightsabers command higher values on the secondary market.

Luke Skywalker (Jedi Knight Outfit), with accessories.

Constructed to represent Luke Skywalker wearing the robes of a formal Jedi Knight—the first of his kind in a generation—this figure exists as one of the finest achievements within the vintage *Star Wars* toy line. With a smart-fitting hooded cloak, a detailed green lightsaber, a color that is finally film-accurate, a superbly sculpted outfit, a nicely rendered blaster pistol, the ability to hold exciting action poses (note Luke's bent left arm), and one of the best facial sculpts of the entire 1980s, this action figure flew off retail shelves. By 1983, Kenner had refined their toy-making abilities, exponentially improving their creative skills during their tenure working on the *Star Wars* license.

This figure represents the culmination of the character's skills and fortitude in the face of adversity. When viewers of *Return of the Jedi* realize that Luke (a former moisture farmer who wants little to do with the Empire), finally becomes an expert practitioner of the ways of the Force, aficionados can finally observe the powers of a Jedi Knight. Luke is so consumed by devotion that he constructs his own lightsaber, one with a green blade—contrasting the blue one he inherited from his father.

Having learned much about the nature of the Force from Obi-Wan (see Ben [Obi-Wan] Kenobi) and Yoda, (see Yoda) Luke continues his studies alone—cultivating his Force sensitivity, striving to achieve his long-term goal of becoming a Jedi Knight, while ultimately desiring to one day confront and again challenge Darth Vader, and perhaps even Emperor Palpatine himself, for the fate of the galaxy (see Anakin Skywalker, Darth Vader, The Emperor, and the many

"You failed, Your Highness. I am a Jedi ... like my father before me."

—Luke Skywalker to the Emperor, showing his faith in his father while relinquishing his lightsaber

Luke Skywalker (Jedi Knight Outfit) body variations.

Jedi Cloak variations; snap variation, far left.

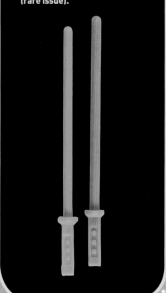

Lightsaber variations: green (standard issue), and blue (rare issue).

other versions of Luke). After a series of adventures—the most prominent of these the rescue of Rebel hero Han Solo (see Han Solo [In Carbonite Chamber])—Luke has proven his mettle, and returns to Dagobah to receive Grand Master Yoda's final instructions before his death.

MOC: *ROTJ* blue saber: **$135-$150+**, green saber: **$75-$100+**; *POTF*: **$225-$260+**; **MLC**: cape with "snap" & blue saber: **$42-$50+**, standard cape & blue saber: **$35-$46+**, cape with "snap" and green saber: **$26-$42+**, standard cape & green saber: **$24-$38+**.

Princess Leia Organa (Boushh Disguise)/Boushh

[Production #70730]

1st carded appearance: 65-back card
Original Retail Price (average): $2.99

- ○ highly detailed body sculpt or lighter detailed body sculpt or the finest detailed body sculpt variations
- ○ four different head sculpt variations
- • with Boushh Helmet, optically enhanced with speech scrambler, unique to the figure
- • with Electrostaff, unique to the figure

Princess Leia Organa (Boushh Disguise), with accessories.

In order to fulfill Luke Skywalker's (see Luke Skywalker [Jedi Knight Outfit]) intricate plan to rescue Han Solo (see Han Solo [in Carbonite Chamber]) from the alien detritus and humanoid refuse lurking in the depths of Jabba's Place (see Jabba the Hutt Action Playset) on the desert planet Tatooine, Princess Leia Organa chooses to arrive at the palace in a clever disguise. She carefully selects the guise of a recently deceased bounty hunter by the name of Boushh.

Boushh is a successful male Ubese bounty hunter—a race of graceful yet frail near-humans with fair skin, no facial hair whatsoever, dark hair atop their heads, a narrow facial structure sporting high cheekbones and eyes that appear too large for their heads. With a characteristic quiet voice mimicked expertly by Princess Leia, the Ubese can't produce vocal sounds any higher than a coarse whisper—and so the Ubese develop a complex system of sign language utilized between members of their race. Furthermore, due to the oxygen-depleted air quality on his home planet of Uba IV, when Boushh arrives upon an oxygen-rich, Type I world, he is forced to don a breath mask or breath filter to process the too-powerful atmosphere (re: Boushh's helmet with built-in respirator).

Throughout his career, Boushh adopts his peoples' distrust toward other races, yet his skill as a game hunter and melee combatant leads him to roam the Outer Rim territories for years following bounty contracts. Occasionally, Boushh pursues contracts for one of the largest criminal organizations in the galaxy, Black Sun; however, the syndicate eventually finds the Ubese's demands and violent, vengeful streak too much for their liking, and have Boushh killed.

A short time after Boushh's demise—a death that is kept secret—a member of Black Sun donates his armor to Princess Leia Organa for a mission she undertakes to Coruscant that serves the criminal organization's interest. In 4 ABY during the events that transpire at the beginning of *Return of the Jedi*, she dons the armor one last time, and brings Chewbacca in front of Jabba Desilijic Tiure to retrieve the Hutt's bounty on the Wookiee. Leia as Boushh threatens the entire court with a Merr-Sonn Munitions, Inc. Class-A thermal detonator, a highly unstable military weapon similar to a grenade with a blast radius of twenty meters, unless Jabba the Hutt meets her contract demands.

MOC: *ROTJ:* $60-$75+
MLC: $14-$22+

Rebel Commando
(a.k.a. Alliance Special Forces Corp, SpecForce)

`[Production #70740]`

1st carded appearance: 65-back card
Original Retail Price (average): $2.99

- o flesh-toned head or brown-toned head with painted face variations*
- o 4 bands with small belt pocket with "1st backpack" or 3 bands with large belt pocket with "2nd backpack" variations
- o many rifle variations
- • with Commando Rifle and strap, a.k.a. A280 blaster rifle or "Longblaster," unique to the figure

*Note: If you find a Rebel Commando with a face that is molded flesh-color and not painted, this is a highly desirable variant. Loose samples of this molded face figure sell for over $50 each. Carded samples of this variation are impossible to find, since the figure may only appear on "Tri-Logo" foreign packages.

The Rebel Commando is a figure used to represent a generic, yet elite, soldier of the Rebellion, specifically a member of the elite Alliance Special Forces. Featured in *Return of the Jedi*, the trooper is one of the members of General Han Solo's highly skilled Endor strike team; a commando force placed on the Sanctuary Moon (a.k.a. forest moon of Endor) via the stolen Imperial Shuttle *Tydirium* (see Imperial Shuttle). A team of highly trained Rebel Commandos under the command of Major Bren Derlin (see Rebel Commander) fight savagely alongside a native tribe of Ewoks against Imperial forces, and are able to destroy the

Empire's shield generator on the Sanctuary Moon in order to allow the Rebel Fleet to destroy the second Death Star.

Rebel Commandos come equipped with jungle fatigues, backpacks (molded onto the figure), modified E-11 blaster rifles to allow for a higher firing rate, comlinks, low-feedback scanners and sensor scramblers, and a whopping amount of explosives such as proton grenades and thermal detonators (see Princess Leia, Boushh Disguise) with which they can destroy the shield generator. Of these various accoutrements, only one accessory was included with Kenner's Rebel Commando action figure: the A280 blaster rifle.

The Rebel Commandos' preferred weapon is the A280 blaster rifle, as produced by BlasTech Industries. Known as a "longblaster" due to its elongated barrel, which helps to improve the weapon's accuracy, the A-280 is a powerful and fairly heavy weapon, reputably able to slice an armored Imperial Stormtrooper in half at 150 yards; the maximum range of the gun is 300 meters (!). Depictions of the A280 have differed over the years as it is portrayed in various iterations within the *Star Wars* universe—with some collectors willing to accept the fact that these are many different modifications of essentially the same weapon.

Rebel Commando, with Commando Rifle and strap.

Rebel Commando painted face vs. molded face variations.

MOC: molded face: **$62-$75+**; *ROTJ* painted face: **$35-$45**; **MLC:** molded face: **$45-$52+**, painted face: **$10-$14**.

Ree-Yees

[Production #70800]

1st carded appearance: 65-back card
Original Retail Price (average): $2.99

- flesh-molded arm (common) or brown-molded arm (rare) variations
- dark green booted or green booted variations
- with gold-colored Ree-Yees Blaster-Staff

Ree-Yees, with Ree-Yees Blaster-Staff.

A member of Jabba Desilijic Tiure's court (see Jabba the Hutt Action Playset), the criminal known as Ree-Yees, a phoneticism of "Three-Eyes," is a male Gran—a sentient mammalian humanoid native to the pastoral planet of Kinyen. As a member of the Gran race, Ree-Yees has three eyes mounted on short stalks, a goat-like snout, a stocky build, and other characteristics possessed by earthbound bovids such as an herbivorous diet (Gran enjoys eating Goatgrass, a local flora found on the plains of Kinyen), and a multi-chambered stomach that digests difficult-to-absorb plant matter like most ruminants. Ree-Yees personally suffered from an uncommon Granian genetic mutation, which causes his hands to swell and appear deformed.

Although by and large Gran society is peaceful, Ree-Yees is the exception that proves the rule: he is a vicious criminal fleeing prosecution for murder on Kinyen, hiding on the desert planet Tatooine. There, he is featured in many scenes within the palace in *Return of the Jedi*, since he is prominent member of Jabba's court, responsible for taking care of the Hutt's hideous-looking Frog-dog pet named Bubo—a species of sentient reptiles with both frog and dog-like features.

In order to keep Ree-Yees "loyal," the crafty Hutt crimelord plants a short-range explosive device within him and when Jabba speaks a particular phrase, the Gran will explode to bits. This bomb serves two purposes: to murder Ree-Yees if disloyal, and to thwart an assassination attempt if a potential assassin comes too close to his resident Frog-dog walker. However, as a result of the abuse and risk involved in attending Jabba during Ree-Yees' time at court, he conspires with Tessek (see Squid Head) to murder their master aboard his large sail skiff, the *Khetanna*. Unfortunately, Ree-Yees perishes when Luke Skywalker and Princess Leia Organa destroy the *Khetanna* and all of the entities aboard.

Ree-Yees molded flesh arms vs. painted flesh hands variations.

MOC: *ROTJ*: $26-$32;
MLC: $7-$10.

Squid Head, with accessories.

Squid Head (a.k.a. Tessek)

[Production #70770]

1st carded appearance: 65-back card
Original Retail Price (average): $2.99

- o lighter paint on wristbands and hands or darker paint on wristbands and hands variations
- o bright[er] blue eyes and light plastic or blue eyes and darker plastic variations
- with gray Bespin Blaster (DH-17 blaster pistol)
- with tan fabric Squid Head Cape made with two different materials, unique to the figure
- with cream fabric Squid Head Skirt, unique to the figure
- with gray plastic Squid Head Belt, unique to the figure

One of several fascinating species hailing from the planet Dac, dubbed "Mon Calamari," "Calamari," or "Mon Cala" by off-worlders, the Quarren (a.k.a. Qarren) are sentient aquatics that inhabit their planet's ocean-covered surface and sport squid-like heads, leathery skin that requires moisture for maintenance, a small mouth with two fangs/teeth protruding outward with a long tongue between them, and four or more prehensile tentacles that can manipulate food. With two holes on the sides of the neck most likely for breathing purposes, two sac-like organs that hang on the back of their heads for reasons unknown, and two triangular flaps that jut out from the sides of their heads with built-in gills that assist in the hearing process, the Quarrens have an exceptionally unique physiology. As aquatic creatures, they can descend to the depths of 300 meters without use of breathing apparatus.

The Quarren male known as Tessek was once a supporter of the Republic, yet when the Galactic Empire invades his home planet of Dac (see Admiral Ackbar), he escapes the conflict. Always a crafty opportunist with conflicting loyalties, Tessek finds his way to the desert planet of Tatooine—a world largely ignored by the Empire—where he joins the court of interplanetary gangster Jabba Desilijic Tiure (see Jabba the Hutt Action Playset) as his accountant. Although miserable on Tatooine due to the effect of the planet's blistering heat on his delicate skin (he needs to soak in a tub for many hours a day) and the fact that his master is an abusive sociopath, Tessek hatches a complex scheme to kill him. Although successfully avoiding death when Luke Skywalker and Princess Leia Organa destroy

Jabba's large skiff, the *Khetanna*, and all of the entities aboard, the accountant met his doom a bit later.

Upon returning to the Palace after Jabba's death, Tessek's brain is forcibly removed from his body, and placed into the mechanical body of a B'omarr Monk—becoming a member of the B'omarr Order. As a mysterious religious organization that believes cutting oneself off from all physical sensation is the only way to achieve enlightenment, the B'omarr Monks allow their brains to be removed from their bodies. Therefore, the disembodied brains of the order's members are placed into specially modified BT-16 perimeter droids and left to ponder the mysteries of the cosmos.

MOC: *ROTJ*: **$35-$45+**;
MLC: **$11-$15**.

Squid Head cape and armband color variations.

Weequay, with Skiff Guard Vibro Ax.

Weequay (a.k.a. Pagetti Rook)

[Production #70760]

1st carded appearance: 65-back card
Original Retail Price (average): $2.99

- o dark or light brown paint application variations
- • with Skiff Guard Vibro Ax, a.k.a. "BD-1 Cutter Vibro-Ax"

The original production designation for the character Weequay and his race, also named the Weequay, is the phonetically similar production nickname "Queequeg," based on the character's resemblance to the roughly attired cannibal and extraordinary harpooner Queequeg, who sails aboard the *Pequod* in Herman Melville's magnum opus, *Moby Dick*. It takes thirty years for this character of the Weequay race to obtain its official name of Pagetti Rook, as told in the informative 2013 article, "Inside Jabba's Court," featured in *Star Wars Insider* that discusses the secrets of Jabba's Palace (see Jabba the Hutt Action Playset)—specifically, what goes on behind the scenes at the Tatooine citadel in *Return of the Jedi*.

One of the few Kenner action figures posed in a dynamic position, able to place both hands upon his melee weapon—the DD-1 Cutter vibro-ax (a.k.a. Skiff Guard vibro-ax [see Klaatu])—Pagetti Rook hails from the planet Sriluur located in the Outer Rim. A desert planet similar to where he works on Tatooine, Sriluur's environment is responsible for its inhabitants' leathery skin, lipless mouths, excellent sense of smell, ruddy skin tone, and recessed eyes to protect their

vision from the atmosphere's adverse elements.

Since Weequays communicate speechlessly among each other via the transfer of pheromones, many humanoids think the race unintelligent; verbal speaking is a secondary form of communication to Weequay such as Pagetti Rook. Clan identity trumps that of the individual, which leads to the idea of expendability among Rook's people; sacrificing the one for the greater good is of paramount importance. Nevertheless, Rook is witnessed prodding Luke Skywalker with his vibro-ax, encouraging the Jedi to walk the skiff's plank (see Tatooine Skiff). He is killed by Skywalker when the Jedi returns to the vehicle.

MOC: *ROTJ:* $25-$32; **MLC:** $7-$10.

Sy Snootles and the Rebo Band Action Figure Set

[Production #71360]

1st packaged appearance: 77-back [shadow] box
Original Retail Price [average]: $11.99

This is the only three-piece action figure "set" offered by Kenner in the original line. What follows are their individual entries.

MISP: *ROTJ*: **$110-$145+**, prices of this sealed set vary based upon packaging condition; **MIP**: **$75-85+**; **MLC**: **$54-65+**.

Droopy McCool (a.k.a. Snit)

[Production #71360]

1st packaged appearance: 77-back shadow box
Original Retail Price: Only sold via three-pack

- with Droopy McCool Flute, a.k.a. chidinkalu flute, unique to the figure, black or silver variations

Droopy McCool, with Flute.

With a name utterly incomprehensible to most sentient beings due to its delivery in the manner of a series of whistles, the Kitonak with the alias of "Snit" was born on his homeworld of Kirdo III, yet is sold off planet into servitude by a slaver company. Snit is bought by impresario Evar Orbus, the talented lead singer of a popular musical group, and follows Orbus to the desert planet of Tatooine, where they pursue a gig at an infamous Wookiee-managed hotspot: Chalmun's Spaceport Cantina (a.k.a. the Mos Eisley Cantina, see Cantina Adventure Set *or* Creature Cantina). Due to an unfortunate incident, their engagement at the Cantina does not work out, so they audition for Jabba Desilijic Tiure (see Jabba the Hutt's Action Playset) and are awarded exclusive rights to perform at his palace.

Snit is a laid-back, casual musician who is quite talented on his chosen instrument—the chidinkalu flute, yet early on the Kitonak becomes dissatisfied with his

stage name until Sy Snootles suggests "Droopy Mc-Cool," which he promptly adopts. Possessing an aloof, quasi-mystical behavior, he does not fit in with the rest of Jabba's court; Droopy is an outsider who speaks to almost no one but Sy for years, until the death of Jabba and most of the gangster's entourage during the Battle of Carkoon. Following this incident, the Max Rebo Band breaks up and goes their separate ways—with Droopy wandering off into the desert.

MIP: *ROTJ*: n/a; **MLC**: **$25-$32**.

Max Rebo (a.k.a. Siiruulian Phantele)

[Production #71360]

1st packaged appearance: 77-back shadow box
Original Retail Price: Only sold via a
three-pack

- with Max Rebo Microphone, lower-level stand,
  unique to figure, black or silver variations
- with Max Rebo Organ, a.k.a. "Red Ball Jett"
  organ, or nalargon

Max Rebo, with lower-
level Microphone.

Max Rebo
Organ.

The talented musician who goes by the stage name of "Max Rebo" is an Ortolan: a species of bipedal pachydermoids (elephant-like humanoids) who possess trunks, beady black eyes, floppy ears, thick fuzzy skin that resembles hanging blue velvet, and hands that end in odd suction-cupped fingers (and similarly-adapted toes) which allow Ortolans to absorb food through these digits, as well as their mouths.

With a magnificent sense of hearing that reaches into the subsonic range and an advanced sense of smell due to their homeworld's dearth of available food, many Ortolans such as Siiruulian Phantele (Max's real name) engage in a lifelong pursuit of both music and food: chefs and musicians. Hence, Max becomes a *gourmand*, as well as a world-class organist.

Relative to other Ortolans, Max is actually quite lithe, yet his obsession with food certainly handicaps his business dealings as a musician, where he plays his famous Red Ball Jett Organ (a.k.a. nalargon, a 22-keyed air-powered organ with circular keyboard). Pursuing work on the planet Tatooine, Max is forced into the position of band leader since the group's singer and true "frontman," Sy Snootles, wishes to protect her anonymity (and her life) when engaged in typical yet deadly underhanded business negotiations. Unfortunately, when arbitrating a contract with Jabba Desilijic Tiure, Max "sells" the band to Jabba (see Jabba the Hutt

Action Playset) for the promise of unlimited food in perpetuity—yet no monetary compensation whatsoever.

Max, along with the rest of the members of the band, who disband following the death of Jabba the Hutt, eventually becomes a wealthy restaurant owner of a chain of Max's Flangth House franchises on seven different worlds—serving the mysterious yet nutritious food known as *flangth* (alternatively, *flanth*).

MIP: ROTJ: n/a, **MLO:** C12 $16.

109

Sy Snootles (a.k.a. "Mrs. Snooty")

[Production #71360]

1st packaged appearance: 77-back shadow box
Original Retail Price: Only sold via a
three-pack

- with Sy Snootles Microphone, higher-level stand, unique to the figure, black or silver variations
- with plastic Sy Snootles Skirt, unique to the figure

Sy Snootles, with accessories.

The sultry, lipsticked Pa'lowick crooner known as Sy Snootles, originally dubbed "Mrs. Snooty" during the production of *Return of the Jedi*, is a sapient amphibian hailing from the planet of Lowick in the Outer Rim. As a Pa'lowick, she possesses a body shape that is perfectly suited for Lowick's semi-aquatic environment: lithe arms and legs, powerful lungs, round and husky central masses, stalked eyes, and a long proboscis (*not* a snout) that ends in a pair of lips. Since storytelling is a prime aspect of Pa'lowick culture, their people write songs to satisfy a powerful creative impulse; singing is both a pastime and a sacred ritual.

Sy is a former part-time bounty hunter, tragic lover and killer of Jabba the Hutt's traitorous uncle Ziro Desilijic Tiure, and also functions as the lead singer for the Max Rebo Band—which, although the group is named after their keyboardist, Sy leads them from the shadows, allowing Max Rebo to attract the unwanted attention garnered by a band leader that travels in precariously criminal circles. Throughout her tenure in the band, she functions as a double agent for Jabba (see Jabba the Hutt Action Playset), feeding his enemies false information provided to her by the crime lord's majordomo (see Bib Fortuna).

After the death of Jabba and most of the gangster's entourage during the Battle of Carkoon, Sy and her bandmates gotheir separate ways, and she devotes her life to minor singing gigs. It is worth noting that in the original film, Sy is portrayed by a puppet; in the Special Edition and afterward, the Pa'lowick chanteuse is rendered by CGI-animation.

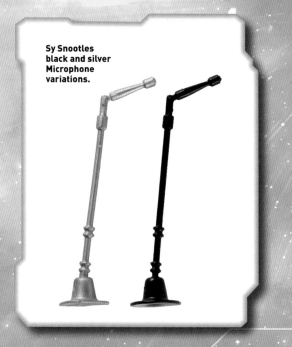

Sy Snootles black and silver Microphone variations.

MIP: *ROTJ*: n/a; **MLC**: $18-$22.

8D8 (a.k.a. Atedeeate)

[Production #71210]

1st appearance: (Sears Exclusive) The Jabba the Hutt Dungeon action playset, gray base
1st carded appearance: 77-back card
Original Retail Price (average): $2.99

○ four different leg variations

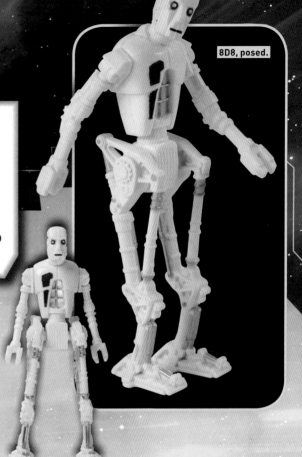

8D8, posed.

Working in conjunction with the dominant supervisor/interrogator droid known as EV-9D9 (see her separate entry) in the "cyborg operations" section—and one-time boiler room—within the lower levels of Jabba Desilijic Tiure's stronghold on the desert planet of Tatooine, the area is essentially retrofitted to accommodate a makeshift torture facility for disobedient droids. Along with EV-9D9, these two droids eradicate the original programming of any victims brought to the facility, then re-tool and re-outfit these droids for staunch obedience.

Originally dedicated to working in facilities that extracted metal ore, Atedeeate is one member of the 8D-series of smelter droids (a.k.a. 8D Smelting Operators) that are manufactured by the Verpine species of brilliant sentient insectoids who inhabited the Roche asteroids. Heat-resistant, fireproof, fiercely strong yet simple-minded, these droids closely resemble the tall, lanky humanoid members of the Muun species (Palpatine's Sith Master Darth Plagueis is a Muun), instead of their insectoid creators.

Sporting attenuated limbs and complex leg joints, Atedeeate rarely interacts with sentient beings after Jabba has him reprogrammed as a torturer of both droids and organic creatures. Possessing a crude personality and an intense dislike of those droids more intellectually able than himself, Atedeeate nurses a secret grudge against EV-9D9 … yet he does his job to the best of his ability.

MOC: ROTJ. $40-$45; MLC: $7-$10.

No. 71210   Ages 4 and up

STAR WARS
RETURN OF THE
JEDI

8D8.

Kenner

8D8 MOC.

Klaatu (In Skiff Guard Outfit)/ Klaatu (Skiff Guard Outfit)

[Production #71290]

1st appearance: (Sears Exclusive) The Jabba the Hutt Dungeon action playset, gray base
1st carded appearance: 77-back card
Original Retail Price (average): $2.99

- with Skiff Guard Force Pike, unique to the figure

Klaatu (in Skiff Guard Outfit), with Skiff Guard Force Pike.

Although the Klaatu (in Skiff Guard Outfit) action figure's facial features bear more than a passing similarity to the other Klaatu (see Klaatu) toy released, it has been canonically established that the two are completely separate characters, yet both are members of the Nikto race—"Green Nikto" to be exact (see Nikto). Regardless of the striking similarity between these two Kadas'sa'Nikto, who serve Jabba Desilijic Tiure (see Jabba the Hutt Action Playset), the first Kenner figure, the Klaatu sporting a fabric skirt, brown tunic, and bladed vibro-ax, is actually named "Wooof," while this second version produced by Kenner as Klaatu (in Skiff Guard Outfit), with his white jumpsuit, cream-colored hat and shoulder pads, and a large force pike, is the character who should truly be called "Klaatu."

As a character, Klaatu is Barada's (see Barada) number-one assistant and can often be found repairing the skiffs in Jabba's motor pool. During the Battle of Carkoon, Klaatu mans the huge cannon atop his master's large sail skiff, the

CLOSE-UP

Skiff Guard Force Pike.

Khetanna—a weapon that proves Jabba and his retinue's undoing. The weapon included with this figure is *markedly* different from the accessory included with Klaatu (a.k.a. Wooof), Lando Calrissian (Skiff Guard Disguise, a.k.a. Tamtel Skreej), and Weequay (a.k.a. Pagetti Rook). This accessory—often referred to as a Skiff Guard force pike—has no discernible blade, yet functions as a vibrostave weapon (see Gamorrean Guard), with a complex arrangement of modifications: an apparent power pak, an Ultrasonic generator, and a sophisticated shaft.

MOC: *ROTJ*: $32-$40; **MLC:** $8-$10.

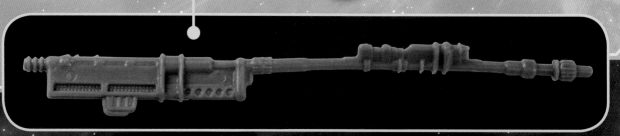

Nikto

[Production #71190]

1st appearance: (Sears Exclusive) The Jabba the Hutt Dungeon action playset, gray base
1st carded appearance: 77-back card
Original Retail Price (average): $2.99

- o lighter face and hand spray figure or darker face and hand spray figure variations
- o with Skiff Guard Battle Staff

The ancient reptilian humanoid species known as Nikto possesses fierce tempers, cold, calculating reptilian eyes, and leathery skin, which is actually comprised of thousands of protective scales that overlap upon one another. Nikto are derived from the planet Kintan where, due to massive bursts of radiation from a nearby dying star, there manifests five different sub-species, all of which are capable of interbreeding.

The five sub-species of Nikto may be distinguished by differing facial features and skin color: the first and most prominent group are *Red Nikto* (a.k.a. *Kajain'sa'Nikto*)—adapted to the desert regions of Kintan and having forehead ridges and small facial horns framing their faces, as well as adaptations to allow for living in a sandy environment; Green Nikto (a.k.a. *Kadas'sa'Nikto*)—adapted to the forest regions of Kintan, possessing noses and visible scales, with smallish horns around their eyes (see Klaatu); Mountain Nikto (a.k.a. *Esral'sa'Nikto*)—with large, fin-shaped ears, smooth skin, and a nasal membrane (lacking a visible nose) similar to the Red Nikto; Pale Nikto (a.k.a. *Gluss'sa'Nikto*)—this white/gray-skinned sub-species inhabits the island areas of Kintan and has eye-horns like the Green Nikto, yet sports fin-like ears similar to the Mountain Niktos; and Southern Niktos (a.k.a. *M'shento'su'Nikto*)—with no horns whatsoever, a nasal membrane, smooth

Nikto, with Skiff Guard Battle Staff.

skin which varied from a jaundiced yellow to pale orange, and several pairs of breathing tubes.

The character pictured on Kenner's card front is a Red Nikto who goes by the name of Lathe. One of the few members of Jabba the Hutt's staff who works at the palace voluntarily, this henchman is an information broker with dreams to leave the desert planet of Tatooine one day. Unfortunately, he is killed by Luke Skywalker at the famous Battle of Carkoon during *Return of the Jedi*.

MOC: *ROTJ:* **$32 $38**; *POTF:* **$900-$1,100**; **MLC: $8-$10**.

The Emperor
(a.k.a. Darth Sidious, Galactic Emperor Palpatine)

[Production #71190]

1st appearance: Mail-Away
1st carded appearance: 77-back card
Original Retail Price (average): $2.99

○ fine detailed robe & hands + darker gray plastic, or soft detailed robe & hands + lighter gray plastic variations
• with Emperor's Cane, a.k.a. Sith artifact

The Emperor, with Emperor's Cane.

Yet another in a long line of fabulous vintage mail-away *Star Wars* action figures, with five proof-of-purchase seals, collectors could obtain "The Emperor" from *Return of the Jedi* who is, according to the promotional advertisement, the "Leader of the Imperial Forces, ruler of Darth Vader, and Supreme Master of the Dark Side of the Force." After submitting your POPs to Kenner, within 10 to 12 weeks, a small white shipping box arrived at your door that contained a *ROTJ* product catalog and an Emperor action figure sealed within a transparent baggie with his glossy black cane accessory, but *without* the usual standard one-page insert that described who the character was within the context of *Star Wars* canon. Why include this sheet anymore, when this mail-away Emperor Palpatine toy was not created to *tease* the film, but to garner repeat visits to the theater?

Kenner's action figure of "The Emperor" is based upon a young man who was born in 82 BBY to the noble House Palpatine of the planet Naboo, who, as an adolescent, becomes fascinated by dark side artifacts. One day, this ambitious young man meets the secret Sith Lord Darth Plagueis (of the tall, thin Muun species) who convinces the fledgling Palpatine to train under him in the ways of the Sith. Palpatine embraces Plagueis' tutelage, and so the Sith Master convinces his young apprentice to murder his own father and formally adopt the name Darth Sidious; thus Palpatine develops a sophisticated double life—one where he spends his observable hours immersed in local politics, yet while in seclusion he devotes the rest of his time to the manipulation of the dark side of the Force. Eventually, Palpatine grows in power and influence

Palpatine: "We have a new enemy, the young Rebel who destroyed the Death Star. I have no doubt this boy is the offspring of Anakin Skywalker."

Darth Vader: "How is that possible?"

Palpatine: "Search your feelings, Lord Vader. You will know it to be true. He could destroy us."

—The Emperor speaks to Darth Vader about Luke Skywalker's origin

<blockquote>
The Emperor mailer box, with ephemera.
</blockquote>

and adopts a trainee of his own, the Sith assassin Darth Maul. Following "the Rule of Two" doctrine—a guiding principle of the Order of the Sith Lords that states that there can only exist two Sith at one time (a Master and an Apprentice)—Palpatine plans to eliminate Darth Plagueis. The Rule of Two exists so that once an Apprentice is powerful enough to "take" the title of Master (through murder), only then will they be considered worthy. After dispatching Darth Plagueis, who Palpatine kills in his sleep, Darth Sidious set his designs on taking over the Galactic Republic.

Since ambassador Palpatine is also a power-hungry politician, he eventually ascends to the post of Senator Palpatine of the planet Naboo. The senator's ambition combines with his total lack of morality and allows him to manipulate those closest to him and therefore, the Galactic Senate elected Palpatine to the position of Supreme Chancellor.

It was Supreme Chancellor Palpatine who, through a series of machinations, resuscitated the dangerous Sith Order of force-sensitives (who utilize the dark side of the Force), and the sect blossoms and grows to eclipse the entire galaxy. Consequently, after General Grievous' death on Utapau, Darth Tyranus' murder above Coruscant, and the expendable Darth Maul's apparent

death on Naboo, and following the Great Jedi Purge and the extermination of the leaders of the Confederacy of Independent Systems by Palpatine's newfound apprentice Darth Vader, the Supreme Chancellor has himself crowned Emperor at the galactic capital of Coruscant—which he has re-formed into the core of the first Galactic Empire.

Sporting his trademark glossy black cane that allows the Emperor to appear weak, when in fact he is more powerful than his enemies could imagine, Palpatine ushers in a new age of oppression as his Galactic Empire allows him total control over the entire galaxy, amassing some of the most impressive armies ever seen. He rules through threats and terror, constructing two Death Star space stations, while using his Apprentice Darth Vader to enforce his indomitable will (see Darth Vader).

MISB: All contents sealed in mailer: **$35-$40+**; **MIB**: w/all included pieces & sealed figure: **$28-$30**; **MIB**: w/all included pieces & non-sealed figure: **$20-$22+**; **MOC**: *ROTJ*: **$35-$42**; *POTF*: **$85-$100+**; **MLC**: **$7-$12**.

AT-ST Driver
(a.k.a. Lieutenant Arnet or Major Marquand)

[Production #71330]

1st carded appearance: 77-back card
Original Retail Price (average): $2.99

- gray helmet with matte black gloves and darker plastic variation
- darker gray helmet with glossy black gloves and lighter plastic variation
- with gray or gray/blue Endor Blaster (Merr-Sonn Munitions DD6 "Light" Blaster Pistol)

AT-ST Driver, with Endor Blaster.

The position of AT-ST driver (or more accurately, AT-ST "pilot") is given to only the most talented of all the recruits of the Imperial Army. In order to qualify for the position, an AT-ST pilot (see Scout Walker [vehicle]) must possess an extraordinary sense of balance that can transfer their ability to control the bipedal vehicle over rough ground. An AT-ST pilot's conception of how to drive their dexterous vehicles over craggy terrain is an important aspect of their vocations.

The gray Army trooper uniform worn by Kenner's AT-ST Driver action figure is standard for the characters featured in *ROTJ*. In the film, when two AT-ST crew members, gunner Lieutenant Watts and pilot Major Marquand, are ousted from *Tempest Scout 2*, their personal AT-ST (call sign 17-B) by Chewbacca (see Chewbacca) and two Ewoks, Widdle Warrick and Wunka, their uniforms are fully observed. Thus, an AT-ST pilot wears the following accoutrements: an open-faced helmet with chinstrap and attached goggles, black boots, a gray pocketed jumpsuit with a black Imperial emblem stenciled onto each shoulder, and black gauntlets.

MOC: *ROTJ*: $30-$35; *POTF*: $40-$42+; **MLC:** $14-$16.

B-Wing Pilot

[Production #71280]

1st carded appearance: 77-back card
Original Retail Price (average): $2.99

- less-detailed helmet wire variation
- dark brown helmet + unpainted top of chin strap + smooth chest variation
- light brown helmet + fully-painted top of chin strap + fine chest variation
- square pocket and 1-piece boot strap or curved pocket and sectioned boot strap variations
- with gray or gray/blue Endor Blaster (Merr-Sonn Munitions DD6 "Light" Blaster Pistol)

B-Wing Pilot, with Endor Blaster.

Having developed a reputation as the easiest vintage figure to obtain Mint On Card on the secondary market due to the figure's ubiquity, this ease of availability combined with the toy's (debatable) lack of fine detailing led Kenner's B-wing Pilot figurine to be regarded as an afterthought to most collectors.

Apart from of the toy's ill repute, B-wing pilots develop the same sterling reputation as every other Alliance pilot in the Rebel fleet: brave in the face of often insurmountable odds, and fairly well trained due to their superiors' (see Admiral Ackbar) decision to educate recently recruited aviators via impromptu missions which afford them the chance to fly through abandoned factories. These unsanctioned runs quickly help to improve the basic skills, combat instincts, and enduring resolve of a new Rebel pilot's combat instincts.

B-wing pilots wear red flight suits with flak vests and a life box mounted on the chest, and a unique flight helmet with a visor that has access to a projected targeting program, which is nearly always decorated with the Alliance Starbird. Furthermore, B-wing pilots are required to retain a high level of skill relative to other Alliance aviators, since the B-wing heavy assault starfighter (see B-wing Fighter) is quite large, heavily armed with an unusually large payload for its size, lack both agility and speed, and its unique rotating hull system is quite difficult to control. Before the Battle of Endor (4 ABY), few pilots are qualified to fly the B-wing.

MOC: *ROTJ:* $30-$38; *POTF:* $45-$55; **MLC:** $11-$14.

B-Wing Pilot uniform variations.

Han Solo (In Trench Coat)

[Production #71300]

1st carded appearance: 77-back card
Original Retail Price (average): $2.99

- well-detailed body and face sculpt or less-detailed body and face sculpt
- with camouflaged cloth trench coat/jacket, with or without camouflaged lapels
- with true black Rebel Blaster (DL-44 heavy blaster pistol)

Han Solo (in Trench Coat), with accessories.

Although reckless at times, over the course of the original trilogy, his formerly selfish nature gives way to myriad acts of selfless heroism and noble gallantry; the daring risks Solo takes to courageously save his friends' lives and to preserve the integrity of the Rebellion affords him a military promotion: Alliance General Han Solo is a natural leader, and an inspiration to the young troops he commands.

Dressed in the uniform he wears when plotting a strike against the Imperial bunker that safeguards the shield generator for the second Death Star, General Solo essentially leads a suicide mission armed with volunteers that have little to no hope of success. Armed with stolen Imperial codes in order to land a captured shuttle (see Imperial Shuttle vehicle) on the Sanctuary Moon,

Solo achieves the initial piece of the puzzle: they land on the forest moon of Endor without incident. Once there, however, it becomes obvious that the collective forces of his small commando strike team are no match for the Empire's well-armed Stormtroopers, Biker Scouts with their Speeder Bikes, and AT-ST Drivers with their AT-STs.

However, thanks to Princess Leia's (see Princess Leia Organa [In Combat Poncho]) chance encounter with a native member of a local tribe of Ewoks (see Wicket W. Warrick), Solo's Alliances forces join with Chief Chirpa's gutsy, resourceful tribe and ultimately shut down the shield generator—allowing for Lando Calrissian (see Lando Calrissian [General Pilot]), Nien Nunb, and Admiral Ackbar to destroy the second Death Star.

MOC: *ROTJ*: **$60-$65**; *POTF*: **$290-$310**; **MLC**: **$15-$22**, depending upon condition.

Han Solo (in Trench Coat) figure variations.

Trench Coat variations.

Princess Leia Organa (In Combat Poncho)

[Production #71220]

1st carded appearance: 77-back card
Original Retail Price (average): $2.99

- o sharply detailed body sculpt or softer-detailed body sculpt
- with camouflaged cloth Princess Leia Combat Poncho, unique to the figure
- with Princess Leia Battle Helmet, unique to the figure
- with black plastic Princess Leia Belt, with "two settings" (similar to Luke Endor's belt), unique to the figure
- with gray or gray/blue Endor Blaster (Merr-Sonn Munitions DD6 "Light" Blaster Pistol)

Princess Leia Organa (in Combat Poncho), with accessories.

This, the final action figure based upon the character of Princess Leia Organa, features the daughter of Anakin Skywalker and Padmé Amidala as she appears on the Sanctuary Moon—the forested moon of Endor. Similar in design to that of the later-released Luke Skywalker (In Battle Poncho), Leia eschews her position as a Rebel leader and volunteers as a member of Han Solo's commando strike team (see Han Solo [In Trench Coat] and Rebel Commando) to extinguish the shield generator in order for the Rebel Fleet to successfully destroy the second Death Star. With a magnificent, removable helmet (if only Luke's were removable as well), slick black belt, camouflaged poncho, and light blaster, the princess is ready for action.

Although successful in their mission, it is Leia's friendship and diplomacy with the native species of Ewoks that ultimately saves the day: when Leia befriends a young Ewok (see Wicket W. Warrick)

after losing her speeder (see Speeder Bike vehicle), her charisma, combined with the assistance of her friends (C-3PO in particular), convinces the Ewoks' tribal chieftain (see Chief Chirpa) to pledge his peoples' assistance in the Rebels' fight against the Empire. Without the Ewoks' backing, the strike team assembled by Leia and Han would never have achieved their objective, and the Rebel fleet would have failed.

It is worth mentioning that later in the canon, Princess Leia's full name becomes "Princess Leia Amidala Skywalker Organa Solo"—she marries Han Solo and has three children with him: Jaina, Jacen, and Anakin.

Princess Leia Organa (in Combat Poncho) figure variations.

MOC: *ROTJ:* $55-$60; *POTF:* $70-$80+; **MLC:** $18-$26, depending upon condition.

Prune Face (a.k.a. Orrimaarko)

[Production #71320]

1st carded appearance: 77-back card
Original Retail Price (average): $2.99

- o finely detailed sculpt with light legs or softer sculpt with dark legs variations
- • with hooded tan cloth Prune Face Cape, unique to figure
- • with Prune Face Rifle and sling, unique to the figure

Prune Face, with accessories.

A noted leader of his planet's struggle against Imperial forces, the xenophobic resistance fighter Orrimaarko, nicknamed "Prune Face" due to his characteristic facial qualities, is a member of the Dressellian race—a species of tall, thin, sentient humanoids with wrinkled skin and bulbous, hairless skulls. Dressellians originally maintain a peaceful presence in the galaxy, existing in isolation from all other races until the Empire threatens Prune Face's homeworld. This threat forces the people of Dressel to reluctantly join the Alliance to Restore the Republic, and eventually, the New Republic.

In conjunction with their old allies, the Bothans (a species of short, furry, humanoid mammalians) Orrimaarko and his Dressellian brethren develop his species' favored weapon: the Dressellian projectile rifle. Issued with its distinctive sling, this firearm—although considered primitive when compared to the blasters used by Rebel and Imperial soldiers—still packs a wallop, able to pierce the tough plastoid armor of an Imperial Scout Trooper with relative ease.

MOC: *ROTJ*: **$25-$28**; **MLC**: **$8-$10**, depending upon condition.

Prune Face, posed.

Rancor Keeper
(a.k.a. Malakili [of the Circus Horrificus])

[Production #71350]

1st carded appearance: 77-back card
Original Retail Price (average): $2.99

- with Rancor Keeper Hood, unique to the figure, two color variations
- with Rancor Keeper Vibroblade (a.k.a. Gaderffii "Gaffi" Stick), three different stick variations, unique to the figure

Known to *Star Wars* fans everywhere as the Rancor Keeper, this character was born on Corellia, the capital planet of the Corellian system and birthplace of famed smuggler Han Solo, and heroic member of Rogue Squadron, pilot Wedge Antilles. Known for its lightning-fast starships, accomplished merchants, and fearsome pirates, Corellia also gave birth to the human male known as Malakili, a young man who becomes fascinated with wild animals at an early age.

Due to his affinity for peculiar creatures, the talented young man joins Gargonn the Hutt's spectacle, the Circus Horrificus, which, according to Wookieepedia.com, is "a travelling menagerie that displayed monstrous creatures throughout the galaxy." As the show's resident monster handler, Malakili is peerless at his vocation due to his uncanny ability to tame and train nearly any savage beast

he encounters: He is a "monster whisperer."

Eventually, Malakili is transferred (sold, actually) from the world-hopping Circus Horrificus to the citadel of Jabba Desilijic Tiure (see Jabba the Hutt Action Playset) on the desert planet of Tatooine, where the friendly animal wrangler is brought in to train a particularly prickly beast: a bloodthirsty rancor (see Rancor Monster) given to the crime lord as a birthday present from his henchmen (see Bib Fortuna). Malakili resents the fact that such a beautiful creature is held in captivity, and Jabba's rancor steals the trainer's heart and soul, becoming his obsession; he eats meals with the beast, treats its wounds, and devotes many waking hours to its care.

After Luke Skywalker kills the rancor, Malakili openly weeps, falling into the arms of his Kadas'sa'Nikto assistant, Giran. Following the death of Jabba and his entourage aboard the luxury skiff *Khetanna*, he and the palace cook escape and begin their own eatery, the Crystal Moon Restaurant.

It is worth noting that Malakili's weapon—a gaderffii ("gaffi") stick—is given to him by a tribe of Tusken Raiders (see Sand People) when the animal trainer dispatches a mutated womp rat that has taken over one of the Raiders' local caves.

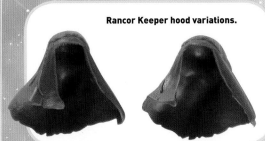

Rancor Keeper hood variations.

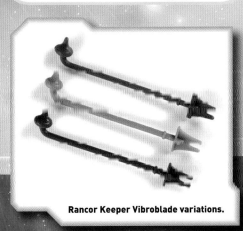

Rancor Keeper Vibroblade variations.

MOC: ROTJ: $22-$30+; MLC: $8-$12, depending upon condition.

121

Teebo [light and dark gray striped (fog-colored and stone-colored) Ewok]

[Production #71310]

1st carded appearance: 77-back card

Original Retail Price (average): $2.99

- o darker gray lines or lighter gray lines variations
- with Teebo Headdress, sporting a skull of a gurreck (horned predator of Endor) and painted feathers of a churi (bird native to Endor), unique to the figure
- with Teebo Stone Ax, unique to the figure
- with Teebo battle horn and sling, unique to the figure

Having spent much of his childhood growing up with Wicket (see Wicket W. Warrick) and Kneesa a Jari Kintaka (Princess Kneesa [see Chief Chirpa]) as his close friends, Teebo, son of Batcheela and Warok (see Warok), possesses the heart of a poet and philosopher. A deep thinker and one of the more prominent Ewoks featured within *Return of the Jedi* (he is distrustful of the Rebel strike force, and is "zapped" by R2-D2 in retribution), Teebo is attuned to the spiritual world. Although relatively young, his naturalistic intelligence, wisdom, and keen intellect lead him to pursue an apprenticeship under the crafty Ewok shaman, Logray (see Logray [Ewok Medicine Man])—yet does not succeed him as shaman upon the elder's banishment (see Paploo). Since many pundits have suggested that Teebo is Force-sensitive, this predisposition may have aided him in pursuing many aspects of Ewok magic (see *Star Wars: Ewoks*), and lends credence to his position as an eventual tribal leader.

Unfortunately, Teebo is portrayed a bit ridiculously in the second season of the animated *Star Wars: Ewoks*—a personality bordering on foolishness, according to famous story editor Paul Dini, that didn't quite mesh with the film delivery of his character, particularly the way the character is portrayed in the fascinating novelization of *ROTJ*—an absolutely essential read for any diehard *Star Wars* aficionado. The Ewoks' depiction in this book provides readers with a far better view of their culture and abilities than their other canonical sources.

Teebo's action figure is quite striking as it features many distinctive accoutrements: with his interestingly striped pelt, trademark authority stick/battle ax, gurreck-skull headdress adorned with churi feathers, and battle horn with shoulder sling, this Kenner figurine is one of their better translations of the diminutive characters from the film.

Teebo, with accessories.

MOC: *ROTJ:* **$38-$45+**; *POTF:* **$200**; **MLC:** **$13-$16**.

Wicket W. Warrick

(a.k.a. Wicket Wystri Warrick) [diminutive Ewok with brown body, and light tan chest, face, and ears]

[Production #71230]

1st carded appearance: 77-back card
Original Retail Price (average): $2.99

- with Wicket Headdress, animal pelt, unique to the figure
- with Wicket Spear, flint-pointed,* unique to the figure

*Note: The spear included with Wicket is different from the one included with Romba.

Brilliantly portrayed by eleven-year-old British actor Warwick Davies, who played the title character in *Willow* and the *Leprechaun* series of horror films, as well as Professor Flitwick in the *Harry Potter* franchise, the character of Wicket W. Warrick, whose middle initial is "Wystri," is the touchstone of the Ewok tribe for younger viewers, who could easily relate to the character.

Introduced in *Return of the Jedi* when Han Solo's commando strike team infiltrates the Ewok's home on the forest moon of Endor, Wicket appears when Princess Leia (see Princess Leia Organa [In Combat Poncho]) falls off of her stolen Imperial speeder (see Speeder Bike vehicle). Initially nervous, after Leia gives the pint-sized Ewok a bit of food, he warms to the Rebel leader. Following a moment of bonding between the two where they both team up to incapacitate an Imperial solider (see Imperial Stormtrooper), Wicket brings Leia back to his tribe at Bright Tree Village (see Ewok Village Playset), where she is treated with all the formality due to her station. Eventually the Ewoks are joined by the rest of

Leia's small band of Rebels (see Han Solo [In Trench Coat], Luke Skywalker [In Battle Poncho], Artoo-Detoo [R2-D2, with Sensorscope], See-Threepio [C-3PO, with Removable Limbs], and Chewbacca), where they are initially distrusted by Wicket's tribe, yet the Ewoks' leader (see Chief Chirpa) allows his people to formally join the Rebellion in their successful fight against the Empire. Wicket plays an instrumental role in the defeat of the Imperial forces on Endor. Following the death of their tribal chieftain, Warrick and his bride, Princess Kneesaa a Jai Kintaka (daughter of Chief Chirpa), rule Bright Tree Village together.

Beyond the impressive role Wicket played in *Return of the Jedi*, he was essentially the main character of many other versions of media proffered by Lucasfilm involving Ewoks. From 1985's *Star Wars: Ewoks* animated series to the two made-for-television live action specials (see Warok), and even a number of children's books and a Marvel Comics Ewoks series targeted for younger readers, Lucasfilm did everything they possibly could to capitalize on the young Ewok's success.

Wicket W. Warrick, with accessories.

MOC: *ROTJ*: **$38-$45+**; *POTF*: **$110-$115+**; **MLC**: **$14-$22**.

Note: Ewoks Lumat and Paploo are often considered to be part of "The Last Seventeen," the final, rare POTF ("Power of the Force") assortment of *Star Wars* action figures, even though these two Ewoks were originally produced on 79-back *ROTJ* cardbacks. Additionally, no date stamp can be found on either Lumat or Paploo. Therefore, they have been included with *Return of the Jedi* assortments in this book.

Lumat* [pursed lips, right arm curved for bow, no belt, tan fur, gray lips]

[Production #93670]

1st carded appearance: (briefly) 79-back card or oftentimes on 92-figure POTF cardback

Original Retail Price (average): $2.99

- with Lumat Bow (maroon brown, different from Warok's deep-dark brown bow), unique to the figure
- with Lumat Hood, hood ends to the lower left, unique to the figure
- With light-brown plastic Lumat Quiver with four painted white arrows, unique to the figure

*Note: Lumat's image was blacked-out on his Tri-Logo (International) cardback to preserve the surprise of his image; furthermore, his name was changed to "Ewok Warrior."

Lumat, with accessories.

Chief woodcutter of his tribe, husband to Zephee and father of Latara, Nippet, and Wiley, Lumat is one of the Ewok's warriors who helps his people to repel Imperial forces from their forest homeland.

Like Paploo, Lumat was originally released on a *Return of the Jedi* cardback, yet was re-released as one of the "last seventeen" in Power of the Force packaging—one of the final seventeen unique *Star Wars* characters released individually packaged. As with every figure solicited on a Power of the Force cardback, when Lumat and Paploo were on these POTF packages, they also came complete with a vac-metallized, chromed collector's coin unique to each figure.

Lumat Power of the Force Collector's Coin.

MOC: *ROTJ:* $75-$85+; *POTF:* $65-$75; **MLC:** $25-$32; **Coin:** $6-$10.

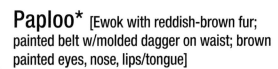

Paploo* [Ewok with reddish-brown fur; painted belt w/molded dagger on waist; brown painted eyes, nose, lips/tongue]

[Production #93680]

1st carded appearance: (briefly) 79-back card or oftentimes on 92-figure POTF cardback
Original Retail Price (average): $2.99

- with cream-colored plastic hood with painted feathers and bones
- with dark-brown Paploo Battle Staff, unique to the figure

*Note: Paploo's image was blacked-out on his Tri-Logo (International) card-back to preserve the surprise of his image.

Paploo Power of the Force Collector's Coin.

Paploo, with accessories.

Hailing from the Sanctuary Moon, a.k.a. the "Forest Moon of Endor," one of nine moons orbiting the planet Endor, the gregarious Ewok scout known as Paploo proves Jedi master Yoda's philosophy true, that "size matters not … "; if it weren't for the youngster's daring act of stealing an Imperial speeder (see Speeder Bike) right in front of its pilot (see Biker Scout), Han and Leia's Rebel commando team may never have succeeded in infiltrating the Imperial bunker.

Although he is the nephew of Chief Chirpa, it is not nepotism that allows Paploo to rise in status within his tribe. When the Ewok's longtime shaman becomes corrupted through an obsession with dark magic, the oppressive Logray is exiled from the tribe by Chief Chirpa, and Paploo succeeds him as the new medicine man, due to his intelligence and profound courage.

For an explanation of his packaging and how he was solicited, see Lumat.

MOC: *ROTJ*: $35-$40; *POTF*: $50-$55 MLC: $20-$24. Coin: $6-$10.

125

POWER OF THE FORCE

In 1984, a year after the premiere of *Return of the Jedi*, the original *Star Wars* trilogy was passing out of the collective consciousness, and a slew of new toy and action figure offerings began crowding *Star Wars* product off retail shelves—such as Hasbro's highly articulated *G.I. Joe: A Real American Hero* toys and their sentient, changing robots known as *Transformers: More Than Meets the Eye*, and Mattel's *Masters of the Universe* (all thanks to Ronald Reagan's deregulation of children's television in 1983)—and so, *Star Wars* action figures had a last gasp in late 1984/early 1985 when Kenner produced the final magnificent action figure assortment of the vintage *Star Wars* line: *Star Wars*, Power of the Force.

Although hailed by *Star Wars* aficionados as some of the best-sculpted and well-rendered of all the action figures, due to waning interest, these toys, packaged with a special silver-colored foil-embossed collector's coin, did not sell very well and were often discounted at retail. Due to their scarcity and limited availability in stores, their high level of detail and ornate packaging, these figures are in exceedingly high demand on the secondary market.

It should be noted that although fifteen all-new action figures (not seventeen, since Ewoks Romba and Warok were initially released at the tail end of the *ROTJ* assortment package within *Return of the Jedi* packaging) were sculpted under the *Star Wars* Power of the Force banner (and one figure, the highly desirable Yak Face, was only available outside of the United States), many popular older figures (Ben Obi-Wan Kenobi, Luke Skywalker: Jedi Knight, C-3PO with Removable Limbs, etc.), were re-released on POTF cards with newly created vac-metallized, chrome-plated POTF collector's coins. Many of these coins and other POTF coins that were only available

as mail-aways off of the figures' package backs are worth their weight in gold—quite literally—on the secondary market. Twenty-seven coins were available only through a Kenner mail-away offer; these are the most difficult to find of all POTF coins.

To capitalize on the poor sales of the POTF assortment and diminishing popularity of the *Star Wars* toy franchise, Kenner decided to tap into the emerging children's programming market by constructing two disparate toy lines with Saturday morning cartoon tie-ins: the *Droids* and *Ewoks* collections. Both toy lines continued the procedure established with Kenner's *Star Wars:* Power of the Force assortment, packaging a foil-stamped collector's coin unique to each figure within the toy's blister card: *Droids* coins were minted in gold; *Ewoks* coins produced in bronze.

Regardless, we should never forget that Kenner sold more than 250 million total figures between 1978 and 1985.

One of the most desirable of all of the action figures in the entire vintage *Star Wars* line is based on Luke Skywalker's Stormtrooper disguise in *Return of the Jedi*. Disney/Lucasfilm/20th Century Fox/Heritage Auctions

Artoo-Detoo (R2-D2) With Pop Up Lightsaber*

[Production #93720]

1st carded appearance: 92-back card POTF cardback
Original Retail Price (average): $2.99

- with paper label/sticker, unique to the figure
- with pop-up green Lightsaber, unique to the figure, no circle on hilt like the '85 Droids version
- with silver POTF "R2-D2/Rebel Droid" coin (coin text: "Barrel-shaped DROID." Functions as a sophisticated computer-repair and information retrieval robot. R2-D2 communicates through electronic sounds and uses C-3PO as his interpreter.")

*Note: Although this R2-D2 figure still possesses a 1977 date stamp, since Kenner utilized their surviving 1978 R2-D2 body mold, this figure was produced in 1984.

R2-D2 with Pop Up Lightsaber
Power of the Force Collector's Coin.

Preserving the same aspects of the original R2-D2 that kids and collectors loved—a vacuum-metallized silver chromed dome, clicking head that rotates 360 degrees, and pair of solid, poseable legs that make the figure stable beyond reproach—the designers at Kenner added one more stunning feature that sent consumers over the moon: a pop-up green lightsaber that, when you turn Artoo's head from left to right, jumps upward.

Finally, kids could reenact the magnificent Battle of the Great Pit of Carkoon (4 ABY), where this "little-astromech-that-could" saves the lives of his Rebel friends when he executes Luke Skywalker's carefully laid plan to perfection. Beyond Artoo's hiding his master's lightsaber, he also possesses a multitude of splendid accessories at his disposal: a sensorscope (see Artoo-Detoo with Sensorscope), an extendible neck, a utility arm carousel that economized space by placing a variety of arms onto a rotating drum (e.g., grasping arm, electro magnetic power charge arm, universal computer interface arm), and even a set of Brooks propulsion rocket boosters for flight—which were damaged by the time R2 is bought by Luke during the events of *A New Hope*.

R2-D2, with Pop Up Lightsaber.

MOC: *POTF*: $185-$200; MLC: $100-$110; Coin itself: $24-$28.

R2-D2's pop-up green Lightsaber.

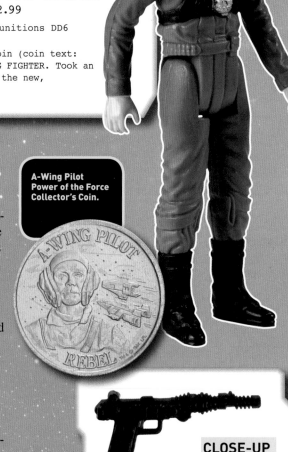

A-wing Pilot
(a.k.a. RZ-1 A-wing Interceptor Rebel Pilot)

[Production #93830]

1st carded appearance: 92-back card, POTF cardback
Original Retail Price (average): $2.99

- with black Endor Blaster (Merr-Sonn Munitions DD6 "Light" Blaster Pistol)
- with silver POTF "A-wing Pilot/Rebel" coin (coin text: "Brave REBEL PILOT of the awesome A-WING FIGHTER. Took an active part in the successful attack on the new, more powerful DEATH STAR.")

Kenner's A-wing Pilot action figure is meant to represent a generic starfighter pilot: one of many members of the skilled piloting corps who fly the Rebellion's premiere spacecraft, the slick, lightning-fast A-wing fighter—a vehicle *never released* in the vintage *Star Wars* line (fans had to wait until 1985's short-lived *Star Wars: Droids* sub-line to obtain the magnificent toy). Since the A-wing is such a responsive ship, the pilots chosen to fly them have to be taken from among the Rebellion's best: they are some of the most physically and intellectually gifted pilots in the Rebel ranks.

The daring A-wing Pilot by the name of Arvel Crynyd leads Green Squadron's stalwart team of quick A-wings (see *Star Wars: Droids*, A-wing Fighter) during the battle over Endor against an Imperial fleet of Star Destroyers with the goal of destroying their ion cannons. Hoping that his squadron's tactics will afford the Alliance Fleet the ability to attack Darth Vader's Star Dreadnought *Executor* (see Darth Vader's Star Destroyer Action Playset) in the middle of a strafing run, Crynyd's A-wing is struck by heavy cannon fire from the powerful capital ship. Since he knows he is about to perish, Crynyd gains control of his starfighter, expertly aiming it through the *Executor's* unshielded command bridge, instantly destroying himself and his ship, yet killing the massive Imperial craft's command crew.

Similar to Kenner's Imperial Gunner figure from their Power of the Force line, the A-wing Pilot (both

A-Wing Pilot Power of the Force Collector's Coin.

CLOSE-UP

A-Wing Pilot's Endor Blaster.

Power of the Force and Droids [see *Star Wars: Droids*] versions of the figurine) only came with a black-colored Endor Blaster: the blue/gray versions were included with other characters.

MOC: *POTF:* **$140-$150+**; **MLC:** **$65-$70**; **Coin itself:** **$12-$15**.

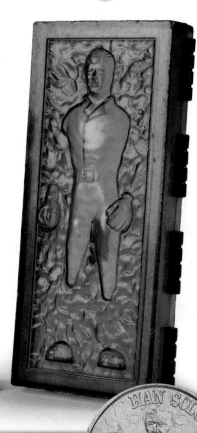
Han Solo (In Carbonite Chamber)

[Production #93770]

1st carded appearance: 92-back card, POTF cardback

Original Retail Price (average): $2.99

- with Carbonite Chamber, unique to the figure
- with silver POTF "Han Solo/Carbon Freeze" coin (coin text: "Smuggler captured by the bounty hunter BOBA FETT and 'frozen' because he owed money to the evil JABBA THE HUTT.")

At the end of *The Empire Strikes Back*, the pig-faced, diminutive Ugnaughts prepare a defiant Han Solo to be encased in a carbonite block by order of Darth Vader on the Cloud City colony of the planet Bespin (see Cloud City Playset). Until this point in history, the process was used only to preserve the bodies of the dead, yet the technologically astute Ugnaughts modify the procedure to (hopefully) work on the living: to observe if a human being can indeed be frozen in carbonite and survive. To that end, in order for the Sith Lord to ensure the carbon-freezing process will not harm his chosen detainee, Vader first tests the procedure on Solo before prepping the chamber for his son, Luke Skywalker, a Jedi Knight who he believes to be too dangerous to transport back to the Emperor without first immobilizing him.

Boba Fett does not want Darth Vader to test the carbon-freezing chamber on Han because he believes the process will murder him and void his bounty for Jabba the Hutt, whose contract demands that Han be brought to his palace on Tatooine alive. Disregarding Fett's contract, Vader allows Solo to undergo this dangerous procedure, which proves successful, and so the famous Rebel leader enters a period of suspended animation for nearly one year. As promised, Vader gives the carbon-frozen Solo over to Boba Fett, who transports the Corellian to Jabba's Palace (see *Slave-1*), earning his bounty and the Hutt crime lord one of his prized possessions.

Han Solo (in Carbonite Chamber) Power of the Force Collector's Coin.

 MOC: *POTF:* **$210-$225+; MLC: $70-$75; Coin itself: $12-$14.**

129

Imperial Dignitary

[Production #93850]

1st carded appearance: 92-back card, POTF cardback
Original Retail Price (average): $2.99

- with silver POTF "Imperial Dignitary/Empire" coin (coin text: "One of the evil men who is close to The Emperor and serves as an advisor in his plans to destroy the REBEL forces.")

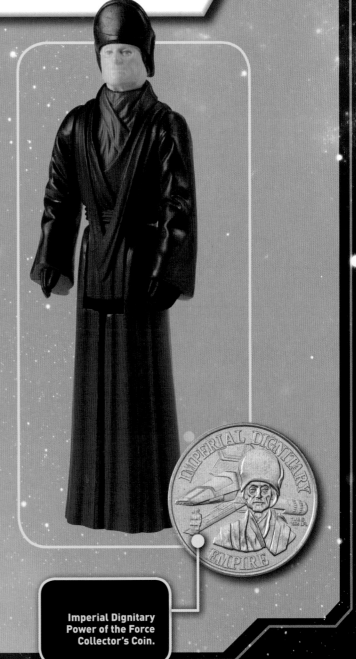

Donning opulent and lavish robes fit for his station—as well as Coruscanti headwear that functions as an homage to his homeworld of Coruscant (hiding his gray hair)—the Imperial Dignitary known as Sim Aloo is present in a few short scenes from *Return of the Jedi*. A Force-sensitive human born on Coruscant, capital planet of the Galactic Republic and symbolic center of the Galactic Empire, Aloo begins as an ally and advisor to Palpatine (see The Emperor) when the Sith Lord is but a member of the Senate. Following Palpatine when he ascends to the position of Supreme Chancellor after the fall of the Galactic Republic, it appears that Aloo backs the right horse, having been promoted to the position of senior political advisor when Palpatine proclaims himself Galactic Emperor. As a member of the Emperor's Inner Circle, Aloo holds this post for the duration of the Imperial era.

Aloo is featured in a brief scene where Darth Vader interrupts Emperor Palpatine when his Sith Master is on an inspection tour of the Death Star. Apparently, the Emperor leaks information to the Rebellion about his presence aboard the battle station, leading to the Alliance launching a full-scale attack on the unfinished second Death Star project— resulting in its destruction and the death of the Emperor.

MOC: *POTF*: $115-$125;
MLC: $35-$42+; Coin
itself: $10.

**Imperial Dignitary
Power of the Force
Collector's Coin.**

Imperial Gunner
Power of the Force
Collector's Coin.

CLOSE-UP
Imperial Gunner's
Endor Blaster.

Imperial Gunner

[Production #93760]

1st carded appearance: 92-back card,
POTF cardback

Original Retail Price (average): $2.99

- with black Endor Blaster (Merr-Sonn Munitions DD6 "Light" Blaster Pistol)
- with silver POTF "Imperial Gunnery/Empire" coin (coin text: "One of the men who controlled the original DEATH STAR's powerful Death Ray. In one single blast, he destroyed the entire planet of ALDERAAN.")

Despite the fact that the Imperial Gunner represents the final "troop builder" action figure produced by Kenner for the company's vintage *Star Wars* toy line, these figurines were prohibitively expensive if collectors chose to amass an army of them. With their black overalls, black gauntlets, Imperial emblem on each upper arm, and black enclosed targeting-computer helmet, these characters look quite mysterious and imposing.

In the original trilogy, they are known as Death Star gunners, functioning as a specialized sub-unit of the Imperial Navy's Imperial pilot corps, and are utilized as weaponeers at the Empire's military bases, on Imperial capital ships (see Darth Vader's Star Destroyer Action Playset), and particularly on the Death Stars (see Death Star Space Station), where the Imperial Gunners ex-

hibited their profound skills working with ion cannons and turbolasers aboard Imperial vessels such as Star Destroyers. Specifically, these characters are featured in scenes when they are commanded to use a Death Star's superlaser.

Like Kenner's A-wing Pilot figure, the Imperial Gunner only came with a black-colored Endor Blaster: the blue/gray versions were included with other characters.

MOC: *POTF:* **$110-$125+; MLC: $55-$65+; Coin itself: $14-$18.**

Luke Skywalker (Imperial Stormtrooper Outfit)

[Production #93780]

1st carded appearance: 92-back card, POTF cardback
Original Retail Price (average): $2.99

- with removable Stormtrooper Helmet, unique to the figure
- with solid black Imperial Blaster (E-11 blaster rifle)
- with silver POTF "Luke Skywalker/Rebel Leader" coin (coin text: "Young adventurer who rescued PRINCESS LEIA from the detention center of the original DEATH STAR battle station.")

One of the most desirable of all of the action figures in the entire vintage *Star Wars* line, Luke Skywalker donning an Imperial stormtrooper's uniform is one of the most popular boy's toys from the 1980s. With the ability to remove his stormtrooper helmet and deliver the now-classic line, "I'm Luke Skywalker. I'm here to rescue you," finding a pure-white sample of this toy on the secondary market is difficult.

Braving the detention levels of the original Death Star, the farm-hand-turned-Rebel-hero daringly rescues Princess Leia Organa from the clutches of Darth Vader for the sake of the Rebel Alliance. If only Kenner made a vintage Han Solo in Imperial Stormtrooper Outfit action figure in 3-3/4-inch scale to accompany this figure. Regardless, this uniform is an intricate, expensive piece of equipment that truly helps him and Han survive the rescue and protects them from the attack of a dianoga while being trapped in the space station's trash compactor.

A stormtrooper's spectacular uniform was comprised of plastoid composite armor worn over a black full-body glove that features the following accoutrements: 1) a utility belt, which holds energy rations, energy sinks that hang to the left and right side of the belt to absorb blast energy, and extra power cell containers/holders), 2) a reinforced helmet with a broadband communications antenna, audio pickup, and artificial air supply nozzles, 3) a Baradium-core code key thermal detonator (note the cylindrical object located on the back of the Kenner action figures' belts, and 4) a power pack with pressurized gas system, which allows the owner to breathe in hostile environments—even within the vacuum of space.

The E-11 BlasTech Standard Imperial Sidearm carried by Luke and Han while wearing these uniforms is a deadly weapon, and can be energized via a removable/replaceable power cell, similar to a rifle's magazine; the cell can hold roughly 100 shots each—with replacement cells worn in containers on the trooper's belt.

Luke Skywalker (Imperial Stormtrooper Outfit) Power of the Force Collector's Coin.

 MOC: *POTF:* $345-$365+; **MLC:** $95-$115+; **Coin itself:** $14-$18+.

CLOSE-UP
Luke Skywalker's Stormtrooper Outfit accessories.

Amanaman [Amani Bounty Hunter]

[Production #93740]

1st appearance: (Sears Exclusive) The Jabba the Hutt Dungeon Action Playset (II), tan base, if obtained via this playset, no POTF coin included
1st carded appearance: 92-back card, POTF cardback
Original Retail Price (average): $2.99
- with large brown Headhunter Staff sporting three white painted skulls, unique to the figure
- with silver POTF "Amanaman" coin (coin text: "Long-armed creature at Jabba's Court, called 'Head Hunter' because of his staff with three heads.")

Amanaman, with Headhunter Staff.

One member of the primitive Amanin species from the woodland world of Maridun, the male Amani known as Amanaman is a bounty hunter who exhibits precisely the same physical traits as the rest of his sentient race: terribly long arms, elongated lithe fingers, short stubby legs, a body resembling that of a planarian (similar to a flatworm), and wrinkled yellow skin on the front of his body—with a dark green hood that runs from the tip of his head to the top of his short legs. To keep their skin moist and protect them against predation, Amanin also secrete a poisonous slime all over their craggy epidermis.

Like the rest of his species, Amanaman's reputation as a "head hunter" is well founded due to the Amanin's tendency to collect the heads of their victims as souvenirs. Amanaman is regularly found at Jabba's Palace, where he sports a fear-provoking staff decorated with three of his favorite victims' heads, while he drags a decapitated, desiccated corpse behind him; the corpse is not included with his action figure.

MOC: *POTF:* $190-$215+;
MLC: $80-$85; **Coin itself:** $12-$14.

Amanaman Power of the Force Collector's Coin.

Anakin Skywalker

[Production #93790]

1st appearance: Mail-Away, if obtained via mail-away, then no POTF coin included
1st carded appearance: 92-back card, POTF cardback
Original Mail-Away Price: FREE (5 proof-of-purchase seals)
Original Retail Price (average): $2.99

- with silver POTF "Anakin Skywalker/Jedi" coin (coin text: "Father of LUKE SKYWALKER and PRINCESS LEIA One-time JEDI KNIGHT and pupil of BEN KENOBI.")

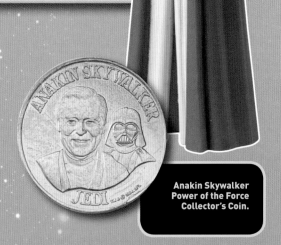

Anakin Skywalker
Power of the Force
Collector's Coin.

This, the final mail-away action figure for the vintage *Star Wars* action figure line, allowed collectors to obtain a representation of the man behind the mask: Jedi Knight Anakin Skywalker, with a design based upon the image of actor David Prowse, who also plays Darth Vader in the original trilogy, before the elder Prowse's image was replaced by young actor Hayden Christensen.

During the course of the character's career as a *padawan* (Jedi in training) and then as a Jedi Knight, Anakin is known as one of the finest pilots in the galaxy, as well as one of the most powerful members of the Jedi Order. Throughout his tenure, debate rages over whether or not the surprisingly potent Anakin is the fabled "Chosen One," a liberator mentioned in an ancient Jedi prophecy as a messianic being who will "… destroy the Sith and bring balance to the force."

Unfortunately, Anakin possesses character flaws. When he experiences a vision of his mother, Shmi, dying at the hands of the Tusken Raiders back on Tatooine, the young Jedi travels back to his home-world and his visions become real, as Shmi is massacred by a clan of Sand People. Allowing the hatred he feels toward the assassins to flow through him, Anakin attacks and slaughters the entire tribe of Sand People, killing warriors, women, and children alike. The Jedi order also underestimates the clever influence of Senator Palpatine upon the young man's passion. Palpatine becomes a mentor to the young Jedi and plays upon Anakin's rage and manipulates the powerful feelings of hatred that run rampant through him, convincing the young Jedi of the unbridled power of the Dark Side of the Force.

Palpatine's guidance reaches a tipping point when, upon hearing Anakin relate the tale of a new vision that he has experienced—a dream that prognosticates the death of his beloved wife, Padmé, in childbirth—the Chancellor plays upon Skywalker's sympathies. Knowing that Anakin will do anything to save her life, Palpatine tells the Jedi that if he turns to the Dark Side of the Force, he can save Padmé. Thus, after chipping away at his self-esteem over time, Palpatine turns Anakin to the Dark Side, involving him in his plans to extinguish the Jedi Order and to assist him in constructing a tyrannical Galactic Empire to succeed the Republic. And Anakin—now dubbed Darth Vader as a newly christened Sith Lord—functions as his strong right hand.

MISB: all contents sealed in mailer: **$50**; **MIB:** w/all included pieces & sealed figure: **$40-$42**; **MIB:** w/all included pieces & non-sealed figure: **$30-$35**; **MOC:** *POTF:* **$2,600-$3,000**, based on the condition of the packaging; **MLC:** **$15-$22**; **Coin itself: $105-$115+**.

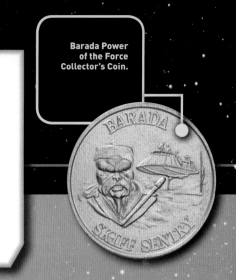

Barada

[Production #93750]

1st appearance: (Sears Exclusive) The Jabba the
Hutt Dungeon action playset (II), tan base, if
obtained via this playset, no POTF coin included
1st carded appearance: 92-back card, POTF cardback
Original Retail Price (average): $2.99

- with Skiff Guard Battle Staff
- with silver POTF "Barada/Skiff Sentry" coin (coin text:
  "One of the many weird creatures who serves as a guard in
  the palace of JABBA THE HUTT.")

There are few explanations of a vintage *Star Wars*
action figure's provenance more complicated than
that of Barada, the head of Jabba the Hutt's (see
Jabba the Hutt Action Playset) motor pool of repulsorlift vehicles (see Desert Sail Skiff, Tatooine Skiff).

Firstly, the character called Barada, Jabba's chief
vehicle expert, is a Klatooinian: Barada is a member of a humanoid race from the planet Klatooine,
a world closely affiliated with the Hutts since
Klatooinians serves as the crime lords' henchmen,
slaves, and mercenary soldiers. Secondly, Barada is
of no relation whatsoever to the previously released
ROTJ character that Kenner named Klaatu (see

Klaatu [In Skiff Guard Uniform]). Klaatu, Jabba's
skiff guard and Barada's first choice as a driver, is
from an entirely different species of humanoid than
Barada: Klaatu's race is that of a Kadas'sa'Nikto
(a.k.a. Green Nikto). So then, Barada's race as a
Klatooinian, and Kenner's use of the name Klaatu
as the proper appellation of a skiff guard, are phonetically similar, yet these similarities are mere
coincidences. Furthermore, the photo based off of a
film still from *Return of the Jedi,* which is plastered
on Barada's POTF package front, is a photo of the
white-shirted Klatooinian named Barada. But the action figure included inside the toy package is sporting
a yellow shirt; the Klatooinian who wore a yellow
shirt in *ROTJ* is actually called Kithaba. So, although
you may believe that the character pictured on the
package front is Barada, the action figure you're re-
ceiving when you open the package is Kithaba.

To complicate things more, you may notice that
Kithaba doesn't wear a backpack in the movie, while
the Kenner action figure does. It is assumed, then,
that Kenner probably chose to give this figure a yellow shirt since the Klatooinian dressed in the yellow
shirt is more noticeable in *Return of the Jedi*—but
they should have omitted his backpack. Discounting
the complex origin of this character, it's up to collectors to determine the fated name used to describe
him—Barada or Kithaba—since evidence exists to
support either of the two characters.

MOC: *POTF*: $90-$100+; **MLC:** $45-
$55; Coin itself: $10.

Barada, with Skiff Guard Battle Staff.

EV-9D9

[Production #93800]

1st appearance: (Sears Exclusive) The Jabba the Hutt Dungeon Action Playset (II), tan base, if obtained via this playset, no POTF coin included
1st carded appearance: 92-back card, POTF cardback
Original Retail Price (average): $2.99

- with silver POTF "EV-9D9/Torture Droid" coin (coin text: "Feared and hated robot who supervised the torture of uncooperative droids in JABBA THE HUTT's dungeon.")

Originally, EV-9D9 was a single unit borne out of MerenData's model line of EV-series supervisor/interrogator droids—a series that is meant to function as, according to Wookieepedia, taskmasters for automated labor pools, such as robots, droids, cyborgs, etc. Unfortunately, the line malfunctioned due to the installation of an incompatible MDF motivator. Without a motivator, a droid will not be able to move—however, this is a type of motivator that should have been installed ONLY into torture droids. This certainly makes the EV-series imbalanced and unstable; however, some unscrupulous consumers respond positively to this (illegal) faulty modification and buy the EV's on the black market, encouraging them to perform their sinister function.

EV-9D9 herself is originally stationed at Cloud City under the purview of Lando Calrissian, the Baron Administrator of the profitable outpost. After a series of mysterious, and sinister, incidences occur that cause the droid to flee, escaping imprisonment for her torturing and destroying a full quarter of all the droids at the colony, she eventually finds her way to the court of interstellar crime lord Jabba Desilijic Tiure (a.k.a. Jabba the Hutt, see Jabba the Hutt Action Playset). Here, EV-9D9 revels in her peerless proficiency to torture helpless droids, a macabre skill that is cultivated and encouraged by her new master.

Inhabiting the boiler room of Jabba's Palace, the area is loosely dedicated to "cyborg operations" within the citadel, and the entire division falls under EV-9D9's oversight. Along with her able assistant Atedeeate (see 8D8), the two droids eradicate the original programming of droids brought to the facility, then re-tool and re-outfit them for obedience. With an opening-and-closing mouth feature, this droid towers over many vintage *Star Wars* action figures.

MOC: *POTF:* **$190-$215+; MLC:** **$80-$90; Coin itself: $12-$15.**

EV-9D9 Power of the Force Collector's Coin.

Lando Calrissian (General Pilot)

[Production #93820]

1st carded appearance: 92-back card, POTF cardback
Original Retail Price (average): $2.99

- with General's Cloak, unique to the figure
- with black Palace Blaster (DL-18 blaster)
- with silver POTF "Lando Calrissian/Rebel General" coin (coin text: "The administrator of CLOUD CITY, LANDO flies the MILLENNIUM FALCON to victory as the REBELS destroy the DEATH STAR.")

Lando Calrissian (General Pilot), with accessories, above; and his Power of the Force Collector's Coin, below.

In the period between *The Empire Strikes Back* (3 ABY) and *Return of the Jedi* (4 ABY), the charming rogue known as Lando Calrissian offers his exceptional skills as an aviator to the Rebel Alliance, co-piloting the *Millennium Falcon* with Chewbacca in the search for his stolen friend Han Solo, and eventually assisting Luke Skywalker in the rescue of the smuggler-turned-hero from the clutches of gangster Jabba the Hutt (see Jabba the Hutt Action Playset) dressed as deceased bounty hunter Tamtel Skreej (see Lando Calrissian, [Skiff Guard Disguise]).

After successfully rescuing Han Solo, productively completing a number of other missions for the Rebellion, and considering his past accomplishments, such as performing a series of brilliant maneuvers within the ice rings of a moon during the Battle of Taanab (0 ABY), Lando is promoted to the rank of General, and tasked to fly the *Millennium Falcon* with a Sullustan co-pilot (see Nien Nunb), while Solo forms a commando strike team to disable the second Death Star's shield generator on the forest moon of Endor. It is Calrissian who saves the lives of the entire Rebel fleet when he perceptively recognizes that the shield protecting the Death Star has not yet been neutralized by Solo's squad. Thanks to his skillful leadership, he gives Han's strike team just enough time to finish their mission, allowing him and Nunb, along with spectacular Rebel pilot Wedge Antilles of Rogue Squadron, to fire the shots that destroy the second Death Star, symbolically bringing an end to the Galactic Empire.

With his beautifully rendered dress cape, General's rank plaque painted in silver, and unique Alliance general's uniform, this Lando Calrissian action figure is a treasured item in many collections.

MOC: *POTF*: $125-$140+; MLC: $55-$65; Coin itself: $10-$12.

Luke Skywalker (In Battle Poncho)

[Production #93710]

1st carded appearance: 92-back card, POTF cardback

Original Retail Price (average): $2.99

- with brown and cream fabric Battle Poncho
- with black plastic belt, with "three settings," similar to Leia Endor's belt, unique to the figure
- with black Palace Blaster (DL-18 blaster)
- with silver POTF "Luke Skywalker/Rebel Leader" coin (coin text: "JEDI KNIGHT and member of ENDOR assault group. On a SPEEDER BIKE, he fearlessly pursued IMPERIAL BIKER SCOUTS.")

Luke Skywalker (in Battle Poncho) Power of the Force Collector's Coin.

After learning of the construction of a second Death Star, Luke follows Han Solo's strike team to the Sanctuary Moon aboard an Imperial shuttlecraft (see Imperial Shuttle vehicle). While-sporting his "battle poncho," Luke assists the Rebels in fending off a squad of Biker Scouts, and befriends a native tribe of Ewoks. However, while Han Solo takes the remaining assault group to secure the Imperial bunker on the forest moon, Luke surrenders himself to Darth Vader, and the two are transported aboard the second Death Star to meet the Emperor. During the Battle of Endor and upon greeting Palpatine, Luke is manipulated into dueling Vader one last time—however, the young man's fighting prowess has grown even more powerful than the highly skilled Sith Lord's, and Vader is defeated. Refusing to kill his father at the behest of the Emperor, the young Jedi Knight declines to duel any longer, and relinquishes his lightsaber.

However, Palpatine does not accept Luke's repudiation of the dark side, and begins to destroy him with powerful bursts of Force lightning. Witnessing the death of his only son, Anakin abandons the dark side, and conquers Darth Vader from within, killing Palpatine to save his son's life—decimating the Galactic Empire as a result. It appears that Anakin is indeed "The Chosen One"; he simply needs a nudge from his son to fulfill the ancient Jedi prophecy and bring balance to the Force.

Oddly enough, this is the only Luke Skywalker action figure produced by Kenner that did not include a lightsaber. Some would argue that in order for it to

Luke Skywalker (in Battle Poncho) accessories.

comfortably fit on a Speeder Bike, Luke's action figure could not have wielded the weapon effectively enough.

MOC: *POTF:* **$105-$115+; MLC: $50-$60; Coin itself: $10-$12**.

Romba [closed mouth showing two white teeth, maroon fur, painted chocolate brown belt]

[Production #93730]

1st carded appearance: 92-back card, POTF cardback
Original Retail Price (average): $2.99

- o very dark brown furred or dark brown furred variations
- • with Romba Spear, flint-pointed*, unique to the figure
- • with Romba Hood, chocolate brown, right hood tassel longer than the left one, unique to the figure
- • with silver POTF "Romba/Ewok" coin (coin text: "An EWOK warrior who uses simple EWOK weapons to protect the planet ENDOR.")

*Note: The spear included with Romba is distinctly different than the one included with Wicket W. Warrick.

In his role as a scout for his tribe of Ewoks who occupy Bright Tree Village (see Ewok Village Playset), Romba is vigilant in his responsibilities to defend the Ewoks from an attacking band of soldiers of the Imperial Army (see AT-ST Driver, Biker Scout, Scout Walker, and Speeder Bike). Setting traps, utilizing bolas to strangulate Imperial troops (see Imperial Stormtrooper), launching catapults against the Empire's AT-STs, Romba is also easily recognized as the Ewok seen mourning over the loss of his friend, Nanta, who was unfortunately killed by artillery fire from a Scout Walker.

Romba Power of the Force Collector's Coin.

Although the Ewoks are prominently featured in *Return of the Jedi*, these diminutive creatures also form the basis of a series of other adventures of dubious canonical authority, such as 1984's successful *Caravan of Courage: An Ewok Adventure*, which focuses on the Towani family being stranded on the Sanctuary Moon of Endor. Its sequel, broadcast in 1985, *Ewoks: The Battle for Endor*, focuses on Cindel, the orphaned Towani child from the first film who assists Wicket (see Wicket W. Warrick) among other members of his tribe to protect Bright Tree Village from the sinister Marauders. Finally, there was ABC's well-received *Star Wars: Ewoks* animated program that takes place shortly before (3.5 ABY) the Battle of Endor (4 ABY), and was story-edited by the brilliant, prolific creator Paul Dini, also responsible for the revolutionary *Batman: The Animated Series*, among endless others, which lasted for two full seasons: 1985 and 1986 (see *Star Wars: Ewoks*).

Romba, with accessories.

 MOC: *POTF:* $85-$105; **MLC:** $50-$60; Coin itself: $10-$12.

Warok [opened mouth shows teeth, head tilt right, tan/gray fur, unpainted lips]

[Production #93810]

1st carded appearance: 92-back card, POTF cardback
Original Retail Price (average): $2.99

- with light-brown Warok Quiver, unpainted, unique to the figure
- with Warok Bow, deeper darker-brown (different from Lumat's maroon bow), unique to the figure
- with Warok Hood, deep dark-brown color; hood ends to the lower left, unique to the figure
- with silver POTF "Warok/Ewok" coin (coin text: "An EWOK warrior who helps the REBELS overcome the deadly SCOUT WALKERS.")

Warok's accessories.

Father of the young philosopher-poet Teebo, the Ewok known as Warok lives in Bright Tree Village (see Ewok Village Playset) with his wife, Batcheela, and daughter, Malani. His first recorded adventure in the canon is fronting a rescue team to retrieve the Ewok village's woklings (young Ewoks) from the evil Duloks and the sinister King Vulgarr. Many years later, Warok is one of the many Ewoks responsible for assisting the Rebel Alliance in defeating the Galactic Empire during the Battle of Endor. However, he is *not* the Ewok responsible for dropping boulders upon an Imperial AT-ST while flying in a glider (see Ewok Combat Glider).

Although George Lucas originally intended that the primitive race assisting the Rebellion to bring about the defeat of the Empire would be Wookiees, since *Episode IV* and *Episode V* had already established that Chewbacca's people were both intimately familiar with and highly proficient with technology, he had to concoct another species: the pocket-sized Ewoks.

Warok Power of the Force Collector's Coin.

Warok, posed with Warok Quiver, Bow, & Hood.

 MOC: *POTF:* $65-$72+; **MLC:** $38-$45; **Coin itself:** $8-$10.

Yak Face [a.k.a. Saelt-Marae] (Tri-Logo exclusive [not sold domestically])

[Production #93840]

1st carded appearance: 92-back card
Original Retail Price (average): $2.99

- with Skiff Guard Battle Staff
- with silver POTF "Yak Face/Bounty Hunter" coin (coin text: "A creature with long facial hair wearing a furry mantle seen in Jabba's Throne Room and on the SAIL BARGE.")

Yak Face, with Skiff Guard Battle Staff.

Yak Face Power of the Force Collector's Coin.

Yak Face is one of the most sought after of all vintage *Star Wars* action figures since he was never distributed in the United States. The action figure was only available on two different packages; two different cards with vastly different values: the first and most common was a Tri-Logo card. This internationally distributed card is dubbed "Tri-Logo" because there are three *Star Wars* logos emblazoned on the card front: English, French, and Spanish. Unfortunately, this Tri-Logo version of Yak Face did not come with a silver-plated collector's coin. The second package—distributed on a Canadian Power of the Force card—featured only English and French languages: "The Power of the Force/Le Pouvoire de la Force" with "SPECIAL Collectors Coin/Piece de Collèction" included. Purchasing this Canadian Power of the Force cardback was the only way to obtain Yak Face's rare collector's coin.

Therefore, Yak Face never saw domestic distribution. Due to the toy's relative scarcity, many collectors rank him as an extremely rare figurine. But while Yak Face is certainly uncommon, he may not actually be rare: perhaps this is simply a case of supply far outweighing demand. Although the figure sometimes did not include any accessories, more often than not, Yak Face could be found either with a Palace Blaster (gray or black) or a Bespin Blaster, yet many more times he was found with a Skiff Guard Battle Staff—precisely the same accessory as the one included with *ROTJ* Nikto and POTF Barada.

Although his character is not given a proper name until the debut of West End Games' magnificent *Star Wars Trilogy Sourcebook, Special Edition*, in the *Star Wars* canon Yak Face is dubbed Saelt-Marae, where the character appears as a member of Jabba's court in *Return of the Jedi*.

As a Yarkora informant and con man, Marae is a highly secretive alien and little information is known regarding his formative existence. It is known he is married, spawned at least one child, yet left his family, as did most Yarkorans, to keep engaged in his favorite criminal enterprises, of which he excels. As an information broker and confidence trickster, Marae's interpersonal intelligence is so advanced that he can wheedle information and data out of his wealthy targets almost effortlessly. Although at one point in his career Marae sells secrets to both the Rebel Alliance and to the Empire, his real profit-making machine is peddling these tidbits to Jabba Desilijic Tiure—and therefore, Marae earns the crime lord's trust. So valuable is he to Jabba (see Jabba the Hutt Action Playset), the gangster keeeps him on as a member of his court where he is handsomely paid. Posing as a simple-minded merchant, Saelt-Marae susses out the disparate plots, conspiracies, and subversions conceived by the other members of Jabba's scheming entourage, and relates every nefarious detail to his Hutt master.

MOC: *POTF* Canadian card, with coin: **$2,300-$2,600++**, Tri-Logo, International card—no coin: **$275-$325++; MLC: $215-$225+; Coin itself**: **$230-$260**, from Canadian card.

POTF Coins
(Figures, re-issued from prior assortments)

These coins could *only* be obtained by purchasing one of these figures at retail—a character from a previous *Star Wars*, *Empire Strikes Back*, or *Return of the Jedi* assortment that was re-released on a Power of the Force cardback.

1. AT-ST DRIVER/EMPIRE
"Driver of the dreaded SCOUT WALKER used in battle against REBELS and EWOKS on ENDOR."
MLC: $22.

2. BIKER SCOUT/EMPIRE
"Imperial soldier who patrolled the planet ENDOR on a SPEEDER BIKE and protected the DEATH STAR's shield generator from REBEL intruders."
MLC: $25-$30.

3. B-WING PILOT/REBEL
"Courageous REBEL flyer who piloted the spectacular B-WING FIGHTER during the final REBEL assault on the EMPIRE's last DEATH STAR."
MLC: $10-$15.

4. CHEWBACCA/WOOKIEE
"A 200-year-old giant WOOKIEE who co-pilots the MILLENNIUM FALCON. Loyal friend of HAN SOLO."
MLC: $25-$30.

5. C-3PO/PROTOCOL DROID
(See-Threepio/C-3PO, with Removable Limbs), "A DROID who translates millions of galactic languages, including electronic tongues spoken by many DROIDS. R2-D2's companion."
MLC: $15-$22.

6. DARTH VADER/ LORD OF THE SITH
"LORD OF THE SITH who personifies the evil of the GALACTIC EMPIRE. Uses powers to seek destruction of REBEL ALLIANCE."
MLC: $32-$38.

7. EMPEROR/ GALACTIC RULER
"Supreme ruler of the GALACTIC EMPIRE, who enlists DARTH VADER's help to turn LUKE SKYWALKER to the dark side of THE FORCE."
MLC: $25.

8. GAMORREAN GUARD/ PALACE SENTRY
"Imposing, pig-like creatures who guarded entrances to JABBA THE HUTT's castle, throne room, and dungeon."
MLC: $50.

9. HAN SOLO/REBEL
(Han Solo In Trench Coat), "Daredevil pilot of the MILLENNIUM FALCON. Technically not a member of the REBEL ALLIANCE. HAN lends his support when most needed."
MLC: $15.

10. JAWAS
"Furry, cloaked inhabitant of TATOOINE who captured R2-D2 and C-3PO and sold them to LUKE SKYWALKER's uncle."
MLC: $25-$30.

11. LUKE SKYWALKER/ JEDI (X-WING PILOT)
"A young farmer who became a REBEL pilot and JEDI KNIGHT. He helped lead the ALLIANCE in their battle against the EMPIRE."
MLC: $20.

12. LUKE SKYWALKER/ JEDI KNIGHT
"As a brave JEDI KNIGHT, LUKE SKYWALKER gained entrance to JABBA THE HUTT's throne room by using a JEDI mind trick on the guards."
MLC: $20.

13. LUMAT
"This older EWOK is an expert wood carver who has used his skills to help build the EWOK VILLAGE and make other EWOK utensils."
MLC: $12.

14. OBI-WAN KENOBI/ JEDI MASTER
"Former JEDI KNIGHT who served in the CLONE WARS long ago. BEN KENOBI teaches LUKE SKYWALKER to utilize the FORCE."
MLC: $40-$45.

15. PAPLOO/EWOK
"Young EWOK Scout whose love of adventure sometimes gets him--and his EWOK friends-into trouble."
MLC: $12.

16. PRINCESS LEIA/REBEL LEADER
(Leia Organa In Combat Poncho), "Once senator and princess on ALDERAAN, PRINCESS LEIA is a dedicated leader of the REBEL ALLIANCE, undaunted in her struggle to overthrow Imperial tyranny."
MLC: $12.

17. STORMTROOPER/ EMPIRE
"One of the many thousands of drones of the GALACTIC EMPIRE. Totally dedicated to THE EMPEROR, they carried out a reign of terror among the worlds of the galaxy."
MLC: $25.

18. TEEBO/EWOK
"A large EWOK who, with WICKET, serves as a guide for the REBELS on ENDOR."
MLC: $15.

19. WICKET/THE EWOK
"Loveable, furry inhabitant of ENDOR who befriended PRINCESS LEIA after her SPEEDER BIKE was destroyed by BIKER SCOUTS."
MLC: $12.

20. YODA/THE JEDI MASTER
"A small creature who dwells on the bog planet of DAGOBAH. The former teacher of BEN KENOBI, YODA has trained JEDI KNIGHTS for over 800 years."
MLC: $60-70+.

1. AT-AT
"Dreaded armored four-legged machines manned by IMPERIAL PILOTS used in attack on the REBELS on HOTH."
MLC: $100.

2. BIB FORTUNA/ MAJORDOMO
"Gruesome-looking, low-life creature who served as JABBA THE HUTT's confidant and right-hand man."
MLC: $125.

POTF Coins
(mail-away)

These exceedingly rare POTF coins could *only* be obtained randomly via Kenner's final mail-away promotion found on a sticker pasted on the front of 79-back and 92-back action figure packages, and it was nearly impossible to obtain a full set of 62 coins this way.

3. BOBA FETT/BOUNTY HUNTER
"The most notorious bounty hunter in the galaxy, BOBA FETT tracks HAN SOLO and returns him to JABBA THE HUTT for bounty."
MLC: $225.

4. Chief Chirpa/ Ewok Leader
"Chief of the EWOK tribe. A brave leader who guides the EWOKS on ENDOR with strength and wisdom."
MLC: $50.

5. Star Wars/Creatures
"Bizarre-looking low life aliens who hang out in local cantinas and are suspicious of all outsiders."
MLC: $125.

6. Star Wars/Droids
"Galactic robots with advanced high-tech features. Programmed for a variety of specialized technical operations."
MLC $125.

7. Emperor's Royal Guard/Empire
"Majestic troops who greeted THE EMPEROR upon his arrival for the inspection of the nearly-completed DEATH STAR battle station."
MLC: $80.

8. FX-7/Medical Droid
"Medical DROID trained in basic first aid. Examined LUKE SKYWALKER after hi escape from the vicious WAMPA beast."
MLC: $190.

9. Greedo/ Bounty Hunter
"An alien creature killed by HAN SOLO in the cantina at MOS EISLEY when he attempted to collect the money HAN SOLO owed JABBA THE HUTT."
MLC: $190.

10. Han Solo/Rebel Fighter (original)
"Heroic friend to the ALLIANCE who is betrayed by LANDO CALRISSIAN and then frozen in carbonite by the EMPIRE."
MLC: $190.

11. Han Solo/ Rebel Hero
(Han Solo, Hoth Battle Gear), "Caring and loyal friend of the REBELS. He braved the icy wilderness of HOTH in search of LUKE SKYWALKER."
MLC: $100.

12. Hoth Stormtrooper/ Empire
(Imperial Stormtrooper, Hoth Battle Gear),"Trained soldiers who relentlessly led DARTH VADER's invasion of HOTH."
MLC: $250.

13. Imperial Commander/ Empire

"One of several of the EMPIRE's high-ranking military leaders who reported to the insidious Commander of the DEATH STAR--MOFF JERJERROD."

MLC: $70.

14. Lando Calrissian/ Rebel General (original)

"Handsome, charismatic con artist, and old friend of HAN SOLO's, who lived in CLOUD CITY and owned a TIBANNA gas mine in the BESPIN system."

MLC: $80.

15. Logray

"Trusted EWOK Medicine Man. With his magical powers, he has the ability to save the tribe from danger."

MLC: $50.

16. Luke Skywalker/ Rebel Leader (original)

"Once a naive farmboy on TATOOINE, LUKE was plunged into the rebellion when encountering BEN KENOBI and PRINCESS LEIA."

MLC: $100.

17. Luke Skywalker/ Rebel Leader

(Luke Skywalker, Hoth Battle Gear), "Rebel pilot who battled the nearly invincible, mammoth AT-ATs on HOTH with the highly maneuverable SNOWSPEEDER."

MLC: $100.

18. Luke Skywalker/ Jedi Knight

(Luke Skywalker, Bespin Fatigues), "Commander of the REBEL FORCES who rushed to CLOUD CITY to rescue his friends. There he battled DARTH VADER in a ferocious LIGHTSABER duel."

MLC: $85-95+.

19. Millennium Falcon/ Star Wars

"HAN SOLO's famous space vehicle used by The REBEL heroes in their attacks on The Empire."

MLC: $100.

20. Princess Leia/ Rebel Leader (original)

"Determined young princess who resourcefully stored the REBEL escape plans in R2-D2 when IMPERIAL FORCES attacked the REBEL BLOCKADE RUNNER."

MLC: $115.

21. Princess Leia/Boushh

"PRINCESS LEIA in disguise as BOUNTY HUNTER to gain entry into JABBA's palace to save HAN SOLO."

MLC: $210.

22. Star Wars/Sail Barge

(or "Sail Skiff"), "JABBA THE HUTT's desert sailcraft used to transport REBELS to the SARLACC pit."

MLC: $700.

23. Star Destroyer Commander/Empire

"Pilot of the EMPIRE's enormous, wedge-shaped STAR DESTROYER, one of the largest and most lethal vehicles in the IMPERIAL fleet."

MLC: $70.

24. TIE Fighter Pilot/ Empire

"Relentless pilot of an IMPERIAL TIE FIGHTER who tried unsuccessfully to stop LUKE SKYWALKER and other REBELS from destroying the DEATH STAR."

MLC: $65.

25. Too-One Bee/ Medical Droid

"Robot surgeon for the ALLIANCE. Programmed to perform operations with precision. Repaired LUKE SKYWALKER's hand after his LIGHTSABER duel with DARTH VADER."

MLC: $105.

26. Tusken Raider/ Sand People

"Desert nomads who inhabited the plains of TATOOINE. When they ambushed LUKE SKYWALKER, he was rescued by BEN (OBI-WAN) KENOBI."

MLC: $170.

27. Zuckuss/ Bounty Hunter

"A battle-scarred human Bounty Hunter summoned by Darth Vader in his pursuit of the Millennium Falcon and its crew."

MLC: $210.

STAR WARS: DROIDS
The Adventures of R2-D2 and C-3PO

The figures released in 1985 under the *Star Wars: Droids (The Adventures of R2-D2 and C-3PO)* banner were directly based upon the animated series of the same name. Although the animation seems pedestrian in comparison to more modern *Star Wars* CGI-animation—such as the brilliant *Clone Wars* cartoon—the story editor of *Star Wars: Droids*, Brett Burtt, incorporated specific allusions used within the narrative of *Droids* episodes in select story elements within the prequel trilogy, since he edited *Star Wars, Episodes I-III*. For instance, the Boonta Eve Classic, the largest annual podrace in the known galaxy, which is featured in *The Phantom Menace*, had been previously established in the premiere episode of *Star Wars: Droids*, "The White Witch," nearly thirty years ago.

Although some insist this program is *not* part of the *Star Wars* canon, the *Star Wars: Droids (The Adventures of R2-D2 and C-3PO)* animated program recounts events that take place during the nineteen-year span between *Star Wars Episode III: Revenge of the Sith* and *Star Wars Episode IV: A New Hope*. The *Droids* cartoon, which ran from 1985 to 1986 on ABC, follows the exploits of the two most popular droids in the *Star Wars* galaxy: the loquacious C-3PO, voiced by Anthony Daniels from the films, and his determined companion, R2-D2, as the two robots serve a series of four different masters over the course of thirteen episodes and one television special, *The Great Heap*.

Kenner's *Droids'* toy line was the closest of the two animated program/toy tie-in spin-offs to the vintage line and included an assortment of twelve action figures, two of which were straight re-issues of *Star Wars* figures in "Droids" packaging (Boba Fett and A-Wing Pilot) and two others used the same molds as their *Star Wars* counterparts, but were rendered in different paint and/or sticker schemes (C-3PO and R2-D2). Kenner also produced three outstanding vehicles for this line: the ATL-Interceptor, the Side Gunner, and the beautifully constructed, highly prized, and very expensive A-Wing Fighter.

It is worth noting that Kenner had planned on producing a second series of Droids figures highlighting

Star Wars: Droids **features the exploits of popular droids C-3PO and R2-D2.**
Disney/Lucasfilm/Nevala/Heritage Auctions

characters that were featured prominently in the animated series. Of these figures, only Vlix ("Vlix Oncard," from his coin text: TIG FROMM'S constant companion and watchdog and the 'best dressed' gangster around) made it to the commercial market, being offered in Brazil by the Glasslite toy company. Due to its ridiculous level of rarity—far rarer than even the double-telescoping lightsabers of Ben (Obi-Wan) Kenobi, Darth Vader, and Luke Skywalker—the Vlix figure is the single hardest-to-find vintage *Star Wars* action figure, commanding upwards of $3,000 in good condition, with mint specimens fetching more than $3,500 each. It is rumored that less than a dozen of these figures exist in the hands of collectors, but the samples of reproduction figures on a reproduction cardback are sometimes utilized for the sake of reference.

R2-D2: Droids version, with Lightsaber.

R2-D2 Collector's Coin.

A-Wing Pilot Collector's Coin.

Artoo-Detoo* (R2-D2)

[Production #71780]

1st carded appearance: Star Wars—Droids cardback, 1985
Original Retail Price (average): $2.99

- with paper "animated details" label/sticker, unique to the figure
- with pop-up green Lightsaber, with circle on hilt, unlike the 1984 POTF version, unique to the figure
- with gold Star Wars: Droids "R2-D2/Rebel Droid" coin (coin text: "A DROID designed for mechanical repair and data storage. He uses his collection of tools to get out of tight situations.")

*Note: Although this R2-D2 figure still possesses a 1977 date stamp, since Kenner utilized the 1978 R2-D2 body mold, this figure was produced in 1985.

A-wing Pilot

[Production #93830]

1st carded appearance: Star Wars—Droids cardback, 1985
Original Retail Price (average): $2.99

- with black Endor Blaster (Merr-Sonn Munitions DD6 "Light" Blaster Pistol)
- with gold Star Wars: Droids "A-wing Pilot/Rebel" coin (coin text: "Brave REBEL PILOT of the awesome A-WING FIGHTER. Took an active part in the successful attack on the new, more powerful DEATH STAR."]

This—the fourth vintage version of the galaxy's favorite astromech droid—is a simple repaint of the POTF version of R2-D2 (Artoo-Detoo, With Pop Up Lightsaber) with a newly designed paper label—and is described on his *Star Wars: Droids* cardback as follows: "A feisty maintenance DROID whose hidden gadgets save him and his friends from galactic perils … special feature: turn head: lightsaber pops-up!" This animated translation of Artoo-Detoo also comes with an all-new *Droids* version of his collector's coin, sporting different text.

This second version of Kenner's A-wing Pilot action figure, described on his cardback as the " … daring and fearless pilot of the speedy A-WING FIGHTER," is exactly like his earlier-released POTF figurine in every detail, except for including a new gold *Droids* version of his coin within his very rare *Droids* cardback—and both he loose, gold-plated coin and a MOC sealed package are impossibly difficult to obtain.

MOC: $250-$265+; **MLC:** with coin: $205-$215+, without coin: $175-$185+; Coin itself: $35-$50+.

MOC: $385-$425+; **MLC:** with coin: $135-$150, without coin: $65-$70; Coin itself: $75-$90+

Boba Fett

[Production #39260]

1st carded appearance: Star Wars—Droids cardback, 1985
Original Retail Price (average): $2.99

- o armor shade variations
- • with solid black Imperial Blaster (E-11 blaster rifle)
- • with gold Star Wars: Droids "Boba Fett/Bounty Hunter" coin (coin text: "The most notorious bounty hunter in the galaxy, BOBA FETT tracks HAN SOLO and returns him to JABBA THE HUTT for bounty.")

Boba Fett Collector's Coin.

Boba Fett: Droids version, with Imperial Blaster.

This iteration of Boba Fett, "the most notorious bounty hunter in the galaxy," is designed exactly like his previously released *Star Wars* action figure; however, there are two new additions to his accoutrements: the collector's coin included within the action figure's very rare *Star Wars: Droids* packaging has a gold-plated metallic finish (not silver, like his mail-away POTF version), while the Imperial blaster included with Fett is cast in jet black—not the common blue/black color of his original weapon.

MOC: $1,250-$1,400+;
MLC: with coin: **$375-$405+**, without coin: **$25-$32+;**
Coin itself: $350-$375+.

Jann Tosh

[Production #71840]

1st carded appearance: Star Wars—Droids cardback, 1985
Original Retail Price (average): $2.99

- • with solid black IG-88 Rifle ("modified" DLT-20A blaster rifle, unique to the figure)
- • with gold Star Wars: Droids "Jann Tosh/Adventurer" coin (coin text: "A teenage orphan who purchases R2-D2, C-3PO and KEZ IBAN at an auction in TYNE's HORKY. Later he helps KEZ IBAN regain his kingdom as MON JULPA, the lost prince.")

Jann Tosh Collector's Coin.

Possessing a uniquely colored IG-88 rifle cast in solid black, Jann Tosh is described as "a teenager who was orphaned in the Clone Wars and now travels with (his) adventurous UNCLE GUNDY." Tosh was an adventurer who, like Luke Skywalker, yearned for something more than what could be found within his simple homeworld.

MOC: $48-$60+; MLC: $40-$45+;
Coin itself: $10-$12+.

Jann Tosh, with IG-88 Rifle.

Jord Dusat

[Production #71810]

- with black Zuckuss Rifle (loosely based on the long BlasTech W-90 concussion rifle]
- with gold Star Wars: Droids "Jord Dusat/Thrill Seeker" coin (coin text: "From the planet ANOO, she aids THALL JOBEN in battling SISE and TIG FROMM's villainous INGO OPERATION.")

With the exact same type of rifle possessed by Zuckuss (well … 4-LOM), the kind-hearted Jord Dusat functions as "THALL JOBEN's best friend—a 'tough' guy who wants to become a speeder racing champion." A first-rate mechanic, he assists Thall and the two droids in fleeing from the Fromm gang.

MOC: $50-$65; MLC: $25-$35+; Coin itself: $10-$12+.

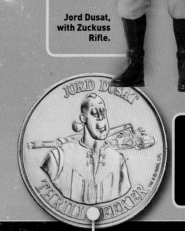

Jord Dusat, with Zuckuss Rifle.

Jord Dusat Collector's Coin.

Kea Moll

[Production #71800]

- with gray Bespin Blaster (DH-17 blaster pistol)
- with gold Star Wars: Droids "Jord Dusat/Thrill Seeker" coin (coin text: "A friend of THALL JOBEN's who helps him rescue R2-D2 and C-3PO from INGO's barren, acid salt flats.")

The resistance fighter known as Kea Moll is described on her package back as a "brave and beautiful teenager from the planet ANNOO who can handle any challenge," and so she allies with Jord Dusat, Thall Joben, R2-D2, and C-3PO on their adventures.

MOC: $45-$55+; MLC: $35-$45+; Coin itself: $8-$10+.

Kea Moll, with Bespin Blaster.

Kea Moll Collector's Coin.

Kez-Iban

[Production #71850]

- with solid black Imperial Blaster (E-11 blaster rifle)
- with blue satchel, unique to the figure
- with gold Star Wars: Droids "Kez-Iban/Lost Prince" coin (coin text: "An Alien from TAMMUZAN who has been stripped of his mind by the evil Vizier ZATEC-CHA. JANN TOSH rescues him from KLEB ZELLOCK.")

Kez-Iban, Droids Collector's Coin.

Armed with an E-11 Imperial blaster rifle that is cast in all-black plastic: just like the ones which came with the Droids version of Boba Fett and Thall Joben; the rifle is not the common blue/black color of the original ubiquitous vintage *Star Wars* weapon. The hidden mystery behind the first animated *Star Wars: Droids* tale, Kez-Iban is essentially "a lost prince (MON-JULPA) who was left to wander from planet to planet after his memory was stripped by an evil vizier."

 MOC: $52-$60; MLC: $35-$40+; Coin itself: $12-$15.

Kez-Iban with accessories.

See-Threepio (C-3PO)

[Production #71770]

- with gold Star Wars: Droids "C-3PO/Droids" coin (coin text: "A protocol DROID conversant in over 6MM forms of communication. He is seeking a new master with his friend R2-D2.")

This marks the rarest version of the melodramatic protocol droid known as C-3PO, and is essentially the exact same action figure as the second version of the Rebel hero—See-Threepio (C-3PO, with Removable Limbs), his arms and legs are removable from his torso—except that instead of vac-metallized golden chrome covering the figurine's body, he has been painted to match the colors he exhibited in *Star Wars: Droids*. His character, however, remains exactly the same, as evidenced by the text on his package back: "(C-3PO is a) protocol DROID and a translator of human/cyborg/alien languages ... a critical, but devoted companion to ARTOO-DETOO (R2-D2)."

 MOC: $300-$320; MLC: $240-$265+; Coin itself: $12-$15.

C-3PO: Droids version, with Removable Limbs.

C-3PO: Droids version, Droids Collector's Coin.

Sise Fromm

[Production #71820]

- with purple pull-over robe, unique to the figure
- with gold Star Wars: Droids "Sise Fromm/Gang Leader" coin (coin text: "A 900-year-old convict who is the notorious leader of an underworld gang of thugs and cutthroats.")

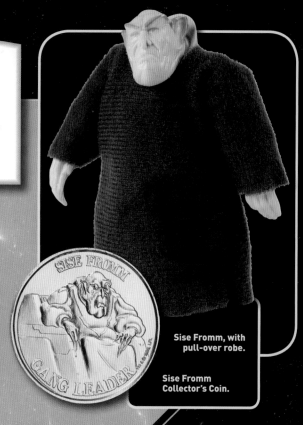

"One of the most notorious gang leaders in the galaxy whose secret desire is to run THE EMPIRE," the sinister Sise Fromm and his Fromm Gang of criminal thugs constructed the Trigon One satellite to subjugate and terrorize the inhabitants of the backwater Mid Rim world known as Ingo: specifically, R2-D2, C-3PO, and their masters Thall Joben and Jord Dusat, along with their ally, Kea Moll.

 MOC: $300-$320; MLC: $225-$245+; Coin itself: $28-$40.

Sise Fromm, with pull-over robe.

Sise Fromm Collector's Coin.

Thall Joben

[Production #71790]

- with solid black Imperial Blaster (E-11 blaster rifle)
- with gold Star Wars: Droids "Thall Joben/Speeder Racer" coin (coin text: "From the planet INGO, THALL is the one-time master of C-3PO and R2-D2. He defeats TIG and SISE FROMM and the TRIGON ONE.")

Thall Joben, with Imperial Blaster.

The protagonist for the first narrative block of *Star Wars: Droids*, Thall Joben and his friend Jord Dusat are teenagers " … from the planet INGO with a passion for speeder racing," prior to podraces taking place in the *Star Wars* canon at the Boonta Eve Challenge in *Episode I.*

 MOC: $50-$002, MLC: $25-$30; Coin itself: $10-$12.

THALL JOBEN Collector's Coin

Tig Fromm

[Production #71830]

- with medical staff
- with gold Star Wars: Droids "Tig Fromm/ Techno-Villain" coin (coin text: "Also known as 'Baby Face,' TIG FROMM is the younger son of SISE FROMM. He overseas the FIENDISH INGO OPERATION.")

Tig Fromm, with Medical Staff.

Tig Fromm Collector's Coin.

Although his cardback states that Tig Fromm is "the leader of an underworld gang of thugs and cutthroats who prey on the weak and helpless of INGO," nothing could be further from the truth: "Tiggy"—a nickname his father's bodyguard, Vlix, would mock him with—exemplified the *worst* qualities of any cartoon villain: he was overconfident, arrogant, incompetent, and foolish.

 MOC: $175-$210+; MLC: $145-$170+; Coin itself: $25-$35+.

Uncle Gundy (Putch Gundarian)

[Production #71880]

- with black-colored Ree-Yees blaster-staff
- with gold Star Wars: Droids "Uncle Gundy/ Prospector" coin (coin text: "Uncle to JANN TOSH and master of C-3PO and R2-D2. The DROIDS help him discover a fortune mining KESHELS.")

Uncle Gundy, with Rees-Yees Blaster-Staff.

Uncle Gundy Collector's Coin.

Orphaned as young boy and with no family to speak of, Jann Tosh became the ward of his father's best friend, Putch Gundarian, on the ore-rich world of Tyne's Horky. Nicknamed "Uncle Gundy," Gundarian was " … an old fortune hunter whose hard luck never discourages him from seeking the 'pot of gold' on every planet," he does eventually strike it rich …

 MOC: $65-$80+; MLC: $42-$55; Coin itself: $12-$14+.

STAR WARS: EWOKS

Following *Return of the Jedi,* Lucasfilm produced two Ewok-based spinoffs for ABC television: 1984's *Caravan of Courage: An Ewok Adventure,* and its sequel, broadcast in 1985, *Ewoks: The Battle for Endor.*

Hoping to capture the imagination of the horde of voracious young consumers who adored the furry, quirky, cute, teddy bear-esque Ewoks, the *Ewoks* animated series was broadcast from 1985 to 1986. Also created by George Lucas and his faithful team, the *Ewoks* cartoon revolves around the antics of Wicket W. Warrick, Princess Kneesaa, and their tribe of Ewoks as they fight against another clan, the sinister Duloks—distant cousins to the Ewoks. Lasting one season longer than *Droids,* ABC's *Ewoks* ran for two full seasons (*Ewoks,* and *All-New Ewoks*) of thirteen episodes each.

The Kenner Ewoks toy line was targeted for younger children, as the figures' lack of poseability and bright colors suggest. Of the two spin-offs cartoons—*Droids and Ewoks*—the Ewoks line is least similar to the original vintage *Star Wars* action figures. Although only six characters from the cartoon were released at retail (more were planned), no vehicles or playsets accompanied these toys. Rather than engage in the costly process of repackaging older *Star Wars* vehicles and playsets under the Ewoks banner, Kenner simply re-solicited Ewok-themed toys from *Star Wars'* Power of the Force and *Return of the Jedi* assortments and offered them on (yet not boxed inside) Ewoks packaging, so the Return of the Jedi Ewok Village, Ewok Combat Glider, Ewok Assault Catapult, and the Power of the Force Ewok Battle Wagon wound up on a 1985 *Star Wars: Ewoks* card back.

The six characters released as action figures were: Wicket W. Warrick, a friendly and inquisitive young Ewok who loves adventure; Logray, the wise old medicine man who aids the Ewoks with magic spells and potions; King Gorneesh, the conniving king of the Duloks who hopes to enslave the Ewoks; Urgah Lady Gorneesh, the sly mate of King Gorneesh who aids him in his devious plans; Dulok Scout, a loathsome, villainous, swamp-dwelling creature who spies on the Ewoks; and finally, the Dulok Shaman, an inept "witch doctor" who uses nasty tricks to attempt to frighten or outwit the Ewoks. Unfortunately, like the Droids line, many important characters were not produced, such as Morag, the Tulgah Witch, due to the short period of the toys' release.

The Ewoks were such popular characters that they earned their own cartoon. *Disney/Lucasfilm/Nelvana/ABC*

Dulok Scout, with
Dulok Club.

Dulok Scout

[Production #71160]

1st carded appearance: Star Wars—Ewoks
cardback, 1985
Original Retail Price (average): $2.99

- with brown Dulok Club, unique to the figure
- with bronze EWOKS "Scout/Dulok" coin (coin text:
  "Typical of the many DULOKS (distant cousins of
  the EWOKS), who live in the swamps on ENDOR.")

Described on the character's cardback as "a loathsome, villainous,
swamp-dwelling creature who spies on
the EWOKS."

 MOC: $32-$45+; MLC:
$18-$32+; Coin itself:
$4-$8.

Dulok Scout
Collector's Coin.

Dulok Shaman, with
Dulok Shaman Staff.

Dulok Shaman (a.k.a. Umwak)

[Production #71150]

1st carded appearance: Star Wars—Ewoks
cardback, 1985
Original Retail Price (average): $2.99

- with long dark brown Dulok Shaman Staff,
  unique to the figure
- with bronze EWOKS "Shaman/Dulok" coin (coin
  text: "The professed DULOK medicine man
  who steals LOGRAY's potions by becoming
  invisible with magic soap.")

Delineated as "an inept 'witch doctor,' who uses
nasty tricks to attempt to frighten or outwit the
Ewoks," the character's name in the animated series
is actually "Umwak."

 MOC: $32-$45+; MLC: $18-$32+;
Coin itself: $4-$8.

Dulok Shaman
Collector's Coin.

King Gorneesh

[Production #71180]

1st carded appearance: Star Wars—Ewoks cardback, 1985
Original Retail Price (average): $2.99

- with long gray Dulok Chieftain Staff, unique to the figure
- with bronze EWOKS "King Gorneesh/Dulok" coin (coin text: "King of the evil DULOKS who leads them in attacks on their distant cousin, the EWOKS.")

King Gorneesh with Staff.

The character's cardback describes Gorneesh as follows: "The conniving king of the Duloks who hopes to enslave the Ewoks."

 MOC: $42-$58+; MLC: $26-$40+; Coin itself: $9-$13.

King Gorneesh Collector's Coin.

Logray: Ewoks version

[Production #71260]

1st carded appearance: Star Wars—Ewoks cardback, 1985
Original Retail Price (average): $2.99

- with brown Ewok Shaman Staff, unique to the figure
- with bronze EWOKS "Logray/Ewok Shaman" coin (coin text: "An old EWOK medicine man, LOGRAY's wisdom and magic are used to avert all kinds of crises on ENDOR.")

Logray, with Ewok Shaman Staff.

This second version of the Ewok medicine man, who is eventually ousted from the clan, is delineated on his package back as follows: "Wise old medicine man who aids the Ewoks with magic spells and potions."

 MOC: $60-$75+; MLC: $35-$48+; Coin itself: $9-$13.

Logray Collector's Coin.

Lady Gorneesh.

Urgah Lady Gorneesh

[Production #71170]

1st carded appearance: Star Wars—Ewoks cardback, 1985
Original Retail Price (average): $2.99
- with bronze EWOKS "Urgah/Dulok" coin (coin text: "KING GORNEESH's consort and partner in his dirty deeds against the EWOKS.")

The only female figure of this line, she is described on her character's cardback as the "sly mate of King Gorneesh, who aids him in his devious plans."

MOC: $42-$60+; MLC: $22-$32+;
Coin itself: $4-$8.

Lady Gorneesh Collector's Coin.

Wicket W. Warrick, with Ewok Spear.

Wicket W. Warrick: Ewoks version

[Production #71250]

1st carded appearance: Star Wars—Ewoks cardback, 1985
Original Retail Price (average): $2.99
- with light tan Ewok Spear, unique to the figure
- with bronze EWOKS "Ewok/Ewok Scout" coin (coin text: "WICKET's friendly adventurous and mischievous nature makes him a leader among other young EWOKS."

The key character in nearly every iteration of media involving the Ewoks, Wicket is succinctly described on his action figure's package back as "a friendly and inquisitive young Ewok who loves adventure."

MOC: $125-$150+; MLC: $60-$78+;
Coin itself: $15-$20.

Wicket Collector's Coin.

Apart from the language utilized on the toy packages, it should be mentioned that collectors have run into problems with these figures and their removable boots. Originally, figures such as Luke Skywalker, who did not have socks or stockings as a barrier between their supple plastic "skin" and their soft plastic boots, came with a paper notice inserted into their packages: "IMPORTANT—to remove and replace action boots, simply sprinkle a little talcum powder into back of boots."

Large Size R2-D2, opened secret compartment.

Artoo-Detoo (R2-D2)

[Production #38630]

1st packaged appearance: late 1978
Original Retail Price (average): $7.99
Action Features:

- 7-1/2" poseable figure
- "Chromed" head "clicks" when turned
- button opens door to secret compartment
- Death Star Plans card
- Simulated "electronic circuits" card
- Authentically detailed
- Roll R2-D2 on wheels

The two included accessories that are hidden within R2-D2's panel are not simply labeled as "Death Star Plans": one represents these Death Star Plans, while the other represents an Electronic Circuit Card. Fans should also take heed that this version of R2-D2 is not the remote-controlled version of the toy, a fact emblazoned all over the toy's box. Like his original 3-3/4-inch counterpart, large size R2-D2 is subject to yellowing when exposed to sunlight or heat—so please make sure to purchase samples that possess little to no yellowing to his white plastic.

Large Size R2-D2's easily lost and removable accessories: removable "Death Star Plans" (flat panel #1 with label), simulated "Electronic Circuit" Card (flat panel #2 with label).

MISB: $675-$725+; **MIB:** pure white plastic: **$135-$160+**, plus some mild yellowing: **$90-$110**; **MLC:** pure white plastic: **$50-$65+**, some mild yellowing: **$24-$32**.

R2-D2's "Electronic Circuit" Card, left, and "Death Star Plans" panel to its right.

Ben (Obi-Wan) Kenobi

[Production #39340]

1st packaged appearance: 1979
Original Retail Price (average): $10.99
Action Features:

- 12″ poseable figure
- Lightsaber
- Moveable arms, legs, shoulders, and neck
- Clothed in black turtle neck, white gown, and hooded cloak
- Authentically detailed

CLOSE-UP
Ben (Obi-Wan) Kenobi's yellow lightsaber.

Fans may "create the fun and excitement of *Star Wars* with poseable Ben (Obi-Wan) Kenobi figure … relive Ben (Obi-Wan) Kenobi's encounter with Stormtroopers," reenacting " … his battle with Darth Vader." Collectors should beware of reproduction lightsabers ($5-$10 each), since they are of far inferior construction, selling for a quarter of the value of Ben's original saber ($35-$40+ each). Oddly enough, this figure came with a yellow lightsaber, while 12-inch Luke came with a blue one— the exact reverse of their 3-3/4-inch counterparts.

Large Size Ben Kenobi's easily lost and removable accessories: black turtleneck, yellow lightsaber, hooded brown cloak, white tunic/gown, pair of brown boots.

Large Size Ben (Obi-Wan) Kenobi, with yellow lightsaber.

 MISB: $240-$285+; **MIB:** $115-$125+; **MLC:** $70-$85+.

Boba Fett's "See-thru" viewport lens.

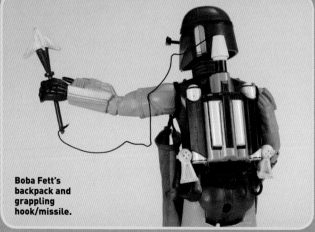

Boba Fett's backpack and grappling hook/missile.

Boba Fett

[Production #39140]

1st packaged appearance: 1979 (SW packaging); 1980 (ESB packaging)
Original Retail Price (average): $10.99
Action Features:

- 13" poseable figure
- fold-down "See-thru" viewport lens in helmet, targeting rangefinder w/holographic targeting display, (borrowed from Kenner's Six Million Dollar Man toy technology)
- "Clicking" pretend range finder on helmet
- Backpack containing grappling hook with attached rope, and swiveling jet pods
- Laser pistol and utility belt
- Wookiee scalps
- Removable cape
- Lensatic "life support" indicator in chest plate, marked by a label only—not an actual "part"
- articulated head, shoulders, elbows, wrists, knees, and hips

Large Size Boba Fett.

It is worth noting that this is "everyone's favorite" large size figure due to its fabulous appearance, brilliant accessories, and wonderful articulation, and as such garners high prices on the secondary market. Unfortunately, combining his popularity with the fact that the figurine possessed a bevy of loose parts, many unscrupulous sellers will include reproduction parts (Wookiee scalps, capes, etc.) with the figure and pass if off as authentic—so please be careful to examine loose specimens carefully. There are also three labels that are often found missing on samples: a round sticker, a white rectangular logo dead center of his chest, and a badge off to the right: there have never been reproduction labels produced for these indicators.

Large Size Boba Fett's easily lost and removable accessories: backpack (Mitronomon Z-6 jetpack with grappling hook with attached rope with hard plastic circle, and swiveling jet pods [directional thrusters]), laser pistol (EE-3 carbine rifle w/scope and fast-draw shoulder sling), cape, utility belt, Wookiee scalps.

MISB: $1,550-$1,750+; MIB: $235-$260+; MLC: $165-$195+.

Boba Fett's accessories.

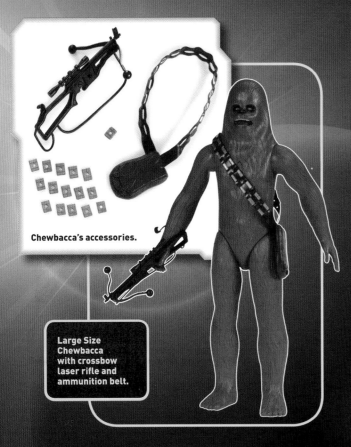

Chewbacca's accessories.

Large Size Chewbacca with crossbow laser rifle and ammunition belt.

Darth Vader's Cape and lightsaber.

Large Size Darth Vader, posed with red lightsaber and wearing cape.

Chewbacca

[Production #38600]

1st packaged appearance: 1978
Original Retail Price (average): $10.99
Action Features:

- 15" poseable figure
- cartridges snap onto crossbow laser rifle
- ammunition belt with removable cartridges (bandolier, i.e., utility belt)
- authentic crossbow laser rifle (Bowcaster, "Wookiee Crossbow")

Large Size Chewbacca's easily lost and removable accessories: Bandolier Strap (pliable plastic with slots) with attached hard plastic pouch, bowcaster/crossbow, and 16 Bandolier cartridges (a few of which are almost always found missing in loose samples).

 MISB: $375-$400+; MIB: $120-$135+; MLC: $55-$70.

Darth Vader

[Production # 38610]

1st packaged appearance: 1978
Original Retail Price (average): $10.99
Action Features:

- 15" poseable figure
- Red lightsaber
- Removable extra large cloth cape, with tie
- Authentically detailed

Large Size Darth Vader's easily lost and removable accessories: Cape and lightsaber.

 MISB: $475-$525+; MIB: $115-$135; MLC: $60-$75+.

Han Solo

[Production #39170]

1st packaged appearance: 1979
Original Retail Price (average): $10.99
Action Features:

- 11-3/4" figure
- Authentically styled shirt, vest, and pants
- Removable gun belt and boots
- Laser Pistol
- Rebel Alliance Medal of Honor

Large Size Han Solo.

It is worth noting that assorted dealers will sell reproduction accessories for these large size action figures. Although this Han Solo figure was removed from a boxed sample, the fabric material comprising his Medal of Honor's ribbon was subject to sun fading; hence, a reproduction Medal of Honor accessory was bought to substitute for the original when displaying the figure. However, the provided image shows the obvious differences between the two.

Large Size Han Solo's easily lost and removable accessories: Blaster (DL-44 Heavy Blaster Pistol, modified), soft plastic black boots, gun belt with holster to hold his blaster, Medal of Honor (chromed plastic with red ribbon), black pants, white shirt, and spacer's vest.

MISB: $550-$625+; **MIB:** $220-$265+; **MLC:** $115-$125+.

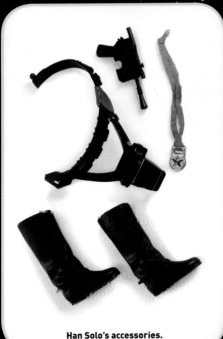

Han Solo's accessories.

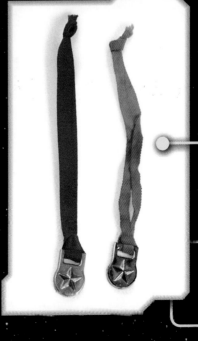

Note the distinct differences between Han Solo's Medal of Honor reproduction, left, vs. the original, at right

Jawa

[Production #39350]

1st packaged appearance: 1979 (Star Wars packaging)
Original Retail Price (average): $7.99
Action Features:

- 8″ poseable figure
- Bright yellow eyes
- Laser Rifle
- Removable ammunition belt
- Hooded cloak
- Authentically detailed

Large Size Jawa, MIB.

This figure possesses remarkable detailing for his bigger size, and his robe and bandolier are expertly crafted. He also has wrists that swivel—a characteristic not possessed by many other figurines in this line. Make sure to see the original entry for the character's mini-action figure to obtain more information about this curious species of bipeds.

Large Size Jawa's easily lost and removable accessories: soft tan rubber Bandolier strap, brown hooded robe, and ionization Blaster (black rifle).

MISB: $325-$350+; MIB: $95-$110+; MLC: $42-$55+.

Jawa's Bandolier strap, Ionization Blaster (black rifle).

Large Size Jawa with Bandolier Strap and Ionization Blaster.

Luke Skywalker

[Production #38080]

1st packaged appearance: 1978 ([early release] Star Wars packaging)
Original Retail Price (average): $10.99
Action Features:

- 11-3/4″ poseable figure
- Authentic Tatooine Desert Costume
- Lightsaber
- Grappling Hook
- Utility Belt

With his authentically styled "farm boy Luke" uniform, this interpretation of everyone's favorite Rebel hero gave collectors the detailed accessories they demanded—ones they would never see at a 3-3/4-inch scale. For instance, this marked the only time that Kenner produced a vintage Luke Skywalker action figure with his appropriately colored blue lightsaber: Kenner's 12-inch Obi-Wan came with a yellow lightsaber—the opposite of their 3-3/4-inch equivalents.

Large Size Luke Skywalker's easily lost and removable accessories: black belt (with room for hook and lightsaber), white boots, grappling hook with string, blue lightsaber, beige pants, white shirt.

MISB: $430-$465+; MIB: $145-$165+; MLC: $60-$72+.

Large Size Luke Skywalker, posed.

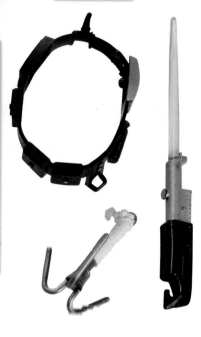

Large Size Luke Skywalker's accessories.

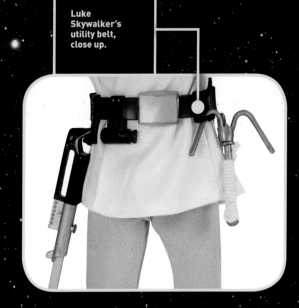

Luke Skywalker's utility belt, close up.

Princess Leia's plastic donut for hairstyling purposes.

Princess Leia's accessories.

Large Size Princess Leia Organa.

Princess Leia Organa

[Production #38070]

1st packaged appearance: 1978 ([early release] Star Wars packaging)
Original Retail Price (average): $10.99
Action Features:

- 11-1/2" poseable figure
- Alderaanian Cape
- Royal Belt
- Comb and Brush
- Styling Star Puffs and other hairdos (and 2 "plastic donuts")

One of the fascinating aspects of this Princess Leia action figure is her magnificently rooted hair. With the two included "hair donuts," collectors could construct a wide variety of hair styles for Leia—many featured in a splendid pack-in booklet included within the figure's window box, *Beautiful Hairstyles for Princess Leia*, almost always found missing in loose samples.

Large Size Princess Leia Organa's easily lost and removable accessories: hard plastic silver belt, blue brush, blue comb, two donuts (brown, hard plastic, for

hairstyles), hairstyle booklet, hooded white long gown, soft plastic white shoes, and a pair of white stockings.

MISB: $340-$380+; **MIB**: with all accessories: **$140-$165+**, without brush, comb, and hairstyle booklet: **$95-$115**. **MLC**: with all accessories: **$65-$80+**, without brush, comb, and hairstyle booklet: **$50-$65+**, hairstyle booklet alone: **$15-$20**, set of plastic donuts: **$18-$24**.

See-Threepio (C-3PO)

[Production #38620]

1st packaged appearance: late-1978
Original Retail Price (average): $10.99
Action Features:

- 12" poseable figure
- Gold metallic finish
- Authentically detailed

Large Size C-3PO.

Although this action figure only sported five points of articulation, it was still a necessary purchase since his body sculpt was so exceptionally detailed. Take care to find samples where his vac-metallized finish is not worn or damaged in any way.

The Large Size See-Threepio did not have any easily lost and removable accessories.

 MISB: $175-$225+; **MIB:** $60-$75+; **MLC:** $28-$40+.

Stormtrooper

[Production #39180]

1st packaged appearance: 1979
Original Retail Price (average): $10.99
Action Features:

- 12" poseable figure
- Moveable arms, legs, and wrists
- Distinctive white and black armor
- Laser Rifle can be held in hand or hung on belt
- Authentically designed

One of the more curious accoutrements placed on any *Star Wars* action figure at any point in history is the Large Size Stormtrooper's "holster": an odd loop of black string jutting out of the soldier's right side. Since many kids had no idea what this loop was for, it can be found either cut or removed entirely from loose samples. Like his original 3-3/4-inch counterpart, Large Size stormtroopers are also subject to yellowing when exposed to sunlight or heat, so please make sure to purchase samples that possess little to no yellowing to the white plastic.

The Large Size Stormtrooper's lone easily lost/removable accessory was his Laser Rifle (BlasTech E-11 Imperial Blaster Rifle).

Large Size Stormtrooper, posed.

 MISB: $325-$405+; **MIB:** pure white armor: $95-$115+, some mild yellowing, $70-$90. **MLC:** pure white armor: $68-$82+, some mild yellowing. $48-$60+.

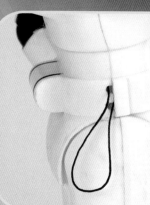

CLOSE-UP

Stormtrooper's belt holster.

Stormtrooper's laser rifle.

IG-88 (Bounty Hunter)

[Production #39960]

1st packaged appearance: 1980
Original Retail Price (average): $10.99
Action Features:

- 15" authentically detailed bounty hunter
- Laser pistol
- Laser rifle
- Cartridge belt
- Articulated head, arms, wrists, and hips.

Oddly enough, the "Laser Rifle" included with the Large Size Stormtrooper action figure and the "Laser Pistol" included with this IG-88 figure are supposed to be the same model of gun: the BlasTech E-11 Blaster Rifle. Not only are these accessories cast from totally different molds, the Stormtrooper's weapon is far larger.

The Large Size IG-88 action figure's easily lost/removable accessories: Laser Rifle (BlasTech DLT-20A Blaster Rifle), Laser Pistol (BlasTech E-11 Imperial Blaster Rifle), Bandolier/Removable Cartridge Belt (soft plastic), four hard plastic, red cartridges/mines, almost always missing in loose samples.

MISB: $1,750-$1,800+;
MIB: $450-$475+;
MLC: $175-$210+.

Large Size IG-88, posed.

The Large Size IG-88's accessories.

PART II
ACCESSORIES
CREATURES, PLAYSETS, AND VEHICLES

Collector's Action
Stand, complete.

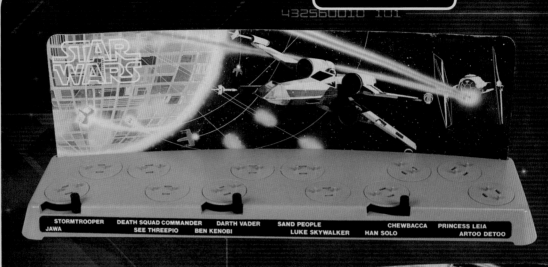

STORMTROOPER | DEATH SQUAD COMMANDER | DARTH VADER | SAND PEOPLE | | CHEWBACCA | PRINCESS LEIA
JAWA | SEE THREEPIO | BEN KENOBI | LUKE SKYWALKER | HAN SOLO | | ARTOO DETOO

Collector's Action Stand, with
original 12 *Star Wars* figures.

Collector's Action Stand/
Action Collector's Stand/
Action Display Stand (Mail-Away)

[Production #39990]

1st packaged appearance: 1978
Original Retail Price (average): mail-
away ($2 shipping & handling + 2 proof-of-
purchase seals, or 12 POP seals alone)

First offered in March 1978 via a coupon that was placed into the small white mailer box of the four action figures sent to those who participated in the Star Wars Early Bird Certificate Package promotion and then offered on the cardbacks of the original twelve *Star Wars* action figures, this Action Display Stand encouraged kids and collectors alike to display (and more importantly, PURCHASE) the first twelve action figures that Kenner produced in grand fashion: with a chipboard backdrop featuring a TIE Fighter chasing an X-wing Fighter as the Rebel spaceship makes its run at the Death Star. Each of the original twelve figures can be mounted onto the stand via their foot pegs, which were one of Kenner's ingenious strategies that was used on accessories, some vehicles, and nearly every playset.

There were three different variations of this mail-away exclusive/retail product: one offered via mail-away, a very rare *Star Wars* retail boxed version, and an impossibly rare *Empire Strikes Back* (potentially retail) boxed version which may have been a prototype. With interlocking gears that allowed you to move each character via a series of action levers, and three levers which rotate four figures per lever, this collector's stand is a wonderful way to display the first dozen figurines produced by Kenner.

Easily lost/removable parts: backdrop, usually found quite worn, 12-figure stand circles, three levers, base, front label, usually found worn.

Mailer box: **MISB: $850-$1,000**; **MIB: $225-$250**; **MLC: $50-$65+**.

SW retail box: **MISB: $3,400-$3,800+**; **MIB: $1,400-$1,600**; **MLC: $50-$65+**.

ESB retail box: **MISB: $6,500-$7,200**; **MIB: $4,400-$4,600**; **MLC: $2,600-$2,800**.

Cantina Adventure Set, complete.

Cantina Adventure Set (Sears Exclusive)

```
[Production #38861]
1st packaged appearance: 1978
Original Retail Price (average): $8.99
```

Cantina Adventure Set, with included figures; Snaggletooth, blue jumpsuit.

Although this playset is modeled after the Mos Eisley Cantina, specifically, based upon the Wookiee Chalmun's Spaceport Cantina, it is simply known as "The Cantina" to many casual *Star Wars* fans. The following flavor text describing "The Cantina" is excerpted from the Sears' 1978 *Christmas Wish Book*, since the Cantina Adventure Set was a Sears exclusive: "Star Wars Cantina Adventure Set—SET INCLUDES: Recreate the bizarre adventures and create new ones with four fully poseable plastic figures; Greedo, Snaggletooth, Hammerhead, and Walrus Man. Graphics depict various characters and activity outside the Cantina. Ages 4 and up. CONSTRUCTION: Made of cardboard. Scene is 18 x 7 inches high."

The Cantina Adventure Set contained four action figures: Greedo, Hammerhead, Snaggletooth, and Walrus Man. Although all four of these figures were available at other retail outlets as individually packaged specimens, one variation of these four figures was exclusive to Sears: "Blue Snaggletooth" —a specimen commanding high prices on today's secondary market (see Snaggletooth, blue jumpsuit, for more information) The figures included with this set were shipped either in a four-pack box or in dual two-pack boxes.

Although the Sears *Wish Book* description states that the Cantina Adventure Set is made of cardboard, this is not entirely accurate. For those collectors buying this piece on the secondary market and expecting a nice, solid piece of corrugated cardboard as the playset's backdrop, they'll be sorely disappointed. The playset is actually comprised of a lightweight, yet quite sturdy, chipboard material rendered in three-dimensions: like a pop-up book.

This mostly chipboard Sears exclusive Cantina Adventure Set should not be confused with the more common mostly plastic-molded Creature Cantina Action Playset—the latter of which was available at mass retail.

The Cantina Adventure Set includes the following easily lost/removable parts: three-dimensional Cantina backdrop, Greedo action figure, with blue/black Rebel Blaster (DL-44 heavy blaster pistol), Hammerhead action figure with blue/black Imperial Blaster (E-11 blaster rifle), Snaggletooth action figure, with either "red jumpsuit" or "blue jumpsuit," and with blue/black Rebel Blaster (DL-44 heavy blaster pistol), Walrus Man action figure with blue/black Imperial Blaster (E-11 blaster rifle), and 12 white foot pegs; 11 are needed for the playset—1 is extra.

MISB: $850-$1,000; **MIB**: with figures and blue Snaggletooth: **$190-$245+**, with figures and red Snaggletooth: **$110-$115+**, without figures: **$90-$110**; **MLC**: with figures and blue Snaggletooth: **$150-$210**, with figures and red Snaggletooth: **$75-$80+**, without figures: **$60-$75+**.

Death Star Space Station, MIB.

Death Star Space Station

[Production #38050]

1st packaged appearance: 1978
Original Retail Price (average): $17.99

Based upon a cross-section of the Death Star battle station (its actual name was the DS-1 Orbital Battle Station) featured in the original *Star Wars* film, *A New Hope*, this playset was the premiere playset for the first few years of Kenner's *Star Wars* line. As with most *Star Wars* playsets, there are many foot pegs featured throughout the Death Star Space Station for you to  stand up your action figures into action poses. Thankfully, this intricate playset's package front provides collectors a list of the items contained within the box: "Working Elevator, Exploding Laser Cannon, Trash Compactor with Moving Wall, Alien Trash Monster, Opening Light Bridge, Trap Door, Rope Swing to Safety... Trash Compactor Unit also removable for individual play."

Individual photos of the playset's action features lit-

Death Star Space Station, isometric view.

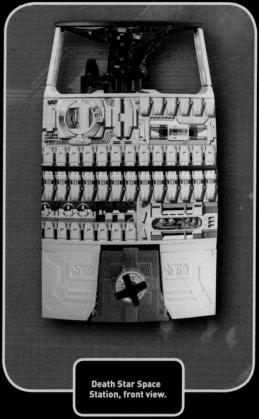

Death Star Space Station, front view.

IN ACTION

Our Rebel heroes are crushed in the trash compactor, until they trip the escape hatch.

ter the box, featuring an "Exploding Laser Cannon," the ability for kids to "Pretend Ben (Obi-Wan) Kenobi turns off tractor beam" and allow the *Millennium Falcon* to escape, an "Opening Light Bridge," and an opportunity to "Rope Swing to safety for Luke and Leia." Furthermore, the Death Star Space Station's "Working Elevator travels to all 4 floors" (Note: you open the elevator by turning the transparent door, and you may lift the elevator manually, it locks into place at each level), a "Trap door that helps Han Solo and Chewbacca es-

cape Darth Vader," and a "Trash Compactor [that] has a moving wall, foam 'Garbage,' Alien Trash Monster and Escape Hatch."

It is worth mentioning a few interesting aspects of the Station's third floor—specifically, its *enormous* cannon. Firstly, in order for a collector to man the exploding laser cannon back in 1978 with a generic Imperial soldier, they would have to utilize either an Imperial Stormtrooper or a Death Squad Commander/ Star Destroyer Commander; Kenner did not produce

Luke and Leia use the rope to "swing across" the chasm.

C-3PO and R2-D2 await to use the Space Station's four-story elevator.

Death Squad Commanders arm the gun battery.

a proper Imperial Gunner action figure until 1985's Power of the Force releases. Secondly, since the toy cannon's launching mechanism and the cannon barrel itself are both extraordinarily fragile, collectors will discover that there are far more broken/damaged cannon tips and launchers than perfectly intact specimens for sale on the secondary market.

The cannon included on the third level not only raises, lowers, and turns, but if you push an action lever, the cannon will eject from its slot. But it's not, as some might believe, one of the Death Star's superlasers: it is simply a gun battery, albeit a huge one, and one of many used to defend the station against Rebel starfighters. Unfortunately, in this playset, we do not witness one of these superlasers which were borne out of the mind of Grand Moff Wilhuff Tarkin—a highly important character, but one not to see an action figure until 1997's Power of the Force II assortment concocted by Hasbro.

Please note that within the next section, the accessories/pieces are arranged by the level they appear on, when the Death Star Space Station is assembled into four disparate levels/stories:

INCLUDES:

Basement: Elevator Shaft; Basement Support Walls (white, left and right, x 2); Trash (3 "pre-cut" square foam sheets in 3 different colors: blue-gray, black-gray and tan-yellow)*; Trash Compactor with escape hatch, two plastic windows, sliding wall, turning crank assembly; Trash Monster ("Dianoga").

First Floor: Bridge Support Column (gray-white); First Floor Columns (gray-white x 3); Instrument Panel #1** (chipboard—labeled in small back letters on the non-glossy side: "PART NO. 314040," X-wing fighter printed on viewscreen); Trap Door.

Second Floor: Bridge Assembly, two-piece (forms "retracting drawbridge"); Second Floor Columns (black x 3); Roof; Rope (blue); Instrument Panel #2** (chip-

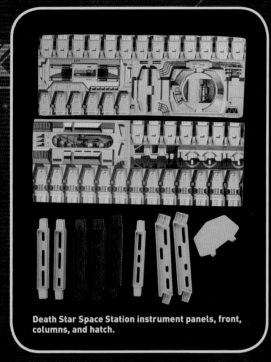

Death Star Space Station instrument panels, front, columns, and hatch.

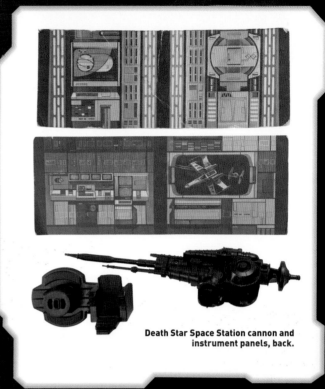

Death Star Space Station cannon and instrument panels, back.

Death Star Space Station parts, loose foam trash, Dianoga monster, rope.

Death Star Space Station parts, elevator ledge, support walls, sealed foam trash, trash compactor.

board—labeled in small back letters on the non-glossy side: "PART NO. 314033").

Third Floor: Third Floor Columns (gray-white x 2); Laser Cannon; Tractor Beam Panel Ledge (gray-white). Label Sheet***.

* The myriad foam pieces of trash/garbage deteriorate over time. Only sealed samples will be perfectly intact, but even then, there is often degradation—similar to the swamp featured in the *Empire Strikes Back* Dagobah action playset. Finding intact piece of foam

garbage for the compactor is rare.

** The two Instrument Panels included with this playset are of slightly different sizes when placed next to one another; panel #1 is a tiny bit *longer* than panel #2.

*** This playset has no instructional guide to apply its included labels—one of the few vintage *Star Wars* toys that does not have this form of reference.

MISB: $1,200-$1,400; MIB: $350-$425; MLC: $125-$150+.

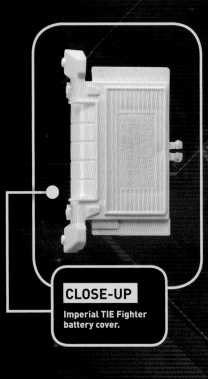

CLOSE-UP
Imperial TIE Fighter
battery cover.

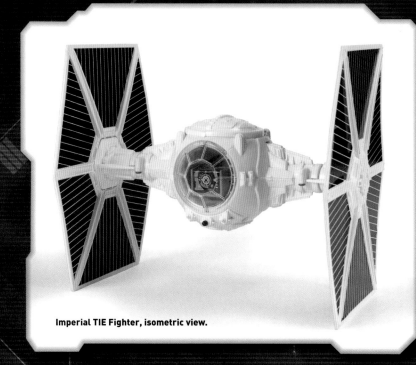

Imperial TIE Fighter, isometric view.

(Imperial) TIE Fighter

[Production #38040]

1st packaged appearance: 1978
Original Retail Price (average): $14.99

The Imperial TIE Fighter—a.k.a. the TIE ("Twin Ion Engine") Starfighter, or the TIE/LN (or TIE/line) starfighter—was created by Sienar Fleet Systems to function as a space superiority fighter. Unlike the Rebel Alliances' craft, the Empire's short range TIE fighter was missing its hyperdrive unit, ejection system, combat shields, and even life-support systems (see TIE Fighter Pilot), yet the craft's superior engine design "reduced the mass of the fighter and conferred *exceptional* maneuverability … " upon these magnificently designed "eyeballs," a Rebel nickname for the TIE, which possessed a pair of powerful, chin-mounted SFS L-s1 laser cannons (Single or Fire-Linked) as armaments.

Kenner's bright white TIE fighter toy leapt off retail shelves; however, the original TIEs featured in *ANH* are not white at all, they're a muted gray—yet perhaps Kenner wished to utilize a body color that would provide a nicer contrast in body to the wings' solar panels. Apart from the vehicle's peculiar color, the TIE fighter

possessed the following action features: "flashing 'laser' light and space sound!" a pilot's hatch that opens while a remote lever raises the seat, and the most distinctive feature of the TIE Fighter: its battle-damaged effect provided by the toy's ability to eject both solar array wings at the push of a button—a feature utilized in every iteration of the toy, from the Darth Vader TIE Fighter (1979) to the "Battle-Damaged" Imperial TIE Fighter vehicle (1982), and finally, with the TIE Interceptor vehicle (1983).

The TIE fighter includes the following removable/easily lost parts: 2x Solar Array Wings, Main Cockpit, 2x Ingress/Egress Hatch Flaps, 1x Hatch Opener/Seat Raiser, Battery Cover.

MISB: $460-$510+; **MIB**: $100, working electronics; **MLC**: $30-$35+, working electronics.

CLOSE-UP

Land Speeder engine.

Land Speeder, isometric view.

Land Speeder (a.k.a. Landspeeder)

[Production #38020]

1st packaged appearance: 1978
Original Retail Price (average): $4.99

Luke Skywalker's famous ride on Tatooine was that of a civilian landspeeder: model X-34, with an open-air cockpit. Manufactured by SoroSuub Corporation, this landspeeder sported three turbine engines (one engine had its cowling cover removed), a Duraplex windscreen, and possessed a repulsor-field generator that yielded "repulsor counterbalances," which existed for smooth and steady travel over rough terrain. With a maximum altitude of 1 meter, its standard cruising altitude was roughly 10 cm above ground level.

Kenner's Land Speeder (note the two-word designa-

tion) toy was a marvel of engineering, which they sold millions of units of these standard vehicles, and possessed the following action features: a shift lever that lowers its spring-loaded wheels, which simulate the toy's floating ride/suspension, and the vehicle's hood opens for access to its turbo reactor and space hatch storage compartment.

The Kenner Land Speeder was also packaged with a sticker sheet and a *Star Wars* catalog (it did not come with an instruction sheet), and includes the following removable/easily lost part: Duraplex Windscreen (removable windshield).

MISB: $260-$300+; **MIB**: $38-$45; **MLC**: $18-$22.

Sonic Land Speeder isometric view, with R2-D2 "Clicker."

Regular Land Speeder vs. Sonic Land Speeder size comparison.

Sonic Land Speeder parts.

Sonic Controlled Land Speeder

[Production #38540]

1st packaged appearance: 1978
Original Retail Price (average): $10.97

Based upon the same model of land speeder utilized by Luke Skywalker in *A New Hope* (SoroSuub Corporation's model X-34, with an open-air cockpit), the Sonic Controlled Land Speeder was quite a bit larger than the standard version of the vehicle. Solicited as a J.C. Penney catalog exclusive, the local production number for this toy was "925-9789," and it could *only* be ordered via J.C. Penney's 1978, 1979, and 1980 Christmas catalogs. At more than double the price of the standard Land Speeder— compare the widely released Land Speeder's cost of $4.99 to Penney's deluxe model at $10.97—the excessive cost for such a toy was prohibitive in the late 1970s.

However, the toy itself was fantastic and utilized no existing parts from its previously released predecessor. Featuring drivewheel technology that locked into four different positions, by inserting four "AA" alkaline batteries into the Sonic Controlled Landspeeder's two slots only (note that the R2-D2-shaped "sonic controls" clicker did not require batteries to operate), and then turning the vehicle's switch to "on" (located between the seats), the vehicle moved and kids could make the

toy change directions from up to 16 feet away (!).

Fabulously enough, the vehicle functioned with four figures aboard the craft: two figurines in the pilot and co-pilot seats (see Luke Skywalker and Ben Kenobi), while two foot pegs on its back deck allowed the droids to hitch a ride as well (see Artoo-Detoo and See-Threepio).

The Sonic Controlled Land Speeder includes the following removable/easily lost parts: R2-D2 clicker/remote, battery covers (x 2—left and right), drive unit (sometimes this falls out—it must be *carefully* replaced), seat, sonic controller (R2-D2 clicker), windshield. Some collectors also believe that the blue plastic adjusters included with the vehicle's extra instruction sheet should be counted as well; however, these are unnecessary to compose a complete Sonic Controlled Land Speeder.

MISB: **$1,000-$1,200+**; **MIB**: contents sealed: **$425-$475+**, contents loose, working electronics: **$185-$210+**; **MLC**: working electronics: **$125-$140+**.

X-wing Fighter

[Production #38030]

1st packaged appearance: 1978
Original Retail Price (average): $14.99

The Incom Corporation's T-65 X-wing was the all-purpose starfighter of the Rebel Alliance and a favorite vehicle of Rebel pilots, existing as the preeminent fighting symbol of the Alliance to restore freedom to the galaxy during the time of the Galactic Civil War.

A trademark feature of the X-Wing Fighter was the characteristic "X" symbol, which the wings activated, and in essence, became, when engaged in high-stress or combat situations. Technically dubbed "S-foils," a.k.a. Strike foils, Stability foils, or X-foils, these movable wings were attached to the starboard and port sides of the iconic starship, while the wingtips were mounted with four Taim & Bak KX9 laser cannons that could operate inside and outside of space—and would fire independently of each other all at once, or in offset pairs. Dual launch tubes rounded out the vehicle's armaments, allowing the X-wing to fire proton torpedoes: "energized torpedoes that carried a devastatingly powerful blast from a proton-scattering warhead." Unfortunately, during the beginning of the First Galactic Civil War (2 BBY-19 ABY), the Rebellion had limited resources, and since proton torpedoes were prohibitively expensive, the Rebels owned a limited quantity of these costly missiles. This explains why, during his run on the first Death Star during the Battle of Yavin, Luke Skywalker

can't fire dozens upon dozens of proton torpedoes repeatedly into the thermal exhaust port of the Death Star.

The X-wing had a bevy of special features: the Landing Skid, located under the front section of the plane, pulls down and pushes back up out of sight, flashing "laser" light and space sound triggered via the use of two "AA" batteries (not included), and collectors could also spread the wings of the fighter just like they saw in the movie—push down on R2-D2's head to bring the wings back to the original position and the central blue button to return.

However, the R2-D2 located atop the hull of the X-wing toy is simply a button—a trigger for an action feature—and is entirely non-removable, a fact that served to denigrate the special relationship of a Rebel pilot and his astromech droid.

The vehicle's easily lost/removable parts include: canopy (translucent, clear and different from the tinted canopy used on the "battle-damaged" X-wing Fighter, 1982), and laser cannons (x4).

 MISB: $520-$550+; **MIB**: working electronics: $85-$110; **MLC**: working electronics: $38-$50+.

X-Wing Fighter "locked" (opened) s-foils/x-foils for attack position

X-Wing Fighter canopy and laser cannons

Creature Cantina, front view.

Creature Cantina Action Playset

[Production #39120]

1st packaged appearance: 1979
Original Retail Price (average): $7.99

The 1979 Kenner toy product catalog promotes their Creature Cantina Action Playset as follows: "Recreate the exciting action from that weird cantina scene. Find adventure by pushing the floor button to swing open the Cantina door so the Stormtrooper can enter. Move the action lever and Ben Kenobi defends Luke Skywalker against Snaggletooth. Move another action lever and Han Solo knocks over Greedo in mock battle. Use the foot pegs around the bar to pose your action figures." What this description effectively does is encapsulate the degree of weirdness that most casual fans felt when introduced to the cantina scene in *A New Hope*.

Located at 3112 Outer Kerner Way, in the large spaceport town of Mos Eisley on the desert planet of Tatooine, the canonical name of the Creature Cantina is Chalmun's Spaceport Cantina, a.k.a. Mos Eisley Cantina, The Cantina or double-c/ceecee, by the local constabulary. With its slack interpretation of the law and vast assortment of beverages from around the galaxy, this prominent drinking establishment was a popular haven for pirates, smugglers, soldiers-of-fortune, bounty hunters, spacers, mercenaries and other assorted characters who lived on the fringe of civilized society. This watering hole is run by the Wookiee proprietor Chalmun, who is loyal and protective of his regulars, yet won't allow droids entry into the one-story building. The owner rarely enforces the bar's rules, and shootings and other crimes are fairly common, such as Han Solo's quick dispatch of Greedo and Ben Kenobi's slicing off Ponda Baba's arm, two exceedingly lawless events, which occur in the same afternoon.

This playset includes the following easily lost/ removable parts: Cantina base with Circular Bar, Chipboard Backdrop with pictures of Star Wars Cantina Band, Battle-Action Lever Bases and Mounts (10 pieces total), Opening Front Door (4-piece door assembly = frame, 2 door halves, elastic band).

MISB: $550-$585+; **MIB**: $80-$95+; **MLC**: $35-$45.

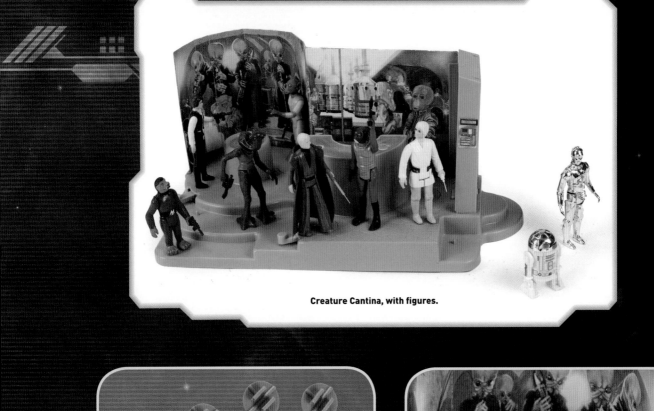

Creature Cantina, with figures.

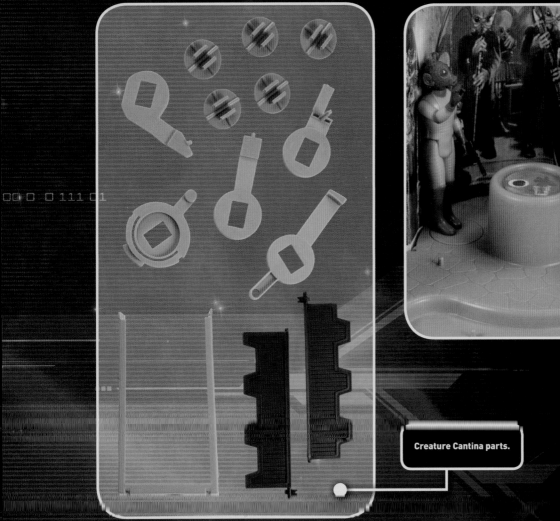

Creature Cantina parts.

Han Solo fires his blaster at Greedo.

Darth Vader
TIE Fighter,
isometric view.

Darth Vader TIE Fighter
(a.k.a. TIE Advanced x1, Vader's TIE)

[Production #39100]

1st packaged appearance: 1979
Original Retail Price (average): $14.99

Utilized by Darth Vader during the Battle of Yavin, the Darth Vader TIE Fighter—clinically known as the *TIE Advanced x1*—is hailed as the logical successor to the Empire's standard "eyeballs": those stock-released TIE/LN starfighters produced by Kenner as the white-colored TIE Fighter toy in 1978. Equipped with the same reactor and twin ion engines, hence the acronym "TIE," featured on the original TIE/LN, Vader's TIE Advanced x1 sported an all-new, original frame that featured an elongated rear deck and hull that was reinforced by a special metal alloy.

However, the most important modification of the TIE Advanced x1 was the spacecraft's spectacular "bent-wing" solar array wings, similar to those featured on the Imperial TIE/sa bomber, which afforded the ship two advantages: the modified solar panels established an increased surface area, which granted the craft more power, while the wing's curvature lowered the ship's target profile by enemy vessels. Although a bit less maneuverable than the standard TIE fighter, the TIE Advanced x1 possessed a superior targeting system than that of a standard TIE, slightly improved speed, and added resil-

ience in combat. Therefore, it was a better class of TIE altogether, and only the most elite pilots in the Imperial navy flew the craft.

This TIE fighter possesses the following action features: flashing laser light and space sound, which required two AA batteries to operate, a hatch that opened while a lever raised the pilot's seat, and the most distinctive feature: its battle-damaged effect provided by the toy's ability to eject both solar array wings at the push of a button—a feature utilized in every iteration of the toy, from the original Imperial TIE fighter (1978), to the "Battle-Damaged" Imperial TIE Fighter vehicle (1982), and the TIE Interceptor vehicle (1983).

The Darth Vader TIE fighter contains the following removable/easily lost parts: 2x Solar Array Wings, Main Cockpit, 2x Ingress/Egress Hatch Flaps, 1x Hatch Opener/Seat Raiser, and Battery Cover.

MISB: $235-$260+; MIB: working electronics: **$55-$65; MLC:** working electronics: **$38-$50+.**

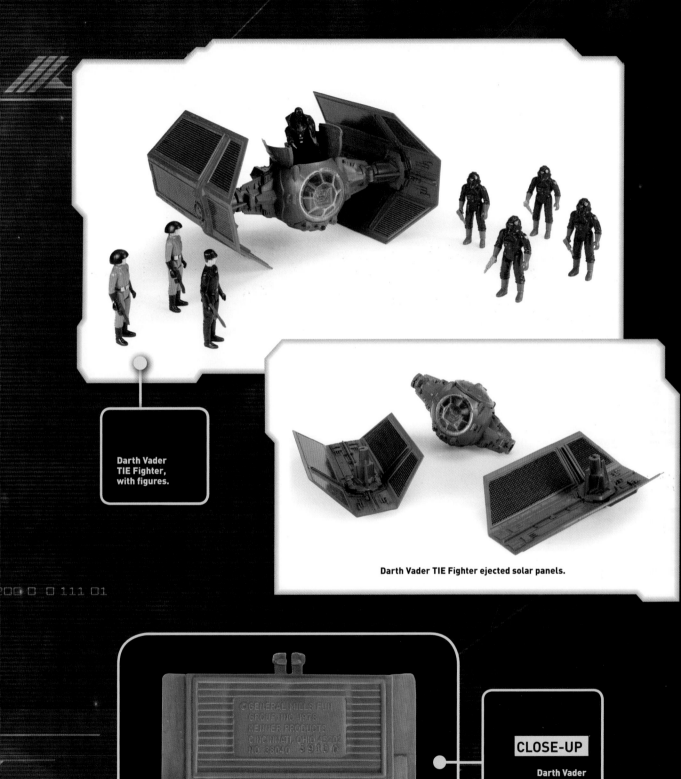

Darth Vader
TIE Fighter,
with figures.

Darth Vader TIE Fighter ejected solar panels.

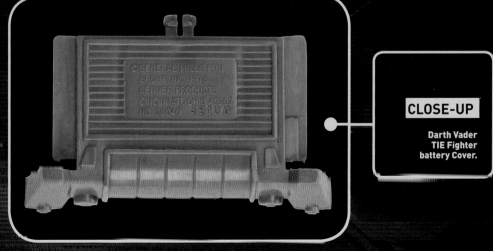

CLOSE-UP

Darth Vader
TIE Fighter
battery Cover.

Droid Factory, with figures.

Droid Factory

[Production #39150]

1st packaged appearance: 1979
Original Retail Price (average): $11.99

Marking the first Kenner-branded toy that afforded *Star Wars* collectors the opportunity to build an R2-D2 action figure with his trademark third leg, the Droid Factory existed as a construction/building playset, as well as an action figure base. Possessing both wow *and* play factor, the toy yielded the following features denoted on the box: its robot parts and pieces are interchangeable, and because of this, you may "build up to 5 different robots at the same time" to "make hundreds of different combinations." With a "robot building instruction booklet included" that allows you to "build your own R2-D2," you may utilize a swivel boom that moves robot parts to an assembly area.

Although this playset is not featured in *Star Wars: A New Hope*, it appears that Kenner was promoting it as part of

the Jawas' purview—if we believe the packaging artwork. Furthermore, the Droid Factory's base, three-piece swivel boom, pivot pin, and hook would be reissued in both Sears exclusive *ROTJ* Jabba the Hutt Dungeon action playsets, with these versions of the four pieces and multiple parts molded in different colors and re-worked: the Droid Factory base is orange-brown, while the boom is dark brown with a black hook; the 1983 *ROTJ* Jabba the Hutt Dungeon ($13.99, originally the one with three *ROTJ* figures) possesses a blue-gray base, while the 1984 Jabba the Hutt Dungeon (the one with three POTF figures) included a sandy-tan base.

The Droid Factory comes with the following parts: base, mast, boom, pivot pin, label sheet, hook, long hydraulic tubing (x2, orange colored—some may be cut into pieces to

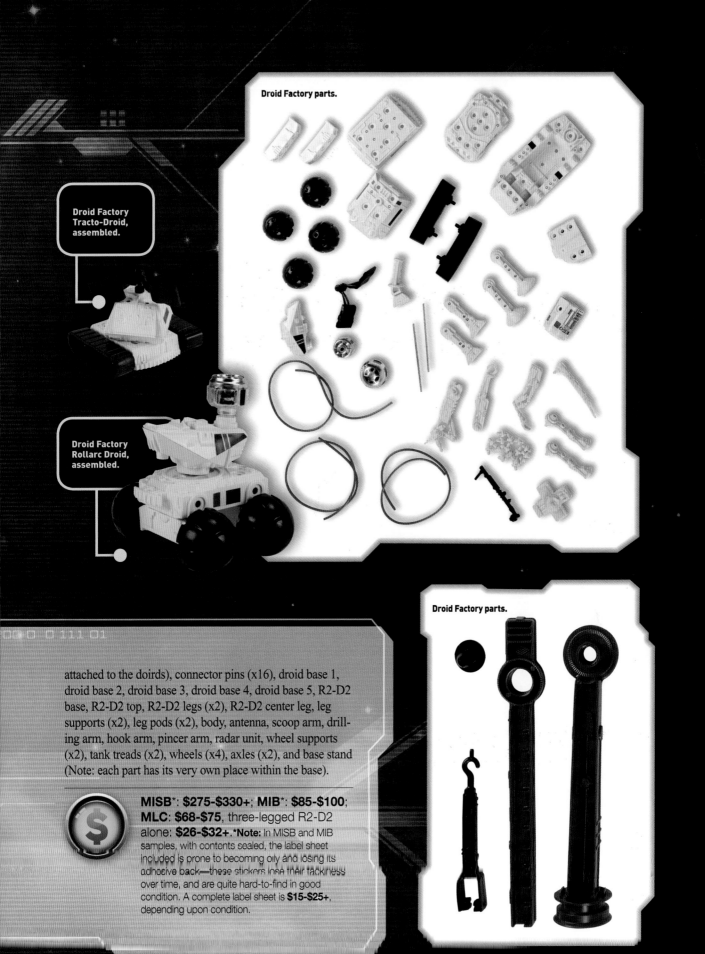

Droid Factory parts.

Droid Factory Tracto-Droid, assembled.

Droid Factory Rollarc Droid, assembled.

Droid Factory parts.

attached to the doirds), connector pins (x16), droid base 1, droid base 2, droid base 3, droid base 4, droid base 5, R2-D2 base, R2-D2 top, R2-D2 legs (x2), R2-D2 center leg, leg supports (x2), leg pods (x2), body, antenna, scoop arm, drilling arm, hook arm, pincer arm, radar unit, wheel supports (x2), tank treads (x2), wheels (x4), axles (x2), and base stand (Note: each part has its very own place within the base).

MISB*: **$275-$330+**; **MIB***: **$85-$100**; **MLC: $68-$75**, three-legged R2-D2 alone: **$26-$32+**.***Note:** In MISB and MIB samples, with contents sealed, the label sheet included is prone to becoming oily and losing its adhesive back—these stickers lose their tackiness over time, and are quite hard-to-find in good condition. A complete label sheet is **$15-$25+**, depending upon condition.

Imperial Troop Transporter

`[Production #39290]`

1st packaged appearance: 1979
Original Retail Price (average): $14.99

One of the few *Star Wars* toys created by Kenner, which does not make an appearance in the original (canonical) film trilogy, the Imperial Troop Transporter is chock-full of nifty special features: a "Swiveling [and synchronized] radar scope and rotating laser cannon [a '50 Megatome Blaster' according to the included storybook] move together, you may "put R2-D2 into [droid] prison compartment," you can "Play original sounds from *Star Wars* [6 original action sounds from the *Star Wars* movie], "place *Star Wars* action figures in [the two] driver-control compartments," use "2 prisoner immobilization units," and the vehicle's "6 side compartments [used to transport Imperial soldiers]."

Oddly enough, the Imperial Troop Transporter came packaged with its own eight-page storybook, perhaps to establish a believable back story for the toy since it did not appear in *Star Wars: A New Hope*. This book features a (non-canonical) narrative that details the events which occurred *immediately after* R2-D2 and C-3PO

crash landed in the "Central Lowlands" of the desert planet of Tatooine in their famously stolen Class-6 escape pod (the pod is included with the Land of the Jawas Playset).

Although the Imperial Troop Transporter never appears within the film canon (there was a similar looking Rebel craft trolling both the Echo Base in *ESB* and the *Home One* frigate in *ROTJ* hangar bays...), the craft does manifest itself in other aspects of the *Star Wars* universe such as the Dark Horse, Marvel, and Marvel UK *Star Wars* comic book series. Finally, in the online adventure *Triplet Threat* published by licensee Wizards of the Coast, talented *Star Wars* author/historian Jason Fry delineates the vehicle as the "Santhe/Sienar Technologies Reconnaissance Troop Transporter."

When comparing 1979's Imperial Troop Transporter to 1981's Imperial Cruiser, you'll notice that the earlier Troop Transporter is far heavier than the lightweight Sears exclusive Cruiser due to the former's vast inner electronics. The Troop Transporter pictured here is darker gray in color, has six red rounded buttons surrounding its top cannon, which can be depressed, three visible Philips-type screws around its laser cannon, thin red-striped stickers on its two front doors,

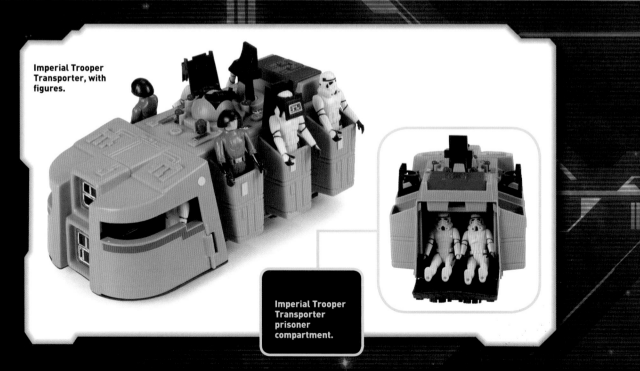

Imperial Trooper Transporter, with figures.

Imperial Trooper Transporter prisoner compartment.

no stickers to the left and right of the battery cover, a small rear prisoner compartment used to transport captured droids, while inside its battery cover are contacts for a size C battery. Finally, and most importantly, the Imperial Troop Transporter's removable battery cover is colored red—the SAME color as the red on its electronic-sound buttons. The Imperial Cruiser's larger prisoner compartment is due to its lack of electronics ... furthermore, the Imperial Cruiser possesses black-colored FLATTENED top buttons (they do NOT trigger sounds—they can't be depressed), while its battery cover is a neutral-orange color; plus, beneath the Cruiser's battery cover is a paper insert that hides a lack of electronic battery contacts.

The toy's easily lost/removable parts includes: red battery cover, doors (x2; left, pilot, and right, co-pilot), personnel pod/side compartments (x6; difficult to remove), prisoner immobilization units (x2), and a radar dish.

MISB: **$325-$350+**; **MIB**: working electronics: **$65-$80+**; **MLC**: working electronics: **$35-$45**.

Imperial Troop Transporter battery cover, radar scope, and two-prisoner immobilization units.

Land of the Jawas Action Playset

[Production #39130]

1st packaged appearance: 1979
Original Retail Price (average): $9.99

Land of the Jawas, front.

Kenner's Land of the Jawas Action Playset is often hailed by many early fans of the franchise as the most memorable of the company's fledgling playsets—quite possibly due to the ingenuity of the Lands' construction, its accoutrements' warm and natural earth tones, and the fact that the toy memorializes one of the more interesting encounters of *Episode IV*, when our heroic pair of droids, R2-D2 and C-3PO, are captured by the hardworking, lovable scavengers known as Jawas.

Oddly enough, it is quite peculiar that in the past, Kenner has often promoted Lucas' Jawa characters from *A New*

Hope—those chirpy, puckish, pint-sized robed and hooded creatures—with almost a childlike enthusiasm. However, this fervor begins to wane when we recognize that those diminutive, clannish humanoid thieves are soon-to-be extensively slaughtered by Darth Vader's Imperial Stormtroopers.

In this playset (and utilizing a cardboard Sandcrawler),

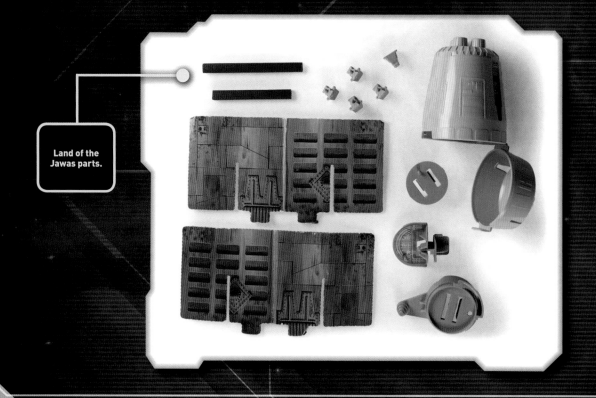

Land of the
Jawas parts.

the Jawas may only use the vehicle as a stationary location: collectors can make the elevator move droids into the underbelly of the vehicle, and may use the front of the vehicle as part of the Tatooine playset—replete with sand dune, small cave, and a landing spot for R2-D2 and C-3PO's "Class-6" escape pod that was fired from Princess Leia Organa's ship, the CR-90 Corvette, the Rebel Blockade Runner known as the *Tantive IV*, as it was boarded by Imperial forces deployed from the Imperial Star Destroyer *Executor*.

The Battle Action Lever located on the far left hand side of the Tatooine Desert Base allows collectors to stand a Jawa action figure on a foot peg atop the circular action stand. Then, by placing a droid on the action button, you can simulate the Jawa firing his ionization blaster to immobilize the droid. Built onto the cardboard Sandcrawler is an elevator that—through the use of a well-placed foot peg—allows collectors to transport figures up into the body of the Sandcrawler and over to the left, out of sight. After these figures are transported inside the Sandcrawler body, there are four action pegs available to them in order for them to remain.

One of the more interesting aspects of this playset is the Escape Pod Rocket ("Class-6 escape pod" according to the canon), an emergency craft which was used by R2-D2 and C-3PO to escape Princess Leia's Tantive IV with the Death

Star plans. It is also worth noting that the plastic base of this playset was utilized many multiple times throughout the tenure of the vintage line: it is used as the base for the Land of the Jawas (tan-colored, 1979), the Hoth Ice Planet Adventure Set (white-colored, 1980), and the Sears exclusive Rebel Command Center (white-colored, 1981).

Includes the following easily lost/removable parts: Action Arm Snapper, Action Button, Action Pegs (tan-colored; x4), Action Stand, Battle Action Lever, Elevator Base, Elevator Guide Rails (brown; x2)*, Elevator Pin, Escape Pod Rocket with Opening Hatch,cardboard Jawa Sandcrawler Backdrop, cardboard Jawa Sandcrawler Body, Jawa Sandcrawler Tread Supports (cardboard; x2), Snapper Cap, base.
*Without the two Elevator Guide Rails (one for each side) to protect the cardboard backdrop, the up-and-down movement of the elevator leading from the tan base to the inside of the Sandcrawler would ruin the integrity of the cardboard's corrugation and cause the elevator to become quite loose. Furthermore, these guide rails are NOT the same length: one is a big longer than the other.

 MISB: $275-$320+; MIB: working: $60-$72+; MLC: working: $38-$45.

Millennium Falcon, isometric view.

Millennium Falcon/
Millennium Falcon Spaceship

[Production #39110]

1st packaged appearance: 1979
Original Retail Price (average): $29.99

Manufactured by the Corellian Engineering Corporation with the call letters "492727ZED" in 60 BBY (Before the Battle of Yavin), the galaxy's most famous YT-1300 light freighter was heavily modified by its most (in-)famous owner, former smuggler, hero of the Rebellion and founding member of the New Republic, Han Solo.

Rather than recount the starship's history prior to Solo's ownership, it is more economical to focus on the role the vehicle plays in the original film trilogy. Named after the quick-flying creature known as the "bat-falcon," the *Millennium Falcon* transfers ownership from Lando Calrissian to Han Solo during a particularly heated game of *sabacc*—a nearly always high stakes, four suited comparing card game (suits: coins, flasks, sabres, staves) similar to, but far more complicated than, the more facile blackjack.

If it weren't for the expert piloting of the *Falcon* by Solo and his first mate Chewbacca toward the

Battle of Yavin's finale (*Episode IV*), during his trench run, Luke Skywalker would never have been able to fire the proton torpedoes that destroy the original Death Star. The *Falcon's* maneuverability also allows Solo and his small band of Rebel friends to evade the entire Imperial Fleet in *Episode V*. In *Episode VI* (4 ABY), during the Battle of Endor, the *Falcon* is flown by former owner Lando Calrissian and his new first mate, Sullustan pilot Nien Nunb, firing the shots at the superstructure of the second Death Star that devastates the battle station and essentially marks the end of the Galactic Empire.

Regarding this oddly shaped yet memorably designed toy (rumor has it that when designing the *Millennium Falcon*, George Lucas based the Falcon's blueprints on a hamburger with an olive placed to one side), the text provided within the instruction sheet reads as follows: you can "re-enact the adventures of *Star Wars*" with a "cockpit that opens to fit two of most *Star Wars* action figures," while "you can raise and lower the ramp for entrances and exits." You may also allow Luke to "…practice his light saber technique with the Light Saber Ball! Have figures play pretend games of

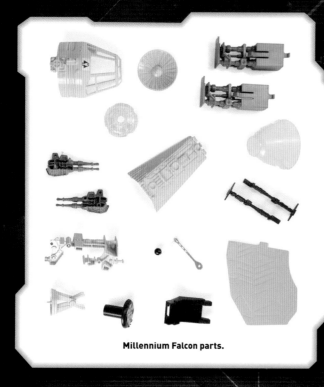

Millennium Falcon parts.

Han Solo smuggles weapons in the hatch.

Obi-Wan trains Luke with a laser remote (lightsaber ball).

Millennium Falcon Dejarik ("Space Chess") table.

Space Chess on the game table." Also, the ship's radar and cannons swivel for action play. Most *Star Wars* action figures could sit on the seat of the cannon and collectors could "push the button on the battery door to make the simulated 'motor sound'." As a former smuggling ship, the *Falcon*'s false floor hides up to three action figures and possesses two landing gears that pull out for pretend landings and a center landing gear that swings down to be used as a handle.

The *Millennium Falcon* includes the following easily lost/removable pieces: AG-2G Quad Laser Cannon (two-piece), battery cover (*usually* non-removable), Vertical Cannon Setup (Cannon Support, Cannon Support Seat [blue], Cannon Window), Cockpit Canopy (*usually* non-removable), Cockpit Canopy Plastic Windshield, False Floor/Secret Compartment, Game Table, Landing Gear (x2), Lightsaber Training Set (Lightsaber Ball-laser remote, Lightsaber Ball Rod, Lightsaber Ball String), Radar Base, Radar Screen, Radar Support, Ramp, Ramp Struts (x2), Removable Outer Hull (flat piece that covers the ship with black circles on top: "Heat Exhaust Vents").

MISB: $2,800-$3,200+; **MIB**: contents sealed: $1,400-$1,600; **MIB**: working electronics: $175-$210+; **MLC**: working electronics: $75-$100.

Patrol Dewback isometric view, with figure.

Patrol Dewback figure

[Production #39240]

1st packaged appearance: 1979
Original Retail Price (average): $10.99

Patrol Dewback harness and saddle.

Working in concert with an Imperial "dewback trooper," a Stormtrooper (see Stormtrooper) operating as a dewback rider, as a light cavalry unit for the Galactic Empire, the four-legged, cold-blooded, omnivores known as dewbacks are large reptiles native to the planet Tatooine's Dune Sea, a monolithic desert that encompasses the surface of the planet's first quadrant. The dewback are hardy creatures, having been birthed in one of the most inhospitable areas on the planet—a region where the average human being will become entirely dehydrated within a half-hour.

Perfectly adapted to the rigors of desert life, dewbacks can be easily domesticated for humanoids looking for riding steeds or fiercely strong beasts of burden. Mainly a solitary animal, perhaps due to the nature of its unwelcoming environment, wild dewbacks can be found searching for food and water in small packs of two to five animals. The dewback species can be further broken down into a variety of different classes: lesser dewback, mountain dewback, grizzled dewback, or the highly aggressive cannibal dewback.

With the ability to move its tail and head side to side, "all four legs articulated for action poses," a "trap door in back that fits most *Star Wars* action figures," and "reins and saddle removable for added play," Kenner's Patrol Dewback creature is a wonderful Imperial mount, and a harness and saddle are its only easily lost parts.

MISB: $165-$190+; **MIB:** $62-$72;
MLC: working: $32-$42+.

Radio Controlled
Jawa Sandcrawler
left side view,
with remote.

Radio Controlled Jawa Sandcrawler

[Production #39270]

1st packaged appearance: 1979
Original Retail Price (average): $29.99

Many thousands of years before the Battle of Yavin, and on occasion since, on the desert planet of Tatooine, assorted corporate interests think the world is ready to host mining operations. Although these companies (Czerka Corporation, Corellia Mining Corp., etc.) make a *substantial* initial investment, a host of issues thwarts their plans: countless violent raids by Tusken Raiders (Sand People), the excavation of poor quality ore, and Tatooine's baking heat and fierce sandstorms drive these corporations off world.

In their impoverished wake and haste to depart, these companies not onlyleave behind a slew of mining equipment, but also the massive tracked vehicles on which they conduct their operations: what is currently known as the Jawas' Sandcrawler. One of the great traits of the mysterious Jawa race is their supreme adaptability, and the diminutive scavengers saw in these vehicles the perfect opportunity for both safety and profit, immediately adjusting them to serve their culture. Fitted with electric cranes, working elevators, the ability to travel over a vast distance, functional workshops, and room for ample living quarters as well as droid/junk storage, these Sandcrawlers were adapted to become the prime mode of transportation and defense for Jawa culture.

Specifically, the version of Sandcrawler translated into plastic by Kenner Toys was the Corellia Mining Corporation digger crawler produced and distributed by TaggeCo (the Tagge Company). Sufficiently stable enough to withstand the sandstorms and adverse weather of Tatooine, these Sandcrawlers are powered by a nuclear fusion engine, and possess heavy-duty tracked treads, which enable them to cross the planet's massive sand dunes.

After major sandstorms, Jawas venture into remote territories in search of ancient, wrecked spacecraft, building ad hoc processing facilities in the field if one

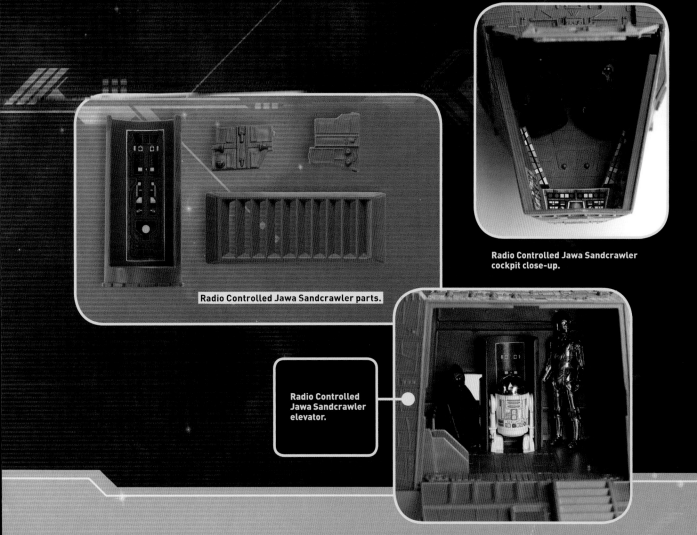

Radio Controlled Jawa Sandcrawler parts.

Radio Controlled Jawa Sandcrawler cockpit close-up.

Radio Controlled Jawa Sandcrawler elevator.

of these ships is discovered, sometimes calling upon other Jawa clans to help them process and dismantle the find. The uppermost front cockpit of the Sandcrawler is the location of the bridge, an area which possesses many small window slits that are monitored by the Jawa 24-7. From this vantage point, if a glint of metal is seen in the distance by one of the clan's scouts, the clan's chief is notified (he usually inhabits the bridge) and the vehicle pursues the sighting. This is also how Jawas locate and encounter droids as they did with R2-D2 and C-3PO in *Episode IV*, which are then captured and moved into the Sandcrawler via an extendable magnetized suction tube originally used for drawing ore from a find by the former owners. For larger items, a retractable front-loading hatch is used (yet on the Kenner toy, only the upper front hatch to allow for the Jawas' bridge crew and one side hatch to allow for droid and materiel storage opened).

On a related note, the Kenner remote-controlled Jawa Sandcrawler is a magnificent toy — and is current-

ly in high demand on the secondary market. It is quite fragile, and has a few interesting action features and a bevy of removable and moving parts. With an elevator used to move droids into the sandcrawler, a flip down ramp with ladder, an opening cockpit that allowed the Jawa chieftain to view the desert while he directed his crew, and a remote control that allowed kids to maneuver the expensive craft, this toy is popular among collectors.

The Sandcrawler possesses the following easily lost/removable parts: elevator, stairs, remote control (body, screw-on antenna, removable battery cover, and long wire), Sandcrawler battery cover, roof hatch (x2), side door/ramp.

MISB: **$3,000-$3,200+**; **MIB**: contents sealed: **$650-$810+**, contents loose, working electronics: **$350-$410+**; **MLC**: working electronics: **$185-$225+**

Star Wars (vinyl) Mini-Figures Collector's Case

`[Production #39190]*`

1st packaged appearance: 1979
Original Retail Price (average): $5.99

*Note: The production number for all of Kenner's vinyl Mini-Figures Collector's Cases is exactly the same: Kenner did not change the assortment number regardless of the year of release: 1979, 1980, 1981, 1982, or 1983.

Due to the small stature of *Star Wars* action figures when released in the 1970s relative to other larger toy lines, Kenner decided to label these toys as "Mini" action figures; the *Star Wars* assortment's shortest characters were 2-1/4-inch tall (R2-D2 and the Jawas), while the tallest figures were 4-1/4-inch tall (Chewbacca and Darth Vader). Therefore, these figurines are a full *four inches* shorter than the most popular action figures of that decade: Mego's Official World's Greatest Super-Heroes.

Yet, thanks to the resounding success of their 3-3/4-inch tall figurines, Kenner concocted the idea of producing transportable, lunch box-style receptacles to hold these miniaturized *Star Wars* characters and their respective accessories. Hence, the vinyl Mini-Figures Collector's Cases were the perfect manner with which to protect and transport the figures, and each vinyl Mini-Figures Collector's Case released at retail from 1979-1983 was "sealed" via a small piece of clear translucent plastic wrapped vertically around the middle of each case, while a small color-printed flier was posted to the cases' blank back via mild, removable adhesive.

Adorned with spectacularly painted artwork that utilizes still photos from the films as inspiration to decorate the front of each of these delicate, heat-sealed vinyl cases—with edges and corners that easily peel and rip—this is the first of many box-shaped portable collector's cases released during the heyday of the vintage Kenner toy line.

Note that the artwork on the collectors case's front is from prominently featured action figures (playsets, and vehicles) that were currently released at retail: Han Solo, Chewbacca, R5-D4, a Power Droid, Walrus Man (in his action figure's generic-looking outfit, yet with a VERY odd rifle), Greedo (also in his action figure's outfit), a Death Star Droid,

Hammerhead, a Jawa (who goes by the name of "Datcha"), Ben "Obi-Wan" Kenobi, two images of Darth Vader, Luke Skywalker, Princess Leia Organa, R2-D2, C-3PO, a Sand Person (Tusken Raider), a Death Squad Commander (Sgt. Derek Torent), Stormtroopers, a moisture evaporator from the Lars homestead, an X-wing Fighter, a TIE Fighter, an Imperial Star Destroyer, and an upside-down Death Star.

Each one of these *Star Wars* Collector's Cases came with a sturdy, four-color paper insert which feature images of the Kenner action figures who were currently available in retail stores, but this paper insert could be laid atop the uppermost of the two trays to stop the figures' weapons from moving around and becoming lost when a child was transporting the case from "A" to "B." However, when we regard the earliest versions of the *Star Wars* Mini-Figure Collector's Case, those that shipped earliest at retail included a rather odd paper insert: this VERY HARD-TO-FIND insert feature a prototype version of Boba Fett; a mold of the bounty hunter's action figure that was never released to the public at any time. Careful collectors will notice that this prototype is almost exactly the same version of the bounty hunter photographed for the Boba Fett mail-away offer advertisement emblazoned on Star Wars 20-back action figure package (i.e., "GET A FREE BOBA FETT ACTION FIGURE").

This case includes the following easily damaged/removable parts: Collector's Case with Color Front Image (blue vinyl inside), Two Stackable Silver-Gray Action Figure Trays, Label Sheet (black-colored), Four-Color Paper Insert (black on both sides), and White Carrying Handle.

MISP: with plastic wrap around the case: **$310-$350+**; **MIP**: with preproduction Boba Fett insert and unapplied labels: **$190-$215+**, with standard insert and unapplied labels: **$40-$45+**; **MLC**: with preproduction Boba Fett insert and labels applied: **$170-$185+**; **MLC**: with standard insert and labels applied: **$18-$22**.

CASE HOLDS 24 **STAR·WARS** MINI-ACTION
FIGURES. COLLECT THEM ALL!

Stormtrooper? · Greedo? · Hammerhead? · Snaggletooth? · Walrus Man? · Stormtrooper?

R5-D4? · Sand People? · Death Star Droid? · Luke Skywalker: X-Wing Pilot? · Boba Fett? · Power Droid?

CLOSE-UP

Insert, prototype
Boba Fett.

STAR WARS

Stormtrooper? · Greedo? · Hammerhead? · Snaggletooth? · Walrus Man? · Stormtrooper?

R5-D4? · Sand People? · Death Star Droid? · Luke Skywalker: X-Wing Pilot? · Boba Fett? · Power Droid?

CASE HOLDS 24 STAR WARS ACTION FIGURES • COLLECT THEM ALL!

CLOSE-UP

Insert, standard
Boba Fett.

**Star Wars Mini-Figures
Collector's Case standard
release Insert, complete.**

Action Figure Survival Kit, mailer box with ephemera.

Action Figure Survival Kit, individual accessories.

Action Figure Survival Kit*

[Production #39632]

1st packaged appearance: 41-back card
Original Retail Price (average): N/A
(5 proof-of-purchase seals)

*Note: Parts of this kit were included in the Rebel Transport vehicle, and assorted playsets and vehicles as bonuses (see AT-AT Imperial All Terrain Armored Transport, Dagobah Action Playset, etc.).

Mailed third class to your home in a white mailer box, with a white instruction sheet describing the items inside, and all of the weapons and accessories packed into a clear baggie, stamped with the "Kenner" logo in blue lettering and "Made in Hong Kong" printed underneath, this "Action Figure Survival Kit" (sometimes singular, sometimes plural) was the one and only time *Star Wars* action figures could receive extra accessories via mail-order with the redemption of five proof-of-purchase seals. The names delineated to the right are considered to be the proper appellations of the accessories, as they have been gleaned from both the insert included within the set's mail-away box AND on the reverse of the Empire Strikes Back 41-back (version "C") action figure card ("Collect all 41!").

The Action Figure Survival Kit includes twelve accessories: 1 Luke Skywalker AT-AT Grappling Hook Belt with Cable and Hook, 1 Jedi Training Harness, 2 Hoth Backpacks, 3 Asteroid Gas Masks, and "5 Assorted Laser Weapons." Specifically, the laser weapons included with the set are: a blue/black Imperial Blaster (E-11 Blaster Rifle), a blue Bespin Blaster (DH-17 Blaster Pistol), a blue Imperial Rifle (DLT-20A Blaster Rifle), a blue Imperial Rifle ("modified" DLT-20A Blaster Rifle with added handle), and a black Hoth Rebel Rifle (BlasTech A295 Blaster Rifle).

The kit includes the 12 easily lost accessories mentioned.

 MISP: $28-$35+; **MIB**: contents sealed in baggie: **$22-$25**, contents not sealed: **$18-$22**; **MLC**: **$15-$20**.

Darth Vader Collector's Case

[Production #39630]

1st packaged appearance: 1980
Original Retail Price (average): $5.99

With the ability to hold 31 action figures and all their myriad accessories within a small "Accessory Storage Chamber" in this imposing-looking transport that expertly captures the three-dimensional visage of one of the most infamous villains in history, Kenner sold *millions* of Darth Vader Collector's Cases, hereafter referred to as the "DVCC," throughout the course of its production run. The toy's inner compartments allow for more room than the smaller, box-shaped vinyl collector's cases that were released from 1979-1983 (see Star Wars [vinyl] Mini-Figures Collector's Case), since within the DVCC, some select units of its 31 compartments are larger than average in order to accommodate figures such as Chewbacca, Darth Vader, and IG-88, while others are smaller to host the likes of Jawas, R2-D2, Snaggletooth,

or Ugnaughts, as a result of the odd shape of Darth Vader's head and shoulders.

When reviewing sealed samples of this toy, you will notice two pieces of transparent tape sealing the top of the case, while a large chipboard skirt was wrapped around the base—a paper sleeve that enveloped Vader's shoulders which may be used to determine the case's release date, whether it is the more common *ESB*-solicited case, or the far rarer *ROTJ* case that was solicited in far fewer numbers due to the fact that Kenner concocted a shiny, all-new case in 1983 (see the See-Threepio Collector's Case). Furthermore, inside the case—separating the two halves of the DVCC—is found a large, four-color paper insert featuring a majority of characters from the newest *Empire Strikes Back* assortment of action figures (or again,

Darth Vader Collector's Case MISB (ESB and ROTJ variations), with insert variations.

195

in rare cases, *Return of the Jedi*), similar in delivery to the four-color action figure inserts placed within the vinyl collector's cases Kenner solicited from 1979-1983. Therefore, there exist different inserts featuring action figures from the latest *ESB* assortments released in 1980, 1981, 1982, and *ROTJ* in 1983. Also included within the case, as with the vinyl collector's cases, was a sheet of self-stick labels with every action figure's name so kids could personalize each compartment. These labels should be affixed to the straps that hold figures in their respective places, in order to identify the figures' compartments.

The DVCC was sold for a long while in *Empire Strikes Back* packaging and there were a number of packaging revisions for the skirt, the labels, and the four-color insert: in 1980 (with the following number of figures on the sleeve's reverse side) featuring 31-back packaging, 32-back, and 41-back; in 1981—with 41-back packaging; and in 1982—with 47-back packaging. It was briefly sold with a *Return of the Jedi* chipboard sleeve in 1983 with 65-back and 77-back packaging. On occasion, in order to stimulate sales, bonus figures were included to spruce things up—sealed samples with these bonus figures add a LOT of extra value to the case on the secondary market. Please consult eBay via a "Completed Items Search," or contact a reputable dealer on the Internet to best gauge these prices.

As a final note, the earliest versions of the DVCC were solicited via a simple cardboard mailer box as catalog exclusives via Sears, Montgomery Wards, etc. More importantly, however, was the fact that the label sheet for these early DVCCs were not branded *ESB*, but simply *Star Wars*, while some of the characters' names on the included label sheet were pre-production names; from "Imperial Snow Stormtrooper" to "Rebel Snow Soldier," from "Ben Kenobi: Obi-Wan" to "Bespin Security Force," from "Assistant Medical Droid: FX-7," to "IG-88 Bounty Hunter," these earlier-released names and the DVCCs themselves are quite fascinating.

The DVCC includes the following features: label sheet, four-color paper action figure insert, and removable support rods (x6; to hold figures and accessories in place).

MISB: *ROTJ*: **$225-$250+**, mailer-box/catalog retailers: **$155-$175+**; *ESB*: **$105-$125**; **MIB**: *ROTJ* with paper sleeve, insert and unapplied labels: **$60-$75**, *ESB* with paper sleeve, insert and unapplied labels: **$38-$50**; **MLC**: with *ROTJ* insert and unapplied labels: **$40-$52+**, with *ESB* insert and unapplied labels: **$25-$40+**, with insert, all labels applied: **$8-$12**.

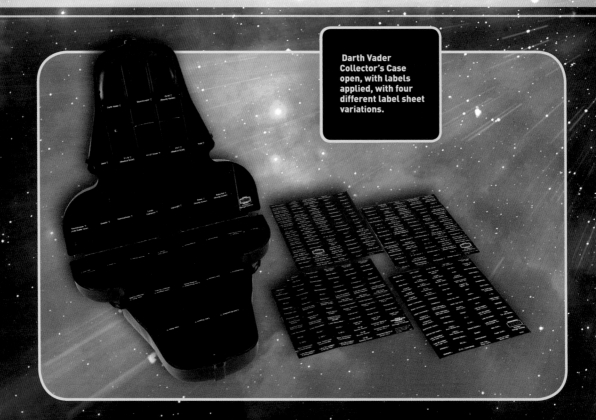

Darth Vader Collector's Case open, with labels applied, with four different label sheet variations.

Darth Vader's
Star Destroyer,
left view.

Darth Vader's Star Destroyer Action Playset

[Production #39850]

1st packaged appearance: 1980
Original Retail Price (average): $17.99

It is worth mentioning that Darth Vader's Star Destroyer Action Playset was created to imitate the spacecraft occupied by the Sith Lord and his crew as Lord Vader pursues the small band of rebels in *The Empire Strikes Back*. However, if we look at the original script and resulting footage for the film, Vader's ship is notably more massive than the five other similar craft surrounding him.

Vader's capital ship, "any armed military starship that possesses a length greater than one hundred meters," is not technically a

Darth Vader's Meditation Chamber.

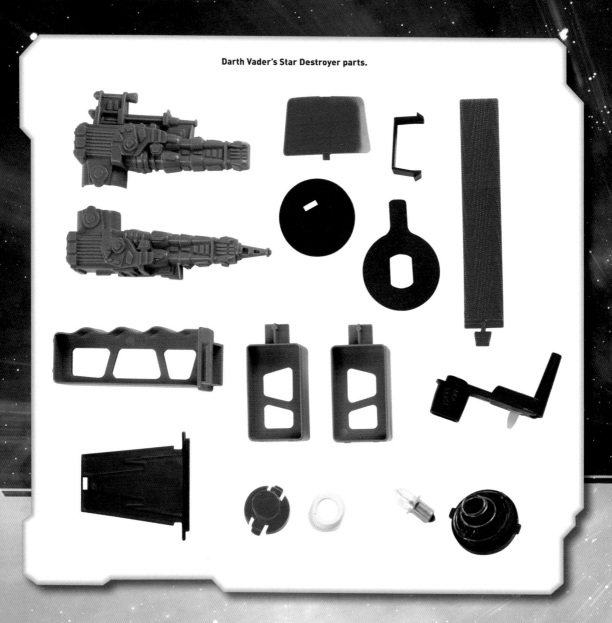

Darth Vader's Star Destroyer parts.

Star Destroyer—colloquially, it is an "*Executor*-class Super Star Destroyer" or an "*Executor*-class Destroyer." However, aficionados and die-hards refer to the ship as the "*Executor*-class Star Dreadnought." As a Star Dreadnought, the *Executor* represents one of a number of the largest and most powerful battleships gleaned from the starfleets of local or regional governments.

Many scenes in *ESB* take place on the decks of the *Executor* and therefore, this Kenner playset: the recruitment of bounty hunters 4-LOM, Boba Fett, Dengar, IG-88, Bossk, and Zuckuss, Darth Vader utilizing the rejuvenating effects of his specially crafted spherical hyperbaric meditation chamber, the

Dark Lord using his HoloNet transceiver projection pod (on the toy, a translucent flip-down "hologram" screen) for communicating with the Emperor, and also, Vader choking the life out of the incompetent Admiral Ozzel via viewscreen—to show filmgoers his limitless power.

This playset allowed collectors to access the following amazing features, such as the ability to "re-live Darth's sending Bounty Hunters after the Rebel Alliance," and also to place a Darth Vader action figure in the Meditation Chamber to increase Darth's Force power by activating the Force light—with the push of a button, and the inclusion of two C batteries, a red glow could engulf Darth Vader's meditation

Princess Leia uses the trapdoor.

Darth Vader meets with bounty hunters on the bridge of the *Executor*.

Darth Vader's Star Destroyer, with figures.

chamber. Imperial Stormtroopers could protect the Star Destroyer with the swiveling laser cannon, Rebel prisoners could push a button to open the door and help Princess Leia through the secret escape hatch, and for those kids who were lifting weights at a young age, the playset's instructions further suggested that the "Star Destroyer can be carried by its landing struts to simulate flight."

Finally, according to the box text, it appears that "Darth talks to the Grand Vizier with the pretend viewing screen ..." by lowering the slide-down translucent piece of red plastic from the roof of the Star Destroyer.

Darth Vader's Star Destroyer Action Playset includes the following easily lost/removable parts:

Front Housing, Landing Struts (x3; two rear [shorter and exactly the same], one front [longer]), Laser Cannon Barrel (two-piece [one-time assembly]), Laser Cannon Lever Hub, Meditation Chamber Assembly (with Meditation Chamber, Lower Half; Computer Console; Meditation Chamber, Upper Half; Battery Cap [two-piece, one-time assembly]; Bulb [labeled "PR-2"]; Red Filter Cover; Red Window), White Reflector, Rear Housing, Star Destroyer Base, Top Housing, Red Hologram, Hologram Retainer Clip (very hard to find), and Trapdoor.

MISB: $550-$610; MIB: $165-$190+; MLC: $58-$75.

Empire Strikes Back
Mini-Figures Collector's
Case, complete.

Empire Strikes Back (vinyl) Mini-Figures Collector's Case

[Production #39190]*

1st packaged appearance: 1980
Original Retail Price (average): $5.99

*Note: The production number for all of Kenner's vinyl Mini-Figures Collector's Cases is exactly the same; Kenner did not change the number regardless of the year of release (1979, 1980, 1981, 1982, or 1983).

This marks the first time Kenner solicited their popular vinyl Mini-Figures Collector's Case with an *Empire Strikes Back* logo on it, even though this is essentially the same case as the original *Star Wars* [vinyl] Mini-Figures Collector's Case sold in 1979. The only differences: 1) the logo on the front of the collectors case's front picture has been changed from *Star Wars* to *Star Wars: The Empire Strikes Back*, 2) the earlier case's sturdy, four-color paper insert featuring action figures and logo from Kenner's *Star Wars* assortment has now been changed to showcase new characters and a logo from *ESB*, and 3) the sticker sheet featuring labels that delineate *SW* characters now has been amended to add figurines from Kenner's new *ESB* assortments.

One of the fascinating aspects of these vinyl Mini-Figures Collector's Cases—apart from their ability to hold 24 vintage action figures and all of their accessories—is the fact that the two inner trays can be stacked (and locked, albeit a bit loosely) on top of one another *ad infinitum* so that if you own ten or more of

these cases, you could potentially stack them exponentially high. These trays also yielded another bit of utility: if you flip over each tray, Kenner added twelve foot pegs on the reverse side of the tray which allowed collectors to pose their action figures on top, since each figure was equipped with two holes on the bottom of their feet: simply turn the trays over to display your collection. Similar to the originally released *Star Wars* case, the four-color paper insert could be place atop the uppermost tray in order to keep your figures' accessories from falling out of their various compartments. A cheaper alternative to the newly-released Darth Vader Collector's Case, this satchel still sold fairly well for Kenner.

This Mini-Figures Collector's Case includes the following easily damaged/removable parts: Collector's Case with Color Front Image (blue vinyl inside), Two Stackable Gray Action Figure Trays, Label Sheet (black-colored), Four-Color Paper Insert (black-colored [Featuring 24 Figures]), and White Carrying Handle.

MISP: with plastic wrap around the case: **$340-$360+**; **MIP**: with paper insert and unapplied labels: **$40-$45+**; **MLC**: with paper insert and labels applied: **$18-$25**.

Hoth Ice Planet
Adventure Set,
with figures.

Hoth Ice Planet Adventure Set

[Production #38770]

1st packaged appearance: 1980
Original Retail Price (average): $10.99

Essentially an update of 1979's Land of the Jawas Action Playset with a different-colored base (a white "snowscape" base instead of desert tan), and a replacement of the Land's cardboard backdrop of a Jawa Sandcrawler with the Ice Planet's cardboard backdrop of an Imperial AT-AT walker, the cardboard AT-AT and printed backdrop is the only unique addition to this playset. The base of the Hoth Ice Planet Adventure Set is *exactly* the same mold as that of the Land of the Jawas: vehicle tread marks and a large divot in the snow are apparent on the right side of the base, while a small cave exists to the left, with a firing trigger in front of said cave. Even the outside and inside of each cardboard backdrop is similar: whether cardboard Sandcrawler or AT-AT, a small manual elevator afforded collectors the ability to move figures inside the belly of the vehicle, where four individual sets of foot pegs allowed

figures to stand. So then, 1980's Hoth Ice Planet Adventure Set utilizes all the same "base" accessories/accoutrements that are included with 1979's Land of the Jawas, yet these pieces are cast in white plastic: the action button, lever and stand, snapper arm and cap, and—of course—the sturdy base. With an "action lever to simulate mock battles" and an elevator that lifts Stormtroopers into the cardboard AT-AT backdrop, this is an entertaining playset. Furthermore, instead of the escape pod that comes with Land of the Jawas, the Hoth Ice Planet Adventure Set comes with a Radar Laser Cannon—a scaled-down version of 1982's larger (and separately sold) "Radar Laser Cannon" weapon system. This smaller "Laser Radar Cannon swivels up and down and turns," adding another action feature to an already interesting play setting.

This set has the following easily lost/removable parts: Action Button, Action Lever, Action Stand, Elevator Front, Elevator Guide Rails (x2)*, Elevator Rear, Pegs (x4), Radar Laser Cannon Assembly (Radar Dish, Lower Base, Turret Left Side, Turret Right Side, Upper Base), Snapper Arm, and Snapper Cap.

*Without the two Elevator Guide Rails (one for each side) to protect the cardboard backdrop, the up-and-down movement of the elevator leading from the white base to the inside of the AT-AT would ruin the integrity of the cardboard's corrugation and cause the elevator to become quite loose. Furthermore, these guide rails are NOT the same length: one is longer.

Hoth Ice Planet Adventure Set parts.

 MISB: $425-$525+; **MIB:** $70-$85+; **MLC:** $48-$62.

Imperial Attack Base
Playset, isometric view.

Imperial Attack Base Playset

[Production #39831]

1st packaged appearance: 1980
Original Retail Price (average): $10.99

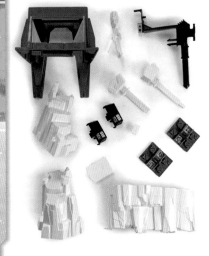

Imperial Attack Base Playset parts.

Still available on the secondary market for a reasonable price (however, collectors should always check for completeness due to the toy's assortment of loose parts), the Imperial Attack Base Playset is an excellent enemy fortification that allows Darth Vader to spearhead the Galactic Empire's mission to overwhelm Rebel forces on Hoth. With a bevy of fabulous action features and a wealth of foot pegs for you to pose Imperial Snowtroopers (a.k.a. Imperial Stormtrooper [Hoth Battle Gear]), Kenner surely constructed a popular and enduring playset. It is because of the quality of planning, the vastness of the invading Imperial army, and the Empire's fierce bunkers such as this base that they score a major victory and the single worst battlefield defeat suffered by the Rebel Alliance to Restore the Republic during the Galactic Civil War.

Although the destruction of the Rebel Alliance's Echo Base hidden on Hoth is assured, due to an important tactical error made by Admiral (Kendal) Ozzel, who leaves lightspeed too close to Hoth and alerts the Rebels of the presence of the Imperial army, the remaining Rebels to flee into space.

Kenner's Imperial Attack Base Playset afforded collectors the opportunity to "defend an Imperial Attack base with the Laser Machine gun," to "simulate battle action with the land mine," and to "pretend you

The Rebel heroes face off against Darth and his Snowtroopers.

Imperial Attack Base Playset command post, intact.

Imperial Attack Base Playset command post, collapsed.

detonate the snow bridge." With a multitude of action features such as the ability to "create battle action with remote levers," to "rotate the cannon for authentic laser sound," and to "simulate a direct hit against the Attack Base by pressing action lever to make Command Post and Snow Bank collapse," kids could effectively recreate the Empire's march on Echo base.

The base contains the following easily lost/removable parts: Cannon with Foot Stand, Command Post, Command Post Hatch Covers (x2), Command Post Lever (marked "S"), Ice Bridge (two-piece), Ice Bridge Lever (marked "I"), Ice Bridge Lever Cover, Land Mine, Land Mine Lever (marked "L"), Monitor #1 (for Land Mine Assembly), Monitor #2 (for Command Post Assembly), and a Snow Bank.

MISB: $265-$290+; **MIB**: $45-$60; **MLC**: $28-$35.

203

Rebel Armored Snowspeeder parts.

Rebel Armored Snowspeeder, isometric view.

Rebel Armored Snowspeeder, back view.

Rebel Armored Snowspeeder

[Production #39610]

1st packaged appearance: 1980
Original Retail Price (average): $14.99

Although outgunned at the Battle of Hoth (ca. 3 ABY) by the Empire's well-armed and heavily armored AT-AT walkers (regard the AT-AT vehicle's own entry), Luke Skywalker and his small band of Rebels need a specialized vehicle that can traverse the inhospitable terrain and frigid cold of the ice planet Hoth.

To accomplish this difficult feat, the Rebellion chooses the Incom Corporation's T-47 airspeeder—a craft originally utilized to transport industrial-sized cargo. The T-47's designers require that the ship possesses a dual cockpit to accommodate both a pilot (in the fore position), and a cargo manager (in the aft, facing backward). It is the cargo manager who uses the harpoon-and-tow-cable assembly mounted on the rear

of the airspeeder to manipulate towed freight. Due to the delicate nature of the pulled cargo, the T-47 also sports high-powered thrust nozzles and mechanical braking flaps, which afford the craft supreme maneuverability for its size.

Necessity being the mother of invention, the Rebels' best technicians modify the transport ship into the Rebel Armored Snowspeeder as we currently know it: a decidedly fit patrol/combat craft. Used for reconnaissance missions on other worlds before its import to Hoth, the Snowspeeder is modified even further to adapt the ship to withstand the torrid cold of the planet's tundra.

So then, during the Battle of Hoth, Rebel Armored Snowspeeders led by Luke Skywalker and the noble pilots of Rogue Squadron—an elite starfighter squadron of the Rebel Alliance, founded shortly after the Battle of Yavin; a successor to Red Squadron—successfully delay the Imperial invasion long enough for the Rebels to evacuate Echo Base.

Collectors could defend their Snowspeeder with [a detachable] laser harpoon cannon [on a cable] … [be-

Tauntaun

`[Production #39820]`

1st packaged appearance: 1980
Original Retail Price (average): $8.99

**Tauntaun, with
Han Solo (in Hoth Outfit).**

**Tauntaun reins
and saddle.**

The indispensable snow-lizard known as a tauntaun serves as a sturdy mount for the many Rebels (see Rebel Soldier [Hoth Battle Gear]), who need personal modes of transportation for reconnaissance missions on the ice planet of Hoth. Hardy beasts, the omnivorous Tauntauns are *reptomammals*—like Rancor, Wampa, and possibly Rodians like Greedo—a class of animal possessing both mammalian and reptilian traits. The tauntaun is an animal whose skin is covered in scales, yet these scales are further coated with shaggy fur, and so at first glance many assume they are mammals. However, they lack mammary glands entirely, and although they engage in live childbirth, for their newborn young they regurgitate a substance similar to "milk," which is produced in their crops.

The single most essential trait of the tauntaun is its highly unusual blood. Fuelled by the animal's four nostrils, which allow the beast to both warm inhaled air and also oxygenate the blood during moments of physical duress, a tauntaun's blood is constructed of a unique mixture that allows the creature to keep its organs from freezing solid, while also affording the species a high level of resistance to the planet's absolutely brutal winds.

Kenner's superbly crafted Tauntaun creature/mount is action-packed and fairly simply to assemble, therefore quite easy to get it ready for action. With moveable front and hind legs, and featuring a trap door in back that fits most action figures, collectors could relive the Rebel Alliance's most important patrol—Han Solo searching for Luke Skywalker.

The Tauntaun only included two easily lost/removable parts made of soft rubber and were quite delicate: a harness and a saddle.

MISB: $85-$115; MIB: $30-$42; MLC: $12-$25, depending upon condition.

---

cause the harpoon] is removable and disengages," an action feature that replicates the harpoon and tow cable scene from *ESB*: essentially an improvised weapon system developed by the genius military tactician, Alliance Commander Beryl Chiffonage, whose "hit it and twist" tactics are used by Luke Skywalker and others in their 1-4/s to successfully defeat Imperial walkers during the Battle of Hoth. After they'd finished with the AT ATs, kids could land their Snowspeeders, and activate the vehicle's landing gear by a remote button, then take their pilot and gunner out of the opening cockpit that held two action figures. Furthermore, with the use of

two C batteries, the Snowspeeder exhibited some of the best "pulsating" laser lights and sounds of any vintage *Star Wars* vehicle.

The Snowspeeder includes the following easily lost/removable parts: Battery Cover, Canopy (with Windshield), 2 Engine Exhaust Cones, Harpoon Assembly (Anchor, Harpoon, String), 2 Laser Cannons 2 Laser Cannon Middle Sections,

MISB: $650-$725+; MIB: working electronics: **$62-$82; MLC:** working electronics: $34-$48

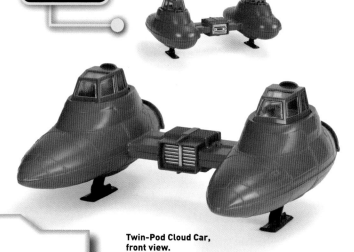

Twin-Pod Cloud Car, rear view.

Twin-Pod Cloud Car, front view.

Twin-Pod Cloud Car parts.

Twin-Pod Cloud Car

[Production #39860]

1st packaged appearance: 1980
Original Retail Price (average): $9.99

The spectacularly designed Storm IV Twin-Pod Cloud Car iks produced by the firm known as Bespin Motors—originally, one branch of the prominent air vehicle manufacturer, the Incom Corporation (see X-wing Fighter). The company is also tasked to construct the impressive outpost of Cloud City itself.

The Storm IV Twin-Pod Cloud Car or more colloquially, the "Twin-Pod Cloud Car," or simply "Cloud Car," is originally designed to patrol the skies surrounding Cloud City: a lucrative mining colony and profitable gambling resort (see Cloud City Playset). The Cloud Car is a highly maneuverable spaceship and serves as a civilian transport, yetcan also function as security and defense. Armed with weapon emplacements that sport two standard blaster cannons that can be swapped out to feature a wide array of different armaments, an advanced navigation system, and a top-notch communications array, the Cloud Car's

superb handling makes it a challenging opponent in combat. With a set of dual cockpits that allow for the ease of enemy engagement (left/port side = main pilot; right/starboard side = gunner), an ion engine that permits the craft to reach speeds of 1,500 kph, and a repulsorlift drive that is utilized to both increase the craft's speed and afford it pinpoint maneuverability, the Storm IV Twin-Pod Cloud Car staunchly defends Cloud City—as evidenced by Han Solo's reaction to the Bespin Wing Guards' firing warning shots next to the *Millennium Falcon*.

As a toy, the Twin-Pod Cloud Car has few easily lost parts, and is found ubiquitously throughout the secondary market and inside collectible stores. Aesthetically, it is quite appealing, and due to its relatively low cost in MLC (Mint, Loose, and Complete) condition, it is one of the few vintage vehicles that you could purchase multiple times for "troop building" purposes.

The Twin-Pod Cloud Car includes the following easily lost/removable parts: two opening cockpits with windshields.

MISB: $225-$265+; **MIB:** $30-$35; **MLC:** $15-$25.

Twin-Pod Cloud Car, with figures.

Action Figure Display Arena (Mail-Away)

[Production #N/A]

1st packaged appearance: 1981
Original Retail Price (average): mail-away ($2 shipping and handling)

With four 7-1/2-inch long "L"-shaped display stands that each hold fourteen vintage *Star Wars* action figures, via an assortment of foot pegs, this mail-away offer was obtainable if collectors purchased any ten action figures and sent the figurines' ten proof-of-purchase seals along with $2 for shipping, handling, and processing. After ten to twelve weeks, these four stands would be shipped to your home along with four reversible backdrops that kids could mount behind each of the four display stands, and would function as different battle scenes when children displayed their collection.

The curious shape of these four stands allowed these stands to "clip" onto one another in a variety of different designs—as an arena (so described in its name): from a long rectangle to a square to a cross to four "Ls" in a row, this was a unique way to provide dedicated collectors a reward for their dedication to the vintage toy line.

The arena includes the following easily lost/removable parts: 4 Interlocking Display Arena Bases, and 4 Reversible Four-Color Backdrops.

MISB: $355-$410+; **MIB:** $125-$155; **MLC:** $48-$62+.

Action Figure Display Arena.

AT-AT, right view.

AT-AT
([Imperial] All Terrain Armored Transport)

[Production #38810]

1st packaged appearance: 1981
Original Retail Price (average): $49.99

Derived from the AT-TE (All Terrain Tactical Enforcer) clone-deploying "tanks" utilized by the Galactic Republic during the Clone Wars (22-19 BBY), the intimidating vehicle known as the AT-AT (All Terrain Armored Transport) is one of the Galactic Empire's menacing motorized behemoths—a four-legged mechanical monstrosity resembling a mythological beast of war—utilized by the Imperial Army to promote terror throughout the galaxy. One of the preeminent vehicles of the Empire's legendary ground forces, these Imperial walkers are heavily armored, well-armed (yet relatively slow), troop-deploying land vehicles that spread destruction and chaos in their wake.

The AT-AT contains a number of different stations, each of which is essential to the assignment of every Imperial walker. The head of the beast is known as the "command section," which is manned by a commander (see AT-AT Commander), pilot (see AT-AT Driver), and gunner, and is equipped with a detailed sensor array, a command viewport, a pair of side-mounted medium repeating blasters, and twin heavy laser cannons that occupy space just underneath the chin (two Taim and Bak MS-1 fire-linked heavy laser cannons)—all of which can be independently operated, while a flexible armored tunnel (for cockpit access, essentially the mechanical beast's bendable "neck") connects the first command section to the AT-AT's second component. The command section houses the vehicle's weapon systems, a holoprojector for the sake of external communications, and holographic targeting systems, which affords the gunner a 360-degree view of the battlefield.

The second "troop section"—the armored trapezoidal body of this mechanical beast—is furnished with a side panel, escape hatch, a large boarding hatch for ease of access, a troop staging area with room for up to forty soldiers (see Imperial Stormtrooper [Hoth Battle Gear]) in its double-tiered passenger section, and a small vehicle bay for deploying speeders and the like (see Speeder Bike); the standard AT-AT can store up to five Imperial speeders *along with* the requisite troops. In lieu of these soldiers however, an AT-AT may hold two semi-disassembled AT-STs (see Scout Walker vehicle).

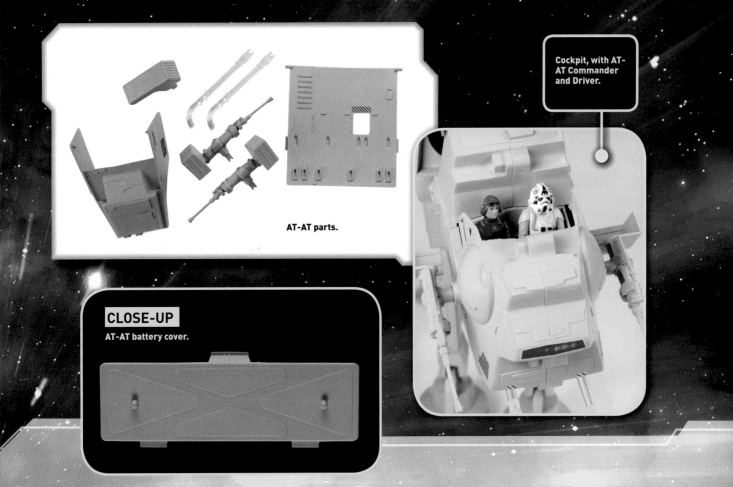

AT-AT parts.

Cockpit, with AT-AT Commander and Driver.

CLOSE-UP
AT-AT battery cover.

Ending in durasteel footpads, the vehicle's four fully articulated, heavily reinforced legs, which require constant repair and maintenance, can bend to kneel at just a few meters above the ground where a boarding ramp is released to dispense Imperial troopers, while two tremendous Kuat Drive Yards FW62 compact fusion drive systems afford the vehicle the ability to move at an remarkable 60 mph. Standing an impressive 22.5 meters (nearly 74 feet) tall, the AT-AT can crush nearly anything in its path as evidenced by the role it plays in the Battle of Hoth.

Unfortunately for the Empire, as Luke Skywalker discovers, the AT-AT's belly armor is far weaker than what sealed the rest of the vehicle. Since a walker can be standing atop its enemies rather quickly, this is a real danger; usually, AT-STs are deployed to protect the AT-AT weak, vulnerable underbelly.

The Kenner toy possesses myriad action features: collectors could "place AT-AT Drivers in the control room," the toy's "clicking machine guns [will] swivel to defend the AT-AT," while "Locat[-ing] your target by positioning the AT-AT head [and] activate [the vehicle's] pulsating,

flashing laser cannons to destroy the Rebel Base by pushing the action button" which requires two "D" Alkaline batteries (not included). Furthermore, kids could "place [an] AT-AT in battle action poses [since its] legs can move at two joints and [its] feet," while the AT-AT's "body holds up to 10 action figures.

Although the impressively scaled AT-AT was released in both *ESB* and *ROTJ* boxes, it was only in the boxes of the later *Empire* released walkers—those late-run *ESB* toy packages emblazoned with or without a $1 rebate offer on the package front—that contained a special bonus offer. Included inside the toy package was a modified version of the über-popular Action Figure Survival Kit promotional that was initially offered as a mail-away on carded action figure packages in 1980, printed on 41-back cards.

The AT-AT includes the following easily lost/removable parts: Battery Compartment Door, 2 Chin Guns (clear), Head Canopy, Light Bulb, Light Bulb Cover, Side Door (for Troop Access), and 2 Side Guns.

MISB: $825-$975+; **MIB**: working electronics. $105-$215+; **MLC**: working electronics. $105-$125+.

Cloud City Playset.

Cloud City Playset, with figures.

Cloud City Playset (Sears Exclusive)

[Production #38781 or 49 59021]

1st packaged appearance: 1981
(1980 *Sears Wish Book*)
Original Retail Price (average): $9.69

The Sears *Wish Book* exclusive Cloud City Playset included the following contents, according to its package: "One backdrop play environment and four action figures with accessories ... Han Solo in his Bespin Outfit, Lobot, Dengar, and Ugnaught"—all-new figures that weren't available anywhere else in the country during that Christmas season; Sears shipped them earlier than anyone else. This hard-to-find three-dimensional play environment was separated into two different chipboard pieces, and also came with a series of white foot pegs to pop into the playset's base—to afford the included figures the ability to stand. The Cloud City Playset afforded collectors the ability to own a playset featuring one of the most famous scenes in *The Empire*

Strikes Back—a three-dimensional representation of what Cloud City's famous carbon-freezing chamber looks like. Combining this playset with the POTF Han Solo (In Carbonite Chamber) figure or Han Solo (Bespin Outfit), Boba Fett, and the bounty hunter's infamous *Slave-1* vehicles could provide collectors with hours of fun. The playset perfectly mimics the carbon freezing chamber facility that is featured in *The Empire Strikes Back*, where many industrious Ugnaught workers mine tibanna. Found in gaseous or liquid form, tibanna comprises the atmosphere of the gas giant known as Bespin, a planet famously hosting Cloud City: the mining facility where Lando Calrissian functions as the chief administrator.

This three-dimensional playset has six holes die-cut within its base in order to allow the included four figures or any other vintage *Star Wars* characters to stand upright when displaying the toy. The number of white

CLOSE-UP

Cloud City Playset foot pegs.

CLOUD CITY PLAYSET FIGURES

foot pegs included with this playset, placed within a sealed baggie inside the small white box which held the four included action figures, have ranged—in sealed samples—from 7 foot pegs (the normal amount—to accommodate the playset's six foot holes, with one extra for good measure) to a baggie containing 12 or 13 foot pegs (unusual, since these pegs may have been repacked from the Early Bird Certificate Package).

The Cloud City Playset* includes the following easily lost/removable parts: Three-Dimensional Cloud City backdrop (two separate pieces), Han Solo (Bespin Outfit) action figure (with blue Bespin Blaster [DH-17 blaster pistol]), Dengar action figure (with blue Imperial Rifle ["modified" DH-20A blaster rifle with added handle]), Lobot action figure (with blue

Bespin Blaster [DH-17 blaster pistol], and Ugnaught action figure (with toolkit and apron/smock [purple or blue variations]), and somewhere between 7-13 white foot pegs (only 6 are needed for the playset—the others are extra).

*Note: For another magnificent representation of Cloud City, please regard Kenner's brilliantly sculpted Micro Collection Bespin World playsets (Bespin Control Room, Bespin Freeze Chamber, and Bespin Gantry).

MISB: $1,200-$1,550+; MIB: with figures: $130-$165+, without figures: $50-$120+; MLC: with figures: $68-$82, without figures: $55-$72+.

Dagobah Action Playset, with figures.

IN ACTION

R2-D2 falls into the "swamp."

Dagobah Action Playset

`[Production #38820]`

1st packaged appearance: 1981
Original Retail Price (average): $10.99

Serving as the "Elba" of exile for Grand Jedi Master Yoda after Emperor Palpatine's Great Jedi Purge (19 BBY) while waiting for "a new hope" to arrive in the form of Luke Skywalker (and his trusty astromech droid, R2-D2, of course), this remote, world of forests, swamps, and fens, possesses little intelligent life other than Yoda himself—although the planet does appear to have pockets of a more sinister nature. It is simply described on its package front as a toy containing "one playset with two action levers, two 'levitation' levers, and two cargo boxes."

Furthermore, although the Dagobah playset was released in both *ESB* and *ROTJ* boxes, it was only in the boxes of the later *Empire* released sets—those late-run *ESB* toy packages emblazoned with or

without a $1 rebate offer on the package front—that contained a special bonus offer. Included inside the toy package was a piece taken from the Action Figure Survival Kit promotional that was initially offered as a mail-away on carded action figure packages in 1980, printed on 41-back cards. The box front sported lettering in a red circle that touted: "Now Includes Jedi Training Back."

Perhaps the most impressively action-packed of any vintage *Star Wars* playset, the Dagobah playset truly captures the spirit of Yoda's home and Luke's training ground. From the bark-like details the toymakers etched onto the massive tree stump to Kenner's ability to accurately capture the textures of "boggy fen" (or quagmire, if you prefer) that surround and encompass Yoda's Hut, this playset's myriad action features are delineated on

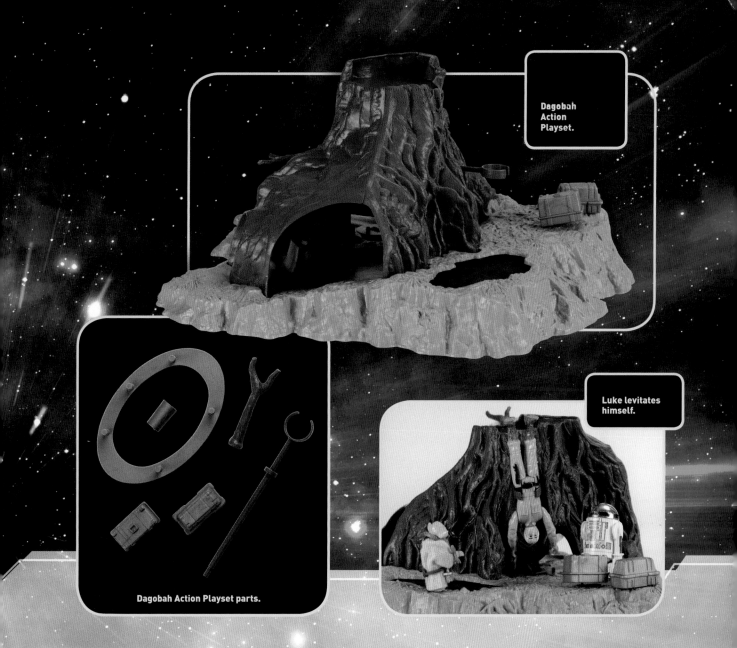

Dagobah Action Playset.

Luke levitates himself.

Dagobah Action Playset parts.

the set's packaging and within the included assembly instructions. Collectors could "recreate Darth's and Luke's Lightsaber battle with these action levers," they would be able to "help Luke master 'The Force' with the 'levitation' action lever," "help Yoda to teach Luke to become a Jedi Knight," or even "pretend to lose your action figure and cargo" in the foam swamp.

However, 95 percent of all Dagobah Action Playset foam swamps have deteriorated over time—the brown foam swamp was not meant to last for decades, only a few short years. You may switch this deteriorating foam swamp with replacement material from a fabric store, or locate replacement swamp materials online. To do this, simply remove the "lower ring" holding in the tattered swamp located on the underside of the Dagobah base, take the old foam out, place your new foam/felt combo back in, replace the lower ring, and your swamp will be functional once again. Conversely, if your sample of the Dagobah Action

Playset has a swamp that appears unscathed, *do not touch it or manipulate it in any way*. It is super-fragile and will deteriorate with the slightest pressure.

Additionally, collectors should take note that the playset's entire tree "stump" is removable and can be taken apart from its base and replaced, since the toy was meant to be disassembled.

The Dagobah Action Playset includes the following easily lost/removable parts: Base, Tree Stump, 2 Action Stands (with 2 Action Levers attached), Two-Piece "Tree" Lever with Branch, 2 Cargo Boxes (both are different sizes), R2-D2 Adapter (allows Artoo to be levitated), Levitation Mechanism, Swamp Ring (Snaps Underneath Swamp Base), Swamp Material (Foam—easily degraded).

MISB: $365-410+; MIB: $65-85+; MLC: $50-60+.

Empire Strikes
Back Mini-Figures
Collector's Case,
complete.

Empire Strikes Back (vinyl) Mini-Figures Collector's Case

[Production #39190]*

1st packaged appearance: 1981
Original Retail Price (average): $5.99

***Note:** The production number for all of Kenner's vinyl Mini-Figures Collector's Cases is exactly the same: Kenner did not change the assortment number regardless of the year of release (1979, 1980, 1981, 1982, or 1983).

This marks Kenner's third "Mini-Action Figure Collector's Case"—and second under the *Empire Strikes Back* logo—that holds 24 exciting figures. With two stackable tan-colored trays to hold the figures and their accessories, a paper insert that featured every figure currently available at retail (41 total at this point), a gray-tan colored label sheet that collectors could use to personalize each compartment, and a sturdy outer casing shrink-wrapped in vinyl (black on the outside, tan on the inside), this *ESB* case was a cheaper alternative to the more expensive Darth Vader Collector's Case.

Note that the magnificent cover artwork on this, the second vinyl *ESB* collector's case's front, is gleaned from the action figures, creatures, playsets, and vehicles that were currently released at retail from Kenner's *Empire Strikes Back* assortments, a viscous image that is detailed as follows: an image of Luke Skywalker atop a Tauntaun using his stolen Imperial binoculars, an AT-AT Driver with AT-AT walker

next to his profile—as a Rebel Armored Snowspeeder utilizing its hook and cable to topple the mechanical beast, Luke in Bespin Fatigues (note the blue lightsaber!) and Darth Vader engaging in a lightsaber duel, a Rebel solider from Hoth (sporting a backpack from the Action Figure Survival kit mail-away) standing in front of a burning DF.9 anti-infantry laser battery turret (from the Turret & Probot playset), a Rebel pilot standing atop a grounded X-wing fighter, a huge profile of Grand Master Yoda, a view of Cloud City featuring the Twin-Pod Cloud Car vehicle with three Stormtroopers (one visible, two shadowed) bringing the body of a frozen Han Solo in carbonite block onto the boarding ramp of Boba Fett's *Slave-1* spacecraft, images of an Ugnaught, Lando Calrissian, Lobot, and a mustached Bespin Guard, a quick shot of medical droids 2-1B and FX-7, a profile picture of Princess Leia (in an unusually-colored purple blouse), and a large image of the four bounty hunters released to date: Dengar, IG-88, Boba Fett, and Bossk.

This case includes the following easily lost/removable parts: Collector's case with color front image (tan vinyl inside), two stackable tan action figure trays, gray-tan label sheet, four-color paper insert (blue on one side, yellow on another, featuring 41 figures), and white carrying handle.

MISP: w/plastic wrap around the case: **$185-$195+**; **MIP**: w/insert and unapplied labels: **$40-$45+**; **MLC**: w/ insert and labels applied: **$18-$25+**.

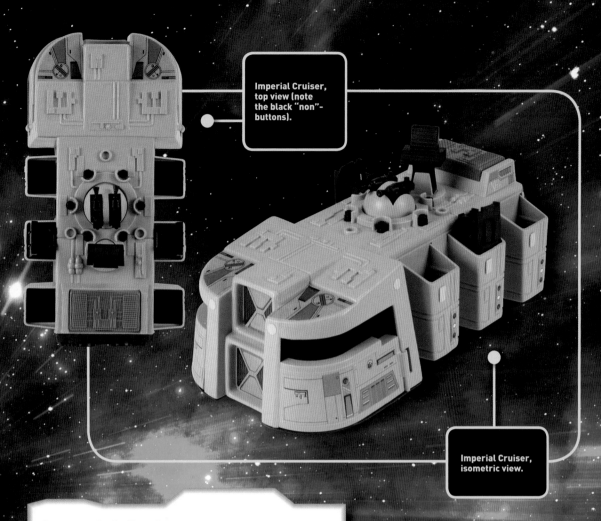

Imperial Cruiser, top view (note the black "non"-buttons).

Imperial Cruiser, isometric view.

Imperial Cruiser (Sears Exclusive)

[Production #93351/59177]

1st packaged appearance: 1981
Original Retail Price (average): $13.99

A Sears exclusive solicited solely in their 1981 and 1982 Christmas *Wish Book* catalogs, the Imperial Cruiser vehicle is essentially a revamped version of 1979's Imperial Troop Transporter. With far different labels than the Troop Transport (note the Cruiser's full-door stickers instead of the Troop Transport's simple red door stripes), the Imperial Cruiser was a fascinating way for Sears to obtain a catalog exclusive: gut the innards out of the Troop Transport—removing all of the toy's electronics and ability to replicate sound—give it a new label sheet, a new box, and change a few colors of the accoutrements, and you have an all-new toy! Unfortunately, the vehicle was prohibitively expensive back in the early '80s, and at nearly $14 a pop, Sears did not sell many of these.

Essentially the Imperial Cruiser is a single vehicle with opening doors, a rotating radar dish with built-in

laser cannon, six side compartments, a weapons storage bin (the former battery compartment when the vehicle was the Imperial Troop Transporter) and a large prisoner compartment. With its "6 side compartments for transporting action figures," the ability to place action figures in its large driver control compartment, since the doors to the front pilot and co-pilot compartments open, you could place action figures (not included) such as an Imperial Stormtrooper or an AT-AT Driver at the controls. Furthermore, Imperial Stormtroopers and captured Rebels can be transported in the six side compartments, while the small black head mounted prisoner immobilization units fit over captured action figures used for the "brainwashing" of prisoners, as "a special rear compartment is used to transport captured rebels." The vehicle's moving laser cannon can also spin a full 360 degrees and move up and

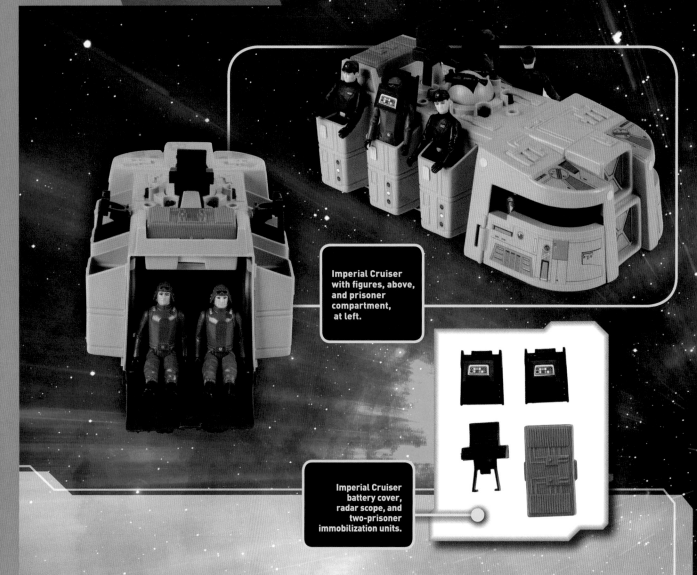

Imperial Cruiser with figures, above, and prisoner compartment, at left.

Imperial Cruiser battery cover, radar scope, and two-prisoner immobilization units.

down, and can be controlled by moving the radar dish in the opposite direction.

Obviously, the vehicle has a bevy of special features, but to charge $13.99 for the toy, just one dollar less than the $14.99 Kenner charged for the far superior Imperial Troop Transporter sold just one year prior, seems counterintuitive. Regardless, the differences between the *Star Wars* Imperial Troop Transporter (1979) and the Sears exclusive *Empire Strikes Back* Imperial Cruiser (1981) can be delineated as follows: the later-released Imperial Cruiser is lighter in weight than its earlier cousin due to a lack of electronics. The Cruiser is a bit lighter gray in color, and has six black flattened buttons surrounding its top cannon, which cannot be depressed, while there are three raised circles around the Cruiser's laser cannon, which has no screws inside. Additionally, inside the Cruiser's "weapons bin cover"

is a non-removable paper insert, and the weapons bin cover is orange. Regarding the Imperial Cruiser's label sheet, there are full-sized stickers on both front doors, and stickers to the left and right of the weapons bin cover. Finally, the Imperial Cruiser's rear prisoner compartment may be used to transport a bevy of captured Rebels, since the compartment runs the length of the vehicle due to the toy's lack of electronics.

This Cruiser comes with the following easily lost/removable parts: doors (x2; left, pilot, and right, co-pilot), personnel pod/side compartments (x6; difficult to remove), Prisoner Immobilization Units (x2), radar dish, orange weapons bin cover (which is hard to find).

MISB: $185-$190+; **MIB**: $55-$68; **MLC**: $16-$22.

MLC-3 isometric view.

MLC-3
(Mobile Laser Cannon, [Rebellion Mini-Rig])

`[Production #40020]`

1st packaged appearance: 1981
Original Retail Price (average): $4.99

This Mobile Laser Cannon, with its tracked chassis and twin blaster cannons, can be manned by a Rebel pilot, via its cockpit, or alternatively, might be operated via remote control. One of the first three *Star Wars* Mini-Rigs to be released, the 1981 Kenner *Toy Fair Catalog* description of this vehicle reads as follows: "MLC-3 is a MOBILE LASER CANNON used by the Rebels to fight off the invading forces on HOTH. It carries one action figure in its manually opened cockpit and has a dome for protection."

The MLC-3 possesses the following easily lost/removable part: domed cockpit.

MLC-3 domed cockpit.

MISB: $90-$105+; **MIB:** $30-$32; **MLC:** $8-$12.

MTV-7
(Multi-Terrain Vehicle, [Imperial Mini-Rig])

`[Production #40010]`

1st packaged appearance: 1981
Original Retail Price (average): $4.99

MTV-7.

The wheeled scouting vehicle known as the MTV-7 features two different configurations ("upright" or "ground-hugging") when utilized as part of Darth Vader's Imperial Army during the Galactic Civil War, specifically as part of the invasion of Echo Base. Due to its small stature and compact nature, the MTV-7 is easy to deploy and requires only one Imperial solider as a pilot—a far cry from installing and maintaining a squad of AT-ST "chicken walkers."

As a toy, collectors could "position the MTV-7 for sneak attacks," and utilize the moveable laser cannon to defend the vehicle. With its spring-loaded dual legs and moveable cannon, this was one of the more popular Mini-Rigs on the secondary market. The MTV-7 was one of the first Mini-Rigs concocted by Kenner.

The MTV-7 possesses no easily lost/removable parts.

MISB: $90-$100+; **MIB:** $18-$21; **MLC:** $8-$12.

PDT-8
(Personnel Deployment Transport [Mini-Rig])

[Production #40070]

1st packaged appearance: 1981
Original Retail Price (average): $4.99

With laser cannons that move to protect the PDT-8 from the enemy, the ability to "position side thrusters to quickly transport action figures from one place to another," a set of "moveable side thrusters [that] can be positioned for takeoff," and "doors that open and close to load most *Star Wars* action figures," the PDT-8 Mini-Rig is one of the more popular of Kenner's lower-priced vehicles.

This two-man personnel/cargo transport was a fine addition to the initial 1981 assortment of Mini-Rigs, and, as the PDT-8's package touts, allowed fans to create Hoth Ice Planet adventures.

It is curious to note that the this Mini-Rig was originally designed to be a transport *solely* for droids, yet this plan was scrapped at the last minute and its name was changed from the original DPT-8 ("Droid Personnel

PDT-8.

Transport") [see *The Complete Star Wars Encyclopedia*] to its current, mass-marketed iteration.

The PDT-8 possesses no easily lost/removable parts; however, the two end flaps/doors may come disengaged sometimes.

MISB: $85-$115+; **MIB**: $16-$24; **MLC**: $8-$12.

Rebel Command Center
Adventure Set (Sears Exclusive)

[Production #69481]

1st packaged appearance: 1981
Original Retail Price (average): $11.99

Far different from the Rebel Command Centers utilized in 2001's *Star Wars: Galactic Battleground*s video game, *The Empire Strikes Back* Rebel Command Center Adventure Set is designed to mimic the gorgeous defense base set up by the Rebellion against the Empire, as established on ice planet Hoth: the iconic Echo Base.

The painting posted on the cardboard/chipboard backdrop of the Rebel Command Center Adventure Set expertly captures the depth of composition of the Echo Base, as well as the meticulous organization of

the upstart Rebels: in the foreground, collectors witness a Rebel Armored Snowspeeder and a Rebel Solider atop his loyal (and indigenous to the planet) Tauntaun, behind them in the background at right you view an X-wing fighter, while in the left center of the painting resides "the fastest hunk of junk in the galaxy": Han Solo and Chewbacca's *Millennium Falcon*. All the while, Rebel troops busy themselves preparing for their exodus from Hoth.

Although a simple playset—with merely a few levers and accoutrements that attach to a flat base along with an ad-hoc backdrop—we must remember it was a Sears exclusive, which bragged three new *ESB* action figures that you could obtain nowhere else on the market: a fabulous Luke Skywalker in his planet Hoth togs, an AT-AT Commander (essentially a "General Veers" figure that was made a troop builder for broader appeal), and an all-new, retooled R2-D2 figure with a protruding "sensorscope." Although it would have been nice to see

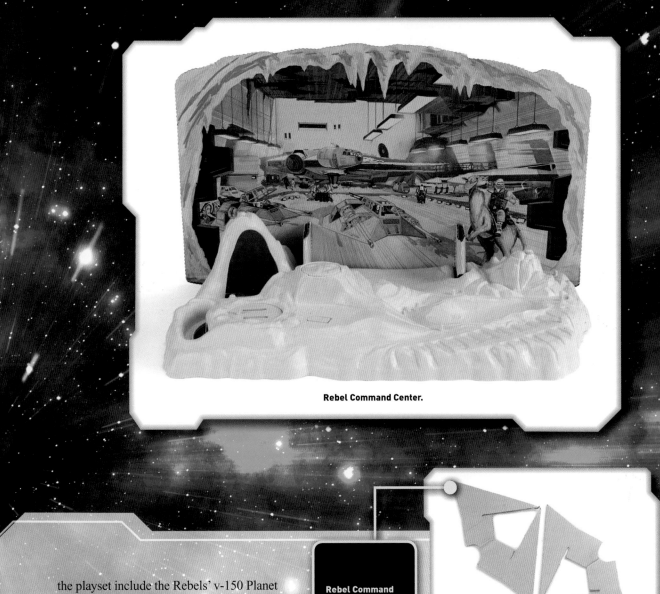

Rebel Command Center.

Rebel Command
Center's two
backdrop tabs.

the playset include the Rebels' v-150 Planet Defender Ion Cannon, shield generator (that spawned a barrier protecting the base from bombardment by the Empire's Star Destroyers), or even an ad-hoc medical facility replete with Bacta tank, this would not happen—although the Micro Collection Hoth Ion Cannon and Hoth Generator Attack sets would include the latter two.

Utilizing all the same "base" accessories/accoutrements that were included with 1979's Land of the Jawas Action Playset and cast in white plastic, this adventure set was produced quickly to meet the demands for a Sears Christmas exclusive in their widely distributed *Sears Wish Book*. Other than the toy's three included action figures, which were also a Sears Christmas season exclusive, the only all-new pieces required to produce this toy was a cardboard/chipboard backdrop.

This set included the following easily lost/removable parts: Action Button, AT-AT Commander action figure (with blue Bespin Blaster [DH-17 blaster pistol]), Luke Skywalker (Hoth Battle Gear) action figure (with black Rebel Rifle with attached strap [BlasTech A295 blaster rifle]), Artoo-Detoo (R2-D2) (With Sensorscope) action figure, Action Lever (with attached handle), Action Stand, Command Center Backdrop (cardboard), Command Center Backdrop, Tabs (x2, cardboard), Command Center Base (plastic, white), Snapper Arm, and Snapper Cap.

MISB: $225-$275+; MIB with figures. $58-$75+, without figures: $35-$45+; MLC: with figures: $40-$45+, without figures: $25-$38.

Slave-1 tinted canopy, cargo ramp, side hatch, and cockpit.

Slave-1, right view.

Slave-1, Boba Fett's Spaceship

[Production #39690]

1st packaged appearance: 1981
Original Retail Price (average): $16.99

One of the most iconic spacecraft in the history of fiction, Boba Fett's *Slave-1* premieres in *Episode V: The Empire Strikes Back*, and although it possesses little screen time, roughly ten to eleven seconds, due to its ludicrous level of underground popularity among collectors, the ship and its infamous owner have appeared in nearly every different iteration of the *Star Wars* franchise: from video games to comic books.

The history of the *Slave-1* is complex. The spacecraft is in actuality a highly modified prototype Firespray-31-class patrol and attack craft, with multiple alterations performed to its weapons systems by both Jango and Boba Fett. Inherited by Boba following the death of his bounty-hunting father, the *Slave-1* was originally designed by Kuat Systems Engineering as a police craft, which was initially utilized as a prisoner transport by the Republic Correctional Authority (dissolved in 19 BBY)—an organization existing at the time of the Galactic Republic, which tracks down dangerous criminals in an attempt to rehabilitate them. As a prisoner transport, the Firespray-31-class possesses everything the Fetts need to transport detainees: it is both armored and well-armed to protect jailbreak assaults; its on-board storage space is ample for conveying multiple prisoners as well as cargo in its hold-

ing cells; its speed rivals the Y-wing starfighter (see Y-Wing Fighter), which allows it to function as a highly-maneuverable *interceptor* (see Droids A-Wing Fighter & ATL Interceptor, the INT-4, and the TIE Interceptor).

Kenner's brilliant *Slave-1* toy possesses a ludicrous amount of special features. Among these are gravity operated wings that rotate between landing and flight positions, a removable side panel to position Boba for take-off, positionable cannons, and an opening rear ramp that allowed fans to relive Boba's taking the frozen Han Solo to Jabba the Hutt.

However, most collectors who pick up loose samples of the *Slave-1* have no idea that within the vehicle's handle there's a top inside trigger, dubbed a "cruise" button, which allows the spacecraft to hold its wings in position and maintain a steady, set flight pattern. This feature mimics the real-world craft whose trademark was to land horizontally with its engines turned toward the surface and its cockpit looking upward.

The *Slave-1* possesses the following easily lost/removable parts: Tinted Canopy, Cargo Ramp (black-colored, hard to find), Han Solo in Carbonite Block, Removable Side Hatch, and two Stabilizer Fins/Wings.

MISB: $975-$1,100+; **MIB**: $95-$120+; **MLC**: $65-$80.

Turret & Probot Playset.

Turret & Probot Playset

[Production #38330]

1st packaged appearance: 1981
Original Retail Price (average): $10.99

The "probot" included with the Kenner Turret & Probot playset is in actuality the more common designation for Arakyd Industries' deep-space Viper probe droid. Capitalizing on the success of an earlier model, Arakyd Industries, manufacturer of the *Star Wars* action figure "Death Star Droid" as well, constructs this all-new Viper probe droid with six "manipulator arms" and several smaller, retractable "sensor arms"—the latter appendages not designed as part of the Kenner toy. Similarly detailed as the toy, the Viper's head is dotted with a vast array of diverse sensors.

When the Galactic Empire launches the Viper to scout the unforgiving, hostile terrain of the ice planet Hoth for the location of the Rebellion's Echo Base, they capitalize upon the probe droid's primary function: to ferret out the location of/gather information on their enemies. In order to accomplish this task, Viper probe droids are fired through hyperspace.

As for the second major part of the popular toy, the "turret" delineated in the playset's title has been perfectly captured in plastic form, Kenner expertly approximating the DF.9 anti-infantry laser battery found in *The Empire Strikes Back* during the Battle of Hoth scene. At the well-defended Outpost Beta—a sentry station located near the Rebel Alliance's Echo Base facility—a modified version of the DF.9 anti-infantry laser battery

is used: the tall, cylinder-shaped turret cannon set atop a tiered pedestal with access door. Manufactured by Golan Arms, the DF.9 is utilized to neutralize or suppress enemy infantry (i.e., Imperial Snowtroopers, see Imperial Stormtrooper [Hoth Battle Gear]). At its most efficient, the DF.9 is manned by three different Rebel Soldiers (see Rebel Soldier [Hoth Battle Gear]): one gunner who sis atop the turret (unfortunately, with his head exposed to sniper fire), while a targeting computer specialist and a power technician inhabit the inside.

Although the "turret" and "probot" are miles away from each other in *ESB*, Kenner decided to package the two concepts together—separated by mere inches in the same playset. Although simple, it is a rather fun playset with the following action features: the ability to "make the Probot Spy fall and action figure turn, with this action lever," while the "turret's door and hatch open to place action figures." Furthermore, you may "defend your 'secret' Rebel base with the clicking gun turret," or "relive Han's being discovered by Darth Vader's Probot spy."

The playset contains the following easily lost/removable parts: Turret Base, Turret Gun, Turret Hatch, and Probot Figure (Two-Piece Head, Body, 5 Assorted Legs).

MISB $365 $100, MID $30-$60,
MIT: $24 $30.

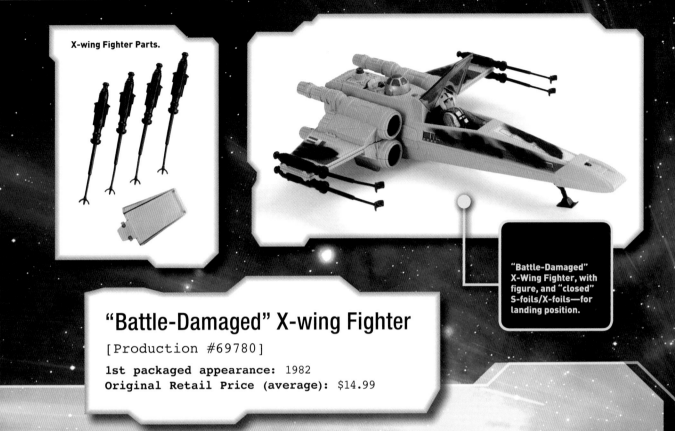

X-wing Fighter Parts.

"Battle-Damaged" X-Wing Fighter, with figure, and "closed" S-foils/X-foils—for landing position.

"Battle-Damaged" X-wing Fighter

[Production #69780]

1st packaged appearance: 1982
Original Retail Price (average): $14.99

With a tracking computer that has a 98.7 percent success rate (perhaps Luke Skywalker shouldn't have turned his off to "use the Force ..."), four impressively powerful wing-mounted Taim & Bak KX9 laser cannons, four Incom 4L4 fusial thrust engines (advanced sublight drive engines, which provide for speeds in advance of 1,300 kilometers-per-hour), two Krupx MG7 proton torpedo launchers, and a hyperdrive that allows the X-wing to venture into depths that the Empire's TIE fighters simply can't, the X-wing Fighter is the "backbone of the Alliance Starfighter Corps": the gold standard by which many all-purpose starfighters are measured.

The "Battle-Damaged" X-wing Fighter is a terrific vehicle to utilize in your Rebel army for collectors to prove that their T-65 class X-wing has suffered minor damage in combat. With a set of six all-new labels, which kids could use to create a "battle-damaged" look, this was a clever way for Kenner to re-solicit the vehicle in 1982 and distinguish it from its original 1978 release. Yet the "Battle-Damaged" X-wing Fighter vehicle still possesses the same special features as its predecessor: You could "Push the R2-D2 button to open wings into attack position," open the pilot's cockpit to accommodate Luke Skywalker (X-Wing Pilot), and trigger the remote release button to close its wings into the normal flight position."

Oddly enough, the box text suggests that there were TWO label applications for the vehicle: with the standard set of X-wing labels only—to make the craft look "brand new," and with the worn labels placed over the standard labels to make the toy complete. But what collector would choose NOT to utilize these "battle-damaged" stickers? Although they were a one-time (non-removable) application, to eschew their use would be peculiar.

Furthermore (and MOST importantly for collectors), upon inspection of these two models of X-wing toys, the two indeed possess some *very* distinct differences. The hull of the original X-wing is molded in white plastic, while the body of the battle-damaged X-wing is gray; the translucent canopy of the original X-wing is clear, while the incredibly hard to find battle-damaged canopy is tinted gray; the inlets for the original X-wing's four engines are white, while on the battle-damaged X-wing, these inlets are black. Beyond the added battle-damaged labels, please make sure you have the proper model X-wing since the later 1982 edition is a harder-to-find toy.

The "Battle-Damaged" X-wing Fighter's easily lost/removable parts include: canopy and laser cannons (x4).

MISB: $415-$425+; **MIB**: working electronics: **$68-$85+**; **MLC**: working electronics: **$52-$65+**.

CAP-2 (Captivator) [Mini-Rig]

[Production #69760]

1st packaged appearance: 1982
Original Retail Price (average): $4.99

CAP-2, isometric view.

This odd-looking, one-man vehicle's box text suggests that collectors "hide CAP-2 in secret places with suction cup feet," and "capture Rebel prisoners and take them to Darth Vader." With a transparent dome, four limbs, two grappling arms ending in claws and two suction-cupped feet, and a small blaster cannon mounted on a ball joint, the peculiar yet dynamic CAP-2 is apparently used by bounty hunters, specifically Bossk, who is pictured on the package front, to obtain their bounties. On the rear of the vehicle, there are two gripping teeth that are used as a vice grip to nab potential enemies. With the addition of the CAP-2 and the INT-4, this *ESB* toy's package flaps proudly tout: "Collect all 5 Mini-Rigs and create your own Star Wars adventures."

The CAP-2's easily lost/removable parts include: 2 Grappling Arms, 2 Suction-Cupped Feet, Blaster Cannon, and a Transparent Dome.

MISB: $120-$130; **MIB:** $25-$32+; **MLC:** $9-$15.

Empire Strikes Back (vinyl) Mini-Figures Collector's Case

[Production #39190]

1st packaged appearance: 1982
Original Retail Price (average): $5.99

Note: The production number for all of Kenner's vinyl Mini-Figures Collector's Cases is exactly the same: Kenner did not change the assortment number regardless of the year of release (1979, 1980, 1981, 1982, or 1983).

Empire Strikes Back Mini-Figures Collector's Case, complete.

This marks Kenner's fourth "Mini-Action Figure Collector's Case"—and third under the *Empire Strikes Back* logo—that holds 24 exciting figures. With two stackable red trays to hold the figures and their accessories, a paper insert that identifies every figure currently available at retail (47 total at this point), a red label sheet that collectors could use to personalize each compartment, and a sturdy outer casing shrink-wrapped in vinyl

223

(black on the outside, red on the inside), this *ESB* case was a cheaper alternative to the higher costing Darth Vader Collector's Case.

This case includes the following easily damaged/removable parts: collector's case with color front image (red vinyl inside), two stackable red action figure trays, red label sheet, four-color paper insert (yellow on both sides, featuring 47 figures), and white carrying handle.

MISP: with plastic wrap around the case: **$195-$205+**; **MIP**: with insert and unapplied labels: **$40-$45+**; **MLC**: with insert and labels applied: **$18-$25+**.

INT-4 parts.

INT-4, isometric view.

INT-4 (Interceptor) [Mini-Rig]

[Production #69750]

1st packaged appearance: 1982
Original Retail Price (average): $4.99

A superbly designed *interceptor* vehicle, a starfighter specifically designed to target, hunt down, intercept, and destroy enemy fighters and bombers, according to Wookieepedia, the Imperial INT-4 possesses the ability to lower its wings to prepare for a scouting mission at Rebel Base, and collectors could open its hatch to place an action figure in the cockpit, while the laser cannon moved to attack the Rebels.

What many collectors don't realize is that an image pictured on one of the INT-4 box's outer flaps is the interesting statement: "AT-AT can carry INT-4 into battle"; apparently, the entire body of the interceptor fits perfectly within the troop compartment of Kenner's Imperial walker (see AT-AT

INT-4, MIB.

([Imperial] All Terrain Armored Transport).

The INT-4's easily lost/removable parts include: two wings (left and right), laser cannon, and hatch (usually non-removable, but can be worked off).

MISB: $95-$105; **MIB**: $25-$38+; **MLC**: $12-$18.

Radar Laser Cannon (a.k.a. "P-Tower")

[Production #93440]

1st packaged appearance: 1982
Original Retail Price (average): $4.99

Radar Laser Cannon.

The nearly three-meter-tall Atgar 1.4 FD (e.g., 1.4 "Fire/Disable number") P-Tower Radar Laser Cannon, nicknamed the "P-Tower," was manufactured by the Atgar SpaceDefense Corporation, a premiere producer of "anti-vehicle weaponry and defense systems." This potent artillery device was featured during the Battle of Hoth as employed by the Rebel Forces, and has been in service since the time of the infamous Clone Wars (22-19 BBY). Although somewhat unreliable (re: firing), the Radar Laser Cannon had an effective range of 2-10 kilometers with varied success which was dependent upon proximity, the cannon could disable an Imperial AT-ST Walker (see Scout Walker) with one shot. Furthermore, the cannon's ammunition was unlimited as long as it was fed by a power generator, such as the one featured during the Battle of Hoth in *The Empire Strikes Back*.

When playing with this simple yet effective toy, with its clicking radar dish and ability to rotate 360 degrees, the toy's instructions state that you " … can pretend that your Radar Laser Cannon toy has been hit by pressing the black 'destruct' button on the top of the cannon base"—and the field gun would collapse into a heap of parts. A pretty nifty battlefield accessory.

The entire assembly of the Radar Laser Cannon is a slew of easily lost/removable parts, which include: radar dish, turret right half, turret left half, and the cannon base.

**MISB: $40-$55+. MIB: $15-$20.
MLC: $6-$10.**

Canon, MIB.

Radar Laser
Cannon
disassembled.

Rebel Transport Vehicle

[Production #69740]

1st packaged appearance: 1982
Original Retail Price (average): $29.99

Produced by Gallofree Yards, a ship manufacturer that is nowhere near as flashy as those produced by Corellian Engineering, Inc., the GR-75 medium transport (a.k.a. Gallofree medium transport) is originally used as re-supply vessels during the Clone Wars (22-19 ABY) and are eventually adapted for use by the Alliance to Restore the Republic as a means to convey a mass of Rebel troopers, without requiring the use of a larger, bulkier freighter. Known as the Rebel Transport, this streamlined craft plays a critical role in *The Empire Strikes Back* during the Battle of Hoth, when the Imperial invasion forces the evacuation of Echo Base.

Although notoriously difficult to maintain due to its constant use, particularly utilizing a maximum load of freight, the Rebel Transport sports a number of unique features, including an upper Command Pod with built-in deflector-shield generator, four twin fire-linked laser cannon turrets, multiple cargo modules, a removable main reactor cowl on the ship's stern, and a top speed of 650 kilometers-per-hour. With a crew of six, and one dedicated gunner, the Rebel Transport has saved the lives of many Rebel soldiers over the years.

One of the most underrated toys in Kenner's arsenal of vintage *Star Wars* toys, the magnificent Rebel Transport possesses the following action features and accoutrements: "…five Hoth backpacks and four as-

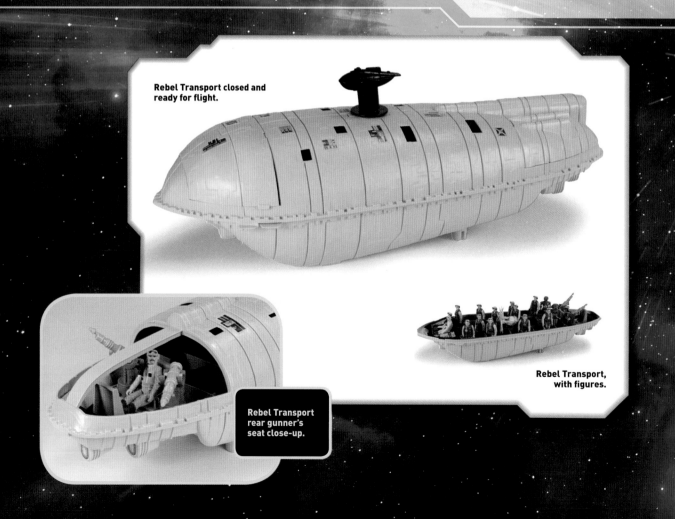

Rebel Transport closed and ready for flight.

Rebel Transport rear gunner's seat close-up.

Rebel Transport, with figures.

teroid gas masks" (see Action Figure Survival Kit), the ability to "…remove [the] top to provide access to [the] crew chamber," and furthermore "remove [the gray plastic] crew chamber to expand [the] play area inside your Rebel Transport." There's also a "…dual cannon assembly [to] protect [the] Rebel Transport," and the "entire cannon assembly is removable to protect your secret land base." Finally, you can pretend that Imperial prisoners can "…get away through the secret escape hatch to tell Darth Vader about the Rebels' new base.

Although many collectors consider the Rebel Transport nothing more than a glorified collector's case, with its removable crew chamber and cockpit canopy cover, detachable cockpit seat, hidden secret storage compartment, removable gunner's seat base and gun turret cover, pop-out shroud cover, detachable

back floor, and removable gunner's seat base consisting of two three-piece gun turret assemblies, which can be separately taken off of the base "for separate play," this deluxe vehicle is truly an underappreciated collectible.

The vehicle's easily lost/removable parts include: 4 Asteroid Gas Masks, Cannon Assembly (2 Cannons/ Gun Turrets, 2 Cannon Supports, Gunner's Platform), "Crew Chamber" Tray, Escape Hatch, Front Cover, 5 Hoth Backpacks, Rear Cover, Top Cover.

 MISB: $265-$295; **MIB**: $78-$95+; **MLC**: $50-$65+, with 5 Hoth backpacks and 4 Asteroid Gas Masks; **MLC**: $40-$48, without backpacks and masks.

Rebel Transport crew chamber and cannon assembly removed.

Rebel Transport vehicle parts.

Scout Walker,
left view.

Scout Walker,
rear view.

Scout Walker vehicle
(a.k.a. AT-ST [All Terrain Scout] Transport)

[Production #69800]

1st packaged appearance: 1982
Original Retail Price (average): $14.99

The spectacular action features possessed by the Scout Walker are delineated on the toy package: Your Scout Walker "can stand unassisted," "open top to place Action Figure inside," "swivel side cannons and hear clicking 'laser machine gun' sounds," and most importantly, collectors would be able to make their Scout Walker run into battle with the hand-operated walking mechanism.

Possessing one of the most cunningly clever feats of toy engineering witnessed in the 1980s, or any other decade for that matter, Kenner's Scout Walker toy can walk, with a switch on the back of the vehicle labeled "Stand" and "Walk." When a button is slid over onto the "Stand" mode, the vehicle may be stood upright (with-

out falling) and posed with a figure inside the cockpit; when the same button is slid over to the right-hand "Walk" mode, the vehicle's legs become weakened and pliable, allowing collectors to depress the rear button up-and-down to move the legs, making the Scout Walker appear to be running.

Although it does not indicate so on the package, the Scout Walker's class is AT-ST: All Terrain Scout Transport. Sometimes dubbed the "chicken walker" due to its characteristic chicken-like ambulatory motion, the AT-ST's small stature (relative to other vehicles) fools the Rebels into believing it is poorly armed, but nothing can be further from the truth. Although lighter than its larger cousin (see AT-AT), the Scout Walker still possesses plenty of speed (up to 90 kilometers-per-hour!) and firepower. To repel other ve-

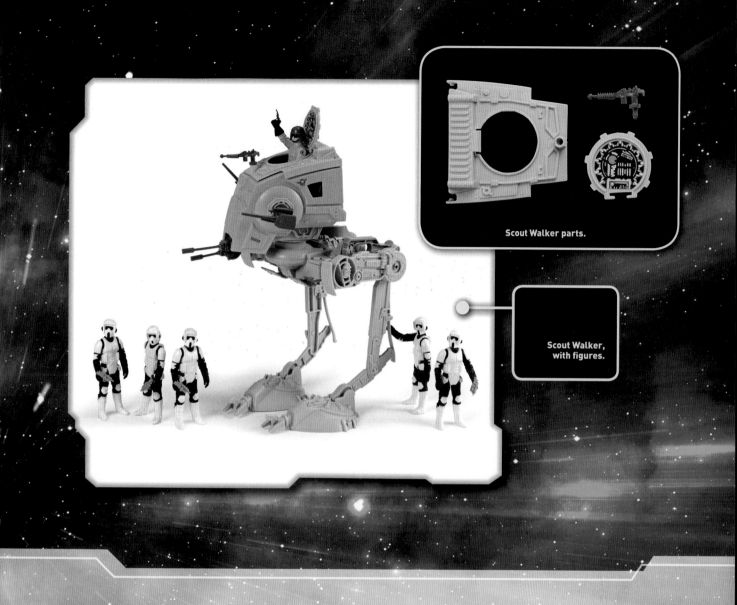

Scout Walker parts.

Scout Walker, with figures.

hicles, the AT-ST comes standard with a front-mounted pair of chin guns, e.g., twin cannons, that have an effective range of two kilometers, while its side-mounted, left-hand grenade launcher and side-mounted, right-hand light blaster cannon takes care of any pesky foot soldiers bold enough to get close to the quick, agile Scout Walker—although the Kenner toy included two side-mounted cannons of the exact same make and model instead. Furthermore, it is worth noting that the AT-ST's feet also possesses a pair of front "claws," which we do not witness the vehicle using in *Return of the Jedi*, that can be utilized for attack or defense.

Unfortunately, although the Scout Walkers are developed and utilized by the Galactic Republic quite effectively during the Clone Wars (ca. 22–19 BBY) and when manned by the Galactic Empire's fierce Blizzard

Force at the Battle of Hoth (3 ABY), the AT-STs' multiple weaknesses are revealed during the Battle of Endor (3 ABY), where the chicken walkers are forced to try their mettle against the tribal skills of a native band of Ewoks and the combined efforts of Rebel troopers. Although branded "All Terrain," the Scout Walkers prove anything but against rolling stones, moving logs, rapidly shifting ground, tree-traps, and its own poorly reinforced roof canopy that can be popped opened if enough force is applied.

The Scout Walker's easily lost/removable parts include: Large Hatch, 2 Side Cannons, Small Hatch, and Top Gun.

MISB: $140-$175+; MIB: $40-$50; MLC: $28-$35.

Tauntaun with Open Belly Rescue Feature

[Production #93340]

1st packaged appearance: 1982
Original Retail Price (average): $8.99

Tauntaun with Open Belly Rescue Feature, with Luke Skywalker (Hoth Battle Gear), posed.

Used in place of their mechanical transports due to the fact that Alliance vehicles will not handle the unbearably cold atmosphere of the ice planet Hoth, tauntauns are utilized as mounts for Rebel troopers on Hoth (see Rebel Soldier [Hoth Battle Gear] and Rebel Commander).

Sporting wide, tridactyled (three-digit) feet with splayed toes, which act as snowshoes for running on the tundra, lightning fast speed (the species has been clocked at nearly 90 kilometers-per-hour), a well-muscled tail for balance during quick movement, swiveling ears that can turn away from the icy wind, clawed feet and hands to better grasp the planet's unlimited supply of ice, a thick layer of blubber for added insulation against the inclement elements, chambered lungs to help with oxygenation, dual nostrils that help to warm inhaled air and further oxygenate the blood, the ability to induce hibernation at night to cope with low nighttime temperatures, and a digestive system that excretes waste materials as oil through the pores of the matriarchal reptomammal's skin—leading to the creature's highly offensive odor.

Although ill-tempered, foul-smelling, and mucus-spitting, if the alpha female of a tauntaun pack can be tamed, this will allow the wrangler access to the domestication of the rest of the pack—such was the case of the Rebel Alliance, who use the creatures as dependable, loyal mounts. If it weren't for the heroic efforts of Han Solo's tauntaun—both before and after its death—Luke Skywalker would never have made it to the swamp planet of Dagobah (see Dagobah action playset), where he is trained to be the first Jedi Knight in a generation. So Kenner immortalized his hardy reptomammalian mount not once, but twice.

This Tauntaun was a fairly revolutionary toy for 1981. Here, Kenner modified the mold of their original 1980 Tauntaun figure to allow the altered toy to sport a pliable "belly" with a slit cut down the middle on the underside of the plastic creature. This allowed fans to reenact the powerful scene in *ESB* where Han Solo borrows Luke Skywalker's lightsaber to slice open the latter's tauntaun mount and stuff Luke inside the creature, essentially keeping him warm overnight, biding time until the two are rescued.

Toy collectors should be aware that most extant copies of this toy have "yellowed bellies" (if you'll pardon the pun): over the course of the past thirty-five years, the white color of the pliable plastic comprising the tauntaun figure's belly has yellowed a bit to heat, sunlight, or simple exposure to air over time. This pliable belly can't be removed and soaked in hydrogen peroxide to whiten it, as it is a softer plastic than standard action figure's plastic resin.

These later-released versions of the figure possess reins and harnesses that are molded in a *slightly* darker color as compared to the earlier, non-open belly releases. Furthermore, the accessories for this Tauntaun are made with plastic that is a bit softer and more pliable than those earlier-released Tauntauns to better resist breakage.

The Tauntaun with Open Belly Rescue Feature only includes two easily lost/removable parts which are made of soft rubber and are quite delicate: a harness and a saddle.

MISB: $175-$195+; **MIB**: no yellowing to "belly": **$110-$135+**, yellowed "belly": **$65-$85+**; **MLC**: no yellowing to "belly": **$32-$45+**, yellowed "belly": **$20-$32**.

Han Solo helps Luke inside the body of the dead Tauntaun to keep him warm and safe until they can be rescued.

Tri-Pod Laser Cannon energizer pack, with power hose inside.

Tri-Pod Laser Cannon, isometric view.

Tri-Pod Laser Cannon parts.

Tri-Pod Laser Cannon
(a.k.a. E-Web Heavy Repeating Blaster)

[Production #93450]

1st packaged appearance: 1982
Original Retail Price (average): $4.99

Manufactured by BlasTech Industries, the Tri-Pod Laser Cannon—known as the E-Web heavy repeating blaster (full name = "Emplacement Weapon, Heavy Blaster") to *Star Wars* aficionados—is one of the most powerful repeating blasters (a.k.a. repeat blasters, repeaters) in the galaxy; a portable weapon that can be disassembled into disparate parts and reassembled in no time on the field. After set-up, optimally the weapon requires two troopers for use: one manning the cannon, the other adjusting and monitoring the Eksoan Class-4T3 power generator, which can be "pre-charged," as witnessed in *ESB*. With myriad parts combined to form this well-designed accessory, it is a popular toy among collectors particularly since the cannon's power hose can be fully stored inside the power unit when not in use.

In *The Empire Strikes Back*, viewers witness a squad of Snowtroopers (see Imperial Stormtrooper [Hoth Battle Gear]) setting up a Tri-Pod Laser Cannon in order to fire upon the Rebels during the Battle of Hoth—even the cannon's hose and power unit are visible. The E-Web is a favorite weapon of the Empire, sporting a laser actuator, three BlasTech TR-62 Autocushion Tripods, a flashback suppressor, an energizer hose, a binocular setting—and sight with infrared adaptor, and a carry handle to add to the weapon's portability.

The Kenner "Tri-Pod laser cannon clicks when moved side to side and moves up and down to destroy its targets," while its "energizer pack and hose are removable," in order that you may utilize "Tri-Pods to open and close to set up your attack bases."

The Cannon's entire assembly is one large mass of easily lost/removable parts, which include: Cannon Base, Cannon Body, 2 Trunnions (Side Handles), 3 Tripod Legs, pliable Power Hose, and the opening/closing Power Unit.

MISB: $35-$46+; MIB: $10-$14; MLC: $5-$10.

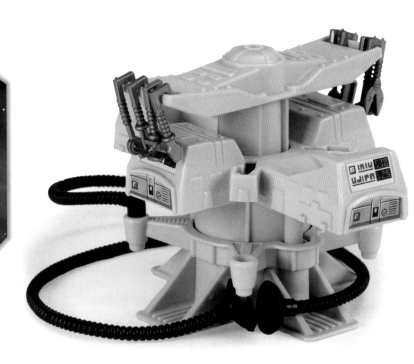

**Vehicle Maintenance Energizer,
top opened for tool access.**

Vehicle Maintenance Energizer toy

[Production #93430]

1st packaged appearance: 1982
Original Retail Price (average): $4.99

Described on its package front as "one accessory with moveable top and eight tools, plus two energizer hoses," the Vehicle Maintenance Energizer, or VME, is the perfect addition to a *Star Wars* fan's vintage toy collection as a means of (faux) repairing mini-rigs and other modes of transportation for the Rebellion, and it looks spectacular parked next to a starfighter (see A-wing, B-wing, X-wing, and/or Y-wing Fighters). With a set of eight unique-looking hydrospanners ("hydrospanner tools" on the toy's instruction sheet), these implements are defined by Wookieepedia.com as "a type of common hand tool used as an all-purpose

socket wrench and bit driver." The Vehicle Maintenance Energizer's eight hydrospanners were not the same—each one possessing a unique head: from pliers to hammers, flathead screwdrivers to socket wrenches, clamps to hand saws, these tools are almost always found missing in loose samples of the VME.

As a collectible, the toy allowed kids to "lift and turn the top to provide access to eight tools and set up a work base," and encouraged children to "attach the energizer hose to your *Star Wars* vehicles for refueling." It is worth mentioning that the two energizer hoses included with this accessory set are a precise match to

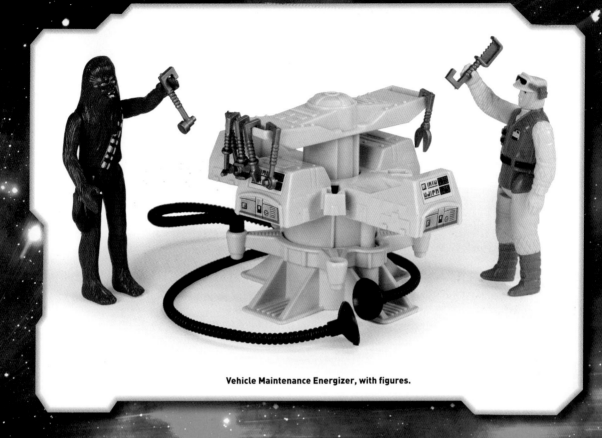

Vehicle Maintenance Energizer, with figures.

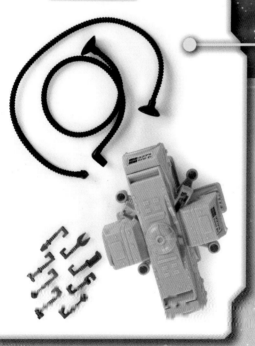

**Vehicle
Maintenance
Energizer parts.**

the power line that came packaged with the Empire's E-Web laser cannon (see Tri-Pod Laser Cannon).

What many collectors might not know is that the Vehicle Maintenance Energizer actually makes a cameo appearance in *Star Wars Episode IV: A New Hope*, where it is utilized at the secret Rebel base on Yavin 4—located on one of three moons orbiting the remote planet of Yavin, a world whose atmosphere provides the setting for one of the most significant battles in galactic history: the *Battle of Yavin*. We can therefore presume that these are ubiquitous at Rebel facilities throughout the galaxy…

The Vehicle Maintenance Energizer Toy's easily lost/removable parts include: 2 hoses, and 8 unique Hydrospanner Tools (all are different from each other).

MISB: $52-$60+; MID. USD $17+.
MLC: $14-$19+.

Wampa, with figures.

Wampa/Hoth Wampa

[Production #69560]

1st packaged appearance: 1982
Original Retail Price (average): $8.99

The vicious, voracious reptomammals (species possessing both mammalian and reptilian traits) known as Wampas roam the tundra of the ice planet Hoth searching for victims that fall prey to either the inclement weather or the beast's sharp claws, craggy teeth, and 6-1/2-foot tall, massive build. Although there are conflicting sources regarding the monster's weight, which ranges from 150 to 200+ kilograms (330-440+ pounds), pundits seem to agree that this ambush-based apex predator walks on all fours, like a polar bear, when moving overland: they only become bipedal when attacking. In devising its attack, the white-furred, dark-pawed Wampa prefer to hide behind a snowbank or slink through a whiteout to disable their prey—if possible, their favorite warm-blooded pack animal known as the Tauntaun (see Tauntaun, or Tauntaun with Open Belly Rescue Feature).

A relatively small toy, just an inch or two taller than most vintage *Star Wars* action figures, Kenner's Wampa was sold packaged within a chipboard box, and not carded as are most products of its size. While Kenner's 6-inch figure of this monster accurately captures the beast's size and girth, the Wampa's facial sculpting is

quite singular: its face appears more similar to a wizened old man than the ravenous beast featured in *The Empire Strikes Back*. Regardless of the figure's aesthetics, collectors could "relive Luke's escape from the Wampa Cave," and to mimic the beast's attack, should "pull back then release the Wampa's arm to create swinging action." Thanks to the figurine's expertly designed hands, which allow the toy to hold onto an action figure's arm or leg, kids were able to "pose the Wampa and pretend that it is carrying Action Figures"—specifically, Luke Skywalker (Hoth Battle Gear).

As a note for collectors, the plastic material Kenner utilized to mold their Wampa action figures is prone to yellowing when exposed to heat and sunlight during the past three decades, so pure white samples of this creature command higher prices on the secondary market. The prices below are for these white samples with no yellowing, since yellowing drastically impacts value—and demand.

MISB: $235-$250; **MIB**: $45-$58; **MLC**: $24-$35+.

AST-5
"pursuit mode."

AST-5 "sentry mode."

AST-5 (Armored Sentinel Transport)
Vehicle [Mini-Rig]

[Production #70880]

1st packaged appearance: 1983
Original Retail Price (average): $4.99

AST-5, with figures.

Although this peculiar yet wonderfully designed mini-rig never makes an appearance in *any* aspect of the *Star Wars* film canon, it appears it is meant to function as a vehicle for mercenaries, such as the members of Jabba the Hutt's retinue to scout for enemies around the perimeter of the gangster's citadel. This vehicle has a few interesting capabilities, as described on the toy package: you could rotate the wings to scout for enemy intruders and open its hatch to place an action figure in the cockpit, while the "laser cannons move to attack enemy forces."

The AST-5 is a well-designed mini-rig since it has the ability to switch from "sentry mode" to "attack mode" to "pursuit mode"—from a position of superiority with the vehicle and its struts facing a vertical direction, to a position where the vehicle's profile is reduced as the cockpit rotates at a 90-degree angle from the grounded struts, to that of a speedy, well-nigh impen-

etrable repulsorlift spacecraft where the engine is positioned directly parallel to the cockpit. According to the toy's box front, the AST-5 is piloted by one of the Hutt's finest aviators: Wooof (see Klaatu), who is featured in the vehicle's form-fitting seat.

The AST-5 has no easily lost/removable parts.

MISB: $85-$115; **MIB:** $25-$35+;
MLC: $14-$18.

"Battle-Damaged" Imperial TIE Fighter ejected solar panels.

"Battle-Damaged" Imperial TIE Fighter, isometric view.

"Battle-Damaged" Imperial TIE Fighter

[Production #70990]

1st packaged appearance: 1983
Original Retail Price (average): $14.99

The "battle-damaged" Imperial TIE Fighter is a spectacular addition to the Imperial Naval fleet for die-hard collectors to prove that their TIE/LN starfighter had suffered minor damage in combat. With a set of six all-new labels, which could be utilized to "… create a 'battle-damaged' look," this was a clever way for Kenner to re-solicit the vehicle in 1983 and distinguish it from its original 1978 release.

Kenner also decided to re-cast this TIE fighter in a more authentic blue-gray color, trying to make up for the bright white color of the original TIE. Beyond this difference in color, the "Battle-Damaged" Imperial TIE

Fighter vehicle still possesses the same special features as its predecessor: by pushing the button on top of the toy's battery compartment, you could trigger battle sounds and a flashing laser light (via two AA batteries), and open the cockpit's hatch and press a lever to raise the seat to accommodate a pilot (see Imperial TIE Fighter Pilot). To further evidence the TIE fighter's "battle-damaged" features, pressing the release buttons on each side of the cockpit hatch would make the wings/solar panels "fly" off of the vehicle, simulating a crash landing or destruction via combat—the most distinctive feature of the "Battle-Damaged" TIE Fighter—a feature utilized in every iteration of the toy, from the original (Imperial) TIE fighter (1978), to the Darth Vader TIE Fighter (1979), and the TIE Interceptor vehicle (1983).

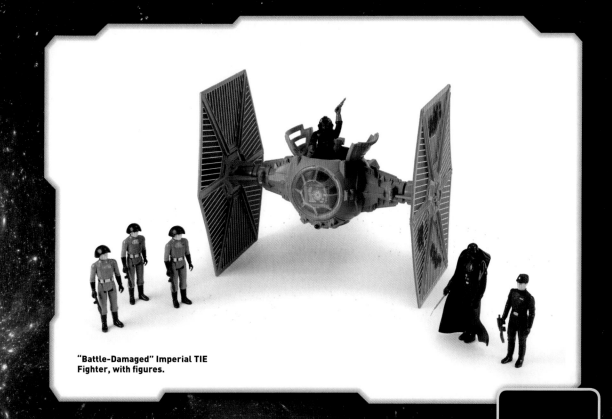

"Battle-Damaged" Imperial TIE
Fighter, with figures.

"Battle-Damaged"
Imperial TIE Fighter
Battery Cover.

Oddly enough, unlike the "Battle-Damaged X-wing
Fighter" from 1982, this TIE's box text does not suggest that there were TWO label applications for the
vehicle: with a standard set of TIE Fighter labels—to
make the craft look "brand new," and then a set of
worn labels, which could be placed over the other to
make the toy complete.

The "Battle-Damaged" TIE Fighter includes the
following removable/easily lost parts: 2x Solar Array
Wings, Main Cockpit, 2x Ingress/Egress Hatch Flaps,
1x Hatch Opener/Seat Raiser, Battery Cover.

MISB: **$345-$365+**; MIB: working
electronics: **$50-$65+**; MLC: working
electronics: **$24-$28**.

Chewbacca Bandolier Strap

[Production #70480]

1st packaged appearance: 1983
Original Retail Price (average): $9.99

According to the always-enlightening Wookieepedia. com, within the canonical *Star Wars* universe, this piece of utilitarian clothing is actually spelled "bandoleer"—although most dictionaries consider both spellings acceptable. Usually employed by soldiers or mercenaries heading into combat, a bandoleer is essentially a broad, long belt worn slung over a shoulder, which fits across the wearer's torso, with multiple pouches attached in order to carry extra ammunition or supplementary equipment that is useful on the battlefield or during paramilitary operations. Bandoleers are popularized by Chewbacca, who wears his as a means to carry extra quarrels for his bowcaster/Wookiee crossbow (see Star Wars ["Large Size"] Chewbacca).

Described in Kenner's 1983 *Return of the Jedi*-themed *Toy Fair* catalog as looking "... just like the one that *CHEWBACCA* wore in the movie. But this bandolier strap is made for kids ... not *WOOKIEES*," the Chewbacca Bandolier Strap is a combination role play item/collector's case, which serves as an interest-

ing manner of transporting and displaying your action figures. With foam-padded clips that can accommodate a maximum of ten action figures and two removable pouches for holding "accessories and secret messages," according to the box text, the Chewbacca Bandolier Strap toy is reminiscent of the band worn by the famous Wookiee co-pilot of the *Millennium Falcon*. Collectors should note that even within factory-sealed samples of this toy, the foam surrounding each of the ten clips has a tendency to deteriorate and become brittle, similar to the brown "swamp" feature of the Dagobah swamp playset (see Dagobah Action Playset). Therefore, it is recommended that if you obtain an intact sample of the strap with little foam degradation, please do not try and fit action figures into the clips—the foam will break apart in your hands.

The Chewbacca Bandolier Strap includes the following removable/easily lost parts: 2 Removable Pouches, 1 Strap (make sure foam for all ten slots has not degraded).

MISB: $30-$40+; **MIB:** $20-$30; **MLC:** $10-$15.

Chewbacca Bandolier Strap, MIB (complete).

C-3PO Collector's
Case, MIB (complete).

See-Threepio (C-3PO)
Collector's Case

[Production #70440]

1st packaged appearance: 1983
Original Retail Price (average): $11.99

The See-Threepio (C-3PO) Collector's Case is described in its promotional material as a "life-size golden sculpting of the world's most popular droid, C-3PO," which "…holds up to 40 Star Wars Action Figures plus accessories and includes a pressure-sensitive label sheet to identify them," while kids and collectors can close the case up and the hidden handle allows a child to carry C-3PO anywhere.

Similar to 1980's Darth Vader Collector's Case (DVCC), which precedes our favorite histrionic droid, this new case came equipped with a set of yellow labels, 77 total, with doubles, to personalize each of the 40 action figure chambers, a four-color paper divider which advertised the action figures currently on sale at retail (65 total), and a small accessory chamber to hold all of the forty figures' various accoutrements dubbed the "special chamber to store accessories."

Hence, this new C-3PO bust smacks of familiarity, yet of improvement as well. Just as with their previous successions of collector's cases, Kenner once again made a marked improvement, when the company's Vinyl Mini

Figures Collector's Cases, which holds 24 characters, had run their course, Kenner replaced these with the infamous Darth Vader Collector's Case, which holds 31 action figures. Now that the DVCC had outlived its usefulness, kids could fit a whopping FORTY figurines into the droid's head and shoulders. Furthermore, the considerable expense it must have incurred Kenner to vac-metallize the entire C-3PO case gave the toy automatic appeal when consumers passed by retail shelves.

Factory-sealed samples of this case come completely shrink-wrapped with see-through plastic wrap, unlike previously offered collector's cases. However, similar to those cases, this, too, possesses a chipboard sleeve that is fitted around the shoulders of this C-3PO bust.

This case includes the following features: label sheet, four-color paper action figure insert, and removable support bars (x8; to hold figures and accessories in place)

MISB: $55-$70+; **MIB**: w/paper sleeve, insert and unapplied labels: **$32-$40**; **MLC**: w/insert and unapplied labels: **$25-$30**

Ewok Village Playset, front view.

Ewok Village Action Playset

[Production #70520]

1st packaged appearance: 1983
Original Retail Price (average): $19.99

Located in the thickly wooded Happy Grove canopy on the Forest Moon of Endor, and directly based upon the roughly 200-member community featured prominently in *Return of the Jedi*, the technical name for this Ewok collective is Bright Tree Village.

With most Ewok huts suspended fifty feet above the forest floor, and the occasional Ewok family—such as the Warricks (see Wicket W. Warrick)—inhabiting the village's ground level, Bright Tree Village affords Luke Skywalker and his small band of Rebel refugees a brief respite before the climactic Battle of Endor. In *ROTJ* and according to Wookieepedia's map of the Ewok community's raised, tree-bound main level, the Ewok Village possesses the following distinct areas: the chief's hut and village meeting place through which pulses the civic lifeblood of the community, a shaman's hut (see Logray) for holding hallowed ceremonies, three huts reserved for "family," with one unconnected to the main village, a food storage hut, a Place of Sickness, a small dwelling for unmarried females and another for unmarried males, a solemn place reserved for

the village elders, and an unattached hut earmarked solely for visitors—where Luke, Leia, Han, Chewie, and the droids stay after they appease the Ewok leaders.

When Kenner translated this setting into toy form, they maintained the integrity and essence of the location. The sheer size of a 200-member community was far too large to slide into a box for sale at a reasonable price point, so the toy company kept the most iconic locations intact. With three large trees acting as pillars to suspend the base

Ewok Village Playset elevator.

Wicket W. Warrick uses the tree slide.

Ewoks gather around the spit and fireplace.

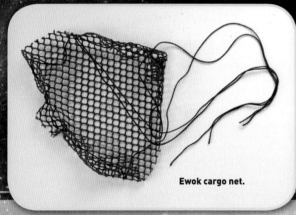

Ewok cargo net.

Ewok Village Playset parts.

of the playset aboveground, three "hut" openings in the trees where the base meets the faux wood, a fabric net which allowed collectors to "pretend to capture the Rebel heroes by activating the net trap," the ability to operate an elevator to get figures into the village above, and an escape chute that made for a quick getaway, this playset is a late jewel in Kenner's *Star Wars* collection.

This playset includes the following easily lost/ removable parts: Drum, Elevator, Fireplace (with label), Main Platform, Netting/Cargo Net, Platform Extension (x3—different sizes: small, medium, and large), Railing #1 (Three-Pole), Railing #2 (Four-Pole), Railing #3 (Five-Pole), Rock, Fire Spit, Spit Assembly Rod (x2), Strings (x4: two long pieces; two short pieces), Support Struts (x3—all are exactly similar), T-Cap (strings are thread through this device; rests upon "split peg"), Throne (two-piece) , Throne Carrier, Tree—Small Sized (with attached, non-re-movable "elevator crank"), Tree—Medium Sized, and a Tree—Large Sized.

Ewok throne, with carrier

MISB: $350-$380+; MIB: $105-$120; MLC: $62-$85.

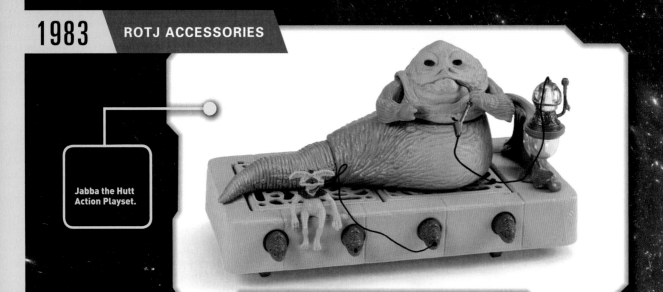

Jabba the Hutt Action Playset.

Jabba the Hutt Action Playset

[Production #70490]

1st packaged appearance: 1983
Original Retail Price (average): $12.99

One of the most popular of all Kenner's many *Star Wars* playsets—currently selling for perhaps far more than it should on the secondary market, since *millions* and *millions* of these sets were produced—this Jabba the Hutt Action Playset expertly captures a highly memorable scene from *Return of the Jedi*: when the corpulent crime lord surrounds himself with his palace's nefarious denizens. Fortunately, the playset features some of the more interesting aspects of Jabba's throne room environment gleaned from the film: collectors can thrill to twist Jabba's waist and watch the creature's tail knock over opposing action figures; kids can chuck Jabba's enemies through the flip-up throne/prison doors and onto the bone-ridden floor of the dungeon below—to meet his deadly, imprisoned Rancor (see the vicious monster's individual *ROTJ* creature entry); fans can pose the cackling Salacious Crumb on the side of throne, allowing the caustic imp to laugh at Jabba's doomed prisoners; and aficionados can accurately pose Jabba to draw at his hookah pipe, sending the Hutt into an intoxicated delirium.

Jabba's pipe and bowl set is not the only screen-accurate piece of this playset: if aficionados carefully scrutinize Jabba's throne, they'll notice that the intricate design/pattern featured on the lever-activated "Prison Doors" expertly reflect the trap doors featured on the floor of Jabba's throne room leading to his pet beast (see Rancor).

Two action figure notes should be mentioned: 1) Oddly enough, Kenner's Jabba figure is designed to possess three fingers on his right hand, yet four fingers on his left, and 2) There are at least two color variations on Jabba: one with a light yellow paint application on his face and chest, and another with darker/thicker yellow paint.

The playset includes the following easily lost/removable parts: Bowl Assembly (Two Bowl Halves, lower—small and no decorations; upper—large with decorations), Bowl Stand, black Bowl String, (Hookah) Pipe, detachable Pipe Bowl Air Intake Stem, Jabba the Hutt figure (both arms are removable*), Jabba's Throne/Base, 2 Throne/Prison Doors*, 2 Throne/Prison Door Levers*, black Throne String, 4 Monster Heads* (two long heads attach to levers, two to Throne String-optional), Salacious Crumb figure (removable tail*), and Slave Collar.

*Although Jabba the Hutt's arms, Salacious Crumb's tail, the Throne's Prison Doors, and the four Monster Heads are not designed to be removable, these accoutrements do, indeed, have a tendency to come off during play—simply replace them when they become separated from their assigned tabs.

MISB: four-color box: **$165-$190+**, catalog two-color box: **$65-$75+**.
MIB: four-color box: **$62-$80**, catalog two-color box: **$48-$55** (mailer box).
MLC: **$25-$32**.

Jabba the Hutt action figure color variations.

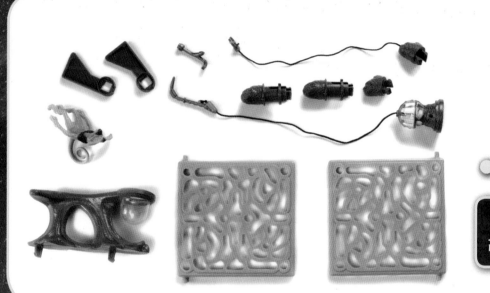

Jabba the Hutt Action Playset parts.

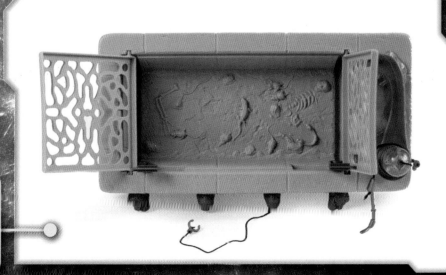

Jabba the Hutt Action Playset, top view.

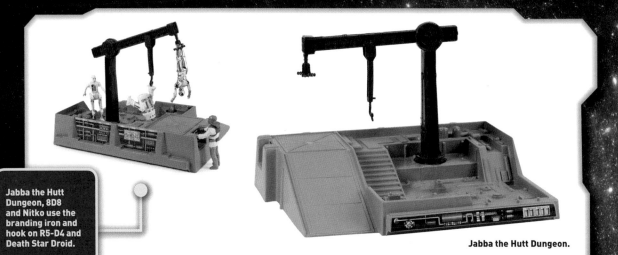

Jabba the Hutt Dungeon, 8D8 and Nitko use the branding iron and hook on R5-D4 and Death Star Droid.

Jabba the Hutt Dungeon.

Jabba the Hutt Dungeon
(Sears Exclusive; blue-gray base, brown boom-and-mast; *ROTJ* figures)

[Production #71381]

1st packaged appearance: 1983
Original Retail Price (average): $11.99

With the proper name of "Jabba Desilijic Tiure," the infamous interstellar gangster better known to the world as Jabba the Hutt is a lone member the *Hutts*: a species of large gastropods (snails and slugs) with short arms, large mouths and bulbous eyes. One of the most feared criminals in the galaxy, "The Bloated One" rules a vast criminal network located in the territory of the Outer Rim, a conglomeration of little-developed frontier planets, while he himself inhabits an opulent palace located in the desert of the planet Tatooine. That is … most of the palace is sumptuous, except for the dungeon.

This Sears exclusive playset was released in 1983 (solicited in Sears' 1984 Christmas season *Wish Book*)

Jabba the Hutt Dungeon parts.

and meant to represent a room within the bowels of Jabba's citadel: a chamber underneath the Hutt crime lord's opulent palace (see Jabba the Hutt Action Playset). As a Sears exclusive in the vein of the Cantina Adventures Set (1978), the Cloud City Playset (1980), or the Rebel Command Center (1981), this newly released playset dubbed "The Jabba the Hutt Dungeon" also contained a few exclusive action figures: 8D8 (a.k.a. Atedeeate), Klaatu (In Skiff Guard Outfit), and Nikto.

Regardless, one thing is clear: this is the earlier version of the playset—the *ROTJ* edition—with a blue-gray base, and a deep brown boom-and-mast assembly, as opposed to 1984's Jabba the Hutt Dungeon, with tan base, POTF figures, and blue-gray boom-and-mast assembly; both playsets are different from 1978's Land of the Jawas Action Playset, with orange base, and maroon-brown boom-and-mast assembly.

The *ROTJ* version of The Jabba the Hutt Action Playset includes the following easily lost/removable parts: 8D8 (a.k.a. Atedeeate) action figure, Klaatu action figure (In Skiff Guard Outfit, with Skiff Guard force pike), Nikto action figure (with Skiff Guard force pike), blue-gray Base Boom (deep brown), black Branding Iron Adapter (two-piece, non-reassembled), black Hook, deep brown Mast, and black Pivot Pin.

MISB: $275-$305+; **MIB**: with figures: $35-$50+, without figures: $45-$60; **MLC**: with figures: $28-$35, without figures: $18-$30+.

ISP-6 (Imperial Shuttle Pod)
[Mini-Rig]

[Production #70890]

1st packaged appearance: 1983
Original Retail Price (average): $4.99

Manufactured by either Cygnus Spaceworks or Sienar Fleet Systems (its provenance is unsure), the ISP-6 is one of the most popular of all Kenner's vintage *Star Wars* low-price-point mini-rigs (or later body-rigs). The magnificently designed ISP-6 vehicle truly allowed the toy company's engineers to showcase their talents and for those kids and collectors (like me) who couldn't afford the glorious shuttle *Tydirium* (see Imperial Shuttle), this Imperial Shuttle Pod was a saving grace. A miniaturized, stripped-down version of the *Tydirium*, this compact vehicle could be deployed from larger transports, and featured two moveable blaster cannons, a rear-view mirror, an open hatch to place the action figure in its one-man cockpit, and wings that folded up when landing.

The ISP-6 includes the following easily lost/removable parts: Cockpit with windshield, 2 Landing Skids (right and left), 2 Side Cannons, and Top Fin.

MISB: $350-$380+; **MIB:** $105-$120; **MLC:** $62-$85.

ISP-6, with figures.

ISP-6, isometric view.

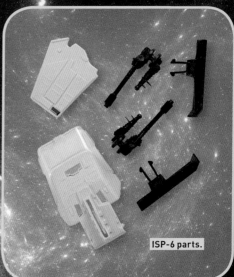
ISP-6 parts.

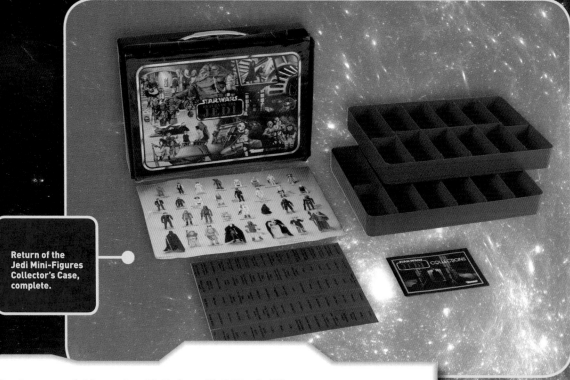

Return of the Jedi Mini-Figures Collector's Case, complete.

Return of the Jedi [vinyl] Mini-Figures Collector's Case

[Production #39190]*

1st packaged appearance: 1983
Original Retail Price (average): $6.49

*Note: The production number for all of Kenner's vinyl Mini-Figures Collector's Cases is exactly the same: Kenner did not change the assortment number regardless of the year of release (1979, 1980, 1981, 1982, or 1983).

The very rare *Return of the Jedi* "Mini-Action Figure Collector's Case" holds 24 *Star Wars* figures and is adorned with spectacularly painted artwork that utilizes still photos from the films as inspiration to decorate the front of each of these delicate, heat-sealed vinyl cases—with edges and corners that easily peel and rip.

Prominently featuring Jabba the Hutt (see Jabba the Hutt Action Playset) on the cover, this collector's case came with an insert that not only features images of the *ROTJ* figures who were currently released at retail, but this paper insert could be laid atop the uppermost of the two trays to stop the figures' weapons from moving around and becoming lost when a child was transporting the case from "A" to "B." For more information on the nature of these cases, please regard earlier Mini-Figures Collector's Cases' entries.

This vinyl case includes the following easily damaged/removable parts: Collector's Case with Color Front Image (red vinyl inside), Two Stackable Red Action Figure Trays, red Label Sheet, Four-Color Paper Insert (yellow both sides, featuring 65 figures), and white Carrying Handle.

MISP: with plastic wrap around the case: **$425-$475+**. **MIP**: with paper insert and unapplied labels: **$65-$80+**. **MLC**: with paper insert and labels applied: **$45-$55**.

Speeder Bike Vehicle

[Production #70500]

1st packaged appearance: 1983
Original Retail Price (average): $6.99

Manufactured by the Aratech Repulsor Company as the 74-Z speeder bike, the Imperial scout squad's lightning-fast Speeder Bike vehicle is a miracle of engineering, capable of reaching a top speed of over five hundred kilometers per hour (310 mph!). Using simple handlebars and foot pedals to control the craft, it is equipped with communication devices, an environmental sensor, comlink, communication jammer, a light blaster cannon, and a powerful boost.

In one of the most spectacular chase scenes in the history of cinema, Luke Skywalker is pursued by a trio of Biker Scouts through the forest, where *Star Wars* fans get to witness some of the Speeder Bike's special features as delineated on its Kenner toy's packaging: the speeder's "rear flaps close bringing Speeder Bike to a safe landing," while the vehicle's "...'brakes' also work when you move the pedals." Furthermore, you could push a button, which looks like a Biker Scout's saddle pack/

knapsack, to create battle damage while flying, yet the "Speeder Bike easily fits back together" for repeated attempts at "crashing."

Speaking to the Speeder Bike's disassembly, collectors should be reminded that nearly every piece can be broken down in order to simulate an "explosion," by depressing the "knapsack" button located behind the vehicle's seat: from the pair of "handlebars" to the "laser gun" mounted underneath of the speeder's hull to the "speed flaps" protecting the bike's engines. These, and the other, larger pieces may become separated from the bike's front extension and body, etc. It should also be mentioned that the speeder's "T-bar" is spring-loaded and will accommodate nearly every *Star Wars* figure atop the vehicle: simply slide the character's legs underneath, and the T-bar will grasp the figure's thighs. From this pseudo-seated position, most characters will also be able to reach the handgrips on the bike's handlebars.

The Speeder Bike's entire assembly is a gaggle of easily lost/removable parts, among these: Front Extension, 2 Handle Bars, Lower Body Shell, Lower Laser Gun, Upper Body Shell, and Upper Fin (mounts onto Front Extension).

MISB: $55-$70+; MIB: $28-$38+; MLC: $16-$26, depending on condition.

Speeder Bike parts: handlebars, upper fin, and front extension.

Speeder Bike, with Biker Scouts.

Speeder Bike

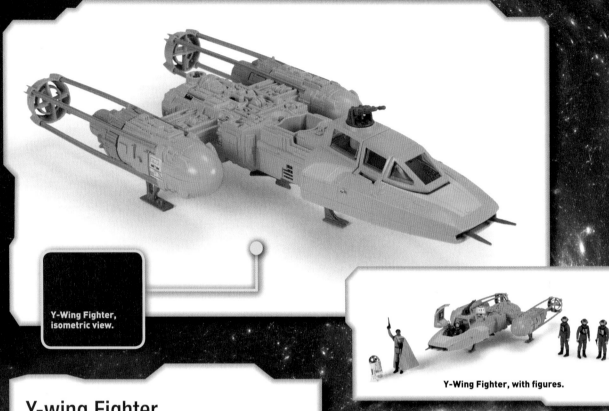

Y-Wing Fighter, isometric view.

Y-Wing Fighter, with figures.

Y-wing Fighter

[Production #70510]

1st packaged appearance: 1983
Original Retail Price (average): $19.99

Created by Koensayr Manufacturing, Y-wings are the workhorses of the Rebel Alliance and fondly known as the "wishbone" to many veteran pilots of the Rebellion. The long-serving BTL Y-wing starfighter, where the provenance of BTL is unknown, is a popular and reliable spacecraft for Alliance pilots due to its staunch, sturdy build—and for its ability to wreak havoc while trudging to a battle, delivering its rather impressive payload, and blasting its way back home.

Every time a Y-wing pilot from Gray Squadron dons his steely jumpsuit and enters his craft's transparisteel alloy canopy (Note: Kenner never produced a "Y-wing Pilot" action figure), he knows his starship is loaded for bear, since it possesses the following armaments: two Taim & Bak IX4 laser cannons, a set of Arakyd Flex Tube Proton-Torpedo Launchers, which fire "energized

torpedoes that carried a devastatingly powerful blast from a proton-scattering warhead," and a pair of ArMek SW-4 Ion Cannons, attached to a rotating top-mounted turret, that possess the ability to paralyze an enemy craft with ion cannon fire without destroying them, according to Wookieepeida.com.

Unfortunately, although the Y-wing is well-shielded and sports a mighty payload due to the tremendous amount of photon torpedoes it can carry, the ship is both sluggish and ungainly in combat: the Alliance needed an upgrade. Hence, the Rebellion creates the B-wing heavy assault starfighter, which should have ended this discussion, but although the B-wing was planned as a phase-out/direct replacement of the Y-wing, the new vessel didn't quite serve its purpose; as a result, the two are used together in assaults against capital ships (see Darth Vader's Star Destroyer Action Playset). Used in conjunction, the two ships are a powerful match.

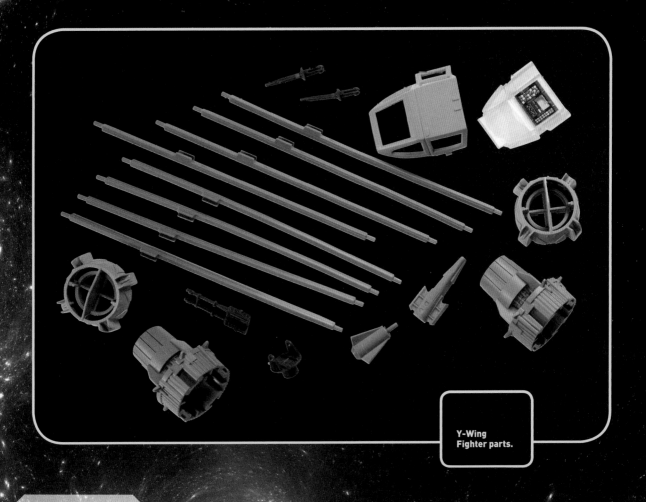

As a toy, one of the most remarkable features of Kenner's Y-wing starfighter is its ability to house an astromech droid in a large socket located immediately behind the cockpit, where the aviator's dependable partner can function as a co-pilot, assisting him with myriad duties, from managing the ship's navigational computers to engaging enemy aircraft via the ship's armaments. The Y-wing marks the only craft in the whole of the vintage toy line that affords collectors this amazing opportunity to hold R2-D2 (whether original, with Sensorscope, with Pop-Up Light Saber, or his Droids variation) or R5-D4 in this socket.

Collectors should note that Kenner's Y-wing vehicle is a bit fragile, with each engine able to be disassembled into six different parts—an exhaust nacelle (x1) that attaches to the base of the ship, four support pylons (x4) that frame each engine, and a disk vectral (x1) that serves as an end cap for both engines. Possessing "automatic LASER CANNONS with real laser sounds

and action" and engine pods that can also be removed to do vehicle maintenance repairs, it also had the ability to take off or land with remote landing gears and capacity to drop "bombs" on enemy targets. Finally, by depressing the vehicle's rear dark gray button, you may activate the top cannon turret motion AND laser cannon sound—a noise triggered by two C batteries.

The Y-wing Fighter's easily lost/removable parts are delineated as follows: Battery Cover, Bomb Assembly (two pieces: front and back), Canopy (with windshield), 2 Front Cannons (hard-to-find on loose samples), 2 Engine Pod Assemblies (2 Exhaust Cones [one each], 8 struts total [4 each], 2 Rear Support Rings [one each]), Top Cannon Assembly (Cannon and Cannon Base).

MISB: $375-$425+; MIB: working electronics: $55-$70+; MLC: working electronics: $40-$52

B-Wing Fighter, front view.

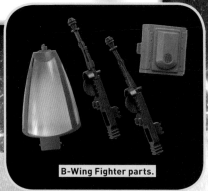

B-Wing Fighter parts.

B-wing Fighter

[Production #71370]

1st packaged appearance: 1984
Original Retail Price (average): $27.99

With its trademark gyro-stabilized cockpit module that allows the craft's dogfighting pilot to remain stationary while the rest of the ship rotates during flight, the B-wing heavy assault starfighter and its impressive payload is a saving grace for the Rebel Alliance as it struggles against the might of the Imperial Navy. Designed by Slayn & Korpil/Verpine, in conjunction with Gial Ackbar, who was then attached to the Shantipole Project (see Admiral Ackbar), the B-wing starfighter (a.k.a. "crosses," due to their distinctive form, or "blade-wings") is originally constructed as a replacement for the BTL Y-wing starfighter (see Y-wing Fighter). Although the B-wing has stronger shields and is better armed than the Y-wing, a few complications prevent this swap of Rebel starfighters from occurring: the B-wing is expensive to produce, it lacks both agility and speed—a necessary aspect for the art of dogfighting, the craft is notoriously challenging to fly, hence the issue of the rotating gyro-stabilized hull is difficult to master, and the larger sized profile of the ship makes it a larger target when in the midst of a battle. Furthermore, although its shields are stronger, the vehicle's armor-plating is weaker than that of the Y-wing.

The B-wing Fighter's toy package touts a bevy of action features, including: laser battle sounds via the use of two AA batteries (not included), "turn the rear engine pad … to move wings into attack position," the "B-Wing Fighter cockpit is gravity controlled and will stay right side up no matter how the wings are rotated," the vehicle's "cockpit opens to accommodate most Star Wars Action Figures" (see B-Wing Pilot), and finally—its "activation lever raises and lowers landing gear." With a non-removable battery door, you may also depress a button between the spacecraft's body and the cockpit in order to trigger the toy's remarkable battle sounds. Another unique feature of the B-wing is its interesting auxiliary wings: simply push in and turn the B-wing's lower right engine nodule (located at the rear of the craft) counter-clockwise in order to raise or lower the starfighter's twin auxiliary wings; for collecting purposes, it is worth noting that these auxiliary wings ARE molded differently from one another—one is labeled "T" (top), while the other is labeled "B" (bottom).

Regardless, the most impressive action feature of all is the B-wing's stunning "gyro cockpit," which remains upright as the vehicle is turned during play.

The B-wing Fighter contains the following easily lost/removable parts: 2 Auxiliary Wings (one top, one bottom), Battery Cover (often non-removeable), Canopy, and 2 Side Guns.

MISB: $425-$475+; **MIB**: working electronics: **$65-$80+**; **MLC**: working electronics: **$40-$55+**.

Desert Sail Skiff [Mini-Rig]

[Production #93520]

1st packaged appearance: 1984
Original Retail Price (average): $4.99

Although similar in construction to the far larger Bantha-II cargo ship (see Tatooine Skiff), Kenner's Desert Sail Skiff toy is a repulsorlift vehicle, which is based directly upon the designs of the Desert Sail-20 Skiff. Accommodating only one pilot, the Desert Sail Skiff sports twin blaster cannons, a moveable sail, a rotating cockpit, and a feature that is spectacular for the toy's small size: kids could "pretend to make *Star Wars* figures walk the plank … when the plank is retracted, *Star Wars* figures will fall over the side." Upon first look, it appears that the Desert Sail Skiff makes an appearance in the sixth episode, "The New King," of 1985's *Star Wars: Droids* cartoon; however, the vehicle in the animated program—dubbed the Floater-935— is missing the Sail-20's weapons and its characteristic red sail.

The Desert Sail Skiff possesses the following easily lost/removable parts: Red Top Sail, Sail Attachment, Two Side Cannons, and Two Side Wings.

MISB: $105-$115+; **MIB**: $38-$50+; **MLC**: $16-$26.

Desert Sail Skiff, with figures.

Desert Sail Skiff parts.

Desert Sail Skiff, isometric view.

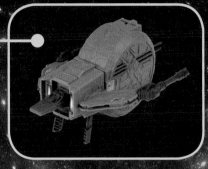

Endor Forest Ranger, rear view.

Endor Forest Ranger, with figure.

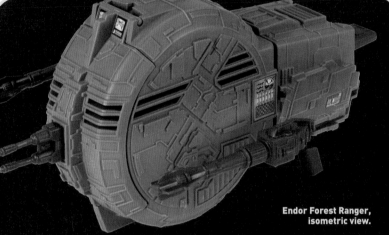

Endor Forest Ranger, isometric view.

Endor Forest Ranger [Mini-Rig]

[Production #93610]

1st packaged appearance: 1984
Original Retail Price (average): $4.99

Endor Forest Ranger parts.

The Endor Forest Ranger's package touts the following action features: "Endor Forest Ranger cockpit is gravity controlled and will stay in flying position no matter how the cannons are rotated," collectors may "Spin laser cannons for spiral firing action," the "vehicle ... has retractable landing gear" and " ... accommodates most Star Wars Action Figures."

Although we never witness the Endor Forest Ranger in *Return of the Jedi*, the toy's title insists upon its appearance on the Sanctuary Moon, if not the film. Furthermore, this odd vehicle also shows up in an issue of *New Mutants Special Edition* #1 (Sept. 1985, P. 39), "Home is Where the Heart Is," where the technology-controlling mutant named Warlock transforms himself into a copy of the vehicle due to artist Arthur Adams' apparent fondness for the toy.

The Endor Forest Ranger possesses the following easily lost/removable parts: Canopy, Front Cannon, and 2 Side Cannons.

MISB: $90-$115+; **MIB:** $40-$50+; **MLC:** $25-$30.

Ewok Assault Catapult

[Production #71070]

1st packaged appearance: 1984
Original Retail Price (average): $4.99

Utilized during the Battle of Endor to defend their homeland, the Ewok Assault Catapult is largely ineffective against the Imperial AT-STs (see Scout Walker), yet can potentially perform far better against ground forces.

Although the package front states it only comes with "one launcher and two boulders," this wasn't exactly true: there were far more moving parts that, if missing, the accessory wouldn't be able to operate. Specifically, the string with attached hook, and the hooked end of the catapult arm are impossible to find on loose samples.

The package text states that collectors may load the Catapult by turning the crank and "when ready to fire, simply pull the string."

The Ewok Assault Catapult possesses the following easily lost/removable parts: 2 Boulders (with holes inside for mounting), Catapult Trigger (with removable hook end), and String with Hook.

Ewok Assault Catapult parts: two boulders, catapult trigger, and (hard-to-find) end hook.

MISB: $80-$90+; MIB: $28-$38+; MLC: $16-$26.

Ewok Assault Catapult parts: black string, hard-to-find hook, crank arm half.

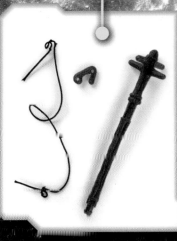

Ewok Assault Catapult.

Ewok Combat Glider

[Production #93610]

1st packaged appearance: 1984
Original Retail Price (average): $4.99

Ewok Combat Glider, with figure.

In the *Star Wars* canon, the Ewoks utilize this vehicle when participating in the defense of the Sanctuary Moon against the Empire during the Battle of Endor. Called the "skin glider" (a.k.a. hang glider or sky-glider) due to its wings being constructed out of the skins of many large animals, one of these transports would take a fairly long time to build, since the dried and stretched skins of many multiple animals must be utilized to create the glider's wings. Originally Ewoks flew this craft for small game hunting from above, yet eventually the vehicle was modified into a defense weapon to dissuade larger native monsters—and eventually proves quite effective against the Imperial Stormtroopers.

Although made for Ewoks to pilot, the Glider will accommodate most *Star Wars* action figures.

Kenner's fascinating yet delicate Ewok Combat Glider possesses a few key easy-to-lose parts and pieces which makes obtaining mint, loose, and complete (MLC) samples of the toy quite difficult: Action Lever, 2 Boulders, Figure Harness, 2 Strings, and X-Brace.

MISB: $75-$80+; **MIB**: $28-$38+; **MLC**: $16-$26.

Ewok Combat Glider parts.

Imperial Shuttle (a.k.a. Shuttle Tydirium)

[Production #93650]

1st packaged appearance: 1984
Original Retail Price (average): $34.99

Kenner's magnificent Imperial Shuttle is directly based upon the designs of the *Lambda*-class T-4a shuttle craft, which is utilized by the ranks of the Imperial military. As a light utility craft, this vessel is developed to transport material, troops, and, as featured in *Return of the Jedi*, high-ranking persons of importance (see Darth Vader, The Emperor, and Imperial Dignitary).

The stolen Imperial Shuttle named *Tydirium*—originally captured by General Crix Madine (see General Madine)—is utilized by Han Solo's Endor strike team, along with a stolen clearance code, in order to insert the Rebel Alliance's commando force onto the Sanctuary Moon (forest moon of Endor) during the Battle of Endor in *ROTJ*. Named after the ore called tydirium, many Imperial spacecraft follows the pattern of naming ships after different minerals, such as the *Shuttle Bandarium* and the *Shuttle Crystilium*.

With the ability for kids and collectors to "press button at rear top of vehicle for 'laser sounds'," and bevy of features such as the ability to "open Imperial Shuttle cockpit," and "adjust wing laser cannons," the Imperial Shuttle toy captures the attention of many diehard *Star Wars* aficionados. Additionally, the spacecraft comes equipped with a sensitive trigger that can be quickly released—via an internal ratchet system—so that its "wings automatically move into flying position," and when the craft lands, the two-part "Imperial Shuttle ramp lowers so action figures can come on board." As if the

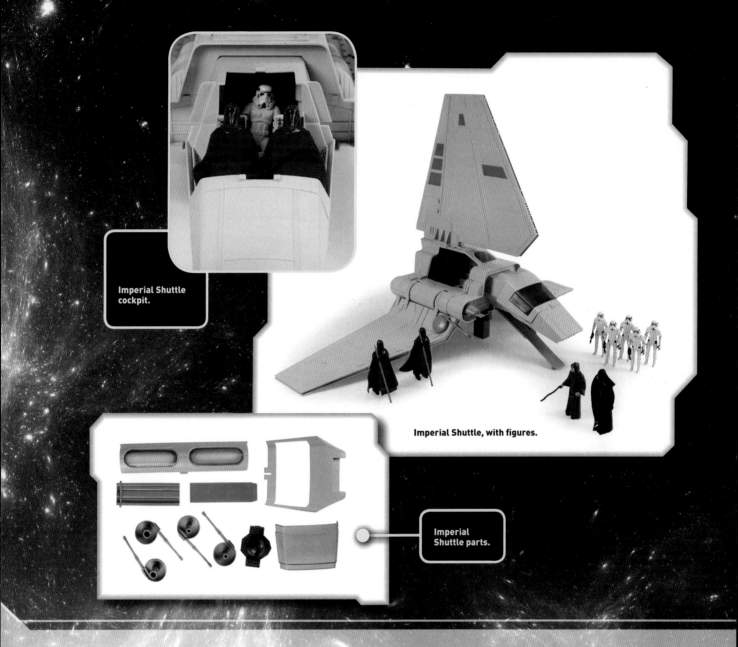

Imperial Shuttle cockpit.

Imperial Shuttle, with figures.

Imperial Shuttle parts.

spaceship needed any more special features, the shuttle's manual landing gear may be released and retracted, while the toy's side panel allows inside access.

However, there is a lone complaint about this toy leveled by collectors in regard to its enormous size and scale when compared to the other toys in the vintage line: The Imperial Shuttle is simply *immense* when paired up with any other Kenner spaceships. A smaller child under the age of ten playing with the toy would have tremendous difficulty holding the ship aloft to mimic the spacecraft's flying motion.

Regardless of its size (22 inches tall with a 3-inch wingspan), the Imperial Shuttle is the largest ship produced for the vintage line, and a prized acquisition for many collectors due to its faithful translation into plastic form. Furthermore, although Kenner's Imperial Shuttle

was released at retail in late 1984/early 1985, this magnificent vehicle was never solicited in any packaging other than *Return of the Jedi*: the toy was never offered in a Power of the Force box.

The Imperial Shuttle includes the following easily lost/removable parts: Battery Compartment, Cockpit Canopy, Plastic Window, Front Cannons (x2; left and right), Handle (non-removable), Landing Gear (x2; left and right), Ramp (two sections; smaller section slides into the larger section), Rear Cannon, Side Hatch Door (not pictured), Vertical Stabilizer (i.e. vertical top wing), Wing Gun (x2; left and right—each Wing Gun has two parts, bottom and top Wing Gun halves)

MISB: $650-$725+; MIB: working electronics. $100–$105 ; MLC: working electronics: $85-$115+.

Jabba the Hutt Dungeon
(Sears Exclusive; tan base, POTF figures)

[Production #59262]

1st packaged appearance: 1984
Original Retail Price (average): $13.99

Specifically, the Sears exclusive Jabba the Hutt Dungeon Playset reflects a combination of two different areas underneath Jabba's Palace (see Jabba Action Playset): 1) the purported "maintenance bay/motor pool" utilized by Jabba's drivers and lackeys to maintain his many skiffs and transports where, during the time of *Return of the Jedi*, the Klatoonian known as Barada is the person-in-charge, and 2) the "cyborg operations" section of Jabba's court hidden deep within the recessed lower levels of the crime lord's palace, where the sinister torture droid known as EV-9D9 wreak havoc on her unfortunate victims. Fortunately enough, the Power of the Force themed version of The Jabba the Hutt Dungeon came with both figures plus a bounty hunter for good measure: motor pool commander Barada, torture droid EV-9D9, and the mercenary known as Amanaman.

Regardless, one thing is clear: although this is the later 1984 version of the Jabba the Hutt Dungeon playset, one that included Power of the Force figures, it was still a *Return of the Jedi* release—with a tan base, and a blue-gray boom-and-mast assembly, as opposed to 1983's Jabba the Hutt Dungeon, with blue-gray base, *ROTJ* figures, and deep brown boom-and-mast assembly. Both playsets are different from 1978's Land of the Jawas Action Playset with orange base, and maroon-brown boom-and-mast assembly.

This version of The Jabba the Hutt Action Playset includes the following easily lost/removable parts: Amanaman action figure (with large brown Headhunter Staff sporting three white painted skulls), Barada (with Skiff Guard battle staff), EV-9D9 action figure, tan Base, blue-gray Boom, Branding Iron Adapter (black, two-piece, non-reassembled), black Hook, blue-gray Mast, and black Pivot Pin.

MISB: $365-$400+; **MIB**: with figures: $150-$190+, without figures: $45-$60; **MLC**: with figures: $135-$145+, without figures: $20-$28+.

Jabba the Hutt Dungeon, with figures.

EV-9D9 uses the hook on Power Droid & 2-1B.

Jabba the Hutt Dungeon parts.

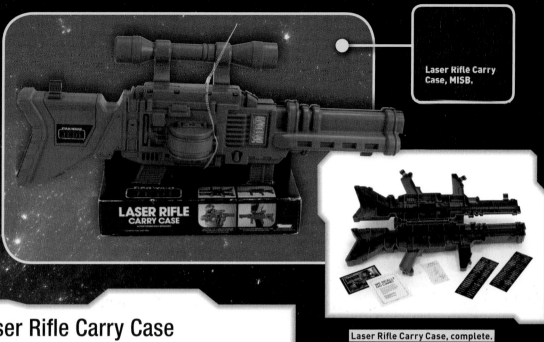

Laser Rifle Carry Case, MISB.

Laser Rifle Carry Case, complete.

Laser Rifle Carry Case

[Production #71530]

1st packaged appearance: 1984
Original Retail Price (average): $13.99

The Laser Rifle Carry Case is the final collector's case made by Kenner for the sole purpose of transporting vintage *Star Wars* action figures and accessories. This Laser Rifle Carry Case marks an evolution in collector's cases. Since the solicitation of the original vinyl Star Wars Mini-Action Figure Collector's Case in 1979—and for those similar boxy, vinyl cases produced every year from 1979-1983—Kenner pushed the envelope of design for collector cases. To wit: The three hard plastic cases the company produced in 1980, 1983, and 1984 appear *far* different from the original, unappealing vinyl ones, since the three newer cases serve two different purposes: utility *and* aesthetics.

For instance, with 1980's Darth Vader Collector's Case and 1983's C-3PO Collector's Case, Kenner constructed collector's cases that could be displayed on your toy shelves after storing your figurines within them: they were essentially three-dimensional sculpted busts of the two popular characters. While the Laser Rifle Carry Case may not have improved upon utility, it did indeed expand upon aesthetics: although you could fit only nineteen action figures and their accessories within the gun (as opposed to Vader's

31, C-3PO's 40, and 24 within the vinyl cases), the Laser Rifle Carry Case existed as a nicely-scaled, youth-sized weapon, with a targeting scope (and inner circular reticle) mounted on the laser rifle, allowing you to actually look through gthe scope while role-playing.

Regardless, here is a description of the carrying case from its small chipboard box attached to the gun with zip ties (a "MISP" Laser Rifle): the "LASER RIFLE Carry Case can be played with like rifles seen in RETURN OF THE JEDI and used as a carrying case," you can "carry your LASER RIFLE Carry Case by holding the see-through scope," and when open via its five clamps, "accommodates 19 STAR WARS Action Figures…," while—like other cases before it—"there is even a compartment for storing accessory items and secret messages."

This Laser Rifle Carry Case includes the following easily lost/removable parts: 2 Long Straps/Holders, 1 Accessory Compartment, and 2 Label Sheets.

MISP: $55-$75+; **MIB**: with chipboard box attached, unapplied label sheet: **$32-$38+**, with chipboard box attached, applied labels: **$25-$30**; **MLC**: with unapplied label sheet: **$22-$28+**, with applied labels: **$10-$14**.

Rancor Monster figure

[Production #71060]

1st packaged appearance: 1984
Original Retail Price (average): $12.99

Rancor Monster, posed.

With the ability for collectors to open the Rancor Monster's jaw by pushing the lever on his back, to "spread [its] spring loaded arms and watch them snap back into position," and to stand the creature in action poses because the "Rancor Monster has movable legs … [and] even has movable wrists," Kenner completely outdid themselves with this magnificent beast featured in *Return of the Jedi*—when Luke Skywalker (see Luke Skywalker [Jedi Knight Outfit]), the doomed dancer, Oola, and a lone, terrified Gamorrean Guard are led down the trapdoor (see Jabba the Hutt Action Playset) into the Rancor's den.

Once there, the victims would face a creature native to the planet Dathomir; Rancors are physically immense, horrifyingly carnivorous beasts that were, in essence, "reptomammals," a combination of reptile and mammal. Although initially viewed as no more than mindless beasts that were utilized as pets or, in rare cases, mounts (for exceptionally brave humanoids), the Rancor race were in actuality capable of acting civilized.

Unfortunately, the Rancor Monster featured in *Return*

of the Jedi is *not* one of those creatures. Kept prisoner by the powerful crime lord Jabba the Hutt, the Rancor Monster inhabiting the pit at Jabba's palace ("Hutt Castle") is little more than a killing machine, laying waste to all of the villain's prisoners who are flung (via trapdoor) from the reception area of his throne room into his pet Rancor's desolate pit …

However, at least one human being fells a strong kinship with Jabba's bellicose pet, a relationship that may evince the creature's sentience: Malakilli, the Rancor Keeper (see Rancor Keeper), who weeps openly when the creature is killed by Jedi Knight Luke Skywalker.

MISB: $245-$275+; **MIB**: $45-$60;
MLC: $28-$35.

TIE Interceptor Vehicle

[Production #71390]

1st packaged appearance: 1984
Original Retail Price (average): $19.99

This final vehicle produced by Kenner for the Empire's TIE series of starfighter utilizes the following action features: "Battle Sound and Flashing Laser Light," and "wing panels pop off to simulate battle damage … easily fit back in place." With its newly designed wings that still possessed Kenner's trademark "pop-off" design, the vehicle is a remarkable feat of toy engineering. Regarding the real-world starfighter,

the Empire needs a better class of starship after they lose nearly 300 standard TIEs to the Rebellion's superior Incom Y-65 X-wing starfighters (see X-Wing Fighter) during one particularly gruesome campaign ca. 1 BBY. Therefore, they wish to create an Imperial craft that has the power of a TIE/Advanced (see Darth Vader TIE Fighter), but *without* the prohibitive cost that makes the TIE/Advanced starfighter far too impractical for mass production.

So then, Sienar Fleet Systems (SFS) manufactures the spectacularly designed TIE Interceptor (a.k.a. TIE/ IN starfighter): a ridiculously quick (maximum speed of 1,250 km/h), highly maneuverable ship that accord-

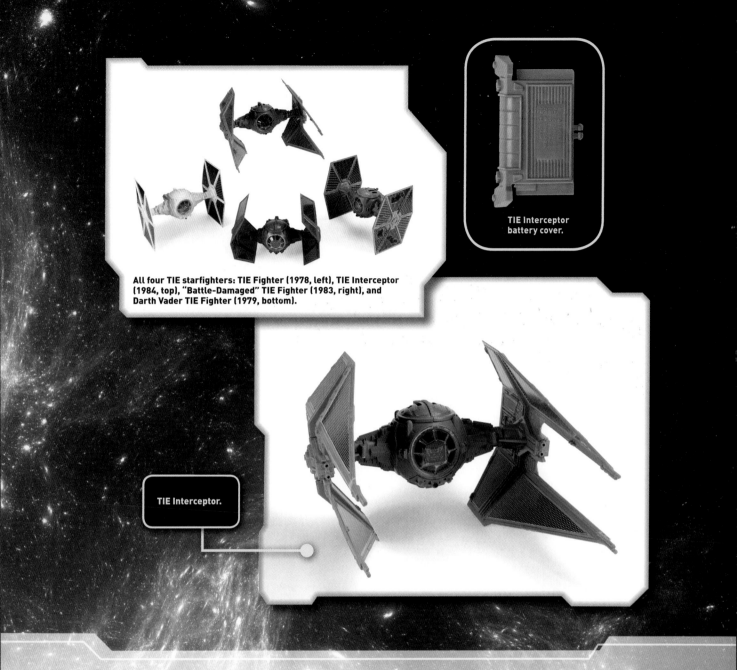

All four TIE starfighters: TIE Fighter (1978, left), TIE Interceptor (1984, top), "Battle-Damaged" TIE Fighter (1983, right), and Darth Vader TIE Fighter (1979, bottom).

TIE Interceptor battery cover.

TIE Interceptor.

ing to Wookieepedia, is specifically designed to "target, hunt down, and destroy enemy fighters and bombers, hence the name *interceptor*." With its distinctively arrow-shaped solar collection panels that are markedly different from the standard hexagon-shaped arrays of the standard TIE fighter (see TIE Fighter), the remarkable TIE Interceptor is one of the fastest ships in the entire galaxy at the time of its production, rivaling even the Rebel Alliance's lightning-quick RZ-1 A-wing interceptor (n.k.a. [see Droids,] A-Wing Fighter).

For toy collectors, it's worth noting that the single most important easily lost part on this vehicle is its battery cover. Please take care not to confuse the TIE Interceptor's battery cover with the battery covers of the other Kenner TIEs on the secondary market. The standard TIE Fighter (1978) is white, the Battle Damaged TIE Fighter (1983) appears blue-gray, the Darth Vader TIE Fighter (1979) is rendered dark gray, while the TIE Interceptor (1984) is light gray.

The TIE Interceptor vehicle includes the following removable/easily lost parts: 2x Solar Array Wings, Main Cockpit, 2x Ingress/Egress Hatch Flaps, 1x Hatch Opener/Seat Raiser, Battery Cover.

MISB: $525-$575+; **MIB**: $80-$105+, working electronics; **MLC**: $55-$65+, working electronics.

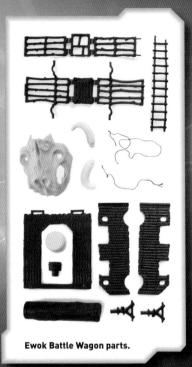

Ewok Battle Wagon parts.

Ewok Battle Wagon, with figures.

Tree Branch Hook with string.

Ewok Battle Wagon, Ewok fort made from sides, etc.

Ewok Battle Wagon

[Production #93690]

1st packaged appearance: 1985
Original Retail Price (average): $22.99

Due to the many fabulous action features and bevy of difficult-to-find accoutrements that comprise the construction of the Ewok Battle Wagon, it is an incredibly difficult piece for collectors to acquire on the secondary market, whether MISB (Mint In Sealed Box), MIB (Mint in Box), MLC (Mint Loose Complete), or even loose and incomplete.

Created by Ewok Erpham Warrick, a powerful warrior and the great-grandfather of Wicket W. Warrick, the Ewok Battle Wagon (aka war wagon) is constructed for attack and defense, particularly in order to combat a local tribe of the aggressive, belligerent barbarians known as the Duloks (see *Ewoks: Dulok Scout, Dulok Shaman, King Gorneesh,* and *Urgah Lady Gorneesh*).

Featured in the tenth episode of the *Star Wars: Ewoks* episode dubbed "Wicket's Wagon," the Ewok Battle Wagon possesses the following action features: a "Battle Ram [which] will help defeat Imperial Scout Walkers," a "Prisoner cage [that] will keep even the

Imperial Sniper [Body-Rig]

[Production #93920]*

1st packaged appearance: 1985
Original Retail Price (average): $4.99

*Note: The Imperial Sniper and the Security Scout possess the exact production number.

Imperial Sniper, with Imperial Gunner.

Although the packaging artwork suggests that these vehicles are utilized during the Battle of Endor, they do not appear in any film. Furthermore, the maintenance hook mounted on the right side of the craft is borrowed exactly from a mini-rig from *The Empire Strikes Back* mini-rig assortment (see CAP-2, [Captivator]).

The Imperial Sniper's package states the following action features and accoutrements: an "action figure can be placed in the seat. Close control panel belt and snap it shut," the Sniper's "wings are movable to alter pretend flight pattern," the "maintenance hook allows for picking up droids and other action figures. Control wheel moves maintenance hook," and if the vehicle's " … seat comes off during play, replace it by inserting tab into slot on seat belt and rotating seat so the top bar snaps into C-clamp."

The Imperial Sniper has one easily lost piece: the Action Figure Seat Belt.

Imperial Sniper Seat Belt.

MOSC*: $125-$150++; MLC: $50-$65+.
*Note: It is almost impossible to obtain a MOSC sample of the Imperial Sniper without the package having a yellowed bubble; for any samples with a clear bubble, add **$50** to the MOSC value.

toughest Imperial soldiers," the ability for Ewoks to direct battles, a "front ramp [that] comes down so the Ewoks can storm enemy strongholds," and a (delicate) prisoner's cage which allowed scouts to " … transport prisoners on their shoulders." Furthermore, the Wagon could carry *many* Ewoks from their home (see Ewok Village Playset)," while its two removable "sides [could] come off to reveal [a] driving pit," whereas collectors could also "Pretend enemy soldiers are moving the Battle Wagon," or finally, "when both vehicle sides are off, you can make an Ewok fort [!].

The Ewok Battle Wagon is quite rare and exceedingly delicate, possessing a number of intricate parts that stop the vehicle from becoming complete on the secondary market. The Ewok Battle Wagon's easily lost/removable parts are listed as follows: Battering Ram Assembly (Ram, 2 Ram Supports, black string, Front Cover [white]), Front Ramp (with long black string), Ladder, 2-piece Prisoner Cage (with black string and impossible-to-find hook), 2 Side Pieces, Skull Assembly (Skull, 2 Removable Tusks), 2 String Cranks, and Table.

MISB. $650 $725+; MIB; $195-$215+; MLO. $165 $185+

One-Man Sand Skimmer [body-rig]

[Production #93920]

1st packaged appearance: 1985
Original Retail Price (average): $4.99

One-Man Sand
Skimmer.

The sandskimmer (aka One-Man Sand Skimmer or one-person sandskimmer) body-rig is featured in two episodes of 1985's *Star Wars: Ewoks* animated program, "The New King" and "The Frozen Citadel," and within the narrative of a few different short stories. This miniature vehicle is utilized to transport one being through an adverse (i.e., desert) environment. Although never featured in any of the *Star Wars* films, the Sand Skimmer body-rig remains quite difficult to obtain on the secondary market.

With the ability to attach an action figure to the foot peg on the base of the vehicle and attach its hands to control the panel handles, the Skimmer's "navigation sail and laser cannon can be moved by activating thumb wheel." Furthermore, "if sail comes off during play, it snaps back into place. Be sure laser cannon and sail are in a straight forward position when inserting peg into hole."

The entire assembly of the One-Man Sand Skimmer is a mess of easily lost parts; however, the Red Sail and Hand Rail are most often found missing.

 MOSC*: $125-$150++; MLC: $50-$65+.
*Note: It is almost impossible to obtain a MOSC sample of the One-Man Sand Skimmer without the package having a yellowed bubble; for any samples with a clear bubble, add **$50** to the MOSC value.

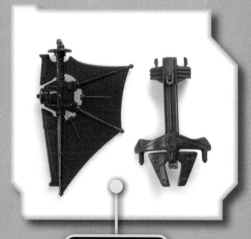

One-Man Sand
Skimmer
navigation sail
and handlebars.

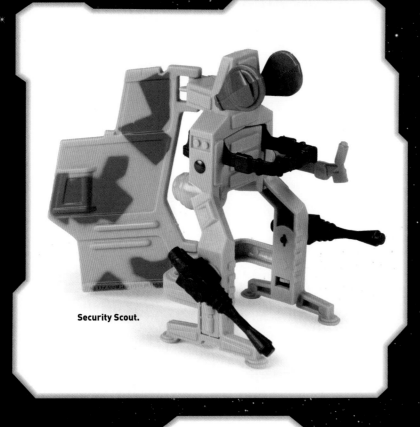

Security Scout.

Security Scout parts.

Security Scout [Body-Rig]

[Production #93920]*

1st packaged appearance: 1985
Original Retail Price (average): $4.99

*Note: The Imperial Sniper vehicle and the Security Scout possess the exact production number.

Piloted by a lone driver in an open cockpit, the Security Scout vehicle is a one-man craft held aloft by repulsorlift technology (see Tatooine Skiff) used by the Rebel Alliance during the fierce Battle of Hoth (3 ABY) for defensive purposes, and later at the Battle of Endor (4 ABY) where its quick maneuverability via its single rudder, forest camouflage, and two blaster cannons assists the native Ewok warriors (see Chief Chirpa and Logray [Ewok Medicine Man]) and the Rebel Alliance's Special Forces Group (see Rebel Commando).

The Security Scout possesses the following action features and accoutrements: you could "slide action figure into body" and "attach hands to control levers and

lower head communications for pretend communications." Also, the vehicle's "rudder can be swiveled for pretend maneuvering," and the Scout's "laser cannons move 360° and make a clicking sound."

The Security Scout has the following easily lost pieces: Head Communications Set, Removable Control Lever, Two Laser Cannons, and Rudder.

MOSC*: $80-$95+; MLC: $45-$60+.
*Note: It is almost impossible to obtain a MOSC sample of the Imperial Sniper without the package having a yellowed bubble; for any samples with a clear bubble, add **$50** to the MOSC value.

Tatooine Skiff, rear view.

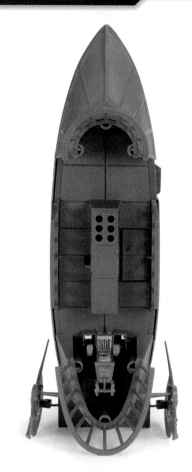

Tatooine Skiff, top view.

Tatooine Skiff

[Production #71540]

1st packaged appearance: 1985
Original Retail Price (average): $15.99

Kenner's Power of the Force Tatooine Skiff is based directly upon the Bantha-II model of cargo skiff manufactured by Ubrikkian Industries and featured in the Battle of the Great Pit of Carkoon scene from *Return of the Jedi*. According to the real-world skiff's schematics, in order for the craft to levitate, the ship utilizes *repulsorlift* technology—a form of anti-gravity technology that is purportedly activated by sub-nuclear "knots" (protuberances) in space-time. These subatomic knots used by the skiff are produced by massive power refineries (i.e., industrial plants located in deep space) that are unmanned due to the perilous danger presented by the manufacturing process.

Named after the horned, stalwart Banthas—those herbivorous hairy beasts of burden found on planets all across the galaxy including Tatooine—this Bantha-II cargo skiff is designed for transporting goods and sometimes sentient species across long distances.

Debatably the rarest, most desirable, and most detailed of the many vehicles produced for the vintage

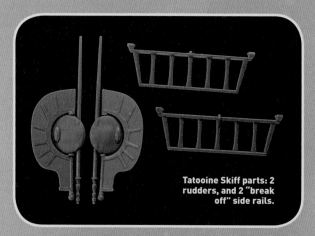

Tatooine Skiff parts: 2 rudders, and 2 "break off" side rails.

Kenner line, the Power of the Force Tatooine Skiff expertly captures the dimensions of the levitating vehicle featured in the fantastic scene that makes this vehicle famous: sailing by the edge of the Dune Sea of Tatooine during a scene that potentially spells

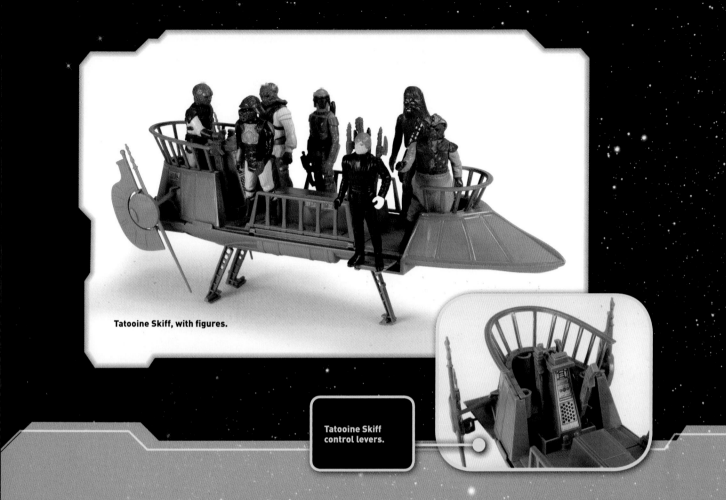

Tatooine Skiff, with figures.

Tatooine Skiff control levers.

doom for Luke Skywalker and his band of Rebel he-roes. While standing poised to "walk the plank," the Jedi Knight hatches a plan to avoid the hungry, gaping maw of the sinister sarlacc—the immense, omnivo-rous, semi-sentient, plant-like, tentacled creature that preys upon Boba Fett after the bounty hunter falls into the Great Pit of Carkoon.

The toy's designers were truly ingenious when con-verting this sophisticated vehicle into plastic form. For instance, many aspects of the Bantha-II cargo skiff in the film are featured prominently on the scaled-down toy, allowing collectors to utilize the model's many spe-cial features: two sliding levers on the rear of the skiff which permitted collectors to move the vehicle's rud-ders to the right and left, a control lever at the right side of the steering column which can be deployed in order to trigger the skiff's landing pods to retract, a left-side control lever on the steering column that activates the skiff's gangplank (note that the edge of the gangplank is hinged and will drop when the lever is pulled), two side rails (left and right) which will fold down to simu-late battle damage, a clever storage area where skiff

guards can stow their large force pikes and staffs, and finally, toward the right-hand side of the ship's bow, and a trapdoor "trigger" that will force an action figure to plummet over the right side of the cargo ship.

Collectors should be mindful that the Tatooine Skiff is perhaps the most delicate vintage *Star Wars* vehicle. For instance, the entire tie rod assembly (tie rods, fin supports, rudders, etc.) is incredibly fragile and prone to damage. Also, the three landing pods retraction sys-tem is subtly difficult to trigger—do not force these up-and-down. Sometimes the rods will not fully retract, yet please do not rest the vehicle flat on the ground without the pods lowered.

The Tatooine Skiff possesses the following eas-ily lost/removable pieces: Gangplank End, 3 Landing Pods (aka Landing Gear Struts), 2 Rudders, 2 Rudder Supports, and 2 "Break Off" Side Rails.

MISB: $525-$575+; **MIB**: $315-$325+; **MLC**: $225-$250+.

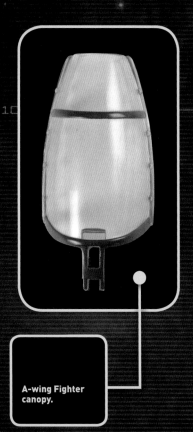

Droids A-wing Fighter, left side view.

A-wing Fighter canopy.

A-wing Fighter

[Production #93700]

1st packaged appearance: 1985
Original Retail Price (average): $9.99

Despite the fact that the vehicle possesses both a hyperdrive unit and shields, at the time of its production by the Rebel Alliance's underground engineers, the RZ-1 A-wing interceptor (a.k.a. the A-Wing Fighter) is one of the fastest ships in the galaxy, speedier even than the Empire's TIE interceptor—which does not sport the same quality of aforementioned features. Therefore, this lightning-quick spaceship is often a Rebel pilot's favorite choice of combat fighter because it is rocket-fast: essentially the A-Wing Fighter is a cockpit attached to a pair of Novaldex J-77 Event Horizon sublight engines. Originally designed as an escort ship with advanced sensors, the A-wing starfighter is the Rebellions' finest ship.

Like its predecessor from the Clone Wars (ca. 22-19 BBY), the Eta-2 *Actis*-class light interceptor, commonly known as the Jedi interceptor (a.k.a. Hasbro's late-model Jedi Starfighter), the A-Wing Fighter requires Rebel aviators possessing exceptional skill to act as pilots, since they can no longer depend upon members of the defunct Jedi Order to fill their ranks after the Great Jedi Purge. Piloting the A-Wing is further complicated by the fact that the vehicle is without the dorsal-mounted astromech droid socket that the Jedi Starfighter possesses—as a result, all of the weapon systems, navigation, and flight controls have to be monitored and maintained by the lone aviator in the cockpit.

With two Dymek HM-6 Concussion Missile Launchers capable of launching six advanced concussion missiles, wing-mounted rotating laser cannons that can rotate in a 360-degree arc, advanced sensory arrays and stealth packages, the ability to fly at speeds up to 1,300 km/h, a sensor jamming unit, and room for one pilot and 40 kilograms of cargo (!), the A-Wing Fighter is powerful enough to engage starships much larger spacecraft than itself ... even capital ships such as Imperial Star Destroyers.

The A-wing Fighter's easily lost/removable parts are: Removable Canopy, 2 Side Cannons.

Note: The A-wing Fighter requires two AA batteries to trigger its laser sounds.

MISB: $475-$510; **MIB:** $165-$185+; **MLC:** $85-$110+.

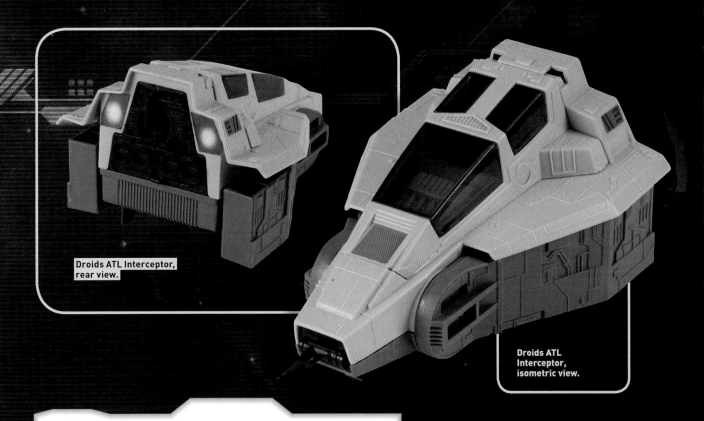

Droids ATL Interceptor, rear view.

Droids ATL Interceptor, isometric view.

ATL Interceptor (a.k.a. Air-To-Land Interceptor)

[Production #69770]

1st packaged appearance: 1985
Original Retail Price (average): $8.99

This fascinating vehicle showcases the level of advancement in toy technology that Kenner had developed over the course of its vintage *Star Wars* product line, particularly when compared to the company's first low-price-point vehicle, the exceedingly simple Land Speeder. With retractable landing gear, a tinted canopy, two different flight modes, a "scout" mode and a "landing" mode, a pair of pop-out side cannons, and button-activated "wings," collectors were most likely pleasantly surprised when nabbing the ATL Interceptor at retail.

The "real-world" version of the ATL (Air-To-Land) Interceptor was built on the planet of Annoo (a.k.a. Gelefil), an agricultural word located in the Outer Rim Territories. Utilized by the Fromm Family of Crime (a.k.a. the Fromm Gang) around 15 BBY, the spacecraft is used by the Fromms (see Droids, Sise Fromm and Tig Fromm) as an *interceptor* (see INT-4 and TIE Interceptor) where the ship functions to protect their weapons satellite, the Trigon One, and to subjugate and terrorize the inhabitants of the backwater Mid Rim world known as Ingo; specifically, R2-D2, C-3PO, and

their masters, Thall Joben and Jord Dusat, along with their ally, Kea Moll (see their individual entries).

The toy's packaging says the ATL Interceptor can accommodate one action figure and "when rear button is activated, wings automatically fall and side laser cannons pop out." The vehicle's scout mode occurs when shields and landing gear are in the up position, and to put the vehicle in landing mode, lower the manual landing gear. Additionally, shields can be lowered for combat mode by pulling the activator toward the rear of the vehicle, and when the shields are activated, the side cannons moved into firing position.

The ATL Interceptor possesses only one easily lost/removable part: a Main Cockpit. However, its front cannon is so fragile, due to the fact that Kenner extended the barrel well past the breakage point that is found broken on 95 percent of loose samples—driving up demand for MISB pieces.

MIGU II107-1110 , MILI 111111-11701 ,
MLC: $50-$65+,

267

Droid Side Gunner parts.

Droids Side Gunner, with Imperial Gunner figures.

Droids Side Gunner.

Side Gunner

[Production #94010]

1st packaged appearance: 1985
Original Retail Price (average): $10.99

Appearing in two episodes of the *Droids* animated program, "Escape Into Terror" and "The New King," as well as the program's title segment, the Imperial *repulsorcraft* (for an explanation, see Tatooine Skiff) dubbed the Side Gunner is a fairly sophisticated bit of toy technology developed by Kenner. With a central pod/main vehicle sporting a one-person cockpit for the craft's pilot and a fabulous sidecar (with Rotational Control Knob) for the vehicle's gunner, this compact vehicle possesses four different cannons: a double-cannon mounted on the front of the sidecar, upper and lower cannons attached to the top and bottom of the central pod's lone wing, and a lower-mounted cannon connected to a post below the cockpit on the main pod.

Collectors should note that although relatively small, it is almost impossible to find the Side Gunner in MLC

condition, forcing aficionados to purchase MISB samples. With a fold-up shroud and removable back protector that fully engulf the gunner, a removable windshield for the central pod, two snap-off wing cannons, and a lower cannon which fits atop the central pod's lone landing gear that is *almost always* found missing on loose samples, since it fits quite loosely—and oddly enough, is NOT PICTURED on the Side Gunner's box.

The Side Gunner's easily lost/removable parts are delineated as follows: Main Pod Hatch, Upper Side Wing Cannon, Lower Side Wing Cannon, Lower Post Cannon (very hard-to-find), and Sidecar Back Shield.

MISB: $125-$145+; **MIB:** $45-$55; **MLC:** $36-$42.

INDEX ACTION FIGURES & ACCESSORIES

2-1B (Two-Onebee), 73
4-LOM/Zuckuss, 80-81
8D8, 111

A

A-wing Fighter, 266
A-wing Pilot, 128, 147
Ackbar, Admiral, 87-88
Action Figure Display
    Arena, 207
Action Figure Survival
    Kit, 194
Amanaman, 133
Arfive-Defour (R5-D4), 43
Artoo-Detoo (R2-D2), 14-15,
    147, 157
    With Pop-Up
        Lightsaber, 127
    With Sensorscope, 76-77
AST-5, 235
AT-AT Commander, 74
AT-AT Driver, 69
AT-AT (All Terrain
    Armored Transport),
    208-209
AT-ST All Terrain Scout
    Transport, 93
AT-ST Driver, 116
ATL Interceptor, 267

B

B-wing Fighter, 250
B-wing Pilot, 117
Barada, 135
"Battle-Damaged" Imperial
    TIE Fighter, 236-237
"Battle-Damaged" X-wing
    Fighter, 222
Bespin Security Guard
    (I), 52
Bespin Security Guard
    (II), 78
Biker Scout, 93
Bossk, 51

C

Calrissian, Lando, 58-59
    General Pilot, 137
    Skiff Guard Disguise, 89
Cantina Adventure Set, 169
CAP-2, 223
Chewbacca, 16-17, 160
Chewbacca Bandolier
    Strap, 238
Chirpa, Chief , 94
Cloud Car Pilot, 79
Cloud City Playset, 210-211
Collector's Action Stand, 168
Creature Cantina Action
    Playset, 178-179

D

Dagobah Action Playset
    212-213
Darth Vader Collector's
    Case, 195-196
Darth Vader's Star
    Destroyer Action
    Playset, 197-199
Darth Vader TIE Fighter,
    180-181
Death Squad Commander,
    32-33
Death Star Space Station,
    170-173
Dengar, 65
Desert Sail Skiff, 251
Droid Factory, 182-183
Dulok Scout, 154
Dulok Shaman, 154
Dusat, Jord, 149

E

Early Bird Certificate
    Package, 12-13
Emperor, The, 114-115
Emperor's Royal Guard, 95
Empire Strikes Back
    accessories, 194-235
Empire Strikes Back action
    figures, 50-85
Empire Strikes Back Mini-
    Figures Collector's Case,
    200, 214, 223-224
Endor Forest Ranger, 252
EV-9D9, 136
Ewok Assault Catapult, 253
Ewok Battle Wagon, 260-261
Ewok Combat Glider, 254
Ewok Village Action
    Playset, 240-241

F

F-X 7, 53
Fett, Boba, 47-49, 148,
    158-159
Fortuna, Bib, 91-92
Fromm, Sise, 151
Fromm, Tig, 152

G

Gamorrean Guard, 96-97
General Madine, 97-98
Gorneesh, Lady Urgah, 156
Greedo, 38

H

Hammerhead, 39
Hoth Ice Planet Adventure
    Set, 201

I

IG-88, 55-56, 166
Imperial Attack Base
    Playset, 202-203
Imperial Commander, 71
Imperial Cruiser, 215-216
Imperial Dignitary, 130
Imperial Gunner, 131
Imperial Shuttle, 234-235
Imperial Sniper, 261
Imperial TIE Fighter
    Pilot, 174

Imperial Troop Transporter,
    184-185
INT-4, 224
ISP-6, 245

J

Jabba the Hutt Action
    Playset, 242-243
Jabba the Hutt Dungeon,
    244, 256
Jawa, 34-35, 162
Joben, Thall, 151

K

Kenobi, Obi-Wan, 22-23, 158
Kez-Iban, 150
King Gorneesh, 155
Klaatu, 99
    Skiff Guard Outfit, 112

L

Land Speeder, 175
Land of the Jawas Action
    Playset, 185-186
Laser Rifle Carry Case, 257
Large size action figures,
    157-166
Lobot, 67
Logray, 100, 155
Lumat, 124

M

McCool, Droopy, 108
Millennium Falcon, 187-188
MLC-3, 217
Moll, Kea, 149
MTV-7, 217

N

Nikto, 113
Nunb, Nien, 90

O

One-Man Sand Skimmer, 262
Organa, Princess Leia,
    20-21, 164
    Bespin Gown, 61
    Boushh Disguise,103
    Hoth Outfit, 70
    In Combat Poncho, 119

P

Paploo, 125
Patrol Dewback, 189
PDT-8, 218
Pilot Blaster, 79, 84, 90
Power of the Force
    accessories, 260-265
Power of the Force action
    figures, 126-145
Power of the Force coins,
    142-145
Power Droid, 46
Princess Leia Blaster, 20,
    61, 70
Prune Face, 120

R

Radar Laser Cannon, 225
Radio Controlled Jawa
    Sandcrawler, 190-191
Rancor Keeper, 121
Rancor Monster, 258
Rebel Armored Snowspeeder,
    204-205
Rebel Command Center
    Adventure Set, 218-219
Rebel Commander, 72
Rebel Commando, 104
Rebel Rifle, 72, 75
Rebel Soldier, 62
Rebel Transport Vehicle,
    226-227
Rebo, Max, 109
Ree-Yees, 105
Return of the Jedi
    accessories, 236-259
Return of the Jedi action
    figures, 86-125
Return of the Jedi Mini-
    Figures Collector's
    Case, 246
Romba, 139

S

Sand People (Tusken
    Raiders), 36-37
Scout Walker, 228-229
Security Scout, 263
See-Threepio (C-3PO),
    28-29, 150, 165
    Removable Limbs,
    82-83
See-Threepio Collector's
    Case, 239
Side Gunner, 268
Skywalker, Anakin, 134
Skywalker, Luke, 18-19, 163
    Bespin Fatigues, 59-60
    Hoth Battle Gear, 54, 75
    Imperial Stormtrooper
        Outfit, 132
    In Battle Poncho, 138
    Jedi Knight Outfit,
        101-102
    X-wing Fighter Pilot, 45
Slave-1, 220
Snaggletooth (Zutton), 40-41
    Blue Snaggletooth,
        40, 41
    Red Snaggletooth,
        40, 41
Snootles, Sy, 110
Solo, Han, 26-27, 161
    Bespin Outfit/Cloud
        City Outfit, 66
    Hoth Battle Gear, 74, 78
    In Carbonite Chamber,
        129
    In Trench Coat, 118
    Sonic Controlled Land
        Speeder, 176

Speeder Bike, 247
Squid Head, 106-107
Star Wars accessories,
    168-193
Star Wars action figures,
    10-49
Star Wars: Droids
    accessories, 266-268
Star Wars: Droids action
    figures, 146-152
Star Wars: Ewoks action
    figures, 153-156
Star Wars Mini-Figures
    Collector's Case, 192-193
Stormtrooper/Imperial
    Stormtrooper, 30-31, 165
    Hoth Battle Gear
        ("Snowtrooper"), 57
Sy Snootles and the Rebo
    Band Action Figure
    Set, 108

T

Tatooine Skiff, 264-265
Tauntaun, 205
Tauntaun with Open Belly
    Rescue Feature, 230
Teebo, 122
TIE Interceptor Vehicle,
    258-259
Tosh, Jann, 148
Tri-Pod Laser Cannon, 231
Turret & Probot Playset, 221
Twin-Pod Cloud Car, 206

U

Ugnaught, 68
Ugnaught apron/smock, 68
Uncle Gundy, 152

V

Vader, Darth, 24-25
Vehicle Maintenance
    Energizer, 232-233

W

Walrus Man (Ponda Baba),
    42-43
Wampa, 234
Warock, 140
Warrick, Wicket W., 123, 156
Weequay, 107

X

X-wing Fighter, 177

Y

Y-wing Fighter, 248-249
Yak Face, 141
Yoda/Yoda the Jedi Master,
    63-64

Z

Zuckuss/4-LOM, 80-81, 85

BIBLIOGRAPHY

Articles and Books

Anderson, Kevin J. "A Boy and His Monster: The Rancor Keeper's Tale." *Tales from Jabba's Palace*. New York: Bantam Spectra, 1996.

Anderson, Kevin J. *Dark Apprentice, Volume 2 of the Jedi Academy Trilogy*. New York: Bantam Spectra, 1994.

Anderson, Kevin J. "Therefore I Am: The Tale of IG-88." *Tales of the Bounty Hunters*. New York: Bantam Spectra, 1996.

Anderson, Kevin J. and Ralph McQuarrie. *The Illustrated Star Wars Universe*. Paperback. New York: Bantam Spectra, 1997.

Beecroft, Simon. *Star Wars Character Encyclopedia*. New York: LucasBooks/DK Publishing, 2011..

Betancourt, John Gregory. "And the Band Played On: The Band's Tale." *Tales from Jabba's Palace*. New York: Bantam Spectra, 1996.

Blackman, W. Haden and Ian Fullwood. *Star Wars: The New Essential Guide to Vehicles & Vessels*. New York: Del Rey, 2003.

Blackman, W. Haden. *Star Wars: The New Essential Guide to Weapons and Technology*. Updated ed. New York: Del Rey, 2004.

Bouzereau, Laurent. *Star Wars: The Annotated Screenplays*. New York: Del Rey, 1997.

Campbell, Drew, et al. *Star Wars Trilogy Sourcebook, Special Edition*. Honesdale, Pennsylvania: West End Games, 1997.

Fry, Jason, and Paul R. Urquhart. *Star Wars: The Essential Guide to Warfare*. New York: Del Rey, 2012. Print.

Hidalgo, Pablo and Michael Stern. *Galaxy Guide 3: The Empire Strikes Back*. 2nd ed. Honesdale, Pennsylvania: West End Games, 1996.

Hodges, Steve. "Snaggletooth's Belt Buckle." Tomart's Action Figure Digest 77. Dayton, Ohio: Tomart Publications, July 2000. (p. 32).

Jenkins, Duncan, and Gus Lopez. *Gus and Duncan's Comprehensive Guide to Star Wars Collectibles*. Liberty: Completist Publications, 2009.

Jeter, K.W. *The Bounty Hunter Wars, Book 1: The Mandalorian Armor*. New York: Bantam Spectra, 1998.

Jeter, K.W. *The Bounty Hunter Wars, Book 3: Hard Merchandise*. New York: Bantam Spectra, 1999.

Lewis, Ann Margaret and R.K. *Post. Star Wars: The Essential Guide to Alien Species*. New York: Del Rey, 2001.

"Mattel Issues a Recall For Toy Space Missiles." United Press International. Atlanta, 11 Jan. 1979.

Newbold, Mark. "Inside Jabba's Court." *Star Wars Insider 143*. Titan Magazines, Inc. 23 Jul. 2013.

Ostrander, John and Tomas Giorello. "No Man's Land." *Star Wars: Republic 62*. Milwaukie, Ore: Dark Horse Comics, 2004.

Pena, Abel G., and Jason Fry. "Kyle Katarn's Tale," *Mission 3: The Blood Moon*. Star Wars Miniatures Game. Wizards of the Coast, April-May 2005.

"Rebel Transport." *The Official Star Wars Fact File #30*. Milan: DeAgostini/Lucas Books. 25 July 2002.

Richardson, Michael and Randy Stradley. "Council of Blood." *Star Wars: Crimson Empire #2*. Milwaukie, Ore: Dark Horse Comics, 1998.

Sansweet, Stephen J. *Star Wars: The Ultimate Action Figure Collection*. New York: Chronicle Books, 2012.

Sansweet, Stephen J. *Star Wars: The Action Figure Archive*. New York: Chronicle Books, 1999.

Sansweet, Stephen J. and Pablo Hidalgo. *The Complete Star Wars Encyclopedia*. 2nd ed. New York: LucasBooks, 2008.

[Sears] Wish Book for the 1978 Holiday Season. Los Angeles: Sears & Roebuck & Co., Nov. 1979. p. 574.

[Sears] Wish Book for the 1979 Holiday Season. Los Angeles: Sears & Roebuck & Co., Nov. 1979. pp. 618-619.

[Sears] Wish Book for the 1980 Holiday Season. Los Angeles: Sears & Roebuck & Co., Nov. 1980. pp. 630-631.

[Sears] Wish Book for the 1981 Holiday Season. Los Angeles: Sears & Roebuck & Co., Nov. 1981. pp. 636-638.

[Sears] Wish Book for the 1982 Holiday Season. Los Angeles: Sears & Roebuck & Co., Nov. 1982. pp. 609-611.

[Sears] Wish Book for the 1983 Holiday Season. Los Angeles: Sears & Roebuck & Co., Nov. 1982. pp. 160-161.

[Sears] Wish Book for the 1984 Holiday Season. Los Angeles: Sears & Roebuck & Co., Nov. 1980. pp. 574-575.

[Sears] Wish Book for the 1985 Holiday Season. Los Angeles: Sears & Roebuck & Co., Nov. 1980. p. 446.

Slavicsek, Bill and Curtis Smith. *The Star Wars Sourcebook*. Honesdale, Pennsylvania: West End Games, 1987.

Smith, Bill, David Nakabayashi and Troy Vigil. *Star Wars: The Essential Guide to Weapons & Technology*. New York: Del Rey, 1997.

Strayton, George and Michael Stern. *Galaxy Guide 5: Return of the Jedi*. 2nd ed. Honesdale, Pennsylvania: West End Games. 1995.

Sudlow, Paul, Michael Stern and Grant S. Boucher. *Star Wars: Galaxy Guide 1: A New Hope*. 2nd ed. Honesdale, Pennsylvania: West End Games, 1995.

Truett, Chuck and Denning, Troy. *Star Wars Galaxy Guide 4: Alien Races*. 2nd ed. Honesdale, Pennsylvania: West End Games. 1994.

Veitch, Tom and Cam Kennedy. "Confrontation on the Smuggler's Moon." *Star Wars: Dark Empire #4*. Milwaukie, Ore: Dark Horse Comics, 1992.

Wallace, Daniel and Ian Fullwood. *Star Wars: The New Essential Guide to Droids*. New York: Del Rey, 2006.

Wallace, Daniel and Denis Cramer III. "Who's Who in Jabba's Palace." *Star Wars Insider 60*. Titan Magazines. July-August 2002.

West Reynolds, David, James Luceno, and Ryder Windham. *Star Wars: The Complete Visual Dictionary*. 2nd ed. New York: LucasBooks/DK Publishing, 2012.

Windham, Ryder. Jedi vs. Sith: *The Essential Guide to the Force*. New York: Del Rey, 2007.

Electronic Sources

"Cyborg." *Dictionary.com Unabridged*. Random House, Inc. 13 Feb. 2014. <http://dictionary.reference.com>.

Fawcett, Chris et al. "Figures/Vehicles/Playsets." *12back.com*. n.p., n.d. Web. Sep. 2013-June 2014.

Fawcett, Chris. "Features: 'Guide to Kenner's Star Wars Figure Card Backs'." *12back.com*. n.p., n.d. Web. Dec. 2013-Jan. 2014. <http://www.12back.com/features/cardbacks/cardbacks.php3>

Fett, Grumpy. "Vintage Kenner Star Wars Action Figure Price Guide: updated 1/10/14." *Vintage Star Wars Action Figure Price Guide*. Squidoo, LLC., 10 Jan. 2014. Web. Feb.-Mar. 2014.

Kemple, Shawn. "Star Wars/Empire/Jedi/POTF/Misc." *Mail Away Guide: Free with Proof of Purchase*. Mail Away Guide, Inc., 2013-2014. Web. Nov.-Feb. 2014.

Lopez, Gus et al. "Archive Database [Toys/Action Figure Related/Small Action Figures, Accessories, Playsets, Vehicles, Miscellaneous, and Large Size Action Figures]." *The Star Wars Collector's Archive*, 1994-2014. Web. Jan. 2013-Mar 2014.

Lopez, Gus. "The Comprehensive Guide to POTF, Droids, and Ewoks Coins." *The Star Wars Collector's Archive*, 1994-2014. Web. Nov. 2013-Mar. 2014. <www.theswca.com/images-coins/coin-chart.html>

Lopez, Gus. "Features: 'Power of the Force Coins'." *12back.com*. n.p., n.d. Web. Jan. 2014-Feb. 2014.

Myatt, D. Martin. "An Interview with Bernard Loomis: Former President of Kenner." *Rebelscum.com*. Philip Wise, Inc., n.d. Web. 07 Jan. 2014. <http://www.rebelscum.com/loomis.asp>

"Search, Completed Listing: 'Star Wars, Vintage'." *eBay: Toys & Hobbies>Action Figures>TV, Movie & Video Games*. eBay, Inc. Feb. 2014. Web. Feb.-Mar. 2014.

"Star Wars (film)." *Wikipedia, The Free Encyclopedia*. Wikimedia Foundation, Inc. 06 Feb. 2014. Web. 07 Feb. 2014.

"Star Wars, Franchises, Total Grosses." *Box Office Mojo*. IMDb.com, Inc. n.d. Web. 20 Dec. 2013.

Star Wars: Droid Database. Wikia, Inc. 04 Aug. 2013-10 Aug. 2013. Web. 02 Feb. 2014. (re: assorted droids, droid gender, etc.) <starwarsdroids.wikia.com/wiki/Star_Wars_Droids_Wiki>

Veekhoven, Tim. "Offscreen, but Not Forgotten: Mini-Rigs, Body-Rigs, and Other Kenner Vehicles." *Starwarsblog.com./Starwars.com*. Lucasfilm Ltd. 14 Oct. 2013. Web. 12 Feb. 2014.

Wikipedia, The Free Encyclopedia. Wikimedia Foundation, Inc. 13 Aug. 2013 to 10 Mar. 2014. Web. May 2013-Mar 2014. (re: characters, events, films, vehicles, etc.). <http://en.wikipedia.org/wiki/Main_Page>

Wise, Phillip et al. "Rebelscum Photo Archive: Older Companies/Kenner." *Rebelscum.com*. Philip Wise, Inc., 1996-2014. Web. Aug. 2013-Mar. 2014.

Woods, Summer J. "The Complete Wermo's Guide to Huttese [and other *Star Wars* languages]." n.p., n.d. Web. Jan. 2014. <www.completewermosguide.com>

Wookieepedia, The Star Wars Wiki. Wikia, Inc. 20 May 2013-10 Mar. 2011. Web. May 2013-Mar 2011. (re: accessories, battles, characters, creatures, events, histories, vehicles, weapons, etc.). http://starwars.wikia.com/wiki/Main_Page

P. 216

Imperial Cruiser, with figures.

Film, Television, Video Games

Caravan of Courage: An Ewok Adventure (a.k.a. *The Ewok Adventure*). Dir. John Korty. Wr. George Lucas (story), Bob Carrau. Nar. Burl Ives. ABC. November 25, 1984. 96 min. Pr. Thomas G. Smith.

Empire of Dreams: The Story of the Star Wars Trilogy. Dir. Edith Becker and Kevin Burns. Wr. Edward Singer. Lucasfilm & Twentieth Century Fox, *Star Wars Trilogy: Special Ed.*, 2004. DVD.

Ewoks: The Battle for Endor. Dir. Jim Wheat & Ken Wheat. Prod. Thomas G. Smith. Story by George Lucas. Screenplay by Jim Wheat & Ken Wheat. ABC. November 24, 1985. 94 mins.

"History of the Sand People." *Star Wars: Knights of the Old Republic*. Microsoft Xbox OS. Nov. 2003. LucasArts. Dec. 2013. Cartridge.

Star Wars Episode IV: A New Hope. Wr. & Dir. George Lucas. Lucasfilm & Twentieth Century Fox, 1977. *Star Wars: THX Trilogy*, 1995. VHS. *Star Wars Trilogy: Special Ed.*, 2004. DVD. *Star Wars: The Complete Saga*, 2011. Blu-ray.

Star Wars Episode V: The Empire Strikes Back. Wr. George Lucas, Leigh Brackett and Lawrence Kasdan. Dir. Irvin Kerschner. Lucasfilm & Twentieth Century Fox, 1980. *Star Wars: THX Trilogy*, 1995. VHS. *Star Wars Trilogy: Special Ed.*, 2004. DVD. *Star Wars: The Complete Saga*, 2011. Blu-ray.

Star Wars Episode VI: Return of the Jedi. Wr. George Lucas & Lawrence Kasdan. Dir. Richard Marquand. Lucasfilm & Twentieth Century Fox, 1983. *Star Wars: THX Trilogy*, 1995. VHS. *Star Wars Trilogy: Special Ed.*, 2004. DVD. *Star Wars: The Complete Saga*, 2011. Blu-ray.

The Star Wars Holiday Special. ABC. Dir. Dave Acomba & Steve Binder. November 17th, 1978. 97 min. George Lucas—story (elements).

Star Wars, Jedi Knight: Dark Forces II. Microsoft Windows OS. Sep. 1997. LucasArts. September 1997. CD-ROM.

Star Wars: The Old Republic. Microsoft Windows OS. 2011. Electronic Arts/LucasArts. Nov. 2013. Web (MMORPG).

"The White Witch," "The New King," "The Trigon Unleashed," "The Great Heep." *Star Wars: Droids—The Adventures of R2-D2 and C-3PO*. ABC. September 7th 1985—June 7th 1986. Nelvana Animation. George Lucas creator. 13 episodes, 1 special. Dir. Raymond Jafelice, Clive A. Smith. 13 episodes, 1 special.

"Wicket's Wagon," *Star Wars: Ewoks/The All New Ewoks*. ABC. September 7th, 1985—December 19th, 1986. 35 episodes. Dir. Raymond Jafelice & Dale Schott. Crea. Prod. George Lucas.